The Nation's Health

The Jones and Bartlett Series in Health Sciences

The Nation's Health

Fourth Edition

Edited by

Philip R. Lee
Carroll L. Estes

Institute for Health Policy Studies
School of Medicine
and
Institute for Health and Aging
School of Nursing
University of California
San Francisco

Nancy Ramsay
Associate Editor
Institute for Health Policy Studies
University of California, San Francisco

Jones and Bartlett Publishers
Boston   London

Editorial, Sales, and Customer Service Offices
Jones and Bartlett Publishers
One Exeter Plaza
Boston, MA 02116
617-859-3900
800-832-0034

Jones and Bartlett Publishers International
PO Box 1498
London W6 7RS
England

Library of Congress Cataloging-in-Publication Data
The Nation's health/edited by Philip R. Lee and Carroll L. Estes.—4th ed.
      p.   cm.
    Includes bibliographical references and index.
    ISBN 0-86720-840-6 :
    1. Public health—United States.   2. Medical policy—United States.
3. Health care reform—United States.   I. Lee, Philip R. (Philip Randolph),
    1924– .   II. Estes, Carroll L.
RA445.N36   1994
362.1'0973—dc20   93-41200
                                     CIP

Acquisitions Editor: Joseph E. Burns
Manufacturing Buyer: Dana L. Cerrito
Cover Design: Design Ad Cetera. Photo © Michael H. Howell, Stock, Boston
Production & Design: Colophon
Composition: LeGwin Associates
Printing and Binding: Edwards Brothers
Cover Printing: New England Book Components

Photo credits: Page 3 © Larry Kolvoord/The Image Works; page 41 © Therese Fiara/The Picture Cube; page 103 © Reuters/Bettmann; page 163 © N.R. Rowan/The Image Works; page 199 © Michael Siluk/The Image Works; page 247 © J.W. Berndt/The Picture Cube; page 293 © J. Griffin/The Image Works; page 313 © Spencer Grant/The Picture Cube; page 345 © Aronson Photographics/Stock, Boston

Printed in the United States of America
98 97 96 95 94   10 9 8 7 6 5 4 3 2 1

❖ Contents

❖ Preface

Health care reform is at the top of the nation's agenda. This volume—edited by two top health policy analysts—includes a practical, in-depth guide to the factors affecting the health of Americans and the precarious circumstances faced by the nation's health care system today.

There is a groundswell of opinion calling for sweeping change in the financing and organization of health care. Clearly, we cannot continue to have our cake and eat it too. At the same time, it is difficult to understand the societal forces at the root of the problems and to go about setting national priorities. How do we evaluate the proliferating proposals for reform, including the plan put forward by President Clinton, and how do we come to grips with terms like *managed competition, capitation, global budgets, the medical-industrial complex, rationing of care,* and *specialization versus family practice?* What is the role of nurses and do we need more? Is it possible to expand access to care and at the same time control relentlessly rising costs?

In addition, what is the relationship of socioeconomic class to health? How important is preventive care? Why do Americans spend over twice as much per capita for health care as other industrial countries and yet rank far behind in infant mortality and life expectancy? And how do we eliminate medical care that is wasteful, inefficient, and unnecessary?

In this book, the nation's leading health policy experts look at the complex web of issues, policies, controversies, hazards, and proposed solutions that surround the health care system.

The fourth edition of *The Nation's Health* represents part of a multidisciplinary program for advanced training and education in health policy and health services research that is conducted by the Institute for Health Policy Studies, School of Medicine, and the Institute for Health and Aging, School of Nursing, University of California, San Francisco. The editors would like to acknowledge the valuable support of the Pew Charitable Trusts, which provided support for a portion of the efforts required to prepare this new edition.

During 1992 when this book was being prepared, Philip Lee was serving as professor of social medicine on the UCSF faculty and as director of the Institute for Health Policy Studies. In July 1993, he was confirmed as Assistant Secretary for Health, Department of Health and Human Services, in the administration of President Bill Clinton. In this role, he has taken part in the national effort to restate the nation's health care agenda in response to many of the problems and issues described in this book and in keeping with many of its themes.

A number of people provided invaluable assistance in the production of this book. Members of the Institute for Health Policy Studies administrative staff have cooperated on every stage of this project. Special appreciation goes to Nancy Ramsay for her critical role in the entire process, from review and selection of articles to final publication; to Ida V. S. W. Red for assistance in developing Chapters 4 and 9, and to Joyce Umamoto who oversaw the preparation of the manuscript and the production process.

Although *The Nation's Health* is a project of the Institute for Health Policy Studies, the Institute for Health and Aging, and the Pew Charitable Trusts, the views expressed are those of the authors only and do not necessarily reflect those of the funding agency or the University of California.

❖ Introduction

In this volume, we have attempted to provide a clear view of the factors affecting the health of people who live in the United States. The emphasis of the fourth edition of *The Nation's Health* is the precarious set of circumstances faced by the nation's health care system in the mid-1990s as we stand on the verge of sweeping health care reform. We intend this textbook to represent a range of views about factors affecting health status, the current state of health care, and the future of the health care system with particular emphasis on the current health care crisis and proposals for change.

During the past 20 years, there has been substantial improvement in many aspects of health care. At the same time, the number of uninsured has grown, miracles of technology have proliferated, and costs have risen relentlessly. Today, more and more people are calling for reforms in health care financing and organization, and indeed a variety of plans are on the table—both nationally and within states.

Expenditures for medical care now exceed $800 billion, representing a record 14 percent of the gross national product (GNP). It is estimated that, unfettered by government action, health care will surpass $1.7 trillion, or 18 percent of the GNP, by the year 2000. The rise in personal health care expenditures can be broken into four components: general inflation; population growth; medical care price inflation above general inflation; and a group of other factors, including increases in volume and intensity of services. Population growth and general inflation accounted for about 55 percent of the increase in the past 20 years, medical care price inflation accounted for 17 percent of the increase, and the volume and intensity of services for approximately 28 percent. These components have been affected by an array of factors, including: increased patient complexity; a tendency in the delivery system toward specialization rather than primary care; concentration of physicians and hospitals in certain urban areas that leads to excess capacity and low productivity; unnecessary and inappropriate care, which some analysts estimate may be as high as 25 percent of health care services; the practice of defensive medicine to avoid the threat of malpractice suits; and, finally, excessive administrative costs.

Rising costs are exacerbated by the fact that the U.S. system insulates both providers and consumers through the cushion of third-party payers, thus avoiding incentives to seek or provide care in a cost-effective manner. A number of failures in the health care market have vastly influenced the way insurance companies try to cope with the rising price paid for health care services. Sometimes costs are shifted from employers to employees and benefits are reduced.

While some economists and policymakers characterize the past decade as a period of increased competition and deregulation, during the same period public programs were exposed to growing regulation. This was particularly important in the Medicare and Medicaid programs, which pay for approximately 33 percent of all personal health care benefits. In 1991, this amounted to $96.5 billion for Medicaid and $120.2 billion for Medicare. In order to control costs, the federal government devised ingenious schemes to limit spending, most notably through the Medicare prospective payment system for hospitals, which was introduced in 1983, and the Medicare fee schedule that went into effect in 1992. Despite efforts in the private sector to stimulate competition and require more and more patients to fit into managed care plans, cost increases were not slowed significantly.

Compounding the problem of rising costs has been a deterioration in access to care. Greater and greater numbers of people across all socioeconomic levels have found it difficult or impossible to obtain health insurance coverage, thus expanding the ranks of the uninsured to over 37 million. Those who hold the pursestrings—third-party payers—have come to dictate treatment plans and hospital stays, as coverage has become increasingly limited. In many cases, people with chronic health problems cannot obtain health benefits. This circumstance has come to be termed a *pre-existing condition*, and in recent years it has become common for insurance companies to exclude coverage for illnesses people are under treatment for at the time they apply for coverage. As Medicaid eligibility shrank in relation to a growing need and other charity care began to decline, the system effectively turned its back on the working poor. Thus, the most vulnerable fared poorest.

Soaring costs and the depletion of financial support for the uninsured and underinsured are a deadly combination existing side by side with the world's most sophisticated and high-priced health care technology. Thus, infant mortality, which is related to access to prenatal and maternity care, is considerably higher for blacks than for whites. It is higher for the poor than for the rich, and it is higher in the United States than in 21 other countries. Sophisticated treatments such as coronary artery bypass graft surgery, coronary angioplasty, and total hip replacement are unavailable to many poor people, the quality of whose lives might be greatly improved by them. Other services often unavailable to the poor are preventive services and management of chronic conditions. These services are critical to good health, as is prenatal care.

At the same time that the health care delivery crisis was playing out, a number of health and social problems swept the nation, decimating the lives of many and cutting at the heart of the health care system. At issue were the epidemics of violence, substance abuse, AIDS, homelessness, and teenage pregnancy, all of them devastatingly expensive in terms of human life, and each with a very high price tag. Concurrently, the number of chronically ill elderly continued to increase, highlighting the lack of provision in our system for serving their special needs.

For many sick people, medicine is the key to life and well being, and thus doctors and hospitals become the arbiters of our most precious commodities. This fact, coupled with the high cost of services and the insulation provided by third-party payers, means that health care does not operate according to classical market principles.

Most observers and participants agree that there is need for fundamental change and restructuring of the health care system. During the primaries and the race leading up to the presidential election in 1992, health care reform was at the forefront of the debate. The public complained bitterly that health care costs too much and that health insurance coverage is difficult to obtain. The candidates discussed proposals to combat inflation in doctor and hospital bills and to ensure comprehensive health care coverage to greater numbers of people. At the same time, numerous reform bills were introduced in Congress, and various states took the initiative to address the same issues. In 1993, President Clinton proposed a vast restructuring of the nation's health care system through a proposal that would provide comprehensive health insurance coverage to all Americans. It was designed to be phased in gradually by the year 2000. Other plans vary from some that are similar to the Clinton plan in combining market forces and regulation to those that propose only minor tinkering and those patterned on the universal care, single-payer systems of other industrial nations.

Many contributors to this volume argue that the nation is confronted by an outmoded system that is the result of failed policies and runaway technological expansion at the expense of the provision of sound basic care for all and effective nationwide programs of prevention and health promotion. Those who are well insured are the beneficiaries of a comprehensive delivery system. Those who suffer its ill effects are children, some of whom are unable to obtain even basic care, including immunizations; the disabled and those who suffer from debilitating chronic illness; and, across all age groups and geographic areas, the poor. In recent years, many institutions of society have abdicated responsibility for footing the bill for care of the nation's neediest. Leading the exodus was the federal government, followed closely by private insurance companies, state governments, hospitals, and other health care providers.

Throughout the 1980s, the nation also experienced an increase in the number and types of corporate for-profit providers. This hotly debated phenomenon has resulted in the proprietary ownership of many hospitals, surgicenters, urgent care centers, clinical laboratories, and imaging facilities. Hospitals and other providers have become increasingly competitive and, as a result, they have begun to operate more like businesses, using techniques such as advertising, marketing, specialization, and productivity monitoring. The effects of this trend are just beginning to be understood.

The irony is that at a time when the poor have been reconciled to society's disparities, a large segment of society has come to expect almost unlimited medical care. Along with the benefits of high-priced care come the pitfalls of overtreatment, overprescribing, unnecessary surgery, and neglect of emphasis on sound preventive measures. Thus, issues related to quality of care are being examined anew. Measuring the effects of medical interventions is a complex and imprecise science. Increasingly, clinicians are asked to interpret medical findings that they are ill-equipped to evaluate. This causes vastly differing treatments from one clinician to another, and the end result is that new issues related to inappropriate care are being investigated today.

In this book, we critically examine the role of modern health care. Rather than merely emphasizing its many contributions in the care of the sick and in improving the health of the population, we look at the complex web of issues, policies, controversies, hazards, problems, and proposed solutions that surround the health care system. While acknowledging the inevitability of death, we would like to explore a means to greater health and longevity for everyone. Despite the advances of science that have contributed to increased life expectancy and reduced mortality, 20th century America faces critical issues if it is to maintain its leadership role in science and health care.

With health care at the top of the nation's political agenda, with medical costs consuming a larger and larger share of the nation's wealth, and with millions of Americans unable to obtain even basic services, the time has come for health care reform. This complex subject is not easily grasped, and the partisan discussions that inundate us through the media often muddy the waters. Some concepts that are at the heart of the debate include managed competition, global budgets, rationing care, employer mandates, and health alliances. This new vocabulary is introduced here, the concepts that underlie these and other issues are outlined, and the hazards and benefits of embarking on each path are explored.

❖ Acknowledgments

❖ Chapter 1

Thomas McKeown. "Determinants of Health." Abridged from *Human Nature*, April 1978. Copyright 1978 by Human Nature, Inc. Reprinted by permission of the publisher.

Robert G. Evans and Gregory L. Stoddart. "Producing Health, Consuming Health Care." Abridged from *Social Science Medicine*, Volume 31, Number 12, 1990. Copyright 1990 by Pergamon Press, Ltd., Oxford, England. Reprinted by permission of the publisher.

M.G. Marmot, George Davey Smith, Stephen Stansfeld, Chandra Patel, Fiona North, Jenny Head, Ian White, Eric Brunner, and Amanda Feeney. "Health Inequalities and Social Class." Abridged from *The Lancet*, Volume 337, 1991, pp. 1387–1392, under the original title "Health Inequalities among British Civil Servants: The Whitehall II Study." Copyright 1991 by *The Lancet*. Reprinted by permission of the publisher and authors.

❖ Chapter 2

Dorothy P. Rice. "Health Status and National Health Priorities." Abridged from and reprinted by permission of *The Western Journal of Medicine* (Dorothy P. Rice, Health Status and National Health Priorities, 1991, (3), Volume 154, pp. 294-302).

Paul R. Torrens and Stephen J. Williams. "Understanding the Present, Planning for the Future: The Dynamics of Health Care in the United States in the 1990s." Abridged from *Introduction to Health Services*, 4th ed., editors: S.J. Williams, P.R. Torrens, 1993, pp. 421–429. Copyright 1993 by Delmar Publishers. Reprinted by permission of Delmar Publishers.

Arnold S. Relman. "The Health Care Industry: Where Is It Taking Us?" Abridged from *New England Journal of Medicine*, Volume 325(12), 1991, pp. 854-859, under the original title "Special Article: 'Shattuck Lecture—The Health Care Industry: Where Is It Taking Us?'" Copyright 1991 by *The New England Journal of Medicine*. Reprinted by permission of the publisher.

Steven A. Schroeder, Jane S. Zones, and Jonathan A. Showstack. "Academic Medicine as a Public Trust." Adapted from *Journal of the American Medical Association*, 1989, Volume 262, Number 6, pp. 803–811. Copyright 1989, American Medical Association.

Select Committee on Aging, U.S. House of Representatives. "Medicare and Medicaid's 25th Anniversary—Much Promised, Accomplished, and Left Unfinished." Abridged from Report of the Select Committee, July 30, 1990, Comm. Pub. No. 101–762, pp. ix-39. U.S. Government Printing Office, Washington, D.C., 1990.

❖ Chapter 3

Theodor J. Litman. "Government and Health: The Political Aspects of Health Care—A Sociopolitical Overview." Abridged from *Health Politics and Policy in Perspective.* Copyright 1984 by John Wiley & Sons, Inc. Reprinted by permission of John Wiley & Sons, Inc.

Philip R. Lee and A.E. Benjamin. "Health Policy and the Politics of Health Care." Abridged from *Introduction to Health Services,* 4th ed., editors: S.J. Williams, P.R. Torrens, 1993, pp. 399–420. Copyright 1993 by Delmar Publishers. Reprinted by permission of the Delmar Publishers.

Carroll L. Estes. "Privatization, the Welfare State, and Aging: The Reagan-Bush Legacy." Abridged from a paper presented at the 21st Annual Conference of the British Society of Gerontology, University of Kent at Canterbury, September 19, 1992. Reprinted by permission of the author.

Richard D. Lamm. "The Brave New World of Health Care." Abridged from *The Annals of Thoracic Surgery,* Volume 52, 1991, pp. 369–384. Reprinted with permission from the Society of Thoracic Surgeons (*The Annals of Thoracic Surgery,* 1991, 52, 369–384) with consent of the author.

❖ Chapter 4

Charlene Harrington, Suzanne Lee Feetham, Patricia A. Moccia, and Gloria R. Smith. "Health Care Access: Problems and Policy Recommendations." Abridged from a monograph published by the American Academy of Nursing, Washington D.C., 1993. Reprinted by permission of the authors.

Linda H. Aiken. "Charting the Future of Hospital Nursing." Abridged from *Image: Journal of Nursing Scholarship,* Volume 22(2), 1990, pp. 72–78. Reprinted by permission of the author.

Claire M. Fagin. "Collaboration between Nurses and Physicians: No Longer a Choice." Abridged from *Academic Medicine,* Volume 64(5), 1992, pp. 295–303. Copyright 1992 by the Association of American Medical Colleges. Reprinted by permission of the publisher.

❖ Chapter 5

Philip R. Lee, Denise Soffel, and Harold S. Luft. "Costs and Coverage: Pressures toward Health Care Reform." Abridged from and reprinted by permission of *The Western Journal of Medicine* (Philip R. Lee, Denise Soffel, Harold S. Luft, "Special Series—Costs and Coverage: Pressures Toward Health Care Reform," Volume 157 (5), 1992, pp. 576–583).

Eli Ginzberg. "Health Care Reform: Where Are We and Where Should We Be Going?" Abridged from *New England Journal of Medicine,* Volume 327(18), 1992, pp. 1310–1312, under "SOUNDING BOARD: Health Care Reform—Where are We and Where Should We Be Going?" Copyright 1992 by *The New England Journal of Medicine.* Reprinted by permission of the publisher.

David Blumenthal. "The Timing and Course of Health Care Reform." Abridged from *New England Journal of Medicine,* Volume 325(3), 1991, pp. 198–200, under "SOUNDING BOARD: The Timing and Course of Health Care Reform." Copyright 1991 by *The New England Journal of Medicine.* Reprinted by permission of the publisher.

John K. Iglehart. "Managed Competition." Abridged from *New England Journal of Medicine*, Volume 328(16), 1993, pp. 1208–1212. Copyright 1993 by *The New England Journal of Medicine*. Reprinted by permission of the publisher.

John K. Iglehart. "The American Health Care System: Managed Care." Abridged from *New England Journal of Medicine*, Volume 327(10), 1992, pp. 742–747. Copyright 1992 by *The New England Journal of Medicine*. Reprinted by permission of the publisher.

George D. Lundberg. "National Health Care Reform: The Aura of Inevitability Intensifies." Abridged from *Journal of the American Medical Association*, Volume 267 (18), 1992, pp. 2521–2524. Copyright 1992, American Medical Association.

❖ Chapter 6

Suzanne W. Letsch, Helen C. Lazenby, Katherine R. Levit, and Cathy A. Cowan. "National Health Expenditures, 1991." Report from the Office of National Health Statistics, Office of the Actuary, Health Care Financing Administration, 1993.

Uwe E. Reinhardt. "Providing Access to Health Care and Controlling Costs: The Universal Dilemma." Reprinted by permission of the author.

Bruce C. Vladeck. "Old Snake Oil in New Bottles." Abridged from *United Hospital Fund: President's Letter*, September 1992. Reprinted by permission of the United Hospital Fund.

Alain C. Enthoven and Richard Kronick. "Universal Health Insurance through Incentives Reform." Abridged from *Journal of the American Medical Association*, Volume 265 (19) 1991, pp. 2532–2536. Copyright 1991, American Medical Association.

❖ Chapter 7

Karen Davis. "Availability of Medical Care and Its Financing." Abridged from a paper presented at the Centennial Symposium, the Johns Hopkins Medical Institutions, Baltimore, Md., February 23–24, 1990. Reprinted by permission of the author.

Emily Friedman. "The Uninsured: From Dilemma to Crisis." Abridged from *Journal of the American Medical Association*, Volume 265 (19) 1991, pp. 2491–2495. Copyright 1991, American Medical Association.

Robert F. St. Peter, Paul W. Newacheck, and Neal Halfon. "Access to Care for Poor Children: Separate and Unequal?" Abridged from *Journal of the American Medical Association*, Volume 267 (20), 1992, pp. 2760–2764. Copyright 1992, American Medical Association.

❖ Chapter 8

David M. Eddy. "Clinical Decision Making: From Theory to Practice." Abridged from *Journal of the American Medical Association*, Volume 263 (2), 1990, pp. 287–290. Copyright 1990, American Medical Association.

Noralou P. Roos and Leslie L. Roos. "Small Area Variations, Practice Style, and Quality of Care." Abridged from *Assessing Quality Health Care: Perspectives for Clinicians*, R.P. Wenzel, ed., Williams & Wilkins, 1992. Copyright 1992 by Williams & Wilkins Co., Baltimore, Md. Reprinted by permission of the publisher and editor.

Jan Blustein and Theodore R. Marmor. "Cutting Waste by Making Rules: Promises, Pitfalls, and Realistic Prospects." Abridged from *University of Pennsylvania Law Review*, Volume 140(5), 1992, pp. 1543–1572. Copyright 1992 by *University of Pennsylvania Law Review*. Reprinted by permission of the publisher.

Chapter 9

S.M. Miller. "Race in the Health of America." Abridged from *The Milbank Quarterly*, Volume 65, Supplement 2, 1987. Copyright 1987 by *The Milbank Quarterly*. Reprinted by permission of the publisher.

Judith Rodin and Jeannette R. Ickovics. "Women's Health: Review and Research Agenda as We Approach the 21st Century." Abridged from *American Psychologist*, Volume 45(9), 1990, pp. 1018-1034, with permission of the author. Copyright 1990 by the American Psychological Association. Reprinted by permission.

Mary K. Zimmerman. "The Women's Health Movement: A Critique of Medical Enterprise and the Position of Women." Abridged from *Analyzing Gender: A Handbook of Social Science Research*, B. Hess and M. Ferree, eds. 1987, pp. 442–473. Copyright 1987 by Sage Publications. Reprinted by permission of Sage Publications, Inc.

The National Commission on Acquired Immune Deficiency Syndrome. "America Living with AIDS: Transforming Anger, Fear, and Indifference into Action." Abridged from the report of the National Commission on Acquired Immune Deficiency Syndrome, 1991, pp. 7–15. Reprinted by permission of the National Commission on AIDS.

❖ PART I

Health and Health Care

❖ Chapter 1

Health Status and Its Determinants

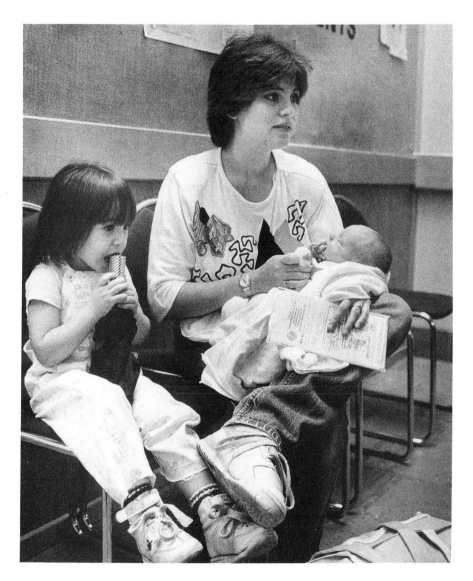

Since the eighteenth century, there has been a dramatic improvement in the health and lifespan of Americans. This largely reflects a decline in the infectious diseases that once claimed the lives of many children. After dramatic declines in mortality from some infectious diseases following the introduction of the sulfanilamides in the 1930s, penicillin in the 1940s, and broad-spectrum antibiotics in the 1940s and early 1950s, progress slowed in the mid-1950s. From the mid-1950s to the mid-1960s, little progress was made in reducing infant mortality or increasing life expectancy. Beginning in the mid-1960s, however, and continuing into the 1980s, America's health improved. Infant deaths dropped to about one half the 1965 level. The life expectancy of those born in 1979 rose more than three years over that of 1965.

Today the leading causes of death are heart disease, cancer, strokes, accidents, homicides, and suicides. In some metropolitan areas, acquired immunodeficiency syndrome (AIDS) has become a leading cause of death, particularly among young adults. These causes result in part from socioeconomic conditions, the ways we choose to live, and the environments we create. Management of these problems requires different strategies than those for the infectious diseases that were the leading killers during the early part of the century. We often cannot rely on the cures of modern medicine or collective public health measures. Today, more than ever, ensuring good health, or the control of disease, requires a focus on both socioeconomic factors, such as social class and individual behavior, and the factors that influence health-related behaviors. For example, a 1992 survey conducted by the American Medical Association found that 66 percent of Americans are overweight and that this was one of a number of indications that Americans are not following good health habits.

The role of health professionals has changed. When cures cannot be effected, medical care can facilitate and encourage healthy behaviors, provide treatment and rehabilitation, offer reassurance, and help us to function as well as possible in the face of serious disease. Current technologies allow people to live many years after contracting an incurable chronic illness, thus prolonging life in a state of compromised health.

The authors in this chapter analyze trends in morbidity and mortality during the 20th century with a view toward understanding the impact of health care and public health on the human lifespan and on the quality of life. These trends are of interest to policymakers and analysts as a means to understand the role of health care and point the direction for future policy decisions. All analysts, however, do not draw the same conclusions from available data and thus the conclusions drawn and the forecasts for future generations vary.

Using primary data on death rates (mortality), the late British physician Thomas McKeown, in his 1978 seminal article "Determinants of Health," reviewed the reasons for the dramatic decline in the death rate since the eighteenth century. He noted that much of the decline in mortality took place before the introduction of specific medical interventions, such as antibiotics. Therefore, McKeown argued, improved nutrition, a safer, cleaner environment, and a change in sexual behavior (smaller family size) were more significant determinants of health than were improvements in medical care. He also suggested that for improvements in health we should look more toward changing our ways of living and personal health habits than to continued reliance on personal health care.

In their article, "Producing Health, Consuming Health Care," Robert G. Evans and Gregory L. Stoddart present an analytic framework for understanding the determinants of health that they contend is more comprehensive and flexible than the traditional framework, which essentially defines health as absence of disease or injury and presents the health care system as a response or feedback mechanism to disease or injury. The authors' broad, complex framework encompasses meaningful categories that are responsive and sensitive to the ways in which a variety of factors interact to determine the health status of individuals and populations. The proposed framework has particular relevance to the current policy debate because it includes a definition of health that reflects the individual's experience as well as the perspective of the health care system; it encourages consideration of both behavioral and biological factors; and it acknowledges the economic trade-off involved in allocating scarce resources.

In "Health Inequalities and Social Class" M.G. Marmot and associates present evidence drawn from the Whitehall II study, an investigation conducted between 1985 and 1988 concerning the degree and causes of differences in morbidity rates in a cohort of over 10,000 British civil servants. This was a follow-up to the original Whitehall study in 1967, which demonstrated an inverse relationship between employment grade and morbidity and mortality. The inferences that can be drawn from these studies are far-reaching, including such factors as the influence on health and longevity of early life environment, leisure-time activity, social networks, housing circumstances, education, and control over the work environment. One of the most important findings relates to the diminished level of healthy behaviors practiced by those in the lower socioeconomic groups, which was reflected in the fact that fewer of those in lower status jobs believed that they could reduce their risk for a heart attack. This group also demonstrated a higher incidence of smoking, less vigorous exercise, more obesity, less healthy diet patterns, and more stressful life events. The study has many important policy implications, including the fact that people in lower socioeconomic groups are not benefiting from our vast knowledge about the close relationship between health status and behavioral factors. It also showed that these socioeconomic factors continue to have a strong influence despite the existence of universal health care coverage.

❖ Determinants of Health

THOMAS MCKEOWN

Modern medicine is not nearly as effective as most people believe. It has not been effective because medical science and service are misdirected and society's investment in health is misused. At the base of this misdirection is a false assumption about human health. Physicians, biochemists, and the general public assume that the body is a machine that can be protected from disease primarily by physical and chemical intervention. This approach, rooted in 17th-century science, has led to widespread indifference to the influence of the primary determinants of human health—environment and personal behavior—and emphasizes the role of medical treatment, which is actually less important than either of the others. It has also resulted in the neglect of sick people whose ailments are not within the scope of the sort of therapy that interests the medical professions.

An appraisal of influences on health in the past suggests that the contribution of modern medicine to the increase of life expectancy has been much smaller than most people believe. Health improved, not because of steps when we are ill, but because we become ill less often. We remain well, less because of specific measures such as vaccination and immunization than because we enjoy a higher standard of nutrition, we live in a healthier environment, and we have fewer children.

The utmost in healing can be achieved when there is unity, when the internal spirit and the external physical shape perfect each other.
>   —The Yellow Emperor
>   China, 1000 BC

For some 300 years, an engineering approach has been dominant in biology and medicine and has provided the basis for the treatment of the sick. A mechanistic concept of nature developed in the 17th century led to the idea that a living organism, like a machine, might be taken apart and reassembled if its structure and function were sufficiently understood. Applied to medicine, this concept meant that understanding the body's response to disease would allow physicians to intervene in the course of disease. The consequences of the engineering approach to medicine are more conspicuous today than they were in the 17th century, largely because the resources of the physical and chemical sciences are so much greater. Medical education begins with the study of the structure and function of the body, continues with examination of disease processes, and ends with clinical instruction on selected sick people. Medical service is dominated by the image of the hospital for the acutely ill, where technological resources are concentrated. Medical research also reflects the mechanistic approach, concerning itself with problems such as the chemical basis of inheritance and the immunological response to transplanted tissues.

No one disputes the predominance of the engineering approach in medicine, but we must now ask whether it is seriously deficient as a conceptualization of the problems of human health. To answer this question, we must examine the determinants of human health. We must first discover why health improved in the past and then go on to ascertain the important influences on health today in the light of the change in health problems that has resulted from the decline of infectious diseases.

It is no exaggeration to say that health, especially the health of infants and young children, has been transformed since the 18th century (Figure 1). For the first time in history, a mother knows it is likely that all her children will live to maturity. Before the 19th century, only about three out of every 10 newborn infants lived beyond the age of 25. Of the seven who died, two or three never reached their first birthday, and five or six died before they were six. Today, in developed countries fewer than one in 20 children die before they reach adulthood.

The increased life expectancy, most evident for young children, is due predominantly, to a reduction of deaths from infectious diseases (Figure 2). Records from England and Wales (the earliest national statistics available) show that this reduction was the reason for the improvement in health before 1900 and it remains the main influence to the present day.

But when we try to account for the decline of infections, significant differences of opinion appear. The conventional view attributes the change to an increased understanding of the nature of infectious disease and to the application of that knowledge through better hygiene, immunization, and treatment. This interpretation places particular emphasis on immunization against diseases like smallpox and polio, and on the use of drugs for the treatment of other diseases, such as tuberculosis, meningitis, and pneumonia. These measures, in fact, contributed relatively little to the total reduction of mortality; the main explanation for the dramatic fall in the number of deaths lies not in medical intervention but elsewhere.

Deaths from the common infections were declining long before effective medical intervention was possible. By 1900, the total death rate had dropped substantially, and over 90 percent of the reduction was due to a decrease of deaths from infectious diseases. The relative importance of the major influences can be illustrated by reference to tuberculosis. Although respiratory tuberculosis was the single largest cause of death in the mid-19th century, mortality from the disease declined continuously after 1938, when it was first registered in England and Wales as a cause of death.

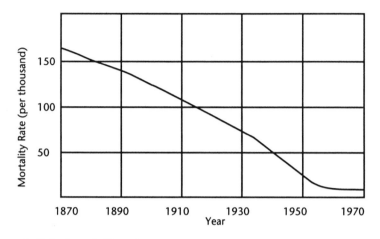

Figure 1. Infant mortality rate.

Robert Koch identified the tubercle bacillus in 1882, but none of the treatments used in the 19th or early 20th centuries significantly influenced the course of the disease. The many drugs that were tried were worthless; so, too, was the practice of surgically collapsing an infected lung, a treatment introduced about 1920. Streptomycin, developed in 1947, was the first effective treatment, but by this time mortality from the disease had fallen to a small fraction of its level during 1848 to 1854. Streptomycin lowered the death rate from tuberculosis in England and Wales by about 50 percent, but its contribution to the decrease in the death rate since the early 19th century was only about 3 percent.

Deaths from bronchitis, pneumonia, and influenza also began to decline before medical science provided an effective treatment for these illnesses. Although the death rate in England and Wales increased in the second half of the 19th century, it has fallen continuously since the beginning of the 20th. There is still no effective immunization against bronchitis or pneumonia, and influenza vaccines have had no effect on deaths. The first successful treatment for these respiratory diseases was a sulfa drug introduced in 1938, but mortality attributed to the lung infections was declining from the beginning of the 20th century. There is no reason to doubt that the decline would have continued without effective therapeutic measures, if at a far slower rate.

In the United States, the story was similar: Thomas Magill noted that "the rapid decline of pneumonia death rates began in New York State before the turn of the century and many years before the 'miracle drugs' were known." Obviously, drug therapy was not responsible for the total decrease in deaths that occurred since 1938, and it could have had no influence on the substantial reduction that occurred before then.

The histories of most other common infections, such as whooping cough, measles, and scarlet fever, are similar. In each of these diseases, mortality had fallen to a low level before effective immunization or therapy became available.

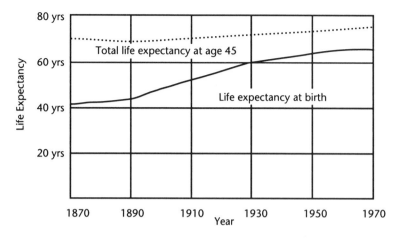

Figure 2. Life expectancy.

In some infections, medical intervention *was* valuable before sulfa drugs and antibiotics became available. Immunization protected people against smallpox and tetanus; antitoxin treatment limited deaths from diphtheria; appendicitis, peritonitis, and ear infections responded to surgery; Salvarsan was a long-sought "magic bullet" against syphilis; intravenous therapy saved people with severe diarrheas; and improved obstetric care prevented childbed fever.

But even if such medical measures had been responsible for the whole decline of mortality from these particular conditions after 1900 (and clearly they were not), they would account for only a small part of the decrease in deaths attributed to all infectious diseases before 1935. From that time, powerful drugs came into use and they were supplemented by improved vaccines. But mortality would have continued to fall even without the presence of these agents; and over the whole period since cause of death was first recorded, immunization and treatments have contributed much less than other influences.

The substantial fall in mortality was due in part to reduced contact with microorganisms. In developed countries, an individual no longer encounters the cholera bacillus, he is rarely exposed to the typhoid organism, and his contact with the tubercle bacillus is infrequent. The death rate from these infections fell continuously from the second half of the 19th century when basic hygienic measures were introduced: purification of water, efficient sewage disposal, and improved food hygiene—particularly the pasteurization of milk, the item in the diet most likely to spread disease.

Pasteurization was probably the main reason for the decrease in deaths from gastroenteritis and for the decline in infant mortality from about 1900.

In the 20th century, these essential hygienic measures were supported by improved conditions in the home, the work place, and the general environment. Over the entire period for which records exist, better hygiene accounts for approximately a fifth of the total reduction of mortality.

But the decline of mortality caused by infections began long before the introduction of sanitary measures. It had already begun in England and Wales by 1838, and statistics from Scandinavia suggest that the death rate had been decreasing there since the first half of the 18th century.

A review of English experience makes it unlikely that reduced exposure to microorganisms contributed significantly to the falling death rate in this earlier period. In England and Wales that was the time of industrialization, characterized by rapid population growth and shifts of people from farms into towns, where living and working conditions were uncontrolled. The crowding and poor hygiene that resulted provided ideal conditions for the multiplication and spread of microorganisms, and the situation improved little before sanitary measures were introduced in the last third of the century.

A further explanation for the falling death rate is that an improvement in nutrition led to an increase in resistance to infectious diseases. This is, I believe, the most credible reason for the decline of the infections, at least until the late 19th century, and also explains why deaths from airborne diseases like scarlet fever and measles have decreased even when exposure to the organisms that cause them remains almost unchanged. The evidence demonstrating the impact of improved nutrition is indirect, but it is still impressive.

Lack of food and the resulting malnutrition were largely responsible for the predominance of the infectious diseases, from the time when men first aggregated in large population groups about 10,000 years ago. In these conditions an improvement in nutrition was necessary for a substantial and prolonged decline in mortality.

Experience in developing countries today leaves no doubt that nutritional state is a critical factor in a person's response to infectious disease, particularly in young children. Malnourished people contract infections more often than those who are well fed and they suffer more when they become infected. According to a recent World Health Organization report on nutrition in developing countries, the best vaccine against common infectious diseases is an adequate diet.

In the 18th and 19th centuries, food production increased greatly throughout the Western world. The number of people in England and Wales tripled between 1700 and 1850 and they were fed on home-grown food.

In summary: The death rate from infectious diseases fell because an increase in food supplies led to better nutrition. From the second half of the 19th century this advance was strongly supported by improved hygiene and safer food and water, which reduced exposure to infection. With the exception of the smallpox vaccination, which played a small part in the total decline of mortality, medical procedures such as immunization and therapy had little impact on human health until the 20th century.

One other influence needs to be considered: a change in reproductive behavior, which caused the birth rate to decline. The significance of this change can hardly be exaggerated, for without it the other advances would soon have been overtaken by the increasing population. We can attribute the modern improvement in health to food, hygiene, and medical intervention in that order of time and importance—but we must recognize that it is to a modification of behavior that we owe the permanence of this improvement.

But it does not follow that these influences have the same relative importance today as in the past. In technologically advanced countries, the decline of infectious diseases was followed by a vast change in health problems, and even in developing countries advances in medical science and technology may have modified the effects of nutrition, sanitation, and contraception. In order to predict the factors likely to affect our health in the future, we need to examine the nature of the problems in health that exist today.

Because today's problems are mainly with noncommunicable diseases, physicians have shifted their approach. In the case of infections, interest centers on the organisms that cause them and on the conditions under which they spread. In noninfective conditions, the engineering approach established in the 17th century remains predominant and attention is focused on how a disease develops rather than on why it begins. Perhaps the most important question now confronting medicine is whether the commonest health problems—heart disease, cancer, rheumatoid arthritis, cerebrovascular disease—are essentially different from health problems of the past or whether, like infections, they can be prevented by modifying the conditions that lead to them.

A wise man should consider that health is the greatest of human blessings, and learn how, by his own thought, to derive benefit from his illness.
  —Hippocrates
  460–400 BC

To answer this question, we must distinguish between genetic and chromosomal diseases determined at the moment of fertilization and all other diseases, which are attributable in greater or lesser degree to the influence of the environment. Most diseases, including the common noninfectious ones, appear to fall into the second category. Whether these diseases can be prevented is likely to be determined by the practicability of controlling the environmental influences that lead them.

The change in the character of health problems that followed the decline of infections in developed countries has not invalidated the conclusion that most diseases, both physical and mental, are associated with influences that might be controlled. Among such influences, those which the individual determines by his own behavior (smoking, eating, exercise, and the like) are now more important for his health than those that depend mainly on society's actions (provision of essential food and protection from hazards). And both behavioral and environmental influences are more significant than medical care.

The role of individual medical care in preventing sickness and premature death is secondary to that of other influences; yet society's investment in health care is based on the premise that it is the major determinant. It is assumed that we are ill and are made well, but it is nearer the truth to say that we are well and are made ill. Few people think of themselves as having the major responsibility for their own health, and the enormous resources that advanced countries assign to the health field are used mainly to treat disease or, to a lesser extent, to prevent it by personal measures such as immunization.

The revised concept of human health cannot provide immediate solutions for the many complex problems facing society: limiting population growth and providing adequate food in developing countries, changing personal behavior, and striking a new balance between technology and care in developed nations. Instead, the enlarged understanding of health and disease should be regarded as a conceptual base with implications for services, education, and research that will take years to develop.

The most immediate requirements in the health services is to give sufficient attention to behavioral influences that are now the main determinants of health. The public believes that health depends primarily on intervention by the doctor and that the essential requirement for health is the early discovery of disease. This concept should be replaced by recognition that disease often cannot be treated effectively, and that health is determined predominantly by the way of life individuals choose to follow. Among the important influences on health are the use of tobacco, the misuse of alcohol and drugs, excessive or unbalanced diets, and lack of exercise. With research, the list of significant behavioral influences will undoubtedly increase, particularly in relation to the prevention of mental illness.

Although the influences of personal behavior are the main determinants of health in developed countries, public action can still accomplish a great deal in the environmental field. Internationally, malnutrition probably remains the most important cause of ill health, and even in affluent societies sections of the population are inadequately—as distinct from unwisely—fed. The malnourished vary in proportion and composition from one country to another, but in the developed world they are mainly the younger children of large families and elderly people who live alone. In light of the importance of food for good health, governments might use supplements and subsidies to put essential foods within the reach of everyone, and provide inducements for people to select beneficial in place of harmful foods. Of course, these aims cannot exclude other considerations such as international agreements and the solvency of farmers who have been encouraged to produce meat and dairy products rather than grains. Nevertheless, in future evaluations of agricultural and related economic policies, health implications deserve a primary place.

Perhaps the most sensitive area for consideration is the funding of health services. Although the contribution of medical intervention to prevention of sickness and premature death can be expected to remain small in relation to behavioral and environmental influences, surgery and drugs are widely regarded as the basis of health and the essence of medical care, and society invests the money it sets aside for health mainly in treatment for acute diseases and particularly in hospitals for the acutely ill. Does it follow from our appraisal that resources should be transferred from acute care to chronic care and to preventive measures?

Health signifies that one's life force is intact, and that one is sufficiently in harmony with the social, physical, and supernatural environment to enjoy what is positively valued in life, and to ward off misfortunes and evils.
        —Bantu African Medical Theory

Restricting the discussion to personal medical care, I believe that neglected areas, such as mental illness, mental retardation, and geriatric care, need greatly increased attention. But to suggest that this can be achieved merely by direct transfer of resources is an oversimplification. The designation "acute care" comprises a wide range of activities that differ profoundly in their effectiveness and efficiency. Some, like surgery for accidents and the treatment of acute emergencies, are among the most important services that medicine can offer and any reduction of their support would be disastrous. Others, however, like coronary care units and iron treatment of some anemias are not shown to be effective, while still others—most tonsillectomies and routine check-ups—are quite useless and should be abandoned. A critical appraisal of medical services for acute illnesses would result in more efficient use of available resources and would free some of them for preventive measures.

What health services need in general is an adjustment in the distribution of interest and resources between prevention of disease, care of the sick who require investigation and treatment, and care of the sick who do not need active intervention. Such an adjustment must pay considerable attention to the major determinants of health: to food and the environment, which will be mainly in the hands of specialists, and to personal behavior, which should be the concern of every practicing doctor.

❖ About the Author

The late Thomas McKeown, M.D., was professor emeritus, Department of Social Medicine, University of Birmingham, England, and author of *The Role of Medicine: Dream, Mirage, or Nemesis?*

❖ Producing Health, Consuming Health Care

ROBERT G. EVANS AND GREGORY L. STODDART

❖ Introduction

People care about their health for good reasons, and they try in a number of ways to maintain or improve it. Individually and in groups at various levels—families, associations, work groups, communities, and nations—they engage in a wide range of activities which they believe will contribute to their health. People also attempt to avoid activities or circumstances which they see as potentially harmful. Implicit in such behavior are theories or, more accurately, loosely associated and often inconsistent collections of causal hypotheses as to the determinants of health.

In particular, but only as a sub-set of these health-oriented activities, modern societies devote a very large proportion of their economic resources to the production and distribution of health care, a particular collection of commodities which are perceived as bearing a special relationship to health. The health care industry, which assembles these resources and converts them into various health-related goods and services, is one of the largest clusters of economic activity in all modern states. Such massive efforts reflect a widespread belief that the availability and use of health care is central to the health of both individuals and populations.

In America the passion for physical well-being is general.
—Alexis de Toqueville (1835)

This concentration of economic effort has meant that public or collective health policy has been predominantly health *care* policy. The provision of care not only absorbs the lion's share of the physical and intellectual resources which are specifically identified as health-related, it also occupies the centre of the stage when the rest of the community considers what to do about its health.

Health care, in turn, is overwhelmingly *reactive* in nature, responding to perceived departures from health and identifying those departures in terms of clinical concepts and categories—diseases, professionally defined. The definition of *health* implicit in (most of) the behavior of the health care system, the collection of people and institutions involved in the provision of care, is a negative concept: the absence of disease or injury. The system is in

14

consequence often labeled, usually by its critics but not unjustly, as a "sickness care system."

Yet this definition of health was specifically rejected by the World Health Organization (WHO) more than 40 years ago. Its classic statement, "Health is a state of complete physical, mental, and social well-being, and not merely the absence of disease or injury" expressed a general perception that there is much more to health than simply a collection of negatives—a state of *not* suffering from any designated undesirable condition.

Such a comprehensive concept of health, however, risks becoming the proper objective for, and is certainly affected by, *all* human activity. There is no room for a separately identifiable realm of specifically health-oriented activity. The WHO definition is thus difficult to use as the basis for health policy because implicitly it includes *all* policy as health policy. It has accordingly been honored in repetition, but rarely in application.

Moreover, the WHO statement appears to offer only polar alternatives for the definition of health. Common usage, however, suggests a continuum of meanings. At one end of that continuum is well being in the broadest sense, the all-encompassing definition of the WHO, almost a platonic ideal of "The Good." At the other end is the simple absence of negative biological circumstances—disease, disability, or death.

But the biological circumstances identified and classified by the health care disciplines as diseases are then experienced by individuals and their families or social groups as illnesses—distressing symptoms. The correspondence between medical disease and personal illness is by no means exact. Thus the patient's concept of health as absence of illness need not match the clinician's absence of disease. Further, the functional capacity of the individual will be influenced but not wholly determined by the perception of illness, and that capacity too will be an aspect, but not the totality, of well-being.

There are no sharply drawn boundaries between the various concepts of health in such a continuum, but that does not prevent us from recognizing their differences. Different concepts are neither right nor wrong, they simply have different purposes and fields of application. Whatever the level of *definition* of health being employed, however, it is important to distinguish this from the question of the *determinants* of (that definition of) health.

Here, too, there exists a broad range of candidates, from particular targeted health care services through genetic endowments of individuals, environmental sanitation, adequacy and quality of nutrition and shelter, stress and the supportiveness of the social environment, to self-esteem and sense of personal adequacy or control. It appears, on the basis of both long-established wisdom and considerable more recent research, that the factors which affect health at all levels of definition include but go well beyond health care per se.

Attempts to advance our understanding of this broad range of determinants through research have, like the health care system itself, tended to focus their attention on the narrower concept of health: absence of disease or injury. This concept has the significant advantage that it can be represented through quantifiable and measurable phenomena: death or survival, the incidence or prevalence of particular morbid conditions. The influence of a wide range of determinants, in and beyond the health care system, has in fact been observed in these most basic—negative—measures.

Precision is gained at a cost. Narrow definitions leave out less specific dimensions of health which many people would judge to be important to their evaluation of their own circumstances or to those of their associates. On the other hand, it seems at least plausible that the broad range of determinants of health, whose effects are reflected in the "mere absence of disease or injury" or simple survival, are also relevant to more comprehensive definitions of health.

The current resurgence of interest in the determinants of health, as well as in its broader conceptualization, represents a return to a very old historical tradition, as old as medicine itself. The dialogue between Asclepios, the god of medicine, and Hygieia, the goddess of health—the external intervention and the well-lived life—goes back to the beginning. Only in the 20th century did the triumph of "scientific" modes of inquiry in medicine (as in most walks of life) result in the eclipse of Hygieia. Knowledge has increasingly become defined in terms of that (and only that) which emerges from the application of reductionist methods of investigation, applied to the fullest extent possible in a "Newtonian" frame of reference.

The health care system has then become the conventional vehicle for the translation of such knowledge into the improvement of health—more and more powerful interventions guided by better and better science. Nor have its achievements been negligible in enhanced ability to prevent some disease, cure others, and alleviate the symptoms or slow the progress of many more. Thus, by mid-century the providers of health care had gained an extraordinary institutional and, even more, an intellectual dominance, defining both what counted as health and how it was to be pursued. The WHO was a voice in the wilderness.

But the intellectual currents have now begun to flow in the other direction. There has been a continuing unease about the exclusive authority of classically "scientific," positivist methods, both to define the knowable and to determine how it may come to be known, an unease which has drawn new strength from developments in sub-atomic physics and more recently in artificial intelligence and mathematics. In addition, the application of those methods themselves to the exploration of the determinants of health is generating increasing evidence—in the most restricted scientific sense—of the powerful role of contributing factors outside the health care system.

Simultaneously, the more rigorous evaluation of the health care system itself has demonstrated that its practices are much more loosely connected with scientific or any other form of knowledge than the official rhetoric would suggest. And, finally, the very success of that system in occupying the centre of the intellectual and policy stage, and in drawing in resources, has been built upon an extraordinarily heightened set of social expectations as to its potential contributions. Some degree of disappointment and disillusionment is an inevitable consequence, with corresponding concern about the justification for the scale of effort involved—the rhetoric of "cost explosions."

There is thus a growing gap between our understanding of the determinants of health and the primary focus of health policy on the provision of health care. This increasing disjunction may be partly a consequence of the persistence, in the policy arena, of incomplete and obsolete models or intellectual frames of reference for conceptualizing the determinants of health. How a problem is framed will determine which kinds of evidence are given weight, and which are disregarded. Perfectly valid data—hard observations bearing directly on important questions—simply drop out of consideration, as if they did not exist, when the implicit model of entities and interrelationships in people's minds provides no set of categories in which to put them.

There is, for example, considerable evidence linking mortality to the (non)availability of social support mechanisms, evidence of a strength which House describes as now equivalent to that in the mid-1950s on the effects of tobacco smoking. Retirement or the death of a spouse are documented as important risk factors. Similarly, some correlate or combination of social class, level of income or education, and position in a social hierarchy are clearly associated with mortality. None of this is denied, yet no account is taken of such relationships in the formulation of health (care) policy.

Such policy is, by contrast, acutely sensitive to even the possibility that some new drug, piece of equipment, or diagnostic or therapeutic maneuver may contribute to health. That someone's health may perhaps be at risk for lack of such intervention is *prima facie* grounds for close policy attention and at least a strong argument for provision. Meanwhile, the egregious fact that people are suffering and, in some cases, dying as a consequence of processes not directly connected to health care, elicits neither rebuttal nor response.

Health is a very large term indeed. It goes beyond the condition of the flesh. It's also a condition of the spirit. Everything we do is reflected in the physical. Over a period of years, the strains and stresses residing in the body often manifest themselves as diseases. The opposite can also be true. And ultimately health doesn't just involve isolated parts of the body. It also involves the whole way we live, the way we think, our social responsibility, our attitude toward the world, our enthusiasm for life.
—George Leonard

The explanation cannot be that there is superior evidence for the effectiveness, still less the cost effectiveness, of health care interventions. It is notorious that new interventions are introduced and, particularly, disseminated in the absence of such evidence. If (some) clinicians find it plausible that a maneuver might be beneficial in particular circumstances, it is likely to be used. The growing concern for "technological assessment" or careful evaluation *before* dissemination is a response to this well-established pattern. But those who might wish to restrain application, fearing lack of effect or even harm, find themselves bearing the burden of rigorous proof. If the evidence is incomplete or ambiguous, the bias is toward intervention.

This heavy concentration of attention and effort on a sub-set of health-related activities and *de facto* dismissal of others may be a product of the conceptual framework within which we think about the determinants of health. A simple mechanical model captures the causal relationships from sickness, to care, to cure. The machine (us) is damaged or breaks and the broken part is repaired (or perhaps replaced). Although this mental picture may be a gross oversimplification of reality, it is easy to hold in mind.

By contrast, it is not at all obvious how one should even think about the causal connections between "stress" or "low self-esteem" and illness or death—much less what would be appropriate policy responses. The whole subject has a somewhat mysterious air with overtones of the occult, in contrast to the (apparently) transparent and scientific process of health care. There being no set of intellectual categories in which to assemble such data, they are ignored.

In this paper, therefore, we propose a somewhat more complex framework, which we believe is sufficiently comprehensive and flexible to represent a wider range of relationships among the determinants of health. The test of such a framework is its ability to provide meaningful categories in which to insert the various sorts of evidence which are now emerging as to the diverse determinants of health, as well as to permit a definition of health broad enough to encompass the dimensions which people—providers of care, policy makers, and particularly ordinary individuals—feel to be important.

Our purpose is *not* to try to present a comprehensive, or even a sketchy, survey of the current evidence on the determinants of health. Even a taxonomy for that evidence, a suggested classification and enumeration of the main heads, would now be a major research task. Rather, we are trying to construct an analytic framework within which such evidence can be fitted and which will highlight the ways in which different types of factors and forces can interact to bear on different conceptualizations of health. Our model or precedent is the Canadian government's *White Paper, A New Perspective on the Health of Canadians*, which likewise presented very little of the actual evidence on the determinants of health, but offered a very powerful and compelling framework for assembling it.

We will also follow the *White Paper* in offering no more than the most cursory indication of what the implications of such evidence might be for health policy, public or private. Policy implications will arise from the actual evidence on the determinants of health, not from the framework per se. If the framework is useful, it should facilitate the presentation of evidence in such a way as to make its implications more apparent. But there is, of course, much more to policy than evidence; "the art of the possible" includes most importantly one's perceptions of who the key actors are and what their objectives might be. We will be addressing these issues in subsequent work, but not here.

Finally, we must emphasize that the entities which form the components of our framework are themselves categories with a rich internal structure. Each box and label could be expanded to show its complex contents. One must therefore be very careful about, and usually avoid, treating such categories as if they could be adequately represented by some single homogeneous variable, much less subjected to mathematical or statistical manipulations like a variable. Single variables may capture some aspect of a particular category, but they are not the same as that category. Moreover, in specific contexts it may be the *interactions* between factors from different categories of determinants that are critical to the health of individuals and populations.

❖ Disease and Health Care: A (Too) Simple Foundation

We build up our framework component by component, progressively adding complexity both in response to the demonstrable inadequacies of the preceding stage and in rough correspondence to (our interpretation of) the historical evolution of the conceptual basis of health policy over the last half century. The first and simplest stage defines health as absence of disease or injury and takes as central the relation between health and health care. The former is represented in terms of the categories and capacities of the latter. The relationship can be represented in a simple feed-back model, as presented in Figure 1, exactly analogous to a heating system governed by a thermostat.

In this framework, people "get sick" or "get hurt" for a variety of unspecified reasons represented by the unlabeled arrows entering on the left-hand side. They may then respond by presenting themselves to the health care system, where the resulting diseases and injuries are defined and interpreted as giving rise to "needs" for particular forms of health care. This interpretive role is critical because the definition of "need" depends on the state of medical technology. Conditions for which (it is believed that) noth-

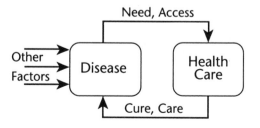

Figure 1.

ing can be done may be regrettable and very distressing, but do not represent "needs" for care. The patient feels the distress, but the health care system defines the need.

Potential "needs" for health care are, however, prefiltered before they reach the care system, an important process which is reflected explicitly neither in Figure 1 nor in most of health policy. Whether people respond to adverse circumstances by contacting the health care system seeking "patient" status will depend on their perceptions of their own coping capacities, and their informal support systems, relative to their expectations of the formal system. These expectations and reactions are thus included among the "other factors" that determine the environment to which the health care system responds.

The health care system then combines the functions of thermostat and furnace, interpreting its environment, defining the appropriate response, and responding. The level of response is determined by the "access" to care which a particular society has provided for its members. This access depends both on the combination of human and physical resources available—doctors, nurses, hospitals, diagnostic equipment, drugs, etc.—and also on the administrative and financial systems in place, which determine whether particular individuals will receive the services of these resources and under what conditions.

The top arrow in Figure 1 thus reflects the positive response of the health care system to disease—the provision of care. But the form and scale of the response is influenced, through a sort of two-key system, both by the professional definition of needs—what should be done to or for people in particular circumstances, suffering particular departures from health—and by the whole collection of institutions which in any particular society mobilizes the resources to meet the needs and ensures access to care.

Those organizing and financing institutions have very different structures from one society to another, but their tasks are essentially similar, as are the problems and conflicts they face. The actual technologies and the institutional and professional roles in health care also show a remarkable similarity across modern societies, suggesting that those societies share a common intellectual framework for thinking about the relationship between health and health care.

The feed-back loop is completed by the lower arrow, reflecting the presumption that the provision of care reduces the level of disease, thereby improving health. The strength of this negative relationship represents the effectiveness of care. These effects include the restoration and maintenance of health (providing "cures"); preventing further deterioration; relieving symptoms, particularly pain; offering assistance in coping with the inevitable; and providing reassurance through authoritative interpretation.

The important role of health care in providing comfort to the afflicted fits somewhat ambiguously in this framework, since services that can clearly be identified as making people feel good, but having no present or future influence on their health status however defined, can readily be seen to include a very wide range of activities, most of which are not usually included as health care.

The provision of services which *are* generally recognized as health care should obviously take place in a context that preserves a decent consideration for the comfort of those served. There is no excuse for the gratuitous infliction of discomfort, and patients should not be made any more miserable than they have to be. But for those services that represent *only* comfort, it is important to ask both: Why should they be professionalized, by assigning "official" providers of health care a privileged right to serve? and Why should the clients of the health care system be awarded privileged access to such services? There are many people, not by any sensible definition ill, who might nevertheless have their lives considerably brightened by comforting services at collective expense.

In this conceptual framework, the level of health of a population is the negative or inverse of the burden of disease. This burden of disease in Figure 1 is analogous to the temperature of the air in a house in a model of a heating system. The health care system diagnoses that disease and responds with treatment; the thermostat detects a fall in air temperature and turns on the furnace. The result is a reduction in disease/increase in room temperature. The external factors—pathogens, accidents—which "cause" disease are analogous to the temperature outside the house; a very cold night is equivalent to an epidemic. But the consequences of such external events are moderated by the response of the heating/health care systems.

The thermostat can, of course, be set at different target temperatures, and the control system of the furnace can be more or less sophisticated depending on the extent and duration of permissible departures from the target temperature. Similarly, access to care can be provided at different levels to meet different degrees of "need" and with tighter or looser tolerances for over- or under-servicing.

The systems do differ, insofar as the house temperature can be increased more or less indefinitely by putting more fuel through the furnace (or adding more furnaces). In principle, the expansion of the health care system is bounded by the burden of remediable disease. When each individual has received all the health care that might conceivably be of benefit, then all needs have been met and "health" in the narrow sense of absence of (remediable) disease or injury has been attained. Health is bounded from above; air temperature is not. The occupants of the house do not of course *want* an ever-increasing temperature, whether or not it is possible. Too much is as bad as too little. Yet no obvious meaning attaches to the words "too healthy." More is always better, a closer approximation to the ideal of perfect, or at least best attainable, health.

The differences are more apparent than real, however, since in practice the professionally defined needs for care are themselves adjusted according to the capacity of the health care system and the pressures on it. The objective of health, René Dubos' mirage, ever recedes as more resources are devoted to health care. As old forms of disease or injury threaten to disappear, new ones are defined. There are always "unmet needs."

Furthermore, obvious meanings *do* attach to the words "too much health care," on at least three levels. First, too much care may result in harm to health in the narrow sense—iatrogenic disease—because potent interventions are always potentially harmful. But even if care contributes to health in the narrow sense—keeping the patient alive, for example—it may still be "too much." Painful interventions which prolong not life but dying are generally recognized as harmful to those who are forced to undergo them. More generally, the side effects of "successful" therapy may, in some cases, be, for the patient, worse than the disease.

Second, even if the care *is* beneficial in terms of both health and well-being of the recipient, it may still represent "too much" if the benefits are very small relative to the costs, the other opportunities foregone by the patient or others. If health is an important, but not the only, goal in life, it follows that there can be "too much" even of effective health care.

And, finally, an important component of health is the individual's *perception* of his or her own state. An exaggerated sense of fragility is not health but hypochondria. Too much emphasis on the number of things that can go wrong, even presented under the banner of "health promotion," can lead to excessive anxiety and a sense of dependence on health care—from annual check-up to continuous monitoring. This is very advantageous economically for the "health care industry," and *perhaps* may contribute in some degree to a reduction in disease, but does not correspond to any more general concept of health.

Unlike a heating system, however, health care systems do not settle down to a stable equilibrium of temperature maintenance and fuel use. The combination of the "ethical" claim that all needs must be met and the empirical regularity that as one need is met another is discovered, apparently *ad infinitum*, leads to a progressive pressure for expansion in the health care systems of all developed societies. It is as if no temperature level were ever high enough. More and more fuel must always be added to the furnace(s).

❖ Concerns about Cost Effectiveness and the Marginal Contribution of Health Care

The result is shown in Figure 2, in which the top arrow, access to health care, has been dramatically expanded to reflect a "health care cost crisis." A comparison of international experience demonstrates that the *perception* of such a crisis is virtually universal, at least in Western Europe and North America. It is interesting to note, however, that the countries which perceive such a crisis actually spend widely differing amounts on health care, either absolutely or as a proportion of their national incomes.

Nevertheless, whether they spend a little or a lot, in all such countries

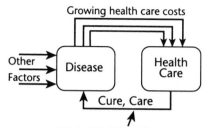

Figure 2.

there is an expressed tension between ever-increasing needs and increasingly restrained resources. Even in the United States, one finds providers of care claiming that they face more and more serious restrictions on the resources available to them despite the egregious observation that the resources devoted to health care in that country are greater, and growing faster, than anywhere else in the world.

We interpret this observation as implying that perceptions of "crises" in health care finance arise from conflicts over the level of expenditure on health care (and thus, by definition, also over the levels of incomes earned from its provision). Such conflicts develop whenever paying agencies attempt to limit the rate of increase of resources flowing to the health care system. They are independent of the actual level of provision of health care to a population or of its expense, let alone of the level of health, however defined, of that population. They also appear to develop independently of the particular form taken by the payment system in a country.

Nor, as the American example shows, does it matter whether the attempts to limit cost escalation are successful. Perceptions of crisis emerge from the attempt, not the result. Accordingly, one should not expect to find any connection between the health of a population and allegations of "crisis" in the funding of its health care—or at least not among the countries of Western Europe and North America.

On the lower arrow, and intimately connected with the perceptions of "cost crisis," we find increasing concern for the effectiveness with which health care services respond to needs. The development and rapid expansion of clinical epidemiology, for example, reflects a concern that the scientific basis underlying much of health care is weak to nonexistent. More generally, the growing field of health services research has accumulated extensive evidence inconsistent with the assumption that the provision of health care is connected in any systematic or scientifically grounded way with patient "needs" or demonstrable outcomes. Accordingly, the greatly increased flow of resources into health care is perceived as not having a commensurate or, in some cases any, impact on health status. Nor is there any demonstrable connection between international variations in health status and variations in health spending. . . .

The combination of virtually universal concern over cost escalation among payers for care with steadily increasing evidence from the international research community that a significant proportion of health care activity is ineffective, inefficient, inexplicable, or simply unevaluated, constitutes an implicit judgment that the "expanding needs" to which expanding health care systems respond are either not of high enough priority to justify the expense or simply not being met at all.

It is not that no "needs" remain, that the populations of modern societies have reached a state of optimum health—that is obviously not the case. Nor is it claimed that medicine has had no effect on health—that too is clearly false. The concern is rather that the remaining shortfalls, the continuing burden of illness, disability, distress, and premature death are less and less sensitive to further extensions in health care—we are reaching the limits of medicine. At the same time, the evidence is growing in both quantity and quality that this burden may be quite sensitive to interventions and structural changes outside the health care system.

These concerns and this evidence are by no means new—they go back at least two decades. Yet most of the public and political debate over health policy continues to be carried on in the rhetoric of "unmet needs" for *health care*. There is a curious disjunction in both the popular and the professional "conventional wisdom," in that widespread concerns about the effectiveness of the health care system and acceptance of the significance of factors outside that system co-exist quite comfortably with continuing worries about shortages and "underfunding."

By the early 1970s, all developed nations had in place extensive and expensive systems of health care, underpinned by collective funding mechanisms, which provided access for all (or, in the United States, most) of their citizens. Yet the resulting health gains seemed more modest than some had anticipated, while the "unmet needs," or at least the pressures for system expansion, refused to diminish.

Simple trend projections indicated that, within a relatively short span of decades, the health care systems of modern societies would take over their entire economies. As public concerns shifted from expansion to evaluation and control, the alternative tradition began to reassert itself. In such an environment, a growing interest in alternative, perhaps more effective, hopefully less expensive, ways of promoting health was a natural response.

The resurgence of interest in ways of enhancing the health of populations, other than by further expansion of health care systems, was thus rooted both in the observation of the stubborn persistence of ill-health and in the concern over growing costs. The latter development has been particularly important in "recruiting new constituencies" for the broader view of the determinants of health. Financial bureaucrats, both public and private, have become (often rather suspect) allies of more traditional advocates.

❖ The Health Field Concept: A New Perspective

The broader view was given particularly compact and articulate expression in the famous Canadian *White Paper* referred to above which came out, presumably by complete coincidence, in the same year as the first "energy crisis." Its "Four Field" framework for categorizing the determinants of health was broad enough to express a number of the concerns of those trying to shift the focus of health policy from an exclusive concern with health care. In Figure 3 this framework is superimposed upon the earlier "thermostat/furnace" model of health care and health.

The *New Perspective* proposed that the determinants of health status could be categorized under the headings of Lifestyles, Environment, Human Biology, and Health Care Organization. As can be seen in Figure 3, the first three of these categories provided specific identification for some of the "other and unspecified" factors entering on the left-hand side of Figures 1 and 2. By labeling and categorizing these factors, the *White Paper* drew attention to them and suggested the possibility that their control might contribute more to the improvement of human health than further expansions in the health care system. At the very least, the health field framework emphasized the centrality of the objective of *health* and the fact that health care was only one among several forms of public policy that might lead toward this objective.

The *White Paper* was received very positively; no one seriously challenged its basic message that who we are, how we live, and where we live are powerful influences on our health status. But the appropriate policy response was less clear because the document could be read in several different ways. At one end of the ideological spectrum, it was seen as a call for a much more interventionist set of social policies, going well beyond the public provision of health care per se in the effort to improve the health of the Canadian population and relieve the burden of morbidity and mortality.

At the other end, however, the assumption that lifestyles and, to a lesser extent, living environments are *chosen* by the persons concerned could be

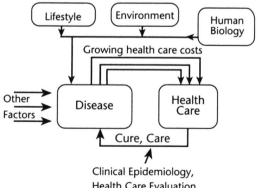

Figure 3.

combined with the *White Paper* framework to argue that people are largely responsible for their own health status—have in fact chosen it. If so, then the justification for collective intervention, even in the provision of health care, becomes less clear. This appears to have been far from the intention of the authors of the paper, but the framework in Figure 3 lends itself to "victim-blaming" as well as to arguments for more comprehensive social reform.

Whatever the original intent, however, the *White Paper* led into a period of detailed analysis of *individual* risk factors, i.e., both individual hazards and individual persons, as contributors to "disease" in the traditional sense. The potential significance of processes operating on health at the level of groups and populations was obscured, if not lost. Smoking, for example, was viewed as an individual act predisposing to specific diseases. Specific atmospheric pollution contributes to lung disease. Genetic defects result in well-defined genetic diseases. The central thermostatic relationship is preserved, with health as absence of disease, and health care as response to disease in order to provide "cures" or relieve symptoms, individual by individual.

The emphasis on individual risk factors and particular diseases has thus served to maintain and protect existing institutions and ways of thinking about health. The "broader determinants of health" were matters for the attention of individuals, perhaps in consultation with their personal physicians, supported by poster campaigns from the local public health unit. The behavior of large and powerful organizations, or the effects of economic and social policies, public and private, were not brought under scrutiny. This interpretation of the *White Paper* thus not only fitted in with the increasingly conservative *zeitgeist* of the late 1970s and early 1980s, but protected and even enhanced the economic position of providers of care, while restricting sharply the range of determinants, and associated policies, considered. Established economic interests were not threatened—with the limited exception of the tobacco industry.

The intellectual framework of the *White Paper*, at least as it has been applied and as represented in Figure 3, has thus supplemented the thermostatic model of health as absence of disease, and health care as response, but has failed to move beyond the core relationship. Since, as noted above, "disease" is defined through the interpretation of individual experience by the providers of health care, it is perhaps not surprising that the Health Care Organization field tended to take over large parts of the other three when they were presented as determinants of disease.

❖ Extending the Framework: Health and Its Biological and Behavioral Determinants

Yet in the years since the publication of the *White Paper*, a great deal of evidence has accumulated, from many different sources, which is difficult or impossible to represent within this framework. The very broad set of relationships encompassed under the label of "stress," for example, and factors protective against "stress," have directed attention to the importance of social relationships, or their absence, as correlates of disease and mortality. Feelings of self-esteem and self-worth, or hierarchical position and control, or, conversely, powerlessness, similarly appear to have health implications quite independent of the conventional risk factors.

These sorts of factors suggest explanations for the universal finding, across all nations, that mortality and (when measurable) morbidity follow a gradient across socioeconomic classes. Lower income and/or lower social status are associated with poorer health.

This relationship is not, however, an indication of deprivation at the lower end of the scale, although it is frequently misinterpreted in that way. In the first place, the socioeconomic gradient in health status has been relatively stable over time, although average income levels have risen markedly in all developed societies. The proportion of persons who are deprived of the necessities of life in a biological sense has clearly declined. But even more important, the relationship is a *gradient*, not a step function. Top people appear to be healthier than those on the second rung, even though the latter are above the population averages for income, status, or whatever the critical factors are.

It follows that the variously interpreted determinants of health that lie outside the health care system are not just a problem of some poor, deprived minority whose situation can be deplored and ignored by the rest of us. *De te fabula narratur*, we are all (or most of us) affected. And that in turn implies that the effects of such factors may be quantitatively very significant for the overall health status of modern populations. The issues involved are not trivial, second- or third-order effects.

Moreover, the fact that gradients in mortality and morbidity across socioeconomic classes appear to be relatively stable over long periods of time, even though the principal causes of death have changed considerably, implies that the underlying factors influence susceptibility to a whole range of diseases. They are general rather than specific risk factors. Whatever is going round, people in lower social positions tend to get more of it, and to die earlier—even after adjustment for the effects of specific individual or environmental hazards.

This suggests that an understanding of the relationship between social position, or "stress," and health will require investigation at a more general level than the aetiology of specific diseases. It also raises the possibility that disease-specific policy responses—through health care or otherwise—may not reach deeply enough to have much effect. Even if one "disease" is "cured," another will take its place.

An attempt to provide a further extension to our intellectual framework, to encompass these new forms of evidence, is laid out in Figure 4.

In Figure 4, two major structural changes are introduced. First, a distinction is drawn between disease, as recognized and responded to by the health care system, and health and function as experienced by the individual per-

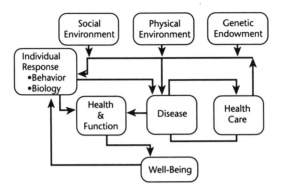

Figure 4.

son. Such a distinction permits us to consider, within this framework, the common observation that illness experienced by individuals (and their families or other relevant social groups) does not necessarily correspond to disease as understood by the providers of care. Persons with "the same" disease, from the point of view of the health care system—similar biological parameters, prognoses, and implications for treatment—may experience very different levels of symptoms and distress, and very different effects on their ability to function in their various social roles.

This is not to say that one perspective is "right" and the other "wrong"; the two modes of interpretation simply have different purposes. The clinician's concept of disease is intended to guide the appropriate application of available medical knowledge and technology, so is formulated in terms of that knowledge and technology. The patient, on the other hand, is ultimately concerned with the impact of the illness on his/her own life. The clinician's disease may be an important part of that impact but is by no means the only relevant factor.

Moreover, from the point of view of the individual's well-being and social performance—including economic productivity—it is the individual's sense of health and functional capacity which is determinative—as shown in Figure 4. The "diseases" diagnosed and treated by the health care system are important only insofar as they affect that sense of health and capacity—which of course they do. But health, even as interpreted by the individual, is not the only thing in life which matters. Figure 4 introduces the category of "well-being," the sense of life satisfaction of the individual, which is or should be (we postulate) the ultimate objective of health policy. The ultimate test of such policy is whether or not it adds to the well-being of the population served.

Going back to the original WHO definition of health, we are relabeling that broad definition as well-being. Our concept of health is defined, in narrow terms but from the patient's perspective, as the absence of illness or injury, of distressing symptoms or impaired capacity. Disease, as a medical construct or concept, will usually have a significant bearing on illness, and thus on health, but is not the same thing. Illness, in turn, is a very important (negative) influence on well-being—but not the only one. The WHO broad definition of "health" is, as noted above, so broad as to become the objective, not only of health policy but of all human activity.

Indeed, progress in genetics is also extending the older picture of a fixed genetic endowment, in which well-defined genetic diseases follow from single-gene defects. It now appears that particular combinations of genes may lead to predispositions, or resistances, to a wide variety of diseases, not themselves normally thought of as "genetic." Whether these predispositions actually become expressed as disease will depend *inter alia* on various environmental factors, physical and social.

The insertion of the host response between environmental factors, and both the expression of disease and the level of health and function, provides a set of categories sufficiently flexible to encompass the growing but rather complex evidence on the connections between social environment and illness. Unemployment, for example, may lead to illness (quite apart from its correlation with economic deprivation) if the unemployed individual becomes socially isolated and stigmatized. On the other hand, if support networks are in place to maintain social contacts, and if self-esteem is not undermined, then the health consequences may be minimal.

The correlation of longevity with hierarchical status may be an example of reverse causality—the physically fitter rise to the top. But it is also possible that the self-esteem and sense of coping ability induced by success and the respect of others results in a "host response" of enhanced immune function or other physiological strengthening. The biological vulnerability or resilience of the individual, in response to external shocks, is dependent on the social and physical environment in interaction with the genetic endowment. While, as noted, the biological pathways for this process are only beginning to be traced out, the observed correlations continue to accumulate. Figure 4 provides a conceptual framework within which to express such a pattern of relationships.

In this extended framework, the relationship between the health care system and the health of the population becomes even more complex. The sense of self-esteem, coping ability, and powerfulness, may conceivably be either reinforced or undermined by health care interventions. Labeling effects may create a greater sense of vulnerability in the labeled, which itself influences physiological function. Such a process was an important part of Ivan Illich's message. Yet the initiation of preventive behavior, or of therapy, may also result in positive "placebo" effects, perhaps reflecting an increased sense of coping or control, independently of any "objective" assessment of the effectiveness of such changes.

The possibility that medical interventions may have unintended effects is inevitable. Our framework includes both placebo and iatrogenic effects in the causal arrow from care to disease. But there is also a potential effect, of ambiguous sign, from care to host response.

At yet another level, the protective sense of self-esteem or coping ability seems to be a collective as well as an individual possession. Being a "winner," being on a "winning team," or simply being associated with a winning team—a resident of a town whose team has a won a championship—all seem to provide considerable satisfaction, and may have more objectively measurable influences on health.

❖ A Further Extension: Economic Trade-Offs and Well-Being

But there is still another feed-back loop to be considered. Health care, and health policy generally, have economic costs which also affect well-being. Once we extend the framework, as in Figure 4, to reflect the fact that the ultimate objective of health-related activity is not the reduction of disease, as defined by the health care system, or even the promotion of human health and function, but the enhancement of human well-being, then we face a further set of trade-offs, which are introduced in Figure 5.

Health care is not "free"; as noted above, the provision of such services is now the largest single industry or cluster of economic activities in all modern societies. This represents a major commitment of resources—human time, energy, and skills; raw materials; and capital services—which are therefore unavailable for other forms of production. To the extent that health care makes a positive contribution to health, it thereby contributes to human happiness both directly and through the economic benefits of enhanced human function and productivity.

The latter effect is frequently referred to as an "investment in health"; spending on health care may even pay for itself through increased capacity

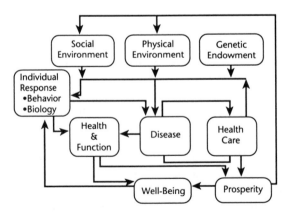

Figure 5.

of the population to work and produce wealth. The increasing concentration of health care on those outside the labor force, the very elderly or chronically ill, has, however, severely weakened this form of linkage. For most health care now provided, the benefits must be found in the value of the resulting improvements in health, not in some further productivity gains.

Whatever the form of the pay-off to health care, the resources used in its provision are inevitably a net drain on the wealth of the community. The well-being and economic progress of the larger society are thus affected *negatively* by the extension of the health care system per se. The fallacious argument frequently put forward by the economically naive, that health care, or any other industry, yields economic benefits through the creation of jobs, rests on a confusion between the job itself—a resource-using activity or cost—and the product of the job, the output. It is in fact an extension into the general economic realm of a common confusion in health care, between the process of care and its outcome.

Yet "job creation" is very easy; one can always hire people to dig holes in the ground and fill them in again. (Keynes suggested burying bottles filled with banknotes, thereby creating opportunities for profitable self-employment.) The creation of wealth, however, depends upon the creation of jobs whose *product* is valued by the recipient. This understanding is implicit in references to "real jobs," as distinct from make-work, or employment purely for the sake of keeping people busy—and remunerated. In a complex modern economy, large numbers of people can be kept busy, apparently gainfully employed, and yet adding little or nothing to the wealth of the population as a whole.

This distinction between the cost of an activity, its net absorption of productive resources, and the benefits which flow from it in the form of valued goods and services, is not unique to health care. It applies to any economic activity, as reflected in the generality of the techniques of cost-benefit analysis. The situation of health care is different, however, for a variety of complex and interrelated reasons, which are implicit in the chain of effects from health care to disease reduction, to improved health and function, to well-being.

As a commodity, health care has characteristics which make it intrinsically different from "normal" commodities traded through private markets, and this is reflected in the peculiar and complex collection of institutional arrangements that surround its provision. As a consequence, both of these intrinsic peculiarities and the institutional responses to them, the mechanisms which for most commodities maintain some linkage between the resource costs of a commodity and its value to users are lacking.

Less obviously, but implicit in Figure 5, the expansion of health care draws resources away from other uses, which may also have health effects. In public budgets, for example, rising health care costs for the elderly draw funds which are then unavailable for increased pensions; rising deficits may even lead to pension reductions. Increased taxes or private health insurance premiums lower the disposable income of the working population. Environmental clean-up programs also compete for scarce resources with the provision of health care.

Once we recognize the importance and potential controllability of factors other than health care in both the limitation of disease and the promotion of health, we simultaneously open for explicit consideration the possibility that the direct positive effects of health care on health may be outweighed by its negative effects through its competition for resources with other health-enhancing activities. A society that spends so much on health care that it cannot or will not spend adequately on other health-enhancing activities may actually be *reducing* the health of its population through increased health spending.

It is not our intent in this paper to lay "The Decline of the West" at the feet of the health care system of the United States, or even those of North America and Western Europe combined. Rather, our point is to show that the framework laid out in Figure 5 is capable of permitting such a relationship to be raised for consideration. Its network of linkages between health, health care, the production of wealth, and the well-being of the population is sufficiently developed to encompass the question, without overwhelming and paralyzing one in the "dependence of everything upon everything."

❖ Frameworks in Principle and in Practice

As noted above, the test of such a framework will be the extent to which others find it useful as a set of categories for assembling data and approximating complex causal patterns. The understanding of the determinants of population health, and the discussion and formulation of health policy, have been seriously impeded by the perpetuation of the incomplete, obsolete, and misleading framework of Figure 1. There is a bigger picture, but clearer understanding and, particularly, a more sensible and constructive public discussion of it requires the development of a more adequate intellectual framework. The progression to Figure 5 is offered as a possible step along the way.

In this paper, we have suggested several important features of such a framework. It should accommodate distinctions among disease, as defined and treated by the health care system, health and function, as perceived and experienced by individuals, and well-being, a still broader concept to which health is an important, but not the only, contributor. It should build on the Lalonde health field framework to permit and encourage a more subtle and more complex consideration of both behavioral and biological responses to social and physical environments. Finally, it should recognize and foster explicit identification of the economic trade-offs involved in the allocation of scarce resources to health care instead of other activities of value to individuals and societies, activities which may themselves contribute to health and well-being.

To date, health care policy has in most societies dominated health policy because of its greater immediacy and apparently more secure scientific base. One may concede in principle the picture in Figure 5, then convert all the lines of causality into "disease" and "health and function" into thin dotted ones, except for a fat black one from "health care." That is the picture implicit in the current emphasis in health policy, despite the increasing concern among health researchers as to the reliability and primacy of the connection from health care to health.

One lesson from international experience in the post-Lalonde era is that appropriate conceptualization of the determinants of health is a necessary, but not a sufficient, condition for serious reform of health policy. Intellectual frameworks, including the one offered here, are only a beginning. Simply put, to be useful, they must be used.

❖ About the Authors

Robert G. Evans is a Professor in the Department of Economics, University of British Columbia, Vancouver, B.C., Canada.

Gregory L. Stoddart is in the Department of Clinical Epidemiology and Biostatistics, Center for Health Economics and Policy Analysis, McMaster University, Hamilton, Ontario, Canada.

❖ Health Inequalities and Social Class

M.G. Marmot, George Davey Smith,
Stephen Stansfeld, Chandra Patel,
Fiona North, Jenny Head, Ian White,
Eric Brunner, and Amanda Feeney

The Whitehall study of British civil servants, begun in 1967, showed a steep inverse association between social class, as assessed by grade of employment, and mortality from a wide range of diseases. Between 1985 and 1988 we investigated the degree and causes of the social gradient in morbidity in a new cohort of 10,314 civil servants (6,900 men, 3,414 women) aged 35–55 (the Whitehall II study). Participants were asked to answer a self-administered questionnaire and attend a screening examination.

In the 20 years separating the two studies there has been no diminution in social class difference in morbidity: we found an inverse association between employment grade and prevalence of angina, electrocardiogram evidence of ischaemia, and symptoms of chronic bronchitis. Self-perceived health status and symptoms were worse in subjects in lower status jobs. There were clear employment-grade differences in health-risk behaviors including smoking, diet, and exercise; in economic circumstances; in possible effects of early-life environment as reflected by height; in social circumstances at work (e.g., monotonous work characterized by low control and low satisfaction); and in social supports.

Healthy behaviors should be encouraged across the whole of society; more attention should be paid to the social environments, job design, and the consequences of income inequality.

❖ Introduction

Inequalities in health are not confined to differences between the rich and the poor. Manual workers have higher mortality rates than non-manual, and in the UK the gap has been widening. Among those in non-manual employment, the lower the social class, the higher the mortality rates.

The Whitehall study of British civil servants—all office workers in stable employment—found that after 10 years of follow-up the highest employment grade (category 1) had about one-third the mortality rate of the lowest (category 6). None of these men was in absolute poverty as it is usually understood. In the Whitehall study, differences in smoking, obesity, physical activity, blood pressure, or plasma cholesterol level could only partly explain differences in mortality. This implies that we have to look beyond the established risk factors for explanations.

The shorter life expectancy among lower socioeconomic groups may be accompanied by a longer period in poor health, and socioeconomic differences in morbidity are similar to those observed for mortality. The use of Registrar-General social classes instead of employment grade may lead to underestimation of the extent of mortality and morbidity differentials.

This study (Whitehall II) was set up to investigate the degree and causes of the social gradient in morbidity, to study additional factors related to the gradient in mortality, and, importantly, to include women. A new cohort of civil servants was established between 1985 and 1988. Particular attention was paid to psychosocial factors which may influence health, with a focus on stressful work environments and lack of social support as they may influence risk of cardiovascular disease.

❖ Methods

Participants

The target population for the Whitehall II study was all men and women aged 35–55 working in the London offices of 20 civil service departments. Members of the target population were invited to participate by letter. The response rate, after excluding those who were ineligible, was 73%. (74% among men, 71% among women). Response rate varied by employment grade, being 81% among the top three employment-grade categories (defined below) and 68% among the lower three categories.

Grade of Employment

We obtained information on grade of employment by asking all participants to give their civil-service grade title. On the basis of salary the civil service identifies 12 non-industrial grades that, in order of decreasing salary, comprise seven "unified grades," and senior executive officer (SEO), higher executive officer (HEO), executive officer (EO), clerical officer, and clerical assistant. Other professional and technical staff are assigned by the civil service to one of these grades on the basis of salary. For analysis, we have combined unified grades 1–6 into one group and the bottom two clerical grades into another, thus producing six categories. Category 1 represents the highest status jobs and category 6 the lowest. The first two categories (unified grades 1–6 and unified grade 7) are roughly equivalent to Administrative grade in the original Whitehall study. SEO, HEO, and EO correspond roughly to Professional and Executive, and the clerical category (which includes a small number of office-support staff) corresponds to the Clerical and "Other" grades in the first study. At January 1, 1987, annual salaries ranged from £62,100 for a permanent secretary to £3,061 for the lowest paid office-support grade.

❖ Results

Morbidity by Grade of Employment

There appears to be no decrease in the difference in prevalence of ischaemia depending on employment category over the 20 years separating Whitehall I and Whitehall II. The relative difference between clerical officers and administrators appears to be greater. For angina pectoris, the difference between grades has changed little in 20 years. The overall prevalence of chronic bronchitis—i.e., cough with phlegm production—is considerably lower for men aged 40–54 in Whitehall II than in the previous study, but the relative difference between the grades is similar. The findings for chronic bronchitis are likely to be related to smoking. Prevalence of smoking among civil servants has decreased, but the striking inverse association with job status persists.

In general, the lower the job status (i.e, the higher the employment category number) the higher the prevalence of ischemic heart disease. Women report higher prevalence of angina than men, despite the lower prevalence of ischemic electrocardiograms (ECGs). Among men there was an inverse association between job status and number of symptoms reported in the last 14 days, likelihood of rating health as average or poor as opposed to good or very good, and a prior diagnosis of hypertension or diabetes. In general, women reported greater morbidity than men. The relation with grade was less consistent. In addition to a higher prevalence of premenstrual bloating, women of lower job status were more likely to report premenstrual irritability and breast tenderness (data not shown).

Sociodemographic Characteristics by Employment Category

Subjects in lower status jobs were less likely to have had higher education, and were more likely to have had fathers in manual social classes, to live in council or rented accommodation, and to have no household access to a car. The higher the job status, the more likely that men were married or cohabiting. Conversely, the highest percentage of married women were in employment category 6.

Potential Explanations: Biological and Behavioral Risk Factors

The grade differences in morbidity parallel those seen previously for mortality. Plasma cholesterol concentrations do not differ by category, and the small inverse association between job status and blood pressure in men was reduced from that seen in the Whitehall I study. There was a significant inverse relation between mean body-mass index (weight/

height) and job status, but, especially in men, the differences were small. However, obesity (body-mass index greater than 30) was more prevalent in lower status jobs, especially in the clerical grade. As in Whitehall I, height correlated with job status. The risk factor that differed most between employment categories was smoking. Women had a higher prevalence of smoking than men in all but the clerical and office-support category. Moderate or vigorous exercise was less common among subjects in lower status jobs. As a rough indicator of dietary pattern, consumption of skimmed and semi-skimmed milk, wholemeal bread, and fresh fruits and vegetables was greatest in higher status jobs. Average alcohol consumption also correlated with job status, strikingly so for women. Reports of parents having had a heart attack were more frequent in higher status jobs; a positive family history of heart attack among siblings was more common in lower status jobs.

Potential Explanations: Psychosocial Characteristics

Fewer of those in lower status jobs report control over their working lives, having varied work, or having to work at a fast pace. Overall, fewer subjects in lower status jobs were satisfied with their work situation.

Social relations are expressed quantitatively as extent of social networks, and qualitatively as the nature of social supports. More subjects in lower status jobs reported visiting relatives once a month or more, while more in higher status jobs visited friends. Fewer people in lower status jobs were involved in hobbies. Fewer men in lower status jobs had a confidante in whom they could entrust their problems or receive practical support; more reported negative reactions from persons close to them. Patterns were less clear in women.

More subjects in lower status jobs were likely to have reported two or more of eight potentially stressful life events in the previous year, and to report difficulties paying bills or with money in general.

Despite their lower rate of heart disease, more of the participants in higher status jobs had type A behavior. It has been suggested that the major component of type A behavior responsible for the link to heart disease is hostility—subjects in higher status jobs had lower scores on the Cook-Medley hostility scale. As one measure of perceived control over their health, fewer participants in lower status jobs believed that it was possible to reduce the risk of heart attack.

❖ Discussion

Our findings show that socioeconomic differences in health status have persisted over the 20 years separating the two Whitehall studies. The relative magnitude of these differences is difficult to assess. In the Whitehall I cohort, grade differences in prevalence of ischaemic heart disease were considerably less than the threefold difference between the lowest and highest grades in ischaemic heart disease mortality found at subsequent follow-up. If the same applies to the Whitehall II cohort, subsequent disease differences will be even greater than those reported here.

The differences between grades in self-perceived ill-health are substantial: compared with those in employment category 1, twice as many in category 6 rate their health as average or worse, nearly twice as many have chronic cough and sputum, and there is a striking excess in the frequency of premenstrual symptoms. The main national figures on morbidity have hitherto come from the General Household Survey questions on longstanding illness. We found that longstanding illness was reported more frequently by lower employment-grade men but not women.

Self-reported data are of special interest. There is an established link between perceived health and other measures of health status. Thus, the question on "overall rating of health as poor or average" is a powerful predictor of mortality, as are the questions on angina pectoris. In addition to their relation to underlying "true" pathology, they reflect a burden of perceived ill-health that shows a clear social class gradient.

We believe that employment grade within the civil service, with its strong relation to income, is a more precise classification of socioeconomic position than Registrar-General's social classes, based on occupation. Homogeneity within grades is high, and differences between grades fairly distinct. We judge, therefore, that ours is a suitable population for exploring reasons for persistent social-class differences in health. It is likely that these findings will apply to white collar employees of other large organizations.

The Black Report, and subsequent discussions, considered that social-class differences could be due to artifact, to selection, to material conditions, or to life-style. In the present study, grade was measured precisely and there is little likelihood of artifact in assignment of social position. Health selection is of course a possibility. Differential recruitment into or exit from grades on health grounds could produce grade differences in health status. An analysis of the relation between speed of promotion and initial health status will be published elsewhere; however, health-related downward mobility has been shown not to account for national social-class mortality differences.

Previously, we concluded that, important though they were, grade differences in established coronary-risk factors could not account for the observed differences in coronary and other diseases. The Whitehall II study throws up a number of possible explanations for these differences.

First, the differences in height by employment category indicate differences in early environment. In the Whitehall I cohort, height was inversely related to mortality. This is consistent with work suggesting that early-life environment predicts disease in adult life. Some of the health risk associated with short height derives from the association between height and socioeconomic position in adulthood. When considering the possible effects of early environment on mortality risk it is important to take socioeconomic position in later life into account, particularly since deprivation in infancy and in adulthood are likely to be strongly related.

Second, grade differences in behaviors were found in both Whitehall studies. The grade difference in frequency of smoking persists. There were also grade differences, favoring the higher status jobs, in leisure-time physical activity and in indicators of healthy eating, though answers to questions on nutrient intake may be more a measure of health consciousness than of actual intake. Consistent with different attitudes to health is the lower degree of belief among those with lower status jobs that they could take action to help prevent a heart attack.

Third, social circumstances differed between employment categories. Because grade correlates with income, those lower down the grade hierarchy were more likely to report financial and housing difficulties and to rent their accommodation. Housing tenure predicts mortality independent of occupationally defined social class. Patterns of social activity differed, with clear indication of less, and less satisfactory, social support among those with lower status jobs.

Fourth, work environment is perceived differently between grades. Impressive evidence has accumulated that jobs characterized by low control, low opportunity to learn and develop skills, and high psychological work load are associated with increased risk of cardiovascular disease. Men with lower status jobs report less control, less use of skills, and less variety at work. To the extent that having to work fast is a measure of psychological work load, those with lower status jobs report having to do this less often. It may, however, also be a measure of job involvement and variety.

A notable exception to the pattern of lower status job—higher risk is type A behavior, the behavior pattern that may predispose to heart disease. There is no hint from these data that differences in type A behavior could account for grade differences in disease. It is worth noting that hostility, which has been associated with heart disease, was more prevalent in those with lower job status.

It should be emphasized that the usual pattern of association between job status and health measures is a gradient. It is not simply that those in the lowest status jobs had the worst health and the greatest clustering of potential risk factors.

It is important to understand the factors determining mortality and morbidity differences. Were it possible to reduce the mortality rate of clerical officers in the civil service to that of administrators, they would have less than half their current death rate. Our data suggest that healthy behaviors should be encouraged across the whole of society, not just among the more privileged. They also suggest that attention should be paid to the social environment, job design, and the consequences of income inequality.

❖ About the Authors

Michael G. Marmot, F.F.P.H.M. is a Professor in the Department of Epidemiology and Public Health, University College and Middlesex School of Medicine, London, UK and is associated with the Department of Epidemiology and Population Sciences, London School of Hygiene and Tropical Medicine.

George Davey Smith is a Lecturer in the Department of Epidemiology and Population Sciences, London School of Hygiene and Tropical Medicine, London, UK.

Stephen Stansfeld, Chandra Patel, M.D., Fiona North, M.B., Jenny Head, M.Sc., Ian White, M.Sc., Eric Brunner, M.Sc., and Amanda Feeney are all with the Department of Epidemiology and Public Health, University College and Middlesex School of Medicine, London.

❖ Chapter 2
Shaping the Health
Care System

In this chapter, we shift our perspective from disease, disability, and death, in order to look at the health care system. As we have seen, the causes for sickness and death have changed dramatically in the last 100 years; so have medical treatment, health professions education, the organization and provision of health care, the costs and methods of payment for health care, the role of government in health care, and the attitudes and values of the American people about health care.

A look at the history of American medicine reveals the societal forces that have shaped modern health care. We began with a system of faith and superstition subscribed to by the colonists and we progressed to a system based on a strong belief in science and the germ theory of disease; a highly developed technology; and deeply held values about individualism, free enterprise, and competition. We can trace two major influences on the evolution of medicine: (1) the free enterprise system with its emphasis on competition, private practice, and fee-for-service payment, as well as the predominance of the private sector, including private practicing physicians, dentists, and pharmacists, nonprofit and proprietary hospitals, drug companies, and nursing homes; and (2) the science-based, disease-oriented system of medical research and education.

Intractable increases in the costs of health care have resulted in various interventions in the traditional system in recent years, including changes in payment systems, and a major revolution is underway in the delivery and financing of health care services. The results of these forces are manifest in a complex structure involving over 7 million health care workers, many of them highly specialized; hospitals that amount to over $300 billion in health care expenditures and that range in size and complexity from small rural hospitals to major urban tertiary care centers that are equipped with streamlined medical electronic systems and technologies for diagnosis and treatment; giant private health insurance companies that serve in some capacity over 80 percent of the population; and federal, state, and local government programs that provide direct care for millions and finance care for the aged and the poor to the tune of over $225 billion a year. The dramatic increase in the size and scope of health care has transformed the medical care of only 50 years ago, when physicians practiced more art than science and prospects for cure were severely limited.

Increasing industrialization, urbanization, and modernization have created a host of new health problems that have replaced some of those that responded earlier to advances in medicine and public health. Many of these problems are as much social as they are medical and they offer new challenges to health care workers as well as to policymakers. Cigarette smoking, for example, accounts for approximately 400,000 deaths annually. Other important causes of preventable morbidity and mortality are alcohol and drug abuse, motor vehicle accidents, violence, pollution, and obesity. Improvements in lifestyle and advances in medical science have contributed to an increase in the number of older Americans. The aging of the population places a greater burden on the health care system, particularly because of the high level of chronic illness among older people. The frail elderly present an exceptional challenge to health care providers and today the fastest growing age group in the nation is composed of those over 85.

In the opening article in this chapter, "Health Status and National Health Priorities," Dorothy P. Rice, a former Director of the National Center for Health Statistics, discusses the implications of current demographic trends as well as changes underway in medical care services, financing, and insurance benefits. Ms. Rice provides a masterly condensation of the state of the nation's health care system, including evolving reimbursement policies, access to medical care, long-term care, and corporate for-profit medicine. Her historical outline and her analysis of the complex forces now at work provide an excellent basis for helping us come to terms with critical issues concerning the future of the nation's health care system. Her conclusion is that universal and affordable health care is the major national health priority requiring a commitment by the people of the United States and its leaders to develop a viable solution.

Paul R. Torrens and Stephen J. Williams state that the purpose of their paper is "to introduce a set of ideas that may possibly explain why there is so much 'activity' in health care in the United States and, at the same time, so little progress in solving our major problems." A worthy endeavor, indeed. In "Understanding the Present, Planning for the Future: The Dynamics of Health Care in the United States in the 1990s" the authors discuss the basic factors behind soaring costs and ultimately lay the blame on the health care system for doing what people want it to do—successfully treat their illnesses and injuries. It is the impact of these high costs, however, that has sent the system into a tailspin wherein nobody is satisfied—not the patients, not the doctors, not the hospitals, and most of all, not the payers. Each group has developed "survival tactics" that are now getting us through the day but do nothing to control costs. The authors conclude that, tragically, until the financing and delivery issues are addressed, the great destiny of the health care system will remain unfulfilled.

In his provocative 1980 paper, "The New Medical-Industrial Complex," Arnold S. Relman assessed the rapid rise of proprietary institutions in health care. He described the trend toward providing health care services for profit through hospitals, nursing homes, diagnostic laboratories, emergency room services, hemodialysis, and a wide variety of other facilities, which raised a number of complex issues regarding the public interest. Dr. Relman suggested that the new "medical-industrial complex" requires close scrutiny and careful monitoring in order to avoid serious abuses, and he cautioned physicians against forging ties with the medical-industrial complex.

In 1991, Dr. Relman took the opportunity of the 101st Shattuck Lecture to the annual meeting of the Massachusetts Medical Society to revisit the entrepreneurial trends he identified 11 years before. That lecture is reprinted here as "The Health Care Industry: Where Is It Taking Us?" His latest assessment of the market-oriented, profit-driven health care system is an important one for patients as well as for providers and policy analysts, as he echoes his earlier cautions to physicians against losing sight of their primary commitment—to serve the best interests of their patients.

The article by Steven A. Schroeder and associates, "Academic Medicine as a Public Trust," is an important contribution to the health policy literature because it is a bold statement on a subject that has been long neglected and rarely addressed. In this article, Dr. Schroeder, Jane S. Zones, and Jonathan A. Showstack, identify a number of ways that academic medicine has failed to live up to its appointed role in society, and they suggest that to the degree that it continues to define its mission narrowly, it not only fails in its responsibility to the public, but it also jeopardizes its future financial viability. The authors recommend that academic medical centers expand their role in addressing problems related to the organization and financing of health services and to issues related to the uninsured and that they generally reexamine their policies and develop new strategies to respond to the rapidly changing health care environment.

Our chapter on the health care system would be incomplete without a discussion of provisions made for older Americans and the poor. A summary of the two key health protection programs financed by the federal government, Medicare and Medicaid, includes a brief history of the programs, the promise that they offered, and their unfinished agendas. This information is included in an abbreviated version of the 1990 report of the Select Committee on Aging of the House of Representatives, "Medicare and Medicaid's 25th Anniversary—Much Promised, Accomplished, and Left Unfinished."

❖ Health Status and National Health Priorities

Dorothy P. Rice

Americans are healthier now than ever before. Death rates for many diseases have declined significantly during the past two decades, and life expectancy has increased. The current health status of the nation is based on decades of progress in sanitation, nutrition, housing, education, income, and medical care. All have contributed to substantial improvements in the health of Americans.

Despite this bright picture, the health status of the nation could be improved:

❖ Compared with other industrialized nations, U.S. life expectancy at birth in 1986 ranked 20th for men and 15th for women, and U.S. infant mortality rates ranked 22nd.
❖ Infant mortality rates for African Americans are more than double those for whites.
❖ Cancer death rates continue to increase.
❖ Accidents are the leading cause of death among children and youth.
❖ Illicit drug use continues to be a major public health problem.
❖ The incidence, prevalence, and number of deaths from the acquired immunodeficiency syndrome (AIDS) have been increasing rapidly, and their toll in human and economic terms is enormous.

These are only a few measures of health status that clearly have significant policy implications. In this article, I briefly examine these and other aspects of the health of Americans and discuss some major policy issues and national priorities that emerge from these data. These policy issues include access to medical care, maternal and child health care, human immunodeficiency virus (HIV) infection, and long-term care.

❖ Health Status Indicators

Various health status indicators highlight the long-term improvements in health status. Many of the same indicators are also markers of serious health problems and of the existing gaps between subgroups of the population. A brief review of infant and general mortality rates, life expectancy, disease risk factors, medical care use, and expenditures will provide the background for identifying the policy issues and directions for developing national health priorities.

45

Infant Mortality

Since the early part of this century, tremendous strides were made in infant survival through improved sanitation and socioeconomic conditions, success against infectious diseases, better nutrition, improved access to prenatal care, and advances in lifesaving technology used in neonatal intensive care units. Between 1950 and 1987, the infant mortality rate declined 65%, from 29.2 to 10.1 per 1,000 live births. The overall infant mortality rate, however, masks the large discrepancy between the mortality of white and African-American infants. In 1987, the African-American infant mortality rate was more than twice that for white infants—17.9 versus 8.6 deaths per 1,000 live births, respectively. From 1975 to 1987, the ratio of African-American to white infant mortality actually increased, reflecting a higher than average annual percent decline for white infants (2.7%) than for African-American infants (2.2%).

About two thirds of all infant deaths occur during the neonatal period, the first month of life. The rate of decline in neonatal mortality between 1975 and 1987 was greater for white than for African-American infants, 47% versus 36%. In 1987, the African-American neonatal mortality rate was more than double the rate for white infants.

The racial differences for postneonatal mortality rates, that is, between the 2nd and the 12th month of life, present a similar picture. In 1987, the postneonatal mortality rate for African-American infants was twice that for white infants.

The pronounced gap in the infant mortality rate between white and African-American infants reflects the more than twofold difference in the proportion of low-birth-weight babies (less than 2,500 grams) in the work groups—5.7% compared with 12.7% in 1987. Some of the factors associated with low birth weights and other major causes of infant deaths are a lack of prenatal care for pregnant women, maternal smoking, alcohol and drug use, age, and the socioeconomic background of the mother.

The United States infant mortality ranks 22nd among other industrialized nations. In 1986, Japan had the lowest infant mortality rate (5.2 deaths per 1,000 live births) and the second lowest perinatal mortality rate (7.3 deaths per 1,000 live births). Finland's perinatal rate was lowest at 6.4 deaths per 1,000 live births. The infant mortality rate for the United States in 1986 was twice the rate for Japan, and the perinatal mortality rate was almost two thirds higher than that for Finland.

Mortality—All Ages

In 1987, 2.1 million persons died in the United States, a rate of 8.7 per 1,000 population. Because the population has been aging, a more accurate picture of mortality trends is provided by the age-adjusted death rate, which eliminates the distortion associated with changing age composition. Thus, the age-adjusted rate in 1987 was 5.4 per 1,000 population. The crude death rate declined 9.5% while the age-adjusted death rate for the total population declined 36% during the 37-year period, 1950 to 1987. Examination of the trend clearly shows two separate periods: a moderate decline from 1950 to 1970, in which the age-adjusted mortality rate declined at an average annual rate of 0.8%; and a more rapid decline from 1970 to 1987 at 1.7% annually.

Heart disease continues to be the leading cause of death in the United States and, as such, is the predominant influence on total mortality. The age-adjusted heart disease death rate decreased 45% from 1950 to 1987. Some suggested explanations for the decline in heart disease mortality include the decreased prevalence of smoking, improved management of hypertension, healthier life-styles, the decreased dietary intake of saturated fats, more widespread physical activity, improved medical emergency services, and a more widespread use and increased efficacy of coronary care units.

The mortality for malignant neoplasms, or cancer, the second leading cause of death, increased 6% since 1950. The highest rate of increase (210%) occurred in cancer of the respiratory system mainly due to the effects of smoking.

Cerebrovascular disease, or stroke, is the third leading cause of death. From 1950 to 1987, the cerebrovascular age-adjusted mortality rates decreased 66%. Factors related to the rapid decline include expanded hypertension screening programs, improved management and rehabilitation of stroke victims, and effective hypertension therapy.

The mortality rates for accidents and suicides, the fourth and fifth leading causes of death in the United States, have declined since 1970, but they remain high. The death rate from HIV infection was 8.3 per 100,000 persons in 1987; in the year ending May 1990, HIV deaths climbed to 39,203, a rate of 15.4 per 100,000 persons, ranking it among the ten leading causes of death in the United States.

Life Expectancy

Since the turn of the century, more than a quarter century has been added to life expectancy at birth. Improvements in life expectancy early in this century have resulted from the control of acute infectious diseases, primarily by reductions in infant mortality. More recent improvements have been due to declining mortality from chronic diseases in the middle and older ages.

There have been and continue to be marked differences in life expectancy at birth for Americans by sex and race. Women live longer than men, and whites live longer than African-Americans. In 1988, white women had the longest life expectancy, 78.9 years, and black men had the shortest, 65.1 years. Although improvements in life expectancy have occurred for all race-sex groups, the amount of improvement varies among these groups. Between 1950 and 1988, life expectancy increased 5.6 years for white men; 6.2 years for African-American men, 6.7 years for white women, and 11.1 years for African-American women.

Increasing life expectancy and declining death rates have resulted in a rapid growth of the population aged 65 and older. This population group will continue to grow at a rapid rate for the remainder of the 20th century and well into the next century. At the turn of the century, there were only 3.1 million elderly people, 4.0% of the total population. By 1980, the elderly population had grown to 25.7 million persons, representing 11.3% of the total population. Because of the aging of the "baby boomers" born between 1946 and 1965, about one out of five Americans will be 65 years of age or older by the year 2030, and the total number is projected to be 65.6 million, more than doubling in the 50-year period, 1980 to 2030.

In the eighth decade of our century, an increasing number of enquiring minds are dissatisfied with the results of bigger and better analyses. They realize that most children born now will grow to maturity. However, when they become adults, physical pains and emotional miseries will probably be so severe that they cannot live without sedatives and tranquilizers.
—Ida Rolf

Like infant mortality rates, life expectancy in the United States is lower than for many industrialized nations, ranking 20th for men and 15th for women in 1986. Japan had the longest life expectancy of industrialized countries, 75.5 years for men and 81.6 years for women.

Health Status

In addition to mortality rates and life expectancy, various measures can be used to depict the health of the population: persons' perception of their health, limitations in their usual activities, and restricted and bed-disability days. Table 1 summarizes these health status measures by family income. For every measure, health status improves with rising incomes. In 1988, 10% of the noninstitutionalized population reported that their health was fair or poor compared with people their age, with the percent declining from 22% for those with family incomes of under $10,000 a year to 4% for those with incomes of $35,000 or more. About 33 million persons, 14% of the noninstitutionalized population, reported limitations of activity—that is, preschool or school activities, employment, or keeping house—due to chronic diseases. The percent suffering a limitation of activity declines with increasing income: 26% for the lowest income group to 8% for the highest income group. Likewise, the percentage of persons unable to carry on their major activity and of those with restricted activity and bed-disability days also declines with increasing income.

TABLE 1. Health Status and Utilization Measures by Family Income, United States, 1988*

Measure	All Persons	Under $10,000	$10,00 to $19,999	$20,000 to $34,999	$35,000 or More
		Family Income			
Health Status					
Percent feeling fair or poor	9.9	22.1	14.3	7.4	4.0
Percent limited in activity†	13.7	26.0	18.1	11.5	7.9
Percent unable to carry on major activity†	4.0	9.1	5.9	2.9	1.5
Restricted-activity days per person†	14.7	26.6	17.8	12.3	9.7
Bed-disability days per person†	6.3	12.2	7.9	4.9	3.8
Utilization					
Physician contacts per person (no.)	5.4	6.6	5.6	5.2	5.3
Percent seeing doctor in past year	76.7	78.0	74.9	76.3	78.9
Short-stay hospital discharges per 100 persons (no.)	11.2	18.7	13.4	10.1	7.7
Average length of stay in short-stay hospitals (days)	6.3	6.9	6.3	5.8	5.4

*From the National Center for Health Statistics.
†Due to chronic conditions.

Disease Risk Factors

Various risk factors have been identified to prevent or to control many diseases and promote good health. The growth in knowledge and awareness of the importance of health promotion and disease prevention in reducing unnecessary illness, disability, and deaths in the United States is the basis for a major focus of activity in the Public Health Service. In 1979, consensus among public health authorities was clearly communicated in *Healthy People: The Surgeon General's Report on Health Promotion and Disease Prevention.* The message was that many major health problems confronting Americans today are rooted in life-style or environmental factors that are amenable to change. Broad national goals for improving the health of American people during the decade of the 1980s were delineated, and 15 areas encompassing 226 specific objectives were identified in which health promotion and disease prevention measures might be expected to achieve further progress through a wide range of public, private, and individual strategies.

A recently published review of the progress made by 1987 on these objectives shows a patchwork of successes, serious failures, and health status areas that fall in between. Five examples of several important failures in progress toward accomplishing the 1990 objectives in which reduced risk factors were identified are listed below.

❖ High blood pressure control: The control of hypertension is one of the most effective prevention efforts to reduce death rates from heart disease and stroke. The control of high blood pressure, redefined to a measurement of 140/90 mm of mercury or higher, has not been reached by 60% of the population at risk, the objective established for 1990. Area studies estimate that only 24% of persons with hypertension have their blood pressure under control. Although there is some decline in sodium intake, a major risk factor for hypertension, progress is difficult to assess. It is also unlikely that the prevalence of overweight persons can be reduced to 10% of men and 17% of women.

❖ Pregnancy and infant health: The progress toward the pregnancy and infant health goals is the most disheartening. The 1990 goals for infant mortality of 9 per 1,000 live births for all races and 12 deaths per 1,000 live African-American infants are unlikely to be met. The infant mortality rate for all races was 10.1 per 1,000 live births and 17.9 for African-American infants in 1987. Rates for low-birth-weight babies, a major risk factor in infant mortality, have had only small declines from 7.1% of all live births in 1978 to 6.9% in 1987. The 1990 objective was set at 5%. The proportion of mothers receiving no pre-natal care in the first trimester of pregnancy, the goal for which was set at 10% by 1990, ranged from 21% for whites to about 40% for African Americans, American Indians, and Hispanics in 1987.

❖ Smoking: Cigarette smoking is the largest single preventable cause of illness and premature death in the United States, amounting to 390,000 deaths each year in the United States. Cigarette smoking is a major risk factor for lung cancer and other cancers, including laryngeal, esophageal, and urinary bladder cancer, and for coronary artery disease, chronic obstructive lung disease, some forms of cerebrovascular disease, spontaneous abortion, retarded fetal growth, and fetal or neonatal death.

Although progress has been made in educating the public about many of the adverse health outcomes associated with smoking, 28.8% of adults smoked cigarettes in 1987; the goal was 24.9% by 1990. The proportion of children and youth aged 12 to 18 years who smoked in 1988 was 12%; the 1990 goal was set at 6%. Knowledge of the adverse effects of smoking during pregnancy is less widespread. In 1985, the percentage of women not aware that smoking during pregnancy increases a woman's chances of having a miscarriage was 26%; of low birth weight, 20%; of stillbirth, 34%; and of premature birth, 30%.

❖ Alcohol and drug abuse: Alcohol and drug use cause or are associated with deaths due to accidents, homicides, suicides, cirrhosis of the liver, and cancer of certain sites. Their use poses special risks among adolescents, young adults, pregnant women, and the elderly.

In 1988, a quarter of adolescents aged 12 to 17 reported using alcohol within the past 30 days. The use of alcohol, marijuana, cocaine, and other illicit drugs has been declining since the late 1970s as awareness of the risks associated with their misuse has been growing. In 1987, about 4.3% and in 1988 about 3.4% of high school seniors reported using cocaine in the past 30 days, compared with 6.7% in 1985 and 6.2% in 1986. These data were collected before the recent increase in crack cocaine use.

A survey of 13 hospitals in eight cities by the Inspector General of the U.S. Department of Health and Human Services found that 8,974 newborns were treated in 1989 for exposure to crack cocaine. Delivery and hospital care of these infants cost $300 million more than normal delivery and care. At least 100,000 crack babies are estimated to be born annually, at a cost of more than $3 billion for medical care.

❖ Sexually transmitted diseases: Although the prevalence rates of traditionally recognized sexually transmitted diseases—gonorrhea, nongonococcal urethritis, genital herpes, and syphilis—have been reduced substantially, the scope and complexity of the sexually transmitted disease problem in the United States have expanded at an alarming rate. Infection with HIV, which was unknown when the 1990 objectives were established, has emerged as a major sexually transmitted disease and presents a major health problem in the nation, as will be discussed further.

Use of Medical Services

The use of medical care has an inverse relationship with family income (see Table 1). In 1988, noninstitutionalized persons in the lowest income group had 6.6 physician contacts (other than contacts as hospital inpatients); those in the highest income class had 5.3 visits. There were 27.1 million discharges from nonfederal short-stay hospitals in 1988, with a total of 170 million days of care. Persons in the lowest income bracket are almost 2 ½ times as likely to be admitted to hospital as those in the highest income bracket. The length of stay for the lowest income group was 1.3 times that of the highest income bracket. It is clear that the health status of persons in the lowest income group is much worse than for those with higher incomes, and their medical care use is significantly higher.

Medical Care Expenditures. During 1960 to 1988, medical care spending increased from $27 billion to $540 billion while its share of the gross national product (GNP) more than doubled, rising from 5.3% to 11.1% (Table 2). Health spending in 1988 amounted to $2,124 per capita, rising from $143 in 1960.

The factors associated with the rise in health care spending are multiple and complex, including the growth in private health insurance and prepay-

TABLE 2. Gross National Product (GNP) and National Health Expenditures by Source of Funds, Selected Years, 1960 to 1988*

| | | National Health Expenditures | | | | | | |
| | | Total | | | Private Funds | | Public Funds | |
Year	GNP $ x 10^{12}	Amount $ x 10^{12}	Per Capita, $	Percent of GNP	Amount $ x 10^{12}	Percent of Total	Amount $ x 10^{12}	Percent of Total
1960	515	27.1	143	5.3	20.5	75.5	6.7	24.5
1965	705	41.6	204	5.9	31.3	75.3	10.3	24.7
1970	1,015	74.4	346	7.3	46.7	62.8	27.7	37.2
1975	1,598	132.9	592	8.3	77.8	58.5	55.1	41.5
1980	2,732	249.1	1,059	9.1	143.9	57.8	105.2	42.2
1985	4,015	420.1	1,700	10.5	245.2	58.4	174.9	41.6
1988	4,881	539.9	2,124	11.1	312.4	57.9	227.5	42.1

*From the Health Care Financing Administration.

ment plans; increased public support of medical care for the aged, disabled, and poor; changing third-party reimbursement methods; increasing population and a rising proportion of elderly requiring more medical care; a shift from the care of acute to more expensive long-term illnesses; the improvement and growth of high-cost technology; higher wages and salary costs in the health care industry; and growth in the supply of health care professionals and facilities. The growing burden on the economy of medical care spending results from all of the above factors as well as higher medical care prices relative to general prices and a slower rate of growth in the general economy compared with continued growth in the health sector. Thus, in the period 1960 to 1988, the GNP grew 9.5 times and health expenditures grew 20 times.

The major portion of health care expenses has in the past been borne by the private sector. In 1960, 27% of total health care spending was paid by private health insurance and philanthropy, 49% of the total comprised direct out-of-pocket payments, and public spending accounted for 25%. The implementation of Medicare and Medicaid, together with increasing coverage of private health insurance, altered these relationships. By 1988, the government's portion rose to 42% of the total. Private health insurance and philanthropy covered 37%, further reducing direct private payments to 21% of the health care bill compared with 49% in 1960. The rise in third-party payments tends to reduce the financial burden of serious illness and patients' concern about the cost of care received and removes the restraining influences from physicians to admit patients to hospitals and use high-cost technologies.

The aged represented about 12% of the population in 1987, but because they tend to be sicker than younger people and use more health care services, they accounted for 36% of expenditures for personal health care. Per capita spending for elderly persons amounted to $5,360 compared with $745 for persons younger than 19 years and $1,535 for adults aged 19 to 64. Almost two thirds of the expenditures for the aged in 1987 (63%) came from public programs, and the remaining 37% came from private payments, out-of-pocket payments, and private insurance, including Medigap policies.

Elderly people approaching death have high expenditures for medical care. In 1982, the top 5% of these decedents accounted for 27% of Medicare reimbursements. Incurring high medical costs at the end of life is not a new phenomenon, and available data do not support the assumption that high medical expenses at the end of life are due largely to aggressive, intensive treatment of patients who are moribund. The data suggest that most sick people who die are given the medical care generally provided to the sick, and sick care is expensive.

A study of health care spending in 24 countries in the Organization for Economic Cooperation and Development (OECD)shows that per capita health expenditures averaged $870 in U.S. dollars, ranging from $140 in Turkey to $1,926 in the United States. U.S. spending exceeded that of Canada by 41%, France by 85%, Germany by 87%, Japan by 131%, Italy by 152%, and the United Kingdom by 171%.

The health share of the gross domestic product (GDP), a better measure for international comparisons than the GNP, ranged from 3.6% in Turkey to 11.1% in the United States. While the health share of the GDP in this country has increased from 10.5% in 1982 to 11.1% in 1986, most of the other six major OECD countries have exhibited stability in their percentages of GDP devoted to health over this three-year period.

❖ Major Policy Issues and National Priorities

The foregoing health status and expenditure data have important policy implications and form the basis for setting national priorities and action. Only a selected few policy issues will be briefly highlighted, including access to medical care, maternal and child health care, AIDS, and long-term care.

Access to Medical Care

Since the enactment of Medicare and Medicaid in 1965, impressive strides have been made in ensuring improved access to the benefits of the health care system for many Americans. More people attained regular access to health services, and a backlog of long-neglected needs, especially among the elderly and the poor, was specifically addressed. Medicaid was successful in improving access to medical services for the population it covers. The poor, however, tend to be sicker than the nonpoor, so that the higher medical care use rates among the poor by the mid-1970s did not necessarily indicate that they received more care given a similar health status. After adjustment for health status, poor persons who reported their health as fair or poor had substantially fewer visits than those in the highest income groups. In addition, those poor not covered by Medicaid continued to lag well behind others in the use of services.

Data from the 1986 Robert Wood Johnson National Access Survey showed a deterioration in access to medical care for the nation's poor, minorities, and uninsured between 1982 and 1986. Physician visits for the low-income group in poorer health declined by 8% compared with an increase of 42% for the nonpoor in similar health status, widening a gap that had almost disappeared. For the elderly poor, physician visits declined 20% during this four-year period. The gap in the number of physician visits among ethnic groups also widened, and there was evidence of an underuse of medical care in 1986 by low-income persons with chronic and serious illnesses.

One of the primary factors in determining access to health care is insurance coverage through both public and private programs. The estimated number of currently uninsured persons younger than 65 ranges between 31 and 37 million. Whatever the precise number of uninsured, two facts are clear: the number and percent of the population without health insurance have grown in the past few years, and access to care is more difficult for these people. The 1986 National Access Survey found that uninsured persons were twice as likely as the insured to be without a regular source of medical care. They had 27% fewer ambulatory visits and a slightly higher rate of medical emergencies.

The National Medical Expenditure Survey reported that 37 million persons, 15.5% of the total population, had no private health insurance coverage in 1987 (Table 3). Persons aged 19 to 24 are least likely to be insured—three out of ten persons in this age group have no public or private coverage. The disparities between the white and minority populations are high—12% of whites, 22% of African Americans, and 32% of Hispanics have no public or private health insurance coverage. The same survey reported that single, divorced, and separated persons are also at high risk for no insurance coverage. Part-time and self-employed persons, workers employed in industries characterized by seasonal employment—agriculture, construction, sales, repair, entertainment, and personal services—were less likely to have employment-related insurance and were more likely to be uninsured. Because the uninsured lack ready access to medical care, these data clearly show that impaired access goes beyond the poor and the unemployed population. Many employed persons in low-paying and seasonal occupations and who work for small businesses are also uninsured. About half of the uninsured are employed either all or part of the year. When their dependents are included, the employed uninsured account for 70% to 75% of the uninsured populations.

In addition to those without any private health insurance protection or coverage under Medicaid or Medicare, many other Americans are underinsured. One study analyzed the 1977 National Medical Care Expenditures Survey and concluded that about 27% of the population, 50.7 million persons in 1977, had inadequate or no insurance coverage. With the continued rise in health care expenditures, the number and proportion of the

TABLE 3. Health Insurance Coverage by Selected Characteristics: Percent with Public, Private, Employment-Related, and No Coverage, 1987*†

Population Characteristics	Population, x 10³	Type of Health Insurance Coverage			
		All Private %	Employment-Related Private %	Only Public %	None, %
Total	237,890	74.5	64.3	10.0	15.5
Age, years					
< 6	21,631	67.5	62.5	15.8	16.7
6 to 18	45,475	71.8	67.8	11.3	16.9
19 to 24	22,675	63.3	55.2	6.5	30.2
25 to 54	98,155	78.8	73.2	5.5	15.7
55 to 64	22,046	79.0	65.2	7.6	13.4
≥ 65	27,909	74.7	35.4	24.4	0.9
Sex					
Male	115,148	75.1	65.9	8.3	16.6
Female	122,743	74.0	62.8	11.7	14.3
Racial/ethnic background					
White	182,794	80.8	69.1	6.8	12.4
African American	28,356	52.9	48.5	25.1	22.0
Hispanic	18,752	50.1	45.9	18.3	31.5

*From the National Center for Health Services Research and Health Care Technology Assessment.
†Numbers may not add to total due to rounding.

population without adequate health insurance protection are likely to be higher now. The shift of the labor force from union to nonunion, from full-time to part-time, and from high- to low-wage jobs contributes to the rise in the numbers of uninsured and underinsured working persons.

The access issue is about the social obligation of government to provide care for low-income people or those who are otherwise uninsured. Although many uninsured persons are poor, they do not qualify for Medicaid because they are not categorically eligible or have incomes above the Medicaid cut-off level for the states in which they reside. Medicaid initially covered more than 60% of the poor but now only covers about 45%.

The recent focus of commissions, policy analysts, states, hospital and health professional associations, and private foundations has been on the uninsured population. The inability of large public hospitals to shift the cost of uncompensated services to patients with insurance has stimulated discussion of this issue. State governments are concerned about rising Medicaid costs. As of February 1988, 15 states had enacted laws establishing health insurance risk pools for people who have been rejected for coverage by at least one insurance company.

The issue of how to provide care to uninsured and underinsured Americans lies at the heart of the access-to-health-care issue. A consensus appears to be emerging among diverse groups that the United States should extend health care to those who do not have access to it. The question is how best to provide and finance such care.

Maternal and Child Health Care

Comprehensive prenatal care results in healthier babies, prevents human suffering, and saves money by reducing the need for high-cost hospital care of low-birth-weight babies. The Office of Technology Assessment estimates that the annual cost of neonatal intensive care in the United States is more than $1.5 billion. A 1985 Institute of Medicine study found overwhelming evidence that prenatal care reduces the incidence of low birth weights. There is also evidence that access to prenatal care has deteriorated in the past few years.

State Medicaid programs are concerned because women living in poverty have a higher risk of having low-birth-weight babies with complex and costly medical problems. Many low-income women do not qualify for Medicaid protection, are not covered by private health insurance, and cannot afford prenatal care. They do not get prenatal care, and their babies are delivered as hospital charity cases, contributing to the problem of hospital uncompensated care. The rate of low birth weight among infants born to women who receive no prenatal care is almost three times that of the general population.

The Omnibus Budget Reconciliation Act (OBRA) of 1989 had several important Medicaid amendments that expanded health coverage for low-income women and children. Under OBRA-1986, states were required to provide Medicaid to pregnant women and infants younger than 1 year whose incomes are at or below 100% of the federal poverty level. The 1989 version required states to extend coverage to pregnant women and children up to age 6 with incomes at or below 133% of the federal poverty income level ($13,380 for a family of three). The Congressional Budget Office estimated that this provision increased by 852,000 the number of children who would participate in Medicaid over the next three years.

The 1989 OBRA also specifically sought to assure that payment levels for obstetric and pediatric services were sufficient to enlist enough providers so that covered services would be available to Medicaid recipients to at least the extent that such services are available to the general population. In addition, the new amendments attempted to improve access to the Early and Periodic Screening, Diagnostic, and Treatment program (EPSDT), a part of Medicaid that provides preventive care and treatment of low-income children; and responded more fully to the health care needs of children by allowing more checkups when an illness or condition is suspected. An important change was a new requirement that states provide any medically necessary follow-up or treatment service that is reimbursable under Medicaid, whether or not the service is included in the state Medicaid plan.

Medicaid income eligibility criteria remain at the discretion of the states. Although these recent Medicaid changes are important, are they sufficient to reach all pregnant women and children? Medicaid still reaches only the very poor; the working poor are still at risk. Of major concern to policy makers is the number of children without any form of insurance coverage—11.3 million children younger than 18 years. It is time that the federal government assumes responsibility for guaranteeing that high-quality, comprehensive, and preventive maternal and child health care be available and accessible to all citizens of the United States needing such services.

Acquired Immunodeficiency Syndrome

Any examination of the health status of the nation and the implications for governmental priorities and actions would be incomplete without discussing HIV-related disease and AIDS, labeled by public health experts as a "world-class epidemic." Between 1981 and the end of May 1990, AIDS was diagnosed in 136,204 persons and more than three fifths died. The World Health Organization estimates that 6 to 8 million people worldwide have been infected with the HIV virus and 15 to 20 million people will be infected by the turn of the century.

The acquired immunodeficiency syndrome clearly is placing an increasing burden on the health care delivery system. In addition to expenditures for medical care and nonpersonal services (direct costs), the value of lost output due to the cessation or reduction of productivity by morbidity and mortality (indirect costs) should also be considered. Scitovsky and Rice estimated the annual direct and indirect costs of AIDS in 1985, 1986, and 1991. According to the authors' best estimates, direct costs, including research and nonpersonal services, will rise from $1.7 billion in 1986 to $10.9 billion in 1991 and indirect costs were estimated to rise from $7 billion in 1986 to $55.6 billion in 1991.

The federal government spent $2.9 billion in 1990 on research, care, and public health programs. The responsibility for paying for AIDS care, however, is shifting to the state and local governments. About 5% of the nation's urban public hospitals are treating more than 50% of persons with AIDS, and a quarter of all AIDS patients have no form of insurance, private or public.

Long-Term Care

Persons who have lost some capacity for self-care because of chronic disease or who suffer disabling physical or mental conditions require a wide range of social, personal, and supportive services in addition to medical care. With the growing number of chronically ill elderly and disabled adults, increasing consideration is being given to alternatives to providing long-term care services and to preventing the need for institutionalization. A wide range of options has been discussed and initiated to eliminate the fragmentation of services and to promote a continuum of care, including social health maintenance organizations; revamping reimbursement incentives to institutional providers to improve quality of care; and changing program incentives from medicalized solutions to social-health support services, such as hospice, home health, day-care centers, residential care homes, rehabilitation centers, and case management. Many of these are being tested under Medicare and Medicaid waivers and state experiments. Such innovative approaches are needed to meet the growing long-term care needs of the elderly and to promote a continuum of care in a cost-effective manner.

❖ Conclusion

With the continued rise in medical care spending, we are forced to ask whether we are getting full value for our investment in health. We can assess the value received for our health care dollar on a macro basis by comparing our health status and health care spending with those of other nations. Americans spend 2.2 times as much per capita for health care as the average for 21 OECD countries. Yet, we rank 22nd in infant mortality rates, 20th in life expectancy for men, and 15th for women. Japan has half our infant mortality rate, the longest life expectancy at birth, and its per capita expenditure for health is less than half of ours.

Access to care is the key indicator of the availability of services to the general population. All of the OECD nations, including our northern neighbor, Canada, have national health insurance or a national health service making medical care available to all their citizens. In our country, from 31 to 37 million Americans are uninsured and are denied basic medical care.

It is not difficult to conclude that the vast expenditures for medical care in this country are providing neither universal access nor the higher health status that many other developed countries enjoy for a proportionately smaller expenditure. Nor is it difficult to conclude that providing universal and affordable health care is the major health priority, requiring a commitment by the people of the United States and its leaders.

❖ About the Author

Dorothy P. Rice, sc.d., is Professor in Residence, Institute for Health and Aging and Department of Social and Behavioral Sciences, School of Nursing, University of California, San Francisco.

❖ Understanding the Present, Planning for the Future: The Dynamics of Health Care in the United States in the 1990s

PAUL R. TORRENS AND STEPHEN J. WILLIAMS

❖ Health Care in the United States: A Continuous Circular "Gaming" System

The model that best describes the current American health care system is that of a continuous, circular "gaming" system. In this model, the rapid rise in health care costs sets off a series of events that ultimately affect the entire U.S. health care system and eventually lead to even higher health care costs in the future. Briefly stated, the rise in health care costs has an impact on those organizations and agencies (employers and insurance programs, primarily) that pay the health care bills and forces them to take cost-containment actions. These efforts of the payors to contain health care costs (to contain health care *expenditures*, more accurately) have an impact on the providers of care, particularly hospitals and physicians. These providers find their sources of revenue being constrained as a result of the payors' health care cost-containment efforts, so they then take actions of their own in reaction to the efforts of the payors. These actions of the health care providers, in turn, often affect patients and communities which must then try to take whatever actions they can to lessen the impact.

The result of this chain of events is a circular system that merely passes along the effects of one particular set of changes to another part of the system, which in turn takes actions of its own to pass the problem along further. The end result of this set of dynamic forces is a continuous, circular system that encourages (some would even say, forces) each individual part of the system to figure out how to play the "game." Each individual part of this circular "gaming" system expends a tremendous amount of effort to solve its particular limited problems and very often does so with an elaborate display of talent, energy, and sophistication. Unfortunately, this limited and somewhat self-interested set of individual solutions to limited problems does not really succeed in containing the rise in health care costs, and this inevitably leads to a new round of individualized efforts by payors to contain the new increases in health care costs. Tragically, the need for each individual part of the circular "gaming" system to deal with its limited problems, and to treat other parts of the system as adversaries, prevents all

59

of the individual parts of the system from coming together to mutually and cooperatively solve systemwide problems that are not amenable to individual, limited solutions. The ultimate tragedy and irony of this circular "gaming" system of health care is that it not only does not solve the initiating problem (the rapid rise in health care costs), but it also prevents any broad, cooperative efforts that would be necessary to solve the problem.

❖ The Reasons for the Rise in Health Care Costs

As a first step in understanding this model of American health care as a circular "gaming" system, it is important to identify the basic reasons for the rise in health care costs in the United States. It is also important to understand that these reasons are the result of significant *successes* and not failures of the individual parts of the American health care system. One of the most unfortunate views of the health care system in the United States today is that there is something "wrong" or "bad" about the rise in health care costs, when the reasons for that rise are directly related to the American society's desire for better health care. Health care in the United States is not a "failure"; it is not providing a product that no one wants. We are not operating a "going-out-of-business" sale in health care. Quite the contrary, in fact. The reasons for the rise in health care costs are that the product (20th-century health care) is very effective and is actively desired by everyone in the United States.

Four particular "successes" have led to the rise in health care costs. The first of these has been the expansion of our supply of hospital facilities and beds, beginning shortly after World War II.

The second reason for the rise in health care costs has been the increasing number of physicians available throughout the United States, again beginning in the 1950s. At that time, it was felt that there was a "shortage" of physicians in the U.S., particularly in rural areas and in such fields of medicine as general practice/family practice. The solution to this perceived shortage of physicians was to expand the country's capacity to produce them.

The third major "success" leading to the rise in health care costs has been the phenomenal expansion of health insurance coverage to the American people, again a post–World War II occurrence. While it is true that the United States does not have universal insurance coverage of its population, it is estimated that more than 85 percent of the population does have access to health insurance of one kind or another.

The fourth major "success" underlying the rise in health care costs has been the remarkable growth in medical science and health care technology since the end of World War II. American society has provided immense sums of money for the development of medical science and technology, primarily through funding the National Institutes of Health and related researchers throughout the country.

American society has actively supported each of these four separate "success" stories. These were not events that were forced on a reluctant or unwilling public, but rather were seen as important social advances. The "failure" of our society, however, has been its lack of willingness to develop a system that would integrate and, to some degree, supervise and control these individual developments.

The rapid rise in health care costs in recent years and the attempts to control that rapid rise are the central, motivating dynamic in the organization and operation of U.S. health care today. The single most important factor influencing virtually all aspects of the health care system is the rise in health care costs and our various piecemeal attempts to contain it. The following sections of this chapter describe how these dynamics play out in practical terms.

❖ Impact of Rising Health Care Costs on Payors and Actions Taken by Payors in Response to Rising Health Care Costs

The rise in health care costs has had a major impact on the payors of health care expenses, particularly the three major elements in the payor section of the American health care system: Medicare, Medicaid, and corporate employers. With the rise in health care costs, each of these payors has faced tremendous challenges and has had to initiate major efforts to contain their expenditures.

For some years, Part A of the federal Medicare program has been paying out more money each year than it has taken in in revenues. This has resulted in significant operating deficits in Part A of the Medicare program. Since that part is supposed to be self-sustaining (that is, maintained solely by contributions from future beneficiaries and not subsidized by general tax revenues), it has been forced to use accumulated reserves from previous years to meet this deficit.

The Health Care Financing Administration (HCFA) has taken a number of steps to reduce its expenditures in both Part A and Part B. First among these efforts has been the implementation of the diagnosis-related groups (DRG) method for paying hospitals for their care of Medicare beneficiaries. As a result of this new method of payment, hospitals are no longer paid according to the number of individual services they provide or the number of days that Medicare beneficiaries remain in there. Instead, they now receive a fixed sum of money for each admission, that sum being determined by the admitting diagnosis, not by the volume of services provided.

A second major strategy employed by Medicare has been to encourage Medicare recipients to join health maintenance organizations and other forms of prepaid group practice plans. The purpose of this strategy is to move as many Medicare beneficiaries as possible into a form of health care delivery that is covered by a single *per capita* payment for care, regardless of the volume of services delivered. This allows the Medicare program to better predict and control its annual beneficiary expenses.

A third strategy of reimbursement reform that is being used by Medicare is the resource-based relative-value system (RBRVS) format for paying physicians. This system attempts to rationalize Medicare payments to physicians by reducing reimbursement to some physicians (who are currently thought to be overpaid) and to increase reimbursement to other types of physicians (who are thought to be underpaid).

Finally, the Medicare program is also initiating a wide variety of small reforms that influence various aspects of the reimbursement policy and, therefore, various parts of the American health care system. In some cases, for example, the contributions of Medicare beneficiaries for their participation in the Medicare program and for their receipt of health care at the time of service is being increased, thereby shifting more of the cost of medical care back to the beneficiaries themselves, even if only in small amounts. Attempts have also been made to review the Medicare reimbursement practices to teaching hospitals for postgraduate medical education and, at the same time, to review reimbursement practices for hospitals that supposedly have a disproportionate share of poor and indigent patients. Other types of regulatory reform related to physician ownership of laboratory and other ancillary services to which physicians themselves might refer patients are also being put in place.

At the same time that Medicare is trying to protect itself from the effects of rising health care costs, individual state Medicaid programs are also battling to control their expenditures, which now represent a major percentage of each state's government outlays. A typical state Medicaid program reaction has been to reduce or restrict eligibility for services as much as possible. States have also attempted to hold down expenditures by limiting increases in payment rates to physicians and hospitals as much as possible.

Some of the most active cost-containment methods are being put into place by employers and by the health insurance carriers they use to provide coverage for their employees. Many employers are trying to reduce benefit packages seen as overly generous in the past; this has been particularly true in the case of mental health benefits. In other instances, employers have attempted to increase the employee cost sharing for health insurance benefits and for health services, with varying degrees of success; in a number of instances, these efforts to shift some of the cost back to the employee have led to prolonged labor disputes.

Many employers, acting through their insurance intermediaries, have initiated stringent utilization review methods, often employing the new utilization review and control companies that have sprung up for this purpose. After a rather slow start, companies have been strongly encouraging their employees to move into health maintenance organizations and managed care programs of one kind or another; in the case of mental health benefits, some employers have virtually removed the individual fee-for-service aspects of mental health coverage and have substituted managed mental health programs for the entire mental health benefit. Finally, in geographic areas where particular employers exercise control over a significant share of the health care market by reason of the number of their employees, employers have become more active in seeking direct contracts with individual providers at competitive prices for selected high-cost (and usually high-technology) procedures.

❖ Impact of Payors' Actions on Providers and Actions Taken by Providers to Adapt to Payor Efforts

All of these activities by the payors to reduce or control their expenditures have not gone unnoticed by health care providers, particularly physicians and hospitals. In each case, the providers have reacted exactly as one might expect: they have looked for ways to reduce their operating cost or to increase their revenues from other sources.

In the case of hospitals, the change to a DRG system of reimbursement by Medicare has been a strong incentive for improved operational efficiency. This has meant a general downsizing of hospitals and their staffs and has prompted a major attempt by most hospitals to manage their resources and activities more carefully.

At the same time, hospitals have realized that they are participating in an increasingly competitive marketplace, one in which other hospitals are now seen as competitors. Hospitals have developed active marketing and advertising programs to seek new "business" and have worked diligently to develop new "product lines" (new types of services that can attract new patients and/or physicians).

In many instances, hospitals have begun to work more closely with their medical staffs to develop joint ventures; these are undertaken both to attract new business to the physician and the hospital and to strengthen the attachment of physicians to their hospitals. In many instances, hospitals and their medical staffs have developed new types of group-practice arrangements that will allow the hospitals to seek contracts from health maintenance organizations on behalf of physicians and the hospitals together.

At the same time as hospitals are being affected by payors' actions, individual physicians are being affected as well. As physicians see more and more of their fee-for-service patients being siphoned off to health maintenance organizations and other types of managed care programs, these physicians feel forced to sign contracts with such programs to accept their enrollees. Often the physicians feel that if they do not participate in these contracted programs, they may eventually find themselves with fewer patients or none at all.

In the same fashion, physicians may purchase and operate various types of ancillary services, such as clinical laboratories, diagnostic imaging centers, home health agencies, and the like; they may operate these as joint ventures with other physicians or perhaps even with hospitals. At the same time, other physicians are adding various types of laboratory or other testing services in their offices, performing those ancillary services themselves that previously had been sent out of the physicians' offices.

Just as hospitals are feeling the need to draw closer to their medical staffs, individual physicians are beginning to feel the need to draw closer to their hospitals. The medical staffs of many hospitals have taken the lead in developing parallel medical service organizations that are intended to allow hospitals and physicians to enter into business and contractual relations together with outside groups.

In addition to physicians and hospitals, other types of providers are scrambling energetically to maintain their level of economic return, as well as their share of the marketplace. Individual practitioners such as physical therapists and nurses, who previously might have only been employed by institutions, are now developing new outpatient and homecare service programs that they can own and operate themselves.

❖ Impact of Provider and Payor Actions on Patients and Communities and Actions Taken by Patients and Communities to Adapt

As might be expected, as the payors and the providers move to adapt to changing environments, patients and communities have felt the impact of their actions and they have attempted to adapt, too. Unfortunately, in our system of health care, individual patients and their communities are least able to protect themselves from the actions of payors and providers. . . .

Not only has the price of health insurance coverage gone up, the availability of insurance, at any price, has changed. Many individuals have found that they cannot purchase health insurance, either because of previous medical conditions or because of limited small group acceptance by many major health insurance carriers. Individuals are increasingly reluctant to change jobs if they are covered for medical care at one job but are uncertain about the range of coverage at another. As has been well documented by a number of researchers, the number of uninsured has increased significantly in recent years; what has not been as well documented has been the increase in under-insurance of those people whose policies are no longer as broad or as beneficial as in the past.

Communities have found themselves affected by the changes in health care as well. With many state Medicaid programs reducing eligibility for health insurance coverage, the burden of providing care to those who were previously covered now falls to the local government health care system.

❖ Impact of All the Combined Changes on Health Care Costs in the U.S. Health Care System

As was mentioned at the beginning of this chapter, the great irony of all these changes and activities is that they have not resulted in any more significant control of health care costs than previously. It is clear that individual efforts and realignments have had at least some effect on keeping the rise of health care costs from being even worse than it is at present, but it must be admitted that none of the cost-control efforts that have been made, either individually or collectively, has resulted in an orderly, effective system for containing future costs. It is quite clear that costs will continue to rise rapidly and that the "gaming" nature of the individual parts of the health care system will continue, as these individual parts struggle to ensure their survival. Indeed, it seems likely that the dynamics of U.S. health care will continue to be determined by efforts to either contain health care costs or protect and maximize reimbursement.

The dilemma facing future health care in the United States is that there seems to be no relief in sight from the present system, while at the same time there is no agreement on the establishment of a new and better system. Workers in the health care system in the future will continue to be forced to adopt survival tactics until some new type of structure comes along that allows all parties to participate in broader, systemwide solutions. It seems clear that the energies of many capable, well-trained, well-intentioned health care professionals will be focused on fixing leaks in the lifeboats rather than on launching new ships.

Every doctor believes that he should have legal powers to compel his patients to swallow drugs, to have their limbs and breasts cut off, their internal organs extirpated, and their blood provided with exceedingly unpleasant stimulants for the phagocytes (opsonins, resulting from immunization), besides dictating whether they shall stay at home or go out or go to bed.
—George Bernard Shaw

This vision of the American health care system is admittedly a pessimistic one, just at a time when the public should be optimistic about the things that can be accomplished in health care today. At the very moment when the scientific and technological side of health and medical care stands poised to develop and deliver major new breakthroughs in treatment and prevention, the financing and delivery side of the system is facing its worst strains. Unfortunately, until the financing and service delivery aspects of health care can be improved, much of the potential of the marvelous new science and technology may remain unfulfilled.

There is simply no way that this society can begin to unleash the potential of these new technologies; there is simply no way that this society can address the need for newer types of services such as long-term care, mental health services, gene therapy, and other molecular biology advances, unless a way of controlling the rising cost of care is found for the services that we have now. The rise in the cost of the present array of services will soak up so much added revenue that there will be none left to permit movement into new services of any kind. At the same time, individual participants in the system are becoming increasingly frightened about moving away from protecting their part of the system, since they see no better alternative on the horizon and have no desire to commit professional suicide for themselves and their institutions.

It must be stated very directly and firmly that the health care system is bogged down in problems that it did not create by itself and that it cannot solve by itself either. It is clear that the larger society must understand that the system has followed a series of mixed messages from the public in its desire for the best in health care and has found itself caught in a continuous, circular, self-repeating situation that it cannot break. Indeed, the *only* way in which solutions can probably be obtained is for society to come to grips with some important questions, such as the limits of its ability to provide care and its willingness to assume a more supervisory and even regulatory control of a system that can no longer handle its own problems. The ideal circumstance would be for the various parts of the American health care system to come together voluntarily to solve those broad systematic problems that no one can solve separately, but that seems highly unlikely.

The future challenge to health care professionals is to understand the dynamics driving the health care system (the rapidly rising costs of care) and to work at several levels to improve the situation. On one level, *every* health care professional must understand that control of rising health care costs is his or her *primary* responsibility. On a broader level, each health care professional must work in his or her individual practices, institutions, and programs to contain health care costs in an organizational manner. Finally, on the broadest (and possibly most important) level, each health care professional must work actively to make society at large understand its responsibility to create new social forms of organization, supervision, and perhaps even control of the health care system itself. The people of the United States and their various representatives can no longer expect the system to solve its own problems; they must provide a new means and a new format for approaching these problems and creating new solutions.

❖ About the Authors

Paul R. Torrens, M.D., M.P.H., is Professor of Health Services Administration, School of Public Health, University of California, Los Angeles.

Stephen J. Williams, SC.D., is Professor of Public Health and Head of the Division of Health Services Administration, Graduate School of Public Health, California State University, San Diego.

❖ The Health Care Industry: Where Is It Taking Us?

Arnold S. Relman

Eleven years ago, in the Annual Discourse presented before the Massachusetts Medical Society, I first addressed the issue of commercialism in medical care. Referring to what I called "the new medical-industrial complex," I described a huge new industry that was supplying health care services for profit. It included proprietary hospitals and nursing homes, diagnostic laboratories, home care and emergency room services, renal hemodialysis units, and a wide variety of other medical services that had formerly been provided largely by public or private not-for-profit community-based institutions or by private physicians in their offices. The medical-industrial complex had developed mainly as a response to the entrepreneurial opportunities afforded by the expansion of health insurance coverage offering indemnification through Medicare and employment-based plans. Given the open-ended, piecework basis of third-party payment, business ownership of a medical facility virtually guaranteed a profit, provided that practicing physicians could be persuaded to use the facility and that services were limited to fully insured patients.

At that time, I estimated that the new medical-industrial complex had revenues of perhaps $35 to $40 billion, which would have been about 17 to 19 percent of total health expenditures for the calendar year 1979, and I was concerned about the possible consequences of the continued growth of the complex. I suggested that its marketing and advertising strategies might lead to high costs and widespread overuse of medical resources; that it might overemphasize expensive technology and neglect less profitable personal care; that it might skim off paying patients, leaving the poor and uninsured to an increasingly burdened not-for-profit sector; and that it might come to exercise undue influence on national health policy and the attitude of physicians toward their profession. I suggested that physicians should avoid all financial ties with the medical-industrial complex in order to be free to continue acting as unbiased protectors of their patients' interests and critical evaluators of new products and services. Finally, I recommended that the new health care industry be studied carefully to determine whether it was providing services of acceptable quality at reasonable prices and to ensure that it was not having adverse effects on the rest of the American health care system.

Two years later, in a lecture at the University of North Carolina, I expressed increasing concern about the future of medical practice in the new medical marketplace. I said,

The key question is: Will medicine now become essentially a business or will it remain a profession? . . . Will we act as businessmen in a system that is becoming increasingly entrepreneurial or will we choose to remain a profession, with all the obligations for self-regulation and protection of the public interest that this commitment implies?

In the decade that has elapsed since then, the problems posed by the commercialization of health care have grown. So have the pressures on the private practice of medicine, and now our profession faces an ethical and economic crisis of unprecedented proportions as it struggles to find its bearings in a health care system that has become a vast and highly lucrative marketplace.

What I want to do here is, first, describe how the commercialization of health care has progressed since 1980, with a brief summary of the initial studies of the behavior of for-profit hospitals. I shall describe how the investor-owned sector has continued to grow, but in new directions. At the same time, our voluntary not-for-profit hospitals have become much more entrepreneurial and have come to resemble their investor-owned competitors in many ways. I shall then consider how the new market-oriented health system has been influencing practicing physicians and how, in turn, the system has been influenced by them. Medical practice inevitably reflects the incentives and orientation of the health care system, but it also plays a critical part in determining how the system works. Finally, I shall briefly analyze the tensions between medical professionalism and the health care market.

❖ The Medical-Industrial Complex since 1980

Turning first to the recent history of the medical-industrial complex, I am glad to report that my earlier concern about the possible domination of the hospital sector by investor-owned chains was not justified by subsequent events. In 1980 there were approximately 1,000 investor-owned hospitals. Ten years later their number had increased to barely 1,400 of a total of some 5,000 hospitals. In the past few years there has been virtually no growth in the chains. The reason is that hospitals are no longer as profitable as they were in the days before the institution of diagnosis-related groups (DRGs) and all the other cost-control measures now used by third-party payers.

Numerous studies published during the past decade have compared the economic behavior of investor-owned hospitals during the early pre-DRG days with that of similar voluntary hospitals. Most reports (including those of the most carefully conducted studies) have found that the investor-owned hospitals charged approximately 15 to 20 percent more per admission, even when similar cases with similar degrees of severity were compared. This difference was largely attributable to increased use of, and higher charges for, ancillary services such as laboratory tests and radiologic procedures. During that earlier period, investor-owned hospitals were no more efficient, as measured by their operating costs per admission; if anything, their costs were a little higher than those of comparable voluntary hospitals. Furthermore, there was strong evidence that the investor-owned hospitals spent substantially less of their resources for the care of uninsured patients than did the voluntary hospitals. There are few or no published data on whether these differences persisted after all hospitals began to face a more hostile and competitive market, but from what we already know it seems clear that for at least the initial phase of their existence, the investor-owned hospitals did not use their alleged corporate advantages for the public benefit. In fact, by seeking to maximize their revenues and avoiding uninsured patients, they contributed to the problems of cost and access our health care system now faces. A few studies have attempted to compare the quality of care in voluntary and investor-owned hospitals, but quality is much more difficult to measure objectively than economic performance, and there is no convincing evidence on this point.

Although the predicted rapid expansion of for-profit hospital chains did not materialize, investor-owned facilities for other kinds of medical care have been growing rapidly. Most of the recent expansion has been in services provided on an ambulatory basis or at home. This is because there has been much less governmental and third-party regulation of those services, and the opportunities for commercial exploitation are still very attractive. Investor-owned businesses have the largest share of this new sector.

Free-standing centers for ambulatory surgery are a good case in point. Ten or 15 years ago, all but the most minor surgery was performed in hospitals. It has now become apparent that at least half of all procedures, even those involving general anesthesia, can be safely performed on an outpatient basis, and in the past decade there has been a rapid proliferation of ambulatory surgery. Some of it is performed in special units within hospitals, but most of it is done in free-standing centers, of which there are now at least 1,200. Most of the free-standing facilities are investor-owned, with the referring surgeons as limited partners, and many of the in-hospital units are joint ventures between hospitals and their staff surgeons.

Sophisticated high-technology radiologic services, formerly found only in hospital radiology units, are now provided at hundreds of free-standing facilities called "imaging centers." Most of them feature magnetic resonance imagers and computerized tomography (CT) scanners. They usually are investor-owned and have business arrangements with practicing physicians who refer patients to the facilities. Diagnostic laboratory services, formerly provided only in hospitals, are now available in thousands of free-standing laboratories, many of which also have physicians as limited partners. Walk-in clinics, offering services such as those provided in hospital emergency rooms and other services formerly provided in doctors' offices, now flourish on street corners and in shopping centers and are operated by investor-owned businesses that employ salaried physicians. Investor-owned companies now provide all sorts of services to patients in their homes that were formerly available only in hospitals. These include oxygen therapy, respiratory therapy, and intravenous treatments.

Health maintenance organizations (HMOs) are another important part of the ambulatory care sector. Over the past decade they have continued to grow at the rate of 4 or 5 percent per year, and now there are an estimated 40 million patients enrolled in some 570 different plans. Approximately two thirds of these plans are investor-owned. Some investor-owned hospital chains have expanded "vertically"—that is, they offer not only inpatient, out-patient, and home services, but also nursing home and rehabilitation services. One or two of the largest chains have even gone into the health insurance business. The largest now insures more than 1.5 million subscribers, under terms that offer financial incentives to use the corporation's own hospitals.

In short, the investor-owned medical-industrial complex has continued to grow, but in new directions. No one has any clear idea of its present size, but I estimate that its revenues during 1990 were probably more than $150 billion, of a total national expenditure for health care of some $700 billion. This would mean that it represents an even larger fraction of total health care expenditures than it did a decade ago. The absence of reliable data on this point reflects the unfortunate consequence of government indifference and proprietary secrecy. And yet we obviously need such information to make future health policy decisions.

❖ The Commercialization of Voluntary Hospitals

What I had not fully appreciated in 1980 was that the pressures on our voluntary hospitals would lead many of them to behave just like their investor-owned competitors. The growing transfer of diagnostic and therapeutic procedures out of the hospital, the mounting cost-control constraints imposed by third-party payers, which reduced the hospitals' freedom to shift costs, and the general excess of hospital beds resulting from decades of rapid and uncontrolled expansion have all conspired to threaten the economic viability of voluntary hospitals. Philanthropy and community contributions, a mainstay of support when hospital costs were relatively low, are no longer of much help. Hospitals now must pay higher wages and much more money for supplies and equipment, but they cannot count on third-party payers and charitable contributions to cover costs. To compound the problem, those voluntary institutions traditionally committed to caring for large numbers of uninsured patients now find their resources strained to the limit. Private patients covered by the old-fashioned, open-ended kind of indemnity insurance are in ever shorter supply, and the voluntary hospitals now must compete aggressively in an increasingly unfriendly economic climate.

The result of all this has been a gradual shift in the focus of our voluntary hospital system. Altruistic motives that formerly guided the decisions of voluntary hospital management are giving way in many institutions to a primary concern for the bottom line. Hospital administrators have become corporate executives (with business titles such as chairman, chief executive officer, president, and the like) who are required first of all to ensure the economic survival of their institutions. For many hospitals, this means aggressive use of marketing and advertising strategies, ownership of for-profit businesses, and joint ventures with physicians on their staff. Decisions about the allocation of hospital resources, the creation of new facilities, or the elimination of existing ones are now based more on considerations of what is likely to be profitable than on the priorities of community health needs.

Many if not most of our voluntary hospitals now view themselves as businesses competing for paying patients in the health care marketplace. They have, in effect, become part of the medical-industrial complex. Voluntary hospitals have always been tax-exempt because they are not owned by investors and they do not distribute profits to their owners. Because they are tax-exempt, they have been expected to provide necessary community services, profitable or not, and to care for uninsured patients. Many, of course, do exactly that, to the limit of their ability. But, sad to say, many do not, and this has raised questions in some quarters about the justification of their continued tax exemption.

In any case, we are witnessing a pervasive change in the ethos of the voluntary hospital system in America from that of a social service to that of a business. Leaders of hospital associations now commonly refer to themselves as part of an industry, and the management philosophy of private hospitals, investor-owned or not, is increasingly dominated by business thinking. It would be interesting to compare current prices and unreimbursed care in the voluntary and investor-owned hospital sectors. My guess is that much of the earlier difference in price has disappeared, but the voluntary hospitals probably still provide proportionately more uninsured care.

❖ A Market-Oriented Health Care System

What we see now is a market-oriented health care system spinning out of control. Costs are rising relentlessly in a competitive marketplace heavily influenced by private commerce and still largely dominated by more or less open-ended indemnity insurance and payment by piecework. The financial arrangements in such a system inevitably stimulate the provision of service with little or no regard for cost. Unlike the usual kind of market, in which consumer demand and ability to pay largely determine what is produced and sold, the health care market is not controlled by consumers, because most payment comes from third parties and most decisions are made by physicians.

The fraction of the gross national product devoted to health care has been rising steeply ever since the advent of Medicare and Medicaid in the mid-1960s. In 1965 we spent about 6 percent of our gross national product on health care; in 1975, approximately 8 percent; in 1985, about 10.5 percent; and, in 1990, over 12 percent, or approximately $700 billion. Despite the high cost, or maybe because of it, the system is unable to provide adequate care for all citizens. At least 15 percent of Americans have no health insurance, and probably at least an equal number are inadequately or only intermittently insured. After all, a system that functions as a competitive marketplace has no more interest in subsidizing the uninsured poor than in restricting the revenues generated by services to those who are insured.

Evidence of inefficiency, duplication, and excessive overhead is everywhere apparent. Administrative costs have recently been estimated to make up between 19 and 24 percent of total spending on health care, far more than in any other country. Nearly half of all the beds in investor-owned hospitals and from 35 to 40 percent of all the beds in voluntary hospitals are, on the average, unused. On the other hand, expensive high-technology diagnostic and therapeutic procedures are being carried out in hospitals, doctors' offices, and growing numbers of specialized free-standing facilities at a rate that many studies suggest is excessive among insured patients, though probably inadequate among the poor.

❖ Medical Practice as a Competitive Business

Adding to the competition and cost in our health care system is the recent rapid increase in the number of practicing physicians, most of whom are specialists. In 1970 there were 153 active physicians per 100,000 members of the population; in 1980 there were 192; and the number for 1990 was estimated to exceed 220. Among these new practitioners, the number of specialists is increasing more rapidly than that of primary care physicians. When doctors were in relatively short supply two or three decades ago, they worried less about their livelihood. Now, as the economists would say, we are in a buyer's market, in which not only underused hospitals but also specialists—available in increasing, sometimes even excessive, numbers—are forced to compete for the diminishing number of paying patients who are not already part of the managed care network.

How have all these developments affected the practice of medicine? In the first place, they have resulted in more regulation of the private practice of medicine by third-party payers, who are trying to control costs. There is more interference with clinical practice decisions, more second-guessing and paperwork, and more administrative delays in billing and collecting than ever before, as third-party payers attempt to slow down cost increases through micromanagement of the medical care system.

Second, doctors are increasingly threatened by malpractice litigation as a strictly business relationship begins to replace the trust and mutual confidence that traditionally characterized the doctor-patient relationship.

Third, the courts, which formerly kept the practice of medicine out of the reach of antitrust law, now regard the physician as just another person doing business, no longer immune from antitrust regulation. In 1975 the Supreme Court handed down a landmark decision that found that the business activities of professionals were properly subject to antitrust law. As a consequence, physicians can no longer act collectively on matters affecting the economics of practice, whether their intent is to protect the public or simply to defend the interests of the profession. Advertising and marketing by individual physicians, groups of physicians, or medical facilities, which used to be regarded as unethical and were proscribed by organized medicine, are now protected—indeed, encouraged—by the Federal Trade Commission.

Advertising and marketing are just a part of the varied entrepreneurial activities in which practicing physicians are now engaged. Perceiving the trend toward the industrialization of medicine, sensing the threat to their access to paying patients from hospitals, HMOs, and other closed-panel insurance plans, and feeling the pressures of competition from the growing army of medical practitioners, doctors have begun to think of themselves as beleaguered businesspersons, and they act accordingly.

Of course, the private practice of medicine has always had businesslike characteristics, in that practicing physicians earn their livelihood through their professional efforts. For the vast majority of physicians, however, professional commitments have dominated business concerns. There was always more than enough work for any physician to do, and few physicians had to worry about competition or earning a livelihood. Furthermore, it had long been generally accepted that a physician's income should derive exclusively from direct services to patients or the supervision of such services, not from any entrepreneurial activities.

All that seems to be changing now in this new era of medical entrepreneurialism and health care marketing. Increasing numbers of physicians have economic interests in health care that go beyond direct services to patients or the supervision of such services. The American Medical Association (AMA), which formerly proscribed entrepreneurialism by physicians, now expressly allows it, with some caveats, apparently recognizing that a very substantial fraction of practitioners supplement their income by financial interests in all sorts of health care goods, services, and facilities.

The arrangements are too numerous and varied to describe in full here, so I shall simply cite some of them, a few of which I have already alluded to: (1) practitioners hold limited partnerships in for-profit diagnostic-laboratory facilities to which they refer their patients but over which they exercise no professional supervision; (2) surgeons hold limited partnerships in for-profit ambulatory surgery facilities to which they refer their own patients; (3) office-based practitioners make deals with prescription-drug wholesalers who supply them with drugs that the physicians prescribe for their patients and for which they charge retail prices; (4) physicians purchase prostheses at reduced rates from manufacturers and make a profit in addition to the professional fees they receive for implanting the prostheses; and (5) practitioners own interests in imaging units to which they refer their patients. Most of the free-standing imaging units are owned by investor-owned businesses, but some were originally owned by radiologists in private practice who have told me that they were persuaded to form joint partnerships with their referring physicians because these physicians threatened to refer their patients elsewhere.

Such arrangements create conflicts of interest that undermine the traditional role of the doctor. In the minds of some physicians, the old Samaritan tradition of our profession has now given way to the concept of a strict business contract between doctor and patient. According to this view, good physicians are simply honest and competent vendors of medical services who are free to contract for whatever services they are willing to provide and patients or their insurers are willing to pay for. Society has no more stake in the practice of medicine than in the conduct of any other business activity, and therefore no right to interfere with the terms of the private contract between doctor and patient.

❖ The Threat to the Morale of Physicians and Their Social Contract

Given this general climate, it is no wonder that the morale of so many practicing physicians and the enthusiasm of so many young people for careers in medicine are flagging. I believe that the attractiveness of medicine as a career and the rewards experienced by practicing physicians have traditionally depended on four essential elements, and still do. First, medicine requires a desire to be of important service to others at a time when they are in particular need, and in a way that may profoundly affect the quality and length of life. Few other vocations offer the opportunity to do so much good and to earn the everlasting gratitude of those being served. Good doctors truly make a difference in people's lives.

Second, medicine also offers the practitioner a unique opportunity to assume personal responsibility for important decisions that are not influenced by or subordinated to the purposes of third parties. Good physicians, whether in solo practice or group practice, have a mixture of responsibility and personal independence that is hard to equal. Medicine has therefore always appealed to people who have a strong sense of commitment to others as well as confidence in themselves and their ability to make difficult decisions.

Third, medicine is based on science, and it therefore attracts those who are fascinated by the science of human biology and who can respond to the challenge of applying science to the diagnosis, treatment, and prevention of disease. At the same time, medicine is a profoundly human discipline that is intimately concerned with the psyche and soul. Although there are some physicians who do not enjoy personal interaction with their patients, most do. One of the greatest rewards of medical practice is the opportunity to deal with patients as people and to help them through personal crises.

Finally, medical practice, at least until now, has always offered a relatively secure livelihood. Competent, well-regarded physicians have been able to count on making a decent living, regardless of their specialty. The median income of physicians has always been several times higher than that of the average wage-earner, and in some specialties physicians earn far beyond that.

Although I do not underestimate the economic rewards of medical practice as one of its major attractions, I do not believe it is the most important one for the vast majority of people who go into medicine. Physicians expect to be well paid for their efforts, and they should be, but I believe that the other, more personal rewards are at least as compelling.

Today's market-oriented, profit-driven health care industry therefore sends signals to physicians that are frustrating and profoundly disturbing to the majority of us who believe our primary commitment is to patients. Most of us believe we are parties to a social contract, not a business contract. We are not vendors, and we are not merely free economic agents in a free market. Society has given us a licensed monopoly to practice our profression protected in large part against competition from other would-be dispensers of health services. We enjoy independence and the authority to regulate ourselves and set our own standards. Much of our professional training is subsidized, and almost all the information and technology we need to practice our profession have been produced at public expense. Those of us who practice in hospitals are given without charge the essential facilities and instruments we need to take care of our patients. Most of all, we have the priceless privilege of enjoying the trust of our patients and playing a critical part in their lives when they most need help.

All this we are given in exchange for the commitment to serve our patients' interests first of all and to do the very best we can. In my view, that means we should not only be competent and compassionate practitioners but also avoid ties with the health care market, in order to guide our patients through it in the most medically responsible and cost-effective way possible. If the present organization and incentives of our health care system make it difficult or impossible for us to practice in this way (and I believe they do), then we must join with others in examining ways of reforming the system.

What our health care system needs now is not more money, but different incentives and a better organization that will enable us to use available resources in a more equitable and efficient manner to provide necessary services for all who need them. We can afford all the care that is medically appropriate according to the best professional standards. We cannot afford all the care a market-driven system is capable of giving.

❖ About the Author

Arnold S. Relman, M.D., is Professor of Medicine and Social Medicine, Harvard Medical School, a,nd former Editor-in-Chief of the *New England Journal of Medicine.*

❖ Academic Medicine as a Public Trust

STEVEN A. SCHROEDER, JANE S. ZONES,
AND JONATHAN A. SHOWSTACK

The ascendancy of North American medicine in the hierarchy of science and social services is a striking feature of the past half-century. Spurred by rapid advances in knowledge about the causes and treatment of diseases and the application of this knowledge in new technologies, our medical institutions have become a model for the world. The United States is the premier site for advanced medical training, and its biomedical science is second to none. North America also leads the world in achieving spectacular declines in heart disease and stroke death rates, the declines coming in large part from aggressive public health campaigns to stop cigarette smoking, change dietary habits, and control hypertension.

The academic medical center is the most important force behind the increasing dominance of U.S. medicine. Advances in basic science research, an efficient hospital-based educational system, and the sophisticated treatment of disease combine to make academic medicine highly productive and influential. The physician-graduates of our academic medical centers are among the most skilled and knowledgeable in the world, diagnosis and treatment are usually at the cutting edge of technological advances, and research often is path-breaking.

Thousands upon thousands of persons have studied disease. Almost no one has studied health.
—Adelle Davis

Yet, to many observers there are disquieting signs that not all is well within medical academia. During the last four decades academic medicine has responded positively and with outstanding success to society's desire for advances in biomedical science. Today, however, the aging of the population, the increased importance of long-term illness, and changes in the economics and organization of medical care suggest that a redirection of the efforts of academic medicine is needed. Increasingly, academic medical centers are confronted with economic and social challenges that threaten the structure and substance of their educational, patient care, and research missions. Changes in organization and financing, particularly the initiation of

76

prospective payment for hospital care and the development of prepaid health care, directly endanger the financial basis of academic medicine as well as the relevance of its educational programs. The attractiveness of medicine as a profession has waned. The number of applicants to medical schools has fallen 31% since 1977, and there is concern that the quality of the applicants has declined as well. The content of education, patient care, and research also is becoming increasingly discordant with the social, behavioral, and clinical problems commonly presented by today's patients.

Because academic medical centers are supported primarily by public funds, and their educational, patient care, and research missions delegated by society, the health needs of the general population must be considered in decisions about program development. To the degree that academic medicine does not meet the needs of society, resources might have to be diverted to support other institutions that are able and willing to fulfill those needs. The aging of the population, the increasing prevalence of long-term and disabling illnesses with multiple social and behavioral risk factors, concern about quality of care, and the escalating costs of medical care suggest that fundamental changes are needed in the way that academic medicine carries out its mission.

Thus, the challenge to academic medicine is the development of a positive and productive response to the changing needs of society, while maintaining excellence in education, patient care, and research. We herein review the nature of academic medicine as a public trust and examine ways that the needs of society might be addressed more completely by academic medicine.

❖ The Public Trust

Academic medicine is entrusted by society with the responsibility to undertake several important social missions, including education, patient care, and research, toward improving the health of the public. Although this trust is implicit, it is given authority by the generous public funding of academic medicine and the agreement to allow medicine to regulate itself. A distinguishing characteristic of professions is the great extent to which the public permits self-regulation. The education and training of physicians is self-regulated through the certification and accreditation of physicians and hospitals, performed by voluntary professional organizations on behalf of the state.

Academic medicine is supported primarily by public funds. Of the 127 medical schools in the United States, 77 (61%) are public institutions. Even institutions without direct government funding derive a large portion of their financing from public sources. Public subsidies for patient care, tax benefits, and grants and contracts provide more than half the resources of academic medical centers in the United States. Residency and fellowship training in the United States are funded primarily through reimbursement to teaching hospitals for patient care, a substantial portion of which comes from federal and state programs such as Medicare and Medicaid. Full-time faculty often are supported in large part by research grants from the federal government. Although the proportion of medical school revenue derived from federal sources has been declining since the mid-1960s, state contributions have risen appreciably; by 1983 to 1984, federal dollars amounted to approximately one fourth and state contributions to 21% of medical school income. Additional revenue is derived from federal and state assistance to elderly and medically indigent patients. Similarly, local, state, and federal sources constitute more than half of the income of university-owned hospitals.

Medical Education as a Public Trust

A principal function of the academic medical center is to prepare young physicians to meet the nation's health care needs. Appropriate execution of this function requires attention both to the quality of the education provided and to the manpower mix produced. Public funds allow academic medicine to carry out this function.

In 1989, there were more than 65,000 medical students in the United States. Academic medicine invests even more in graduate than in undergraduate medical education. In 1988, there were more than 81,000 residents in training. Of the hospitals with accredited residency programs, 90% are affiliated with a medical school. The bulk of funding for graduate medical education comes from patient-care revenues, including 25% to 30% from Medicare and about 18% from Medicaid. Growth of full-time faculty has outstripped the increases in numbers of students and trainees. In constant dollars, between 1965 to 1966 and 1985 to 1986, salaries for faculty in clinical departments rose by 23% to 78%, while salaries for many faculty in the basic sciences actually decreased.

Patient Care as a Public Trust

Patient care is essential for clinical teaching and for much clinical research. Approximately one in six hospital admissions in the United States is to a teaching hospital. Because many teaching hospitals are located in urban centers, they provide more than half of the nation's uncompensated medical care. Many patients in teaching hospitals cannot afford care elsewhere. Academic medical centers traditionally provided health care without regard for a patient's social status or ability to pay. Economic pressures, however, are creating strong incentives to limit care given to the poor and uninsured. As academic medical centers compete in the new health care economic environment, the poor and disadvantaged may lose access to an important source of care.

The increasingly competitive environment of hospital economics has set in motion a cycle of intense competition among hospitals for patients, especially patients with adequate insurance coverage. This occurs at a time when patient care has become an increasingly important part of the mission of academic medical centers. Indeed, revenues from patient care have been the most important factor behind the recent increases in numbers of faculty members. Although there is a valid concern that teaching hospitals may face difficult financial circumstances, until now academic teaching hospitals have done very well. Under Medicare's Prospective Payment System, their profit margins have increased more than those of any other category of hospital. Although their success in the marketplace has depended on a variety of strategies, the introduction and refinement of highly specialized technologies has played a central role. These include new imaging techniques, invasive procedures for diagnosis and treatment, aggressive protocols for the treatment of patients with cancer and cardiovascular disease, and organ and bone marrow transplantation. As is described later herein, however, successful competitive strategies for hospitals may conflict with the educational role of academic medical centers.

Health Research as a Public Trust

Perhaps the most widely recognized public function of academic medical centers is the production of new scientific knowledge to improve the health of the public. A report by the Institute of Medicine observed that additions to scientific knowledge have been the principal contribution of academic medicine during this century. Since World War II, government-supported basic and applied medical research has assumed expanding significance in academic medicine. National expenditures from all sources on biomedical research in 1985 were more than $13 billion, approximately three times as much in constant dollars as in 1960. The federal government provided half of this amount, about $6.8 billion, of which abut 70% ($4.8 billion) came from the National Institutes of Health (NIH). In 1986, more than 80% of the NIH budget was expended on grants to academic institutions, particularly schools of medicine. The lion's share of grant money for health research is allocated to laboratory-based biomedical research. Heavily endowed by the NIH, the most successful academic medical centers obtain a large proportion of their budgets from peer-reviewed grants, thereby deriving monies essential to support the basic operations of the center. Although research funds continue to be an important source of medical center reserves, their relative contribution actually declined from 25% of total revenues in 1970 to 1971 to 20% in 1986 to 1987, reflecting the large growth in clinical income. In addition, research funds are not spread evenly across medical schools; rather, in 1987 more than 60% of NIH support to medical schools went to only 20% of schools. In many academic medical centers, attention to biomedical research has displaced the previous emphasis on training practitioners.

The Leadership Role

In addition to its critical role in education, research, and patient care, medical academia exerts a dominant influence on all aspects of medical care in the United States. Its current and former faculty write textbooks, edit and determine policy for medical journals, constitute the majority of members of accrediting bodies and certifying boards, introduce and disseminate the newest medical drugs and technology, provide the continuing medical education for the nation's practitioners, direct many of the philanthropic foundations, review proposals for research funding, serve as medical ambassadors to other countries, and train much of the leadership of academic medicine from overseas nations. In short, the current medical care system in this country, with its remarkable strengths, as well as its shortcomings, can be seen as reflecting the priorities and influence of medical academia.

❖ How Well Is Academic Medicine Fulfilling Its Public Trust?

Although academic medicine in the United States has been entrusted with a major leadership role and has been well funded for that purpose, it enjoys remarkable autonomy in exercising its functions. Compared with academic medicine in other industrialized countries, it is remarkably free of systems of public accountability. At least on a national level, American academic medicine has the best of both worlds. On one hand, it is the beneficiary of substantial public funds for education, patient care, and research. Yet, in a system characterized by voluntary oversight, it enjoys the freedom to define how it carries out its public responsibilities.

It is thus fair to ask how well academic medicine has fulfilled its public trust. Our impressions of the performance to date of the U.S. health care system, based on available data and international comparisons, are outlined in Table l. It is instructive to review the contributions of medical academia to the categories shown in Table 1, while recognizing that performance in many of these areas is dictated more by national administrative and financing considerations than by the capacities of medical academia.

❖ Areas of Strong Performance
Advances in Biomedical Research

Accomplishments by academic medicine in biomedical research are the envy of the entire world. Whether judged by Nobel prizes, journal citations, peer reputation, or amount of dollar support, it seems incontestable that the combination of strong, sustained, federal tax support through the NIH, rigorous peer review that has been remarkably free of political interference, the creative partnership between academia and the NIH, and the considerable supplementation from private philanthropies (such as the Howard Hughes Institute and the Markey Trust) and private industry has spurred outstanding achievements in biomedical science. How the increasingly evident entrepreneurial atmosphere of recent academic industrial collaboration will affect this performance is not yet clear.

TABLE 1. Areas of Strong and Weak Performance in U.S. Medicine

Areas of Strong Performance	Areas of Weak Performance
Biomedical research	Health status
Technology development and dissemination	Health care expenditures
	Quality of medical care
Progress against targeted diseases	Health manpower mix and distribution
Heart disease	Long-term care and disability
Hypertension and stroke	Inappropriate model for other countries
Smoking-related diseases	
Acquired immunodeficiency syndrome	
Screening for preventable disease	
Health services research	
Innovations in health care provision	

Technology Development and Diffusion

The United States clearly leads the world in the development, diffusion, and use of medical technology and pharmaceuticals. In no other country is a person as likely to have an imaging procedure performed with such new techniques as magnetic resonance, computed tomography, or ultrasound; to have aggressive treatment of atherosclerotic heart disease, including thrombolytic treatment with tissue plasminogen-activator or streptokinase, coronary angioplasty, and coronary artery bypass surgery; to be a recipient of heterologous heart, liver, or kidney transplants for organ system failure; to receive aggressive chemotherapy for cancer; to undergo treatment for infertility; or to receive medication for hypertension or hypercholesterolemia. Academic medical centers often take the lead in dissemination of individual technologies, first in their development and assessment and then in the publication of early results.

Progress Against Certain Target Illnesses

The United States recently has made impressive progress in lowering death rates from heart disease and stroke, in controlling hypertension, and in reducing the prevalence of cigarette smoking. Faculty of academic medical centers have contributed significantly to this progress by identifying the basic mechanism for atherosclerosis, demonstrating that treating hypertension lowers death rates from stroke, documenting the epidemiologic links between cigarette smoking, cancer, and atherosclerosis, and so on.

Perhaps the most recent example of academic contributions in meeting the challenge of a national public health problem is the acquired immunodeficiency syndrome (AIDS) epidemic. Academic scientists have been instrumental in developing the understanding of how AIDS is transmitted, including

identifying its viral etiology, in developing immunologic tests for AIDS anti-
bodies, and in documenting the spread of AIDS through sexual contacts and
blood exchange. They also have pioneered in characterizing the clinical manifestations of AIDS and in developing incremental treatment strategies that prolong the life and preserve the function of patients with the disease. Clearly,
hopes reside in academic centers and the NIH for developing and testing of a
preventive vaccine as well as for improving epidemiologic knowledge of how
to limit viral spread between infected and uninfected persons.

Disease Prevention: Screening and Other Strategies for Clinical Prevention

The best approach to attacking disease is to detect and treat the
precursors before the disease itself becomes manifest. American medical researchers have pioneered in elucidating the science of disease prevention,
including strategies for screening and the application of screening techniques to populations. Studies have demonstrated the benefits of screening
for colon cancer, hypercholesterolemia, and hypertension. Scientists in the
United States also have played an important role in the eradication of infectious diseases, as in the global eradication of smallpox, and in the development of immunizing agents and the strategies for provision of those agents.
There is probably more activity in disease prevention and screening in the
United States than elsewhere in the world, although actual performance is
still far below target levels set by experts, and the full costs of all recommended screening procedures would be considerable.

Health Services Research

Health services research is performed by clinicians, epidemiolo-
gists, economists, and social scientists. It investigates the process of health
care, including outcomes (e.g., quality and patient satisfaction), costs, and the
distribution of resources and services, with the goal of identifying ways to
improve quality, efficiency, equity, or all three. The contributions of American health services researchers are acknowledged widely as pathbreaking,
both in the conceptual understanding of these issues and in their practical elu-
cidation. Although the profile of health services research is modest in individual health sciences centers and in academia as a whole, by world standards
the United States is the uncontested leader in this field. Colloton recently argued that academic medicine can be more responsive to the needs and expectations of society if it places a high priority on health services research.

Innovations in Health Care Provision

A number of innovative forms of health care provision have
emerged in the United States, including health maintenance organizations;
nurse practitioners and physician's assistants as new forms of medical manpower; the applications of computer technology to improve the retrieval of
patient information, to enhance communications among health profession-

als, and to analyze complex data sets; and the development of community-based support groups for patients with specific diseases or trauma (e.g., Alcoholics Anonymous). It is probable that the development of most of these innovations (for example, health maintenance organizations) owes more to the entrepreneurial and individualistic nature of American culture than to contributions from academia. Nevertheless, in many instances academic scientists took the lead in evaluating or promoting these innovations.

❖ Areas of Weak Performance

In contrast to the areas of strong performance, there are other areas in which the United States health care system is not performing as well (see Table 1). While the major roots of the poor performance do not necessarily lie within academia, addressing the weaker components of the system should be a focus of any institution whose central role and substantial support have been granted by the public. Furthermore, it can be argued that society looks to academic medicine for the expertise to define the best approaches to important health problems. To the extent that academic medicine is relatively uninvolved in areas of weak performance, the public, which funds academia, legitimately can ask for more involvement or seek guidance elsewhere.

National Health Status

Despite its eminence in scientific medicine, the United States lags behind most other developed countries in the traditional measurements of a nation's health, such as infant mortality rates and life expectancy. Although infant mortality rates have declined recently, from 20 deaths per 1,000 live births in 1970 to 10.4 in 1986, the United States still ranks 19th in the world, behind, for example, Hong Kong, Singapore, and Ireland. Even after excluding non-whites, whose infant mortality rates are almost twice as high as those for whites, the United States still ranks only 13th, behind Ireland and West Germany. Longevity in the United States also is relatively poor, with many countries, including Japan, Canada, Sweden, and Australia, having longer life expectancy for citizens at birth. To a large extent, these data reflect the heterogeneous economic, class, and ethnic makeup of American society, with the poor having much higher rates of prematurity, teenage pregnancy, deaths from violence and accidents, and hypertension. It is no less ironic, however, that within the shadows of some of the most prestigious academic medical centers in the United States are populations whose health status is embarrassingly poor.

National Health Care Expenditures

The role of academic medical centers in the medical cost problem is difficult to assess. Much of the recent research showing that it may be possible to reduce costs without jeopardizing quality comes from academic investigators. On the other hand, academic centers tend to be the sites where expensive new technologies are developed and from which they diffuse. It is likely that a major reason for the higher expenditures for health care in the United States is its high rate of expensive operations and invasive diagnostic procedures, the standards for the use of these procedures usually being set at academic medical centers. The dominant clinical paradigm of academic centers "not to miss a case" tends to set the standard for excellence and is not conducive to calls for technological or economic restraint. It is likely that this emphasis, which permeates standard textbooks and continuing medical education, has a major cost-inflating effect. In addition, the fastest growing source of revenue for most academic health center faculties is clinical practice, which, like medical care in general, derives much of its revenues from procedures and operations.

Quality of Medical Care

Concern about quality of care is probably more evident in North America than in any other part of the world. American researchers have led in conceptualizing the approach to quality assessment and assurance and have designed innovative approaches to improving the quality of medical care. Nevertheless, there is ample evidence that the quality of a significant proportion of medical care is substandard. Levels of clinical iatrogenesis among hospitalized patients may be as high as 36%. Variations among hospitals in fatality rates for commonly performed surgical procedures are substantial. The rate at which many of these procedures are performed is much higher in the United States than in comparably developed countries. A large proportion of commonly performed procedures and operations has been judged inappropriate or equivocal when reviewed against established criteria by expert consensus panels. Since a predictable number of patients who undergo these procedures will experience adverse complications, including death, the performance of large numbers of dangerous procedures that are not essential for patient treatment seriously threatens quality of care.

On the other hand, the underuse of medical services by certain populations is a major problem in the United States, as documented by inadequate immunization rates for measles, high rates of unwanted teenage pregnancies, and delayed prenatal care. Furthermore, major causes of premature death and disability continue to be cigarette smoking and substance abuse, occupational and other injuries, and dietary deficiencies. These problems receive remarkably little attention from academic medical centers, as judged by the content of standard clinical texts and university-sponsored continuing medical education courses as well as by recent surveys of medical students concerning the adequacy of educational exposure to these subjects.

The Distribution and Mix of Medical Manpower

Despite major recent increases in the physician-population ratio, rural areas still lag behind. For example, in San Francisco, California, Boston, Massachusetts, and Washington, D.C., there are as many as 600 practicing physicians per 100,000 persons compared with fewer than 100 in Appalachia. Even within metropolitan areas, there are wide differences in the distribution of manpower, with wealthier areas proportionally better supplied than the inner city. In addition to problems of numerical maldistribution, there is increasing recognition that the mix of physicians is becoming unbalanced, with relatively too many specialists and too few generalists. Recent surveys of student preferences indicate a marked decline in medical student interest in generalist careers. It is thus likely that serious shortages of generalists may be imminent and that the ranks of future generalists may be filled by many who have failed to secure residencies in such fields as ophthalmology, orthopedic surgery, or radiology. Furthermore, since many specialists will have to function as part-time generalists, the current hospital-dominant training model is unbalanced.

In contrast to the problems of health status, medical costs, and quality, the undesirable mix and distribution of physicians can be addressed directly by academic medical centers. Although one might think that equitable geographic distribution of physicians would result from the economic forces of the market, this does not seem to occur. True, physician-specialists now are appearing in formerly underserved areas, but this redistribution is occurring at the expense of a heightened gradient between physician-dense and physician-scarce regions. It should be acknowledged that the geographic maldistribution of physicians is a global problem. Nevertheless, by changing the criteria for selecting medical students and providing for their exposure to rural settings during the training period, medical academia could help to reverse this trend. In addition to external factors such as technology, reimbursement, and life-style, a number of biases in the current model of medical education seem to favor the production of specialists as opposed to generalists. These biases include faculty role models, the hospital-based nature of clinical training of medical students and residents, and the funding of graduate medical education through teaching hospitals.

To the extent that geographic and specialty maldistribution of physicians contribute to national problems of excessive medical costs, inadequate health status, poor quality, and insufficient access to medical care, the responsibility for addressing these problems falls to academic medical centers.

Long-Term Care and Disability

During the past half-century, the most striking change in the population of the United States has been the growing proportion of older persons, particularly those older than 84 years, whose numbers have increased by more than 50% in each decade since 1940.

How has medical academia responded to the challenges posed by these impressive demographic shifts? Clearly, extensive research into the pathogenesis and treatment of such common long-term illnesses as atherosclerotic heart disease, dementia, cerebrovascular disease, cancer, and arthritis is occurring at virtually every academic medical center. Although progress in understanding the causes and treatment of these illnesses is being made at variable and sometimes unpredictable rates, it is incontestable that the collective effort of medical academia in studying the biomedical aspects of aging is strong and responsive to the public's interest. Less impressive are research efforts to understand how to improve function in the chronically disabled, particularly those with dementia, mental illness, and drug addiction; to prevent or postpone disability; and to defer or ameliorate institutionalization.

The educational response to the demographic realities of aging and long-term illness also is unbalanced. As mentioned previously herein, clinical education for the past half-century has focused on the care of patients in the acute-care hospital, the clinical paradigm being the search for cure to achieve full return of function. This model is appropriate for 35-year-old patients with acute pneumococcal pneumonia or acute appendicitis, but less so for 80-year olds with chronic dementia or end-stage organ failure. By continuing to structure clinical education along the acute-care model, while neglecting the more difficult problems of how to preserve or improve function in the disabled, medical education has failed to respond to a societal need. Not until a more balanced clinical exposure includes such important sites as home care and extended-care facilities (including the multidisiplinary services intrinsic to those settings), and the curriculum is expanded to support these experiences, will medical education be responsive to this increasingly important societal need. It is hoped that an expanded clinical educational model will produce practitioners more interested in, and capable of responding to, long-term illness in the elderly.

Inappropriate Model for Developing Countries

Health professionals from all over the world come to academic medical centers in the United States for advanced training. More than half of all overseas foreign medical graduates in residency training in the United States in 1987 were in internal medicine, pediatrics, psychiatry, or family medicine. In some of their home countries, the average annual per capita expenditure for health care is less than $50, compared with nearly $2,000 in the United States. Exposure to the technology-intensive patterns of U.S. medical practice is not likely to be helpful for countries that face infant mortality rates of 1 in 10 or life expectancies of 40 years. The experiences of countries that have made great improvements in health status, such as China, Cuba, and Israel, suggest that the first step must be the implementation of programs to improve sanitation, family planning, nutrition, immunization, and the oral rehydration treatment of infantile and childhood diarrheas. The next steps involve controlling risk factors for chronic disease, such as cigarette use and hypertension. Given the structure and interests of academic medical centers in the United States, there is cause for great concern about the relevance of the model presented to foreign visitors. Granted, many of these visitors are drawn to the United States because of training opportunities in technology-intensive medicine or in biomedical research. Nevertheless, it would be important for the future direction of health care in the visitors' countries if their stay in the United States included more exposure to population-based concepts.

❖ The Counterargument and a Rebuttal

Clearly, one can argue that the areas of strong performance of academic health centers are so outstanding that to move away from the dominantly biomedical and technological model of American academic medical centers is unwise.

Given the enormous public funding of academic medical centers and the relative autonomy with which they currently define their scope and mission, only two basic responses seem possible. Academic medicine can choose to define its mission narrowly, but in that case it risks forfeiting some of the financial support it currently enjoys because entities to fulfill those important public functions might be sought elsewhere.

Alternatively, academic medicine can choose to expand its paradigm and interpret its mission more broadly, not to the detriment of its current activities but as an expression and recognition of its public responsibilities. Although this might involve some redirection of current activities—for example, a small decline in basic research support—such a transfer of research activities might be justifiable in terms of cost-effectiveness. It is possible that new constituencies for the expanded mission could generate additional support for those activities. Of the two possible responses, the latter choice is both the most responsive to the public's trust and the most realistic, given the extent of current environmental changes. To assist academic medical centers in carrying out their full public missions, adjustments are needed in the conduct of medical education, patient care, and research. Failure to adjust calls into question the legitimacy of the strong leadership positions currently occupied by these centers and eventually might threaten their funding base.

❖ Accepting the Challenge

Expansion of the Research Domain

Improvements in the health of the public require additional research beyond the biomedical sciences. In the field of preventive medicine, for example, major improvements in population health could come from even small improvements in the ability to help persons quit smoking and to discourage would-be smokers from starting; to prevent exposure to the AIDS virus; to improve compliance with recommendations for control of hypertension, lowering of blood lipid levels, and screening for common cancers; to discourage unsafe automobile driving; and to improve care of patients with long-term conditions to postpone or prevent associated complications, such as blindness due to retinopathy or limb amputations that result from inadequate foot care for persons with diabetes.

New knowledge is needed to improve functioning in persons with incurable long-term illnesses and to improve interactions between health providers and patients. Much more information and understanding is needed about the many conditions that cause great distress but are not conducive to easy diagnosis, such as somatization disorder and chronic fatigue syndrome.

Finally, given that resources available for medical care will continue to be finite and will be exceeded by the demand for those services, research is needed to gain a better understanding of factors that determine the distribution of services. How good is the current quality of medical care and how can it be improved? What will be the cost of improvements in quality and what are the best ways to spend society's resources? How can value be attached to the many medical services provided and, in an era of fiscal limits, what are the risks and benefits of expanding or contracting access to different kinds of medical care? Is it possible to quantify and compare the benefits and costs of such diverse services as home care for the home-bound elderly, intravenous thrombolytic therapy in acute myocardial infarction, liver transplantation, chemotherapy for metastatic cancer, or screening colonoscopy to detect colon cancer before it spreads?

This expanded menu of health-related research clearly is responsive to the health needs of the public. Active research on most of these questions already exists at many academic medical centers; indeed, for many topics the cutting-edge research is being performed in these centers. This is not to assert that one type of research must be chosen over another; indeed, the potential synergism of the new molecular biology and health services research is enormous. For example, breakthroughs in molecular genetics may make it possible to identify those persons with genetic predispositions to colon cancer; in such cases, screening procedures could target the at-risk population, thereby vastly improving cost-effectiveness. At issue, however, is whether such areas of inquiry are recognized as legitimate scholarly pursuits. Some advocate a narrower definition of scholarship that excludes these areas from academic medical inquiry. However, if academic medical centers are to respond to the challenge of improving the public's health under appropriate resource constraints, they must embrace a range of research topics that are as broad as the determinants of health and illness.

Expansion of the Educational Domain

In the preclinical years, rigorous introduction to the population-based sciences should be taught in parallel with the biologic sciences. These subjects can serve as clinical "basic sciences" for the difficult allocative and social decisions that practitioners increasingly will be called on to make. White argues that quantitative skills will be essential for "the critical appraisal of the medical literature and the avalanche of new maneuvers stemming from advances in biomedicine." Assuming that the clinical basic sciences of population-based medicine are introduced in the preclinical years, even more substantial changes will be required in the clinical years for medical students as well as for graduate medical education. To shift some clinical training from hospital to ambulatory and community settings, major adjustments are needed in financing and scheduling, in the traditional clinical teaching model, and in the delegation of clinical responsibility. In many cases, existing faculty will have to be retrained or new ones sought who are experienced in the practice of ambulatory care and who are comfortable and confident teaching in that setting. The need for increased time for ambulatory training is sometimes mistakenly linked only to the primary care specialties; however, it also holds for almost all specialties, including surgery, obstetrics and gynecology, and most of the surgical, pediatric, and internal medicine subspecialties.

In addition, the increasing prevalence of chronic illnesses and disabilities mandate that future physicians be aware of the problems and opportunities in settings where long-term care is provided. This means education about care given in the home and in nursing homes, including the scope, efficacy, and method of payment for long-term care services, the types of professionals involved, and how to assess quality. Since most clinician faculty have been recruited for their expertise in hospital medicine and/or biomolecular research, and since their salaries derive mainly from these activities, it is not surprising that clinical teaching has stayed mainly within the hospital. Nevertheless, demographic and epidemiologic realities dictate that clinical education responsive to the public's needs must adopt an expanded paradigm.

The shift from a clinical paradigm that is almost exclusively hospital based to one that includes ambulatory and long-term care may have subtle but important favorable consequences. Despite the obvious successes of modern scientific medicine, there is growing public criticism that physicians are not sufficiently caring. To some extent this criticism may flow inevitably from the increasing technologic complexity of modern medicine, with its subspecialization and fragmentation of care. It is tempting, however, to believe that the hospital-dominant model of clinical education, which includes the entire continuum from undergraduate training to continuing medical education, reinforces the notion that the prime task of medicine is to cure and, hence, that the caring functions are less important. As clinical education expands to include long-term illness and psychosocial concerns outside the hospital, greater attention may be paid to issues of comfort, function, and the primary, secondary, and tertiary prevention of sickness, disability, and suffering.

The final educational change relates to outcomes: the production of physician-specialists. Whether compared with other developed countries or with estimated need based on disease frequency, the United States stands alone in its reliance on specialists to provide much generalist care. This strategy is costly and conducive to unhappiness for specialists who may be ill-prepared for (and perhaps unenthusiastic about) generalist work. To the degree that a surplus of specialists limits opportunities to practice particular skills, technical quality may deteriorate. To some extent, the current reliance on hospital-based clinical education causes specialty excess, since it determines the numbers of faculty, residents, and fellows required to teach and supervise patient care. Thus, the shift away from the hospital model of medical education may decrease the need to train so many specialists.

Expanded Programs in Patient Care

Historically, the strongest aspect of patient care at academic medical centers has been the development and testing of new technologies for diagnosis and treatment. The combination of scientific expertise, highly trained subspecialists, and concentrated referral patterns can work together to create special areas of excellence. As the market for patients becomes more competitive, however, the referral hospitals of most medical centers have relied increasingly on further differentiation of medical care to preserve their market share, often with undesired results for medical education. As the need to survive in an increasingly competitive hospital marketplace drives teaching hospitals to see patient care more and more as a business venture, there is a danger that one public aspect of these institutions might suffer: care of the indigent.

In addition, from the standpoint of the public's health, the medical needs of a defined population comprise more than the highly technical services offered by the typical teaching hospital. To meet population needs, academic medical centers also must (1) demonstrate better patterns of caring for long-term illness; (2) assess the most cost-effective patterns of care for common diseases and procedures; (3) identify segments of the population that have specific unmet needs and help plan for the provision of necessary services (e.g., prenatal care for indigent mothers and contraception for teenagers); and (4) help in the development and implementation of optimal patterns of clinical prevention. Some argue that the central mission of academic medical centers should be to improve the health of a defined population, thereby requiring assessment of the population health status and medical needs and then evaluating whether existing programs are adequate to meet those needs. Adoption of such mission statements may be easier for medical centers of public universities with well-demarcated geographic areas than for private institutions or public ones with overlapping or ambiguous population areas. Nevertheless, the step of assessing the health status and needs of a defined population creates a powerful imperative for further planning and action, highlighting the inadequacy of a model that defines an institution's clinical mission as limited to what transpires within its hospital and outpatient facilities.

Barriers to the Response and Ways to Surmount Them

Even for medical centers whose leadership might agree with the expanded mission, responding to these challenges is inhibited by at least four barriers to change: financing, faculty resistance to changing traditional patterns of activity, difficulties in changing the clinical educational model, and the intractability of many of the social problems underlying inadequate health status.

The current flow of dollars to academic medical centers favors research efforts in biomedical sciences and clinical education in teaching hospitals. It is well-known and understood that current payment formulas for physicians make it much easier to support faculty members in the technology-intensive specialties than in fields such as psychiatry, pediatrics, or family medicine. Furthermore, teaching hospitals have perceived that it is easier to fill hospitals with paying patients by developing magnet programs in tertiary or quaternary care than by developing ambulatory-care programs. The NIH, however, is increasingly interested in funding research in disease prevention and in examining how elderly persons can maximize function. Potential funds for new directions in clinical education of medical students are available from existing private and state tuition monies. For graduate medical education, the distribution patterns within the hospital of the $3 billion that Medicare paid teaching hospitals in 1988 are not well understood. To the extent that the use of these dollars is not consonant with national health manpower needs, then considerable potential funds for new directions are waiting to be tapped. Finally, new efforts to reform physician payment suggest that the current large differences in income among medical specialties may be modified, thereby providing more flexibility to alter the faculty specialty mix.

Perhaps most important, proponents of the new expanded paradigm must come from the faculty of academic medical centers. Most current faculty have been recruited to carry out the prevailing mission of academic medical centers, and support of faculty derives in large part from highly technical hospital care and from biomedical research. It is not surprising that these faculty, justifiably proud of accomplishments in the areas for which they were hired, are not emerging as champions for changing the missions of medical academia. Although a few faculty development programs, such as the Robert Wood Johnson Clinical Scholars Program and the Henry J. Kaiser Faculty Development Program in General Internal Medicine, are training faculty with skills and motivation to accept the challenge of the expanded paradigm, the numbers are small (only 20 Johnson fellowships and three Kaiser faculty fellows per year). Based on these realities, it is reasonable to assume that it will take external public pressures at the national, state and local levels to expand the current missions of academic medical centers. For example, the specialty of family practice, championed by state legislatures with significant rural populations, has established a significant academic foothold only in state-supported schools. Departments of family medicine exist in 71 (93%) of 76 public medical schools but in only 29 (57%) of 51 private institutions.

The current hospital-based model for clinical education, which dates back to Osler, has endured for good reason. It is efficient in concentrating teachers, students, and patients temporally and spatially. By permitting the faculty to teach at predictable times and for limited periods, it frees them to pursue research and/or independent clinical activities. The group nature of ward teams lends itself to the collegiality of shared work experiences and the theater of team case discussions. Nevertheless, if desired educational objectives can no longer be satisfied by the exclusive reliance on the hospital model, then the considerable creative energies of medical faculties should be harnessed to effect the transition to increased clinical teaching outside the hospital.

Many of the root causes of the inadequate health status of the U.S. population seem intractable: poverty; violence; ignorance; addiction to alcohol, cigarettes, and drugs; unsafe sexual practices; and unsafe eating and driving habits. Similar difficult challenges did not prevent earlier efforts to conquer the infectious diseases, neither are they deterring the search for cures for cancer. To the extent that reductionist problems at the cellular or molecular level are easier to conceptualize and study, problems that result from individual or group behavior will never seem as attractive. Nevertheless, despite their intractability, they loom ever larger as barriers to improving the public's health.

Despite these formidable barriers, there are numerous examples of programs initiated by academic medical centers in response to some of the deficiencies listed in Table 1. Academic clinicians have designed and implemented programs to address the particular health and manpower needs of their communities and regions. Academic researchers have pioneered in elucidating the reasons behind mounting medical care costs and in showing how cost containment does not necessarily jeopardize quality of care. Similarly, academic researchers have helped define, assess, and improve the quality of medical care and have sponsored demonstration projects of quality-assurance programs. Improvements in understanding the problems of long-term care and disability have come from academic researchers, who have developed scales to measure functional impairment to study the epidemiology of dementia and to explore using nursing and community sites for education.

❖ Conclusions

Academic medicine enjoys a special place in American society, stemming from the degree to which it is entrusted with vital national health responsibilities and its substantial degree of public financial support. Today, academic medicine is confronting significant challenges to its ability to educate health professionals, undertake research, and provide sophisticated care. It is the site of training of most physicians, the provider of care for a large segment of the disadvantaged population, and the generator of much scientific knowledge. Changing health needs of the population and increased understanding of the etiology of the major causes of morbidity, disability, and mortality suggest, however, that it might be appropriate to reevaluate the focus and trajectory of academic medicine.

At the heart of the medical profession, academic medicine provides educational, clinical, scientific, and policy leadership. Recent and impending changes in demography, disease burden, and the organization and financing of medical care suggest that the evolution of academic medicine as an institution is inevitable. How well it responds to the changing social and clinical environment will determine, in large part, how well it will be able to continue its current levels of excellence as well as merit its current degree of public trust and support. The functions for which society currently is supporting academic medical centers will continue as enduring national concerns. If academic medical centers choose only to fulfill selected parts of that implicit social contract, however, they risk settling for only a limited portion of current levels of responsibility and financial support.

Colloton recently urged academic medicine to focus some of its best medical minds on the problems of the organization and provision of health services, linking improvements in these areas to the problem of care for the medically indigent. He concluded with the following appeal:

> Through a willingness to help define and address these new challenges, we will meet society's needs, recapture the nation's waning trust in the medical system, and sustain medicine as a respected and sought-after profession.

We urge the leaders of academic medicine to accept this challenge and to couple the powerful resources within their institutions with the immense reservoir of public esteem they still enjoy as they carry out a comprehensive definition of their public trust.

❖ About the Authors

Steven A. Schroeder, M.D., is President of the Robert Wood Johnson Foundation, Princeton, New Jersey.

Jane S. Zones, PH.D., is an Assistant Adjunct Professor in the Department of Social and Behavioral Sciences, School of Nursing, University of California, San Francisco, and she is a member of the board of directors of the National Women's Health Network.

Jonathan A. Showstack, M.P.H., is an Associate Professor in the Institute for Health Policy Studies, Division of General Internal Medicine, and Co-Director of the Health of the Public Program, University of California, San Francisco.

❖ Medicare and Medicaid's 25th Anniversary—Much Promised, Accomplished, and Left Unfinished

SELECT COMMITTEE ON AGING, U.S. HOUSE
OF REPRESENTATIVES

❖ Executive Summary

Twenty-five years ago on July 30, 1965, President Johnson signed into law the Medicare and Medicaid programs as Titles XVIII and XIX, respectively, of the Social Security Act. As enacted, the Medicare program was designed as a national, federally administered program with uniform eligibility and benefits tied to the Social Security program. Part A, the hospital insurance program, provides protection for mostly inpatient acute care; while part B, the supplementary medical insurance fund, covers doctor visits and other ambulatory services.

The Medicaid program is a Federal grant program which is administered by the States and is targeted toward lower income individuals and families. It covers a broad range of hospital, nursing facility, and other medical services.

When these programs were enacted, many persons expected that Medicare and Medicaid would ensure full coverage of all health care services for the elderly, disabled, and the poor. While these programs have gone through many changes in their 25 year history, and much has been accomplished during this time period, this report will indicate that there remain many gaps and weaknesses in the programs.

Accomplishments

The Medicare and Medicaid programs have made many important contributions to the health care needs of the elderly, disabled, and the poor. The following statistics give some indication of this contribution. In 1989, society contributed over $120 billion to parts A and B of the Medicare program, and $54 billion to the Medicaid program. These programs have primarily been funded by the taxpayer through Social Security and general income taxes, and by the elderly through these taxes and through premiums.

Over the years, these programs have served many beneficiaries, and, therefore, have provided them access to health care and protected them from much of the burden of considerable health care costs. In 1989, Medicare served 32.5 million beneficiaries and Medicaid served 23.5 million beneficiaries. An examination of a few key services gives an even better perspective on these programs' contributions. In 1987, Medicare provided nursing home care to 300,000 persons, and physician and other medical services to 23 million persons. For Medicaid in 1988, the number of beneficiaries who received skilled and intermediate nursing home care was 1.59 million and the number who received physician services was 15.26 million.

Enactment of Medicare and Medicaid

Medicare was enacted into law on July 30, 1965, as Title XVIII of the Social Security Act. It was designed as a national, federally administered program with uniform eligibility and benefits and was tied to the Social Security program. The hospital insurance program, part A, provides protection for acute care needs with benefits structured around episodes of illness. It covers all expenses for the first 60 days minus a deductible; for days 61–90, a coinsurance amount is deducted. When more than 90 days are required in a benefit period, a patient may elect to draw upon a 60 day lifetime reserve. A coinsurance amount is deducted for each reserve day.

Part A will also pay for up to 100 days in a skilled nursing facility; after the first 20 days, a daily coinsurance amount is deducted. Subject to need, it also pays for home health visits for homebound individuals.

Medicare part B, the supplementary medical insurance fund, pays 80 percent of approved charges and covered services in excess of an annual deductible. Covered services include doctor visits, such as surgery, consultation, home, office, and institutional visits; other medical and health services, such as laboratory and diagnostic tests, radiation, therapy, outpatient services, artificial devices, physical and speech therapy, and ambulance services; and home health services not covered by part A.

Medicaid was also enacted on July 30, 1965, as Title XIX of the Social Security Act. It is a Federal grant program which is administered and partly funded by the States and is limited to low income individuals and families. It covers those persons eligible for existing welfare programs. In addition, States may provide for the medically needy who are individuals not eligible for cash assistance because of income limits but whose medical bills exceed their income to the point that they meet the States' medically needy standards.

Title XIX requires that every State offer hospital inpatient and outpatient care, laboratory and X-ray services, skilled nursing facility services, physician services, family planning, and early and periodic screening, diagnosis, and treatment for persons under 21 years of age. In addition, States may provide a number of other services at their option, including prescription drugs, eyeglasses, intermediate care facility services, inpatient psychiatric care, physical therapy, and dental care.

The Promise

Many people expected that the enactment of Medicare and Medicaid would ultimately protect the elderly and poor persons from burdensome health care costs. When President Johnson signed these bills, he stated:

> No longer will older Americans be denied the healing miracles of modern medicine. No longer will illness crush and destroy the savings that they have so carefully put away over a lifetime so that they might enjoy dignity in their later years.

Medicaid also had far-reaching goals. The poor were promised that they would soon have access to mainstream medical care and that health care was a basic right. However, the original intent of these programs was primarily to address the acute care needs of the elderly and the poor. Chronic long term care was not included. One reason that long term care was not included was that it was not as great a factor as it is today. To avoid opposition by the advocates of States' rights, Congress further compromised by conceding much of the control and administration of Medicaid to the States. These compromises, as well as many other gaps and weaknesses, mean that this nation is still a long way from meeting the original dreams of Medicare and Medicaid.

❖ Unfinished Agenda: Gaps and Weaknesses in Medicare and Medicaid

Despite the many accomplishments of these two programs, there still remain many gaps and weaknesses that need to be resolved. This section highlights a few key problems.

Rising Health Care Costs

Health care costs have been rising at rates faster than the cost of living for at least the past two decades. This has created problems for the entire health care field; for employers and employees; for the Medicare and Medicaid programs; and for the elderly, the poor, and disabled. For instance, while the Consumer Price Index increased by 23 percent from 1983 to 1989, medical care prices increased by 49 percent during this same time period.

One consequence of medical price inflation is pressure on the Medicare Hospital Trust Fund, now projected to be depleted between 1999 and 2018. The rapid increases for the Medicare and Medicaid programs are motivating policymakers at both the Federal and State levels to search for ways to constrain costs. This could result in the elimination of certain services or the elimination of certain groups from Medicaid. The same scenario is also occurring in the private sector, where employers are cutting back on health benefits.

For the elderly, another consequence of health care cost inflation is that health care costs are consuming an ever greater proportion of their income. Their out-of-pocket costs as a percent of income decreased from 15 percent in 1966 to 12.3 percent in 1977 and then increased to 18.2 percent in 1988. Thus, the out-of-pocket proportion of income is 20 percent greater than when Medicare was first implemented in 1966 and 50 percent higher than in 1977. If present trends continue, the elderly will soon pay out-of-pocket costs representing more than one fifth of their incomes.

For the uninsured, the rise in health care costs has major consequences. Many of them are being denied access to even the most critical care. When they do receive such care, they experience staggering bills, which they are unable to pay or which consume a significant portion of their meager incomes. A majority of the uninsured have incomes that are less than 200 percent of the poverty line; yet their out-of-pocket costs of $430 per year are almost equal to those for the insured who on average have substantially higher incomes. The situation is further exacerbated in that the number of uninsured has increased from 28 to 37 million persons between 1979 and 1986 according to the Census Bureau's Current Population Survey.

Incomplete Quality Assurance

While quality of care has received considerable attention in the last few years, there remain many gaps in monitoring and assurance of high quality medical care. One of the reasons for concern is that there have been reports at Congressional hearings indicating that poor quality care has been delivered. There has also been research showing that, at least for selected surgical procedures, over 30 percent of the cases have been inappropriate.

To date, there has been no definitive assessment of the quality of care provided by health care providers, largely because of the lack of a sufficiently acceptable set of quality measures. The field is only in the beginning stages in the development of outcome measures, which are the most fundamental in assessing the quality of care, and the initiation of effectiveness research which will test whether or not certain medical procedures are more effective than others. Another significant gap is that quality assurance is fragmented between several parties including survey and certification agencies, the peer review organizations, and licensing bodies. There is very little in the way of communications between these entities. Finally, a major limitation is that quality assurance efforts focus on Medicare and, to some extent, on Medicaid, but do very little to protect the privately insured and the uninsured.

Recently, several steps have been taken to improve this state of affairs. For instance, the Omnibus Budget Reconciliation Act of 1987 required the implementation of several quality assurance reforms; e.g., a consumer hotline, patient bill of rights, training of home health aides, and new survey procedures. These procedures are soon to be implemented. Quality assurance for Health Maintenance Organizations is being beefed up, but is still in the early stages of development. Quality assurance for physicians' offices is in the process of early implementation. However, even with these efforts, quality assurance has a long way to go before it fulfills its promise.

Coverage Gaps and Weaknesses

As a result of the repeal of the Medicare Catastrophic Care Act, the Medicare program still has major services uncovered such as extended hospital care, home health care, nursing home care, prescription drugs, and various preventive services. An even greater deficiency is the lack of a really meaningful long-term care benefit, outside of Medicaid, for nursing home, home health, adult day care, and other forms of community-based care including case management services. These are all critically important services for the elderly and the disabled.

Because States establish many of their own Medicaid policies as to eligibility, the Medicaid program covered only 42 percent of poor persons across all the different states as of 1986. With respect to the many elderly who need nursing home care, they are required to spend all of their assets before they are eligible for Medicaid. Furthermore, even with recent changes, States still vary in the amount of income and assets they will protect for the spouses of those persons needing such care.

As indicated earlier, States have substantial latitude on which services they cover under Medicaid. They may choose to include prescription drugs, eyeglasses, dental care, and inpatient psychiatric care. Given this discretion, several states have chosen not to cover these services.

❖ Conclusion

Though the rich history of Medicare and Medicaid is replete with lessons for the future, the question remains as to whether or not this nation will take the time and has the wisdom to learn those lessons. Twenty-five years ago on July 30, 1965, a President and a Congress took the bold and courageous action to enact a protection package for millions of elderly, poor, and disabled. No one then thought Medicare and Medicaid were the perfect solutions, but few doubted that many people's lives would be much better as a result of that bold action. Today, few dispute that millions of Americans are better off due to Medicare and Medicaid.

Looking to the future, the nation has two responsibilities. The first responsibility is one of stewardship over Medicare and Medicaid as they are today. Just maintaining the health and well-being of these two programs will be no minor task for the Administration and Congress. It is a task that will be made more difficult to the extent that it is done in an adversarial environment. Most Americans agree that Medicare and Medicaid are too important to be allowed to fall victim to partisanship and expect their national leaders to fulfill their stewardship responsibilities.

The second responsibility is to those who have yet to benefit from this nation's greatest step forward toward protecting the health of its citizens. When millions live at risk and in fear of a long term disabling illness wiping out the financial and emotional resources of their families, a nation cannot be satisfied with Medicaid as the nation's long term care policy. When millions are forced to seek charity for whatever health care they need, a nation can feel no pride in having the best medical care in the world.

❖ Part II

Health Policy

A Framework for Action

❖ Chapter 3
The Politics of Health

Establishing Policies and
Setting Priorities

Americans place great trust in their physicians, nurses, dentists, and other health care providers; in the insurance companies that pay for much of their care; and in the government that regulates, oversees, and, to a great extent, finances the system. In Part II, we take a look, in one sense, at the underpinnings of this system: the struggle for money and control of various aspects of health services by a variety of groups. Underneath the regulation and legislation is a power struggle, the outcome of which ultimately determines the quality of services we receive. It decides who will care for us when, where, and how; the method by which we will pay for care; how much we will pay; where hospitals will be located; and the size and scope of these facilities. It has great influence on health professions education, and it determines the scope and direction of research.

On the surface, it appears that these decisions emanate from the government. But, in reality, policymakers take their cues for health care legislation and regulation from a variety of sources. Historically, some special-interest groups, such as physicians, have been able virtually to dictate policy in specific areas. This dominant role has changed in recent years as more and more interest groups appeared on the scene, as proprietary organizations proliferated, as consumers took a more active role in attaining public accountability, and as the stakes escalated to sky-high proportions. The four most powerful interest groups are physicians, hospitals, insurance companies, and the drug industry. There are also lobbying groups for dentists, nurses, and many other health professions; for nursing homes and other such institutions; for labor and business groups; and for most other participants in the health care arena. While these groups participate in the high-quality care we receive, they also are helping to ensure that their own interests are served.

The making of health policy across several levels of government and hundreds of programs is complex. Policy students have identified five characteristics of the policy process in the United States: (1) the relationship of government to the private sector; (2) the distribution of authority and responsibility within a federal system of government; (3) pluralistic ideology as a basis of politics; (4) the relationship between policy formulation and administrative implementation; and (5) incrementalism as a strategy for reform. These characteristics are considered from a variety of perspectives in this chapter.

Today, policymakers and citizens are debating about methods to tackle the fragmentation in financing and provision of health care, crippling cost escalations, high expenditures for administration, the commercialization of medicine, the trend toward defensive medicine, the erosion of physician authority, and the lack of access for many citizens. To understand how to address these issues, it may be useful to look at how we got to where we are. In "Government and Health: The Political Aspects of Health Care—A Sociopolitical Overview," Theodor J. Litman provides historical background for government health policy. He documents the growth of the federal government's role in health care contrasted with the role of state governments and ends with an outline of lessons that can be learned from the past.

Dr. Litman's historical analysis is followed by a discussion of health policy and the politics of health care by Philip Lee and A.E. Benjamin. Their analysis leads to the conclusion that a consensus has emerged about what the problems are; it is only on the solutions that dissension exists. They point out that as the political debate heats up, we are in fact at a turning point.

In "Privatization, the Welfare State, and Aging: The Reagan-Bush Legacy," Carroll L. Estes says that aging and health policy represent a major battleground on which the nation's social struggles are being fought. She outlines the various reasons given by government leaders in recent years for refusing to provide long-term care and argues that their line of reasoning essentially is based on the notion that such care should be provided by unpaid women in the families of the elderly. Dr. Estes also contends that the chronic illness burden of the elderly is blamed for crippling the national economy. She raises the question of whether the administration of President Bill Clinton will alter the course set by Presidents Reagan and Bush and begin to shift the cost of health care to public and nonprofit institutions, lift the enormous burden placed on individuals, and stem the tide of profits reaped by the medical-industrial complex.

It is only fitting that we include in this discussion the words of a policymaker—in this case, Richard D. Lamm, who served as governor of Colorado for three consecutive terms, 1975–1987. Prior to that, he served in the Colorado House of Representatives, 1966–1974. Mr. Lamm highlights some of the most treacherous hazards we face. He looks at the high percentage of the national budget spent on health care with a view toward stretching those resources to provide basic services to more people and limiting the frills. He asks the nation to wake up to the fact that we have reached a point in which our infinite medical demands must be reconciled with our finite resources. In other words we have more doctors, hospital beds, medicines, and medical technology than we can afford to use. Ultimately, he suggests, health care is too much of a dominating factor in the nation's economy, and he has recommendations for liberating some resources that now are swallowed up by health so that they can go to work for us in fiscally neglected areas. Mr. Lamm not only calls for prioritizing, he makes suggestions on how this sensitive subject can be approached.

❖ Government and Health: The Political Aspects of Health Care—A Sociopolitical Overview

THEODOR J. LITMAN

When the Eighty-ninth Congress adjourned in 1966, its record of legislative accomplishments made it the most health-minded Congress in U.S. history. Not only had more national health legislation been enacted into law during its first session than had been passed in both sessions of all Congresses in the previous decade, but it had appropriated more money for health in the last 2 years of its term than its predecessors had in the previous 168 years. Never before had one session of Congress produced legislation of such far-reaching implications for the health, education, and socioeconomic welfare of the American people than had been enacted in 1965. So extensive was the legislative activity in terms of the number and scope of health actions taken that one observer depicted the period as a turning point in health law.

As far as health care financing was concerned, the issue was no longer that of public versus private enterprise. According to Anne Somers, that issue had seemingly been settled in favor of the nation's or the United States' unique pluralistic health care economy with its programmatic amalgamation of public and private activities. What had changed was the nature of the mix, which seemed to lean markedly in favor of the public sector. Moreover, with the passage of the National Planning and Resources Development Act (PL 93-641) in 1974, the question of the federal government's right to interfere in the private practice of medicine appeared to be decided, for all intents and purposes, in favor of government.

The role of the federal government in the organization, financing, and delivery of health care services in the United States at mid-decade seemed assured, and the prospects for adoption of some form of national health insurance seemed imminent, if not a foregone conclusion.

But although the federal initiative of the past 20 years or so had been seen by many as a sociopolitical watershed in which the powers and machinery of government were mobilized to improve access to services, to further distribute justice and equity, and to redress social and economic wrongs, times and circumstances change. The heady optimism and faith in the unbridled growth and intervention of the federal establishment of the 1960s and 1970s soon gave way to suspicion, distrust, and disillusionment with government programs. Thus, in spite of a number of notable accomplishments—such as demonstrated gains in access to care and health status among the poor and the elderly, greater rationalization of the health planning process, and increased production of health personnel—skepticism and dissatisfaction with such initiatives began to grow in the face of rising costs, economic stagflation, limited revenues, diminished financial resources, programmatic cutbacks, indifferent if not hostile central administration, and bureaucratic insensitivity to the infringement of federal policies, directives, and regulations on state and local prerogatives, culminating in the Reagan election in 1980.

The response was sudden and pointed. The new chief executive, who had ridden to victory on a promise to get government off the backs of the American people, moved quickly and decisively. Within six months of taking office, through the deft and imaginative use of the budgetary process and with the support of a group of conservative Democrats (known as the Boll Weavils) who were ideologically closer to the Republican party than their own, the president succeeded in gaining congressional approval of a package of budget cuts that repealed and modified scores of programs that had become integral parts of the nation's social and economic fabric, while reversing the federal expansion of the last half-century and reducing the size and scope of government.

And so, as the United States entered the new decade, it seemed to be embarking on a different course, one reflected in the president's commitment to less social planning and regulation, a smaller public and larger private sector in health as well as other aspects of life, and an abrupt reduction in government, especially in federal funding for social programs. Whether the results of the 1980 election marked a major shift in sociopolitical thought in the United States vis-à-vis the relationship of government to the individual and his or her health care, as many early editorial writers suggested, or was merely an aberrational interlude in the United States' continuing flirtation with the adoption of some form of national health program, remains to be seen. Suffice it to say, however, that the answer is likely to lie in an understanding of the peculiar nature and role of government and politics in American life, with the decision reached, the product of a deliberative political process.

❖ Government and Health in the United States

A number of years ago, the noted British social historian T.H. Marshall observed that no modern government could disdain responsibility for the health of its people nor would it wish to do so. Policies, he noted, differ not so much in the aims pursued as in the methods adopted in pursuit of them. But although the notion of a national system of health services has long been a well-established fact in much of the rest of the world, it has been slow to take hold in the United States. Since the first governmental system of health care was established in Germany under Bismarck in 1883, the provision of health and medical care to an entire population on a nationwide basis through some form of national health service or insurance mechanism has been adopted in nearly half of the world's sovereign nations, including most of those in Western Europe. On the whole, this development has generally come about through an evolutionary rather than revolutionary process, a function of the social, cultural, political, and economic fabrics of the various countries involved. In most cases, government programs for the financing of health care services have evolved as part of a broader system of social benefits. To a large extent, each nation's health care system is a reflection of its own particular legacy of traditions, organization, and institutions, and the American experience has been no exception. Thus, to understand where the United States is and may be heading, it is necessary to know something of the past and the nature of the governmental system.

❖ The United States System of Government

As most students of government are aware, ours is a limited system of federalism predicated on the notion of representative government with an emphasis on minority rights, majority rule, and the preservation of individual liberty. Historically, the American conception of freedom has taken the guise of rights to be protected from restraint, rather than duties to be performed, and a suspicion of established authority. Thus, largely in response to government oppression experienced in Europe, the framers of the Constitution provided an extensive system of checks and balances upon the federal establishment. Although Madison and others recognized the need for national supremacy—earlier attempts to rest sovereignty in the state or colonial legislatures as called for under the original Articles of Confederation had proven unsuccessful—they were also aware of the need for protection from the arbitrary use of power by the national government. To pit sovereignty against sovereignty, however, was seen as a formula for disaster.

As set forth under Article 1, Section 8, of the Constitution, the relationship between the states and the federal government was fairly well drawn, with the federal government given certain prescribed delegated powers, other powers reserved for the states, and still others left to be exercised jointly.

But the framers were also farsighted and realized that the United States was bound to change over time. As a result, the Constitution was envisioned to be a flexible document, confined neither in time nor place. Thus, the role of government in American life has evolved over the past 200 years or so in large part through judicial interpretation and response to executive initiatives and legislative action.

❖ Federalism and the Constitutional Relationship between the National Government and the States

The question of the proper role of government in general, as well as the relative distribution of powers among the national, state, and local governments in particular, has been the subject of prolonged philosophical debate in the United States, with the line in any given controversy ultimately drawn by the courts. Such deliberations have ranged from Marshall's Doctrine of National Supremacy (*McCulloch v. Maryland*) to the Doctrine of Dual Federalism of the Taney court (*Cooley v. Board of Wardens*) with the states having concurrent powers in those matters considered to be truly local in character, to the Cooperative Federalism of the Cardozo court (Steward Machine Company case) to the concept of Creative Federalism under President Johnson and the New Federalism and new New Federalism of the Nixon and Reagan administrations.

Before the 1930s, both federal and state legislation in the field of social welfare were invalidated by the courts on the basis of the due process clause. In 1937, however, the Supreme Court reversed itself (*West Coast Hotel Company v. Parrish*) and repudiated the old doctrine that the due process could be used to crush social welfare legislation. Nevertheless, it was Marshall's interpretation of the commerce clause and the supremacy of the central government that served as the basis for much of the legislative initiatives of the New Deal (Roosevelt), the Fair Deal (Truman), the New Frontier (Kennedy), and the New Society (Johnson).

State-Federal Regulations

The role of the states in the U.S. political system has changed dramatically over the past 200 years as events and trends have altered the fiscal, functional, and political balance within the federal system and rekindled debate over the proper division of powers and responsibilities among the constituent units.

The expansion of the federal government's role in U.S. life was neither an historical accident nor an altogether noxious historical legacy, but has come about for good historical reasons.

However, under both the Nixon and Reagan administrations, increasing interest was expressed in the importance of the relations among the various levels of government. At issue was how large the federal government's role should be in its relations with its state and local counterparts. The answer has been caught up in philosophical differences that separate not only Democrats and Republicans but also conservatives and liberals within each party.

Beginning under Roosevelt's New Deal and continuing under the Democratic administrations of the 1960s, a fairly broad agreement was reached in Congress that the federal government should play an active role in areas traditionally within the province of state and local governments, particularly regulation where state laws were either nonexistent or failed to conform to one another. There was also broad agreement that the federal government should have a role in providing financial assistance to states and localities for a variety of purposes, such as fighting poverty, pollution control, local law enforcement, and housing. The issue was no longer legitimacy of whether the federal government should be involved in such areas but rather how it should go about assisting the state and local governments.

Traditionally, federal assistance has been in the form of categorical grants-in-aid made to a variety of governmental and other public and private entities for specific purposes. Such grants-in-aid enable state and local governments to preserve their autonomy within a framework of federal assistance; to assure minimum levels of services regardless of income inequities among states and localities; and to help achieve national objectives that states and localities may be unwilling or unable to pursue as well as stimulate, through federal matching, increased investment of state and local funds. Moreover, since federal taxes are generally more progressive than their state and local counterparts, federal grants help reduce interstate inequities both in the level of government services and the tax burden. As a matter of fact, one of the major reasons for the proliferation of categorical grants programs was that not only could the federal government tap far more revenue sources than the states and localities, but the latter officials could not or would not provide funds to deal with certain problems.

On the other side of the coin, the expansion of federal power at the expense of state and local government is inherent in such revenue-sharing mechanisms, leading to federal domination or control. It was in reaction to just such concerns, as well as the trend toward centralization of government authority in Washington, D.C., that the concept of block grants was developed. Block grants, which are federal payments to states or local governments for specified purposes such as health, education, or law enforcement, were pushed by Republicans in Congress and the executive branch since the 1960s as a way of returning federal decision making to state and local officials. In contrast to categorical grants, which can only be used for specific programs directed by Congress, with block grants state or local officials may make the decisions on how the money is used within the general program area.

The New Federalism   The debate continued with President Reagan's efforts to return many government programs to the states. His proposal, however, although clothed in the mantle of the "New Federalism," represented less a sorting out of functions among the various levels of government than opposition of fiscal conservatives to large-scale public sector spending on particular domestic activities regardless of the level of government. Moreover, although the Reagan proposal to return power and responsibilities to the states has been viewed by some as a watershed in the history of U.S. federalism, critics see the New Federalism and Economic Recovery Act as a device to reduce federal expenditures for key domestic activities, and as an abandonment of the national commitments to certain costly social programs, involving the transfer of responsibility to the states and their political subdivisions without adequate funding.

As states and local units of government have been forced to struggle with the need to provide more human services in the face of ever diminishing financial resources, proposals to return such functions to their control, without a commensurate transfer of funds, have tended to lose much of their aura and appeal, while the debate over the proper role of government in U.S. life continues.

❖ The Growth in the Government's Role in Health and Health Care in the United States
Evolution, Not Revolution

It has long been a truism of U.S. political life that government is only permitted to do that which private institutions either cannot or are unwilling to do. The basic economic justification for government intervention, Blumstein and Zubkoff note, is as a remedy for some market failure. In essence, the traditional basis for government involvement has been a remedial one, that is, when, for whatever reason, the market does not achieve an efficient allocation of resources.

In the area of health and welfare, such a view was perhaps best expressed by a 1965 U.S. Chamber of Commerce Task Force on Economic Growth and Opportunity recommendation on the role of government: "Government programs should be used to help the sick, disabled and aged only if voluntary and private means—truly tried and tested—cannot adequately meet society's needs."

A related corollary to the above would add that with the exception of those powers delegated to it by the Constitution, the growth of the federal government's involvement has generally come about in those areas in which the states have also been found wanting. The Interstate Commerce Act of 1887 was passed only after the states had failed to control the spiraling interstate railroad networks, and enactment of the New Deal came after four years of economic collapse that found the states broke, with only 17 having old age pension plans, most of which were woefully underfunded.

The expansion of government or public intervention in health and health care in the United States has essentially been one of evolution rather than revolution, a function of social, economic, and political forces as well as judicial interpretation.

❖ Historical Development

Over the course of the past 200 years, the role of government in the organization, financing, and delivery of health care services in the United States has evolved from that of a highly constricted provider of services and protector of public health to that of a major financial underwriter of an essentially private enterprise whose policies and procedures have increasingly encroached on the autonomy and prerogatives of the providers of care, as he who pays the piper calls the tune.

Although extensive and, at times, seemingly pervasive, such growth has come about neither capriciously nor because legislators or bureaucrats have had any great desire to interfere in this area of endeavor, but rather because the parties primarily involved—the providers (with the notable exception of organized medicine), consumers, insurance carriers, and politicians—realized and came to recognize the need for assistance and government involvement.

❖ Nature of the Government Role in Health and Health Care in the United States

Both traditionally and historically, responsibility for the medical care of recipients of public assistance, veterans with service-connected disabilities, and other special populations such as native Americans and the armed forces and for public health in the United States has rested with government, whereas responsibility for the cost of facility construction and health personnel training has been shared among various levels of government and the private sector. The provision of direct personal health services, on the other hand, is and has been essentially a private endeavor.

For the most part, government intervention in the health care system has tended to embrace the following features:

1. Financial underwriting in order to assure the availability to all in the population through either contributory insurance (e.g., Medicare), general tax revenues (e.g., Medicaid), or both
2. The development and establishment of various standards and procedures to safeguard the quality of services financed through public funds
3. The provision of services wherever possible through nongovernmental practitioners and institutions
4. Extension toward comprehensiveness in publicly financed services
5. Direct financial support for the modernization, construction, and equipment of health care facilities and for the education and training of needed personnel

Federal Role

As indicated earlier, the federal role in health throughout much of U.S. history has tended to be a constrained one, limited to crisis intervention, the control and prevention of disease in public health. Typically, as Blumstein and Zubkoff have noted, federal intervention in the health area has been on an ad hoc basis without an overall plan, formulation of objectives, or theoretical underpinning. Moreover, in the absence of any specific formulation, national health policy in the United States has been more or less an amorphous set of health goals, derived by various means within the federal structure, with little overall concordance or coordination.

Health Policy at the Federal Level   For the most part, the legislative initiatives in health at the federal level over the course of the past 20 years rested on a set of assumptions and presumptions, many of which were well meaning and seemed to embrace the conventional wisdom of the period but have proven to be overly optimistic, idealistic, or unfounded.

To a large extent, according to Brown of the Brookings Institution, federal health care policy in the United States has tended to embrace two essentially antithetical models or approaches that today are "nurtured in tension." Thus, while "mainstream" equalizing programs continue to receive strong public support, they are challenged by a set of federal proposals based largely on "revisionist" premises concerning constraints on supply and demand for services. As a result, U.S. health care policy has tended to be discontinuous, inconsistent, and, at times, contradictory. Brown goes on to note that by avoiding hard choices and by reconciling in public policy such seemingly contradictory models, we have tended to institutionalize our ambivalence, while preserving the claims of equality of medical services on one hand and delimiting its scope on the other.

Role of the States

In contrast to their federal counterparts, whose influence over health stems in large measure from its enormous fiscal power, the states have rather broad, comprehensive legal authority for a wide variety of programs. As a result, their role in health has taken a number of forms: (1) financial support for the care and treatment of the poor and chronically disabled, including the primary responsibility for the administration of the federal and state Medicaid program; (2) quality assurance and oversight of health care practitioners and facilities, for example, state licensure and regulation; (3) regulation of health care costs and insurance carriers; (4) health personnel training, that is, states provide the major share of the cost for the training of health care professionals; and (5) authorization of local government health services.

Similarly, although historically the power of the governor has been limited, a throwback to the colonists' distrust of the royal governor in the area of public taxation, the states' chief executive appears to exert considerable influence in determining health policy via the power of appointment. A recent review of the statutory authority governing public health decision making in the 50 states found the governor responsible for the appointment of about 91 percent of the 427 positions on the states' boards of health. In 11 states, the members of the board sit at the pleasure of the governor. Moreover, turnover among state health officials has been reported as "brisk," with about 60 percent of them being replaced every 2 years.

State Expenditures for Health   State spending and responsibility in health have traditionally been directed toward broad public health activities, institutional care of the mentally ill, and the purchase of health care services for the economically disadvantaged. During the past 35 years, state spending in health and other human services has been increasingly shaped by federal prescriptions and initiatives, including a variety of apportionment formulas and project grants. As a matter of fact, a familiar characteristic of the U.S. federal system is that many of the programs that carry out national policies are created and operated by the states under rules established by federal legislation and regulations. Moreover, variable methods of federal funding related to purpose, budgetary limits, formulas, and duration impose similar variability on the states' application of funds to the counties.

Like their federal counterpart, state expenditures for health are provided through direct provision of services and indirect purchase of services and have been the subject of considerable political debate over the scope, cost, level of funding, and appropriateness of such expenditures. All this costs money, and the funds may not be readily available in times of economic recession. Thus, while many states found themselves with expanding treasuries during the late 1960s and early 1970s, fueled by inflation and aided and abetted by increased federal revenue sharing and a thriving economy, in the face of a serious economic downturn nationally, declining state revenues, reduced federal aid, rising costs, a heightened demand for health and welfare services, threatened taxpayer revolts, and bulging budget deficits, they were forced to cut back greatly on their programs and allow more and more of the burden to fall back on their local counterparts.

The Impact of Federal Initiatives in Health on States and Localities   Finally, although the evidence on the extent of the impact of federal initiatives on state and local priorities in health is limited, the key to understanding the ways in which federal aid influences state health goals and programmatic activities appears to lie in the political environment of the state. In a study of six states and four public health programs, for example, Buntz et al. found that although federal programs facilitate rather than inhibit the attainment of state health goals, federal influence tends to be secondary to that of the state's political environment. A federal program, they note, may elevate an issue to the state's active policy agenda but need not necessarily lead to formulation of a state policy or goals unless interests within the state are receptive. Moreover, the federal influence on state health policy appears to be both state and program specific, reinforcing changes supported at the state level and altering state goals at the margin. Such changes in state goals, however, are likely to occur only when the political environment of the state is receptive to change. For, although the federal government has the power to force states to pay attention to certain national goals, it cannot force them to shift their goals in any fundamental way nor to accept those goals as legitimate.

Public and Private Financing of Health Care in the United States

Although initial consideration of the adoption of some form of national health insurance in the United States occurred at about the same time as in Europe—at the turn of the century—and in reaction to similar forces—industrialization, urbanization, the demise of the extended family, and employment practices and policies that heightened the threat of work-related injuries and disease as well as unemployment—unlike Europe, the implementation of Social Security in the United States came through selected income maintenance programs and the preservation of the voluntary sector.

Thus, the provision of third-party health insurance coverage in the United States developed primarily on a voluntary basis through Blue Cross-Blue Shield and the commercial insurance industry. The attendant mixture of approaches resulted in a complex pattern of health care financing in which (1) the employed are predominantly covered by voluntary insurance provided through contributions made by their employers and themselves; (2) the aged are insured through a combination of coverages financed out of Social Security tax revenues and voluntary insurance for physician and supplementary coverage; (3) the health care of the poor is covered through Medicaid via federal, state, and local revenues; and (4) special population groups such as veterans, merchant seamen, native Americans, members of the armed forces, Congress, and the executive branch have coverage provided directly by the federal government.

According to Kramer, private health insurance primarily has been a collection of payment mechanisms that supports and reinforces existing patterns of health services. Government spending for health, on the other hand, has been largely confined to filling the gap in the private sector, that is, environmental protection, preventive services, communicable disease control, care for special groups, institutional care for the mentally and chronically ill, provision of medical care to the poor, and support for research and training. The high cost of public medical care programs, Kramer reminds us, owes its genesis to the markedly unique division of risk taking and responsibility between the public and private sector that has thrust upon government the cost of caring for those segments of the population with the highest incidence of illness and greatest need for care; that is, the aged, poor, mentally ill, retarded, chronically ill, and disabled.

Finally, the use of fiscal stimuli through grants-in-aid, the commitment of major financing programs to retrospective reimbursement of costs on a fee-for-service basis, and reliance on peer review for quality assurance reflect a preference for the achievement of public objectives through strategies that offer inducements, persuasion, and positive rewards to providers for compliance rather than impose penalties or costs for failure to comply. Such strategies, however, have been inherently expansive, tending to minimize the need for deliberative allocative choices by increasing the flow of resources into the health care system. Once costs rise and revenues become short, such choices no longer can be put off and questions of constraint and costs are raised.

Problem of Cost versus Services in Government Programs

The amount of money that a nation spends for its health services, Anderson and Newhauser noted in 1969, tends to be a product primarily of a political process arrived at by implicit and explicit public policy decisions within the body politic. An equally appropriate maxim, however, is that whatever government giveth, it can taketh away. In other words, although public programs often initially are enacted on essentially altruistic grounds—for example, increased accessibility to health care services by removing financial barriers to care while defraying costs over a wide segment of the public—once this is done and the costs that originally were borne by patients, their families, and/or the private sector and are now assumed by government rise, there is a strong tendency on the part of the latter to cut back on its commitment by reducing coverage—that is, who and what is covered—and increasing the amount paid by those who use the services.

Thus, as costs rise, the tendency is to cut back on the coverage, especially if the constituency being served is not a very powerful or influential one, such as the poor, the socially and economically disadvantaged and, up to the 1960s, the elderly. For as commendable and needy as a service may be and as legitimate as government involvement is, the question ultimately gets down to a fundamental economic one: the cost of the service given the limited funds (however defined) available for it.

Therefore, beginning in the latter part of the 1960s and early 1970s, the federal government and the states, confronted by escalating costs and depleted resources, began to cut back on the Medicare and Medicaid programs. Thus, in contrast to 20 years ago when the dual programs were first enacted and the primary policy concern was increased access to health care services for more U.S. citizens, ostensibly the aged and economically disadvantaged, the programs were so successful that the budget soon became incapable of containing them. As a result, the policy has taken a 180-degree turn toward greater restriction and control, with often devastating consequences on the provision and receipt of services, in many cases proving to be "penny cheap and pound foolish."

Case of Medicaid

This conflict between costs and services has been especially true of the Medicaid program, whose expenditures tend to be particularly susceptible to the forces of unemployment and inflation. For not only does the size of its clientele, that is, recipients of public assistance and "the medically indigent," vary with the level of unemployment, but the services it renders are purchased in the general medical marketplace and are susceptible to the impact of inflation. In addition, the negative effect of reduced tax receipts on state and local revenues as a result of a national economic recession tends to place both levels of government in a whipsaw as the demand for services on them rises because of heightened unemployment while their capacity to pay for them diminishes.

❖ Conclusion

The growth in government's involvement in health has been an evolutionary one, a response to changes in times and circumstances. Over the past 40 years, there have been major shifts in the role and posture of the federal government in the organization, financing, and delivery of health care services and its relationship with the states in which the following have occurred:

1. The traditional federal role of sharing the cost of health care gradually has been expanded to include programs of care purchased by the government itself as well as the use of federal funding to initiate and develop new forms of delivery; for example, neighborhood health centers and health maintenance organizations (HMOs).
2. An increased use of categorical and project grants in health found the federal government involved in the budget funding of local programs and bypassing local governments considered unresponsive to the needs of the poor.
3. The federal focus has shifted from encouraging the expansion of state programs to assuring their integrity and from concern over improving access to services to control over their costs with both patients and providers often caught in the middle.

The progression in such involvement has been a slow and steady one, a function of the nature of the nation's political process and social and economic systems. Incrementalism, rather than fundamental changes in the structure of the health care delivery system, has been the hallmark of federal policies. What has evolved then, as Anderson has aptly observed, has been a partnership—sometimes rather tenuous and strained—between government (federal and state) and the voluntary system, working together, not as rivals but as partners—not necessarily equally or smoothly, but as partners nevertheless.

Given the experience of the United States over the past half-century with various government entreaties in health, what lessons can be learned? The following are suggested for future consideration:

1. Reform of the health care system in the United States is likely to be incremental, a compromise involving the resolution of a number of interests.

2. National programs require consideration of regional and local problems and needs.

3. Regional variations and the diversity and voluntary-private nature of the health care enterprise make the imposition of national fee schedules, reimbursement formulas, and facility guidelines difficult if not impossible to achieve.

4. Equality in financing is not sufficient to guarantee equal access to medical care.

5. All third-party coverage, whether private or public, such as Medicare and Medicaid, contributes to inflation.

6. All modern national health care systems, predicated as they are on sophisticated technology, are inherently costly.

7. Open-ended reimbursement to providers on the basis of cost is inflationary, whereas unrealistic or picayune controls tend to be self-defeating, leading providers to opt out of the system and leaving recipients a limited range of choices of care.

8. Although any government system is likely ultimately to impose restrictions on the autonomy and prerogatives of providers, such controls can neither be arbitrary nor capricious but should seek the cooperation of professional interests and the use of financial incentives and rewards.

9. A conflict between cost and services is inherent in government programs.

10. Government efforts to reduce expenditures for health services programs by transferring their costs without appropriate financial safeguards to lesser levels of government or recipients of services do not effectively reduce the overall costs of the services but merely shift the financial burden to those least able to bear it while depriving those most in need.

11. Utilitarianism, that is, "put people back to work" and "get them off the welfare rolls and onto the taxpaying rolls," rather than humanitarianism and altruism, underscore the ultimate adoption of most government human services programs.

12. Protection against the financial burden of health and medical care is impossible without the placement of a ceiling on the patient's financial responsibility. Unless the family is guaranteed that its share of the cost of care will not exceed some reasonable fraction of income, the goal of preventing or protecting against the financial burden of health care services cannot be achieved. While what that level of income or ceiling is or should be is open to debate, it should be noted that artificial financial barriers or income cutoffs tend to be highly susceptible to the tyranny of inflation; that is, as dollar amounts soar, real value and purchasing power decline.

13. The use of administrative and regulatory controls, such as Medicare's requirement of a three-day hospital stay before a pa-

tient may be authorized to be admitted to a nursing home, second opinion requirements, inadequate reimbursement to providers, reduction of the tax deduction for health and medical expenditures, and elimination of deductibility for health insurance premiums, rather than civil or criminal penalties, tend to be misdirected, self-defeating, and ineffective.

14. Programs covering only poor people must be carefully designed so as to avoid adverse incentives and inequities in which some people receive substantial assistance and others equally in need or deserving—that is, the near or working poor—receive nothing or practically nothing.

15. Assumptions that the elderly are protected against the cost of long-term care by Medicare are ill-founded and wrong. The only government-provided protection the elderly have against the cost of catastrophic illness is Medicaid—a welfare program.

16. Geographic inequities are bound to occur when states have a major role in setting eligibility and benefit levels.

17. Government health care programs predicated on the virtues of competition and the free marketplace and a preferred single delivery system ignore the fact that one of the major sources for the high cost of hospital care in the United States has been the virtually unfettered costly competition between health institutions for staff, equipment, and so on, which results in a duplication of services, and minimize the value of a diverse pluralistic system of delivery and the variable needs and demands of consumers as well as providers.

18. Whatever the future role of government in health in the United States is to be, it will be the product of a deliberate decision made in the political arena and will likely embrace the unique features of the nation's social, political, economic, and health care systems.

❖ About the Author

Theodor J. Litman, PH.D., is Professor of Health Services Administration, School of Public Health, University of Minnesota, Minneapolis.

❖ Health Policy and the Politics of Health Care

PHILIP R. LEE AND A.E. BENJAMIN

Government plays a major role in planning, directing, and financing health services in the United States. The significance of the public sector is apparent as one considers the following: Public programs account for approximately 40 percent of the nation's personal health care expenditures, most physicians and other health care personnel are trained at public expense, almost 65 percent of all health research and development funds are provided by the government, and most nonprofit community and university hospitals have been built or modernized with government subsidies. The bulk of government expenditures are federal, with state and local governments contributing significant, but much smaller amounts.

Health policies and programs of the U.S. government have evolved piecemeal, usually in response to needs that were not being met by the private sector or by states and local governments. The result has been a proliferation of federal categorical programs administered by more than a dozen government departments. Over the years, new programs have been added, old ones redirected, and numerous efforts made to integrate and coordinate services. In the 1980s a major effort was made by the Reagan administration to significantly diminish the federal role in domestic social policy through the transfer of some programs to the states, reduced federal funding, or elimination of federal support entirely. The effort has been only partially successful and has not changed the basic configuration of publicly supported health programs, although the burden of financing now falls more heavily on state and local governments. Functions of the public and private sectors have become increasingly interrelated, and roles are often poorly delineated. There can be little argument that the primary function of most government programs in health has been to support or strengthen the private sector (e.g., hospital construction, subsidy of medical student training, Medicare) rather than to develop a strong system of publicly provided health care.

Although U.S. government policies have evolved over a 200-year period, most of those affecting health services have developed since the enactment of the Social Security Act of 1935. Many federal health programs evolved because of failures in the private sector to provide necessary support—for example, biomedical research; others arose because results of the free market were grossly inequitable—for example, hospital construction; and some programs, such as Medicare and Medicaid, developed because health care was so costly that many could not afford to pay for necessary health services.

The process by which health policy is made in this country can be best understood by considering a fundamental paradox in American health care: government spends more and more money to support a wide range of health programs, services, and agencies, yet the role of government in the reform of our health care system remains limited and halting. Government is faced with a crisis in health care, defined primarily in terms of rising costs to public treasuries, while solutions are framed in terms that do not address in a comprehensive fashion the sources of demand on the public purse. Indeed, solutions to the cost crisis have combined withdrawing benefits from those very recipient populations whose health care needs justify government intervention with attempts to reduce costs by either stimulating competition or regulating (reducing) payment to hospitals, nursing homes, and physicians. While federal policies may move in one direction, state policies may move in another. To understand this paradox, it is necessary to consider several characteristics of public policy making and thus to explore the sources of the paradox and the nature of policy processes in health.

❖ Dimensions of Policy Making in Health

Policy making in health care crosses several levels of government and hundreds of programs; it is complex, and no single analytical scheme can do it sufficient justice. Still, public policy students have identified five dimensions of the policy process: (1) the relationship of government to the private sector, (2) the distribution of authority within a federal system of government, (3) pluralistic ideology as the basis of politics, (4) the relationship between policy formulation and administrative implementation, and (5) incrementalism as a strategy of reform. Each will be considered in detail.

You would be surprised at the number of years it took me to see clearly what some of the problems were which had to be solved.... Looking back, I think it was more difficult to see what the problems were than to solve them.
　　　　—Charles Darwin

Public and Private Sector Politics

Although the role of government in health care has grown considerably in recent years, that role remains relatively limited. The U.S. government is less involved in health care than are the governments of many other industrialized countries. This circumstance derives primarily from a persistent ideology that identifies the market system as the most appropriate setting for the exchange of health services and from a related belief that private sector support for public sector initiatives can be acquired only through accommodation to the interests of health care providers.

Uncertainty about the role of government in health care has numerous consequences. The primary concern is the absence of any design or blueprint for governmental reform. Instead, the public sector (with its relatively immense capacity to raise revenues) is called on periodically to open and close its funding spigots to stimulate the health care market. Hospital construction and physician education are prominent examples of public activity. Not only is there no blueprint for public sector action, but governments in America harbor grave doubts about the appropriateness of regulation as a public sector activity. Dependence at the federal level, on "voluntary approaches," such as the reduction of hospital costs in the late 1970s, delayed serious consideration of more stringent measures even as the costs to government of hospital care continued to rise dramatically.

A Federal System

The concept of federalism has evolved dramatically in meaning and practice since the founding of the republic more than 200 years ago. Originally, federalism was a legal concept that defined the constitutional division of authority between the federal government and the states. Federalism initially stressed the independence of each level of government from the other, while incorporating the idea that some functions, such as foreign policy, were the exclusive province of the central government, while other functions, such as education, police protection, and health care, were the responsibility of regional units—state and local government. Federalism represented a form of governance that differs both from a unitary state, where regional and local authority derive legally from the central government, and from a confederation, in which the national government has limited authority and does not reach individual citizens directly.

Shifts in responsibilities assigned to various levels of government do not pose a serious problem for health policy if at least two conditions are met: (1) administrative or regulatory responsibilities and financial accountability are consonant, and (2) the various levels of government possess the appropriate capacities to assume those responsibilities assigned to them. Important questions can be raised regarding whether either of these conditions has been met in the development of health policy during the last two decades.

Analysis of federal-state relationships in programs as divergent as Medicaid, provider licensure, and family planning under Title X of the Public Health Service Act have suggested that the structure of these relationships produces outcomes widely held to be dysfunctional (e.g., Medicaid cutbacks) because one level of government (e.g., the states) can do nothing else under the conditions established by another (e.g., the federal government). The disjunction between administrative responsibilities and financial accountability (i.e., the term of federalistic arrangements) in these cases has yielded results for which governments and the recipients of health care ultimately have paid a price. What seems to matter most in the structure of relationships within federalism is not so much the distribution of activities but the relationships among levels of government.

For allocations of authority among levels of government to work, it is important that governments possess those capacities appropriate to the responsibilities they confront. Governments must possess the capacity to generate revenue, the capability to plan and manage policies and programs, and the political will to plan and implement needed reform. State and local governments have been found wanting in each of these respects. Because state governments do not tax as heavily as the federal government, their capacity for generating new revenues is limited. Many states, moreover, are viewed as having inadequate administrative infrastructures, lacking sufficient sophisticated management techniques, and having limited capabilities in the conduct of policy analysis and planning.

Finally, there is evidence that state and local governments may have less political will to make decisions in the public interest than the federal government. Wide variations among states in program outputs (e.g., Medicaid) suggest significant inequities. The argument is not that every state, if freed from federal constraints, would establish standards for health programs that are certain to fall below former federal standards. Rather, it is that some states will surely exceed some federal standards and others will fall far below what is generally considered adequate. At the heart of this problem, many argue, is the reputedly greater susceptibility of state governments to interest group pressures and narrow conceptions of the public good.

The argument regarding centralization and decentralization has not been settled, despite a vigorous debate in the past decade. No agreement has been reached on the vital question of the distribution of authority and responsibility among various levels of government. The federal government finances hospital and medical services for the elderly through Medicare; it contributes at least 50 percent of health care costs for Medicaid beneficiaries, is the major supporter of biomedical research, provides a limited amount of support for a variety of health services (e.g., mental health, family planning, crippled children's services, AIDS, substance abuse), is the sole regulator of the entry of new drugs into the market, and plays a critical role in the regulation of environment and occupational health.

States spend a large portion of their general fund budgets on health care for the poor (Medicaid), on mental health services, on the support of a range of public health programs, and on the education and training of health professionals.

Local governments remain an important provider of health care, particularly hospital, outpatient, and emergency care for the poor; mental health and substance abuse services; and a variety of public health services. Both state and local governments are mandated by higher levels of government (by either regulation or court order) to provide services or implement various environmental health or occupational health and safety regulations.

Pluralistic Politics

Pluralism is a term used by political theorists to describe a set of values about the effective functioning of democratic governments. Pluralists argue that democratic societies are organized into many diverse interest groups, which pervade all socioeconomic strata, and that this network of pressure groups prevents any one elite group from overreaching its legitimate bounds. As a theoretical framework for explaining the political context of policy making, this perspective has been criticized relentlessly and appropriately. As an ideology that continues to influence the way elites and masses view government, pluralism becomes a basis for considering some essential elements of the process of public decision making in this country.

Interest groups play a powerful role in the health policy process. Most federal and state laws designed to address the health care needs of the population are shaped by the interaction among interest groups, key legislators, and agency representatives. Ginzberg has identified four power centers in the health care industry that influence the nature of health care and the role of government: (1) physicians, (2) large insurance organizations, (3) hospitals, and (4) a highly diversified group of participants in profit-making activities within the health care arena.

As the case of Medicare suggests, health policy in the United States has been a product largely of medical politics. Marmor et al. describe the political "market" in health (i.e., institutional arrangements among actors in the political system) as imbalanced. In an imbalanced market, participants have unequal power, and those with concentrated rather than diffuse interests have the greater stake in the effects of policy. At least until recently, provider interest groups have had a far greater stake in shaping health policy than have consumer interests. Recently, large employers have become increasingly important in the health policy debates at the federal and state levels, particularly on issues related to health care cost containment.

Some observers argue that the rising costs of health care may be changing the configuration of interest groups seeking to influence health policy. In recent years, steadily escalating costs have stimulated other interests, especially labor, business, and governments themselves into giving greater attention to health policy and its implications. Polls of public attitudes show a growing dissatisfaction with health care financing in the United States and a strong desire for major reforms. In other words, their interests may be shifting from diffuse to concentrated. The result may be that increased competition in the political marketplace from a more diverse set of participants will lessen the dominance of medical provider groups. The pluralist dream of effective interest groups that prevent any one group from overreaching its legitimate bounds continues to influence our thinking about health care.

Policy Implementation

The nature of the health process is determined not only by the balance between provider and consumer interests but also by the relationships of these interests to government actors. Public policy students have observed that policy making moves through at least three stages: (1) agenda setting, the continuous process by which issues come to public attention and are placed on the agenda for government action; (2) policy adoption, the legislative process through which elected officials decide the broad outlines of policy; and (3) policy implementation, the process by which administrators develop policy by addressing the numerous issues unaddressed by legislation. An important element of the health policy process involves the relative roles of elected officials and professional administrators. As one moves from agenda setting to policy adoption and implementation, it can be argued that the role of elected officials becomes more remote and that of administrators more crucial.

No policy theorist has pressed this argument with more conviction than Lowi. A central theme in what he calls interest-group liberalism is the growing role of administrators in politics. According to Lowi, in a period of resource richness and government expansion, such as the 1960s, government responded to a range of major organized interests, underwrote programs sought by those interests, and assigned program responsibility to administrative agencies. Through this process the programs became captives of the interest groups because the administrative agencies themselves were captured. Interest groups dominate the policy process, he argues, not only through their influence on the legislative process (policy adoption) but also through control of administration (policy implementation). In effect, governments in the United States make policies without laws, and they leave the law making to administrators.

Incremental Reform

The powerful role of administrators in the implementation of policy is derived in part from the broad and ambiguous nature of much federal and state health legislation. Despite dramatic improvements in the capacity of congressional staff to conduct policy analysis, the constraints of politics are such that ambiguity frequently is employed to ensure the passage of legislation.

The public policy process in American government can best be described in terms of an incremental model of decision making. Simply stated, this model posits that policy is made in small steps (increments) and that policy is rarely modified in dramatic ways. Major actors in the political bargaining process, whether legislators, interest groups, or administrators, operate on the basis of certain rules, and these rules are founded in adherence to prior policy patterns. Because the consequences of policy change are difficult to predict and because unpredictability is risky in the political market, policymakers prefer reform in small steps to more radical change.

❖ A Historical Framework: The Development of Health Policy from 1798 to 1988

Although the federal system in the United States has evolved continuously, at certain periods in our history the relationship among the federal, state, and local governments has undergone dramatic change. The major shifts in intergovernment relations were often the result of a crisis (the Civil War, the Great Depression, civil rights issues) rather than the result of a critical examination of the issues.

Public health and health care did not loom large in the policy debate about federalism until the late 1940s, when President Truman advocated a program of national health insurance, and again in the 1960s, when implementation of Medicare transformed the role of the federal government in health care. Over the years, however, health policy issues (e.g., federal regulation of food and drugs, federal support for biomedical research, hospital construction, and health professions education) have raised critical issues about the role of government in health care, intergovernmental relations, and the role of the private sector.

While it is not possible to do full justice to the rich history of health care policy here, an effort is made to present highlights in the development of health policy that reflect the manner in which much has changed and much has stayed the same.

The slow emergence of public policies and programs related to health and health care in the United States has generally followed the pattern of other industrial countries, particularly those in western Europe. At least three stages in the process have been identified:

1. Private charity, including contracts between users and providers, and public apathy or indifference
2. Public provision of necessary health services that are not provided by voluntary effort and private contract
3. Substitution of public services and financing for private, voluntary, and charitable efforts

The role of government at the federal, state, and local levels in public health and health care evolved partly in response to changes occurring in the health care system. With the major changes in health care that have occurred over the past 200 years, particularly those in the past 50 years, has come a transformation in the role of government.

The Early Years of the Republic: A Limited Role for the Federal Government (1798–1862)

During the early years of the republic, the federal government played a limited role in both public health and health care, which were largely within the jurisdiction of the states and the private sector. Private charity shouldered the responsibility of care for the poor. The federal role in providing health care began in 1798, when Congress passed the Act for the Relief of Sick and Disabled Seamen, which imposed a 20-cent per month tax on seamen's wages for their medical care. The federal government later provided direct medical care for merchant seamen through clinics and hospitals in port cities, a policy that continues to this day. The federal government also played a limited role in imposing quarantines on ships entering U.S. ports in order to prevent epidemics. It did little or nothing, however, about the spread of communicable diseases within the nation, a problem that was thought to lie within the jurisdiction of the individual states.

States first exercised their public health authority through special committees or commissions. Most active concern with health matters was at the local level. Local boards of health or health departments were organized to tackle problems of sanitation, poor housing, and quarantine. Later, local health departments were set up in rural areas, particularly in the South, to counteract hookworm, malaria, and other infectious diseases that were widespread in the 19th and early 20th centuries.

The Evolution of Health Policy: The Emergence of Dual Federalism and the Transformation of American Medicine (1862–1935)

The Civil War brought about a dramatic change in the role of the federal government. Not only did the federal government engage in a war to preserve the union, but it also began to expand its role in other ways that significantly altered the nature of federalism in the United States. This changing federal role was reflected in congressional passage of the first program of federal aid to the states, the Morrill Act of 1862, which granted federal lands to each state. Profits from the sale of these lands supported public institutions of higher education, known as *land-grant colleges*. Toward the end of the 19th century, the federal government began to provide cash grants to states for the establishment of agricultural experiment stations. While the federal role generally was expanding, the change had little impact on health care. An important exception occurred in the late 1870s when the Surgeon General of the Marine Hospital Service was given congressional authorization to impose quarantines within the United States.

While the first state health department was established in Louisiana in 1855, it was not until after the Civil War that the states began to assume a more significant role in public health. Massachusetts established the first permanent board of health in 1869. By 1909, public health agencies were established in all the states. During this period there also was rapid development of local health departments. State and local governments based their policy changes and management practices on the rapid advances in the biological sciences. Drawing on these advances, state and local health departments moved beyond sanitation and quarantine to the scientific control of communicable diseases.

The basic policies that created both state and local health departments derived from the police power of state governments. Thus the states, and not the federal government, were the key to translating the scientific advances of the late 19th century into public health policy and the dramatic improvements in public health that followed.

The most significant role played by state governments in personal health care during this period was in the establishment of state mental hospitals.

Hospitals began to evolve in the 19th century from almshouses that provided shelter for the poor. Hospital sponsorship at the local level was either public (local government) or through a variety of religious, fraternal, or other community groups. Thus, the nonprofit community hospital was born; this institution, rather than the local public hospital, gradually became the primary locus of medical care. Physicians provided voluntary services to the sick poor in order to earn the privilege of caring for their paying patients in the hospital. Hospital appointments became important for physicians in order to conduct their practices. Hospitals increased in number in the late 19th century and began to incorporate new medical technologies, such as anesthesia, aseptic surgery, and, later, radiology. Although charity was the major source of care for the poor, public services also began to grow in the 19th century. Gradually, local government assumed responsibility for indigent care.

After the Morrill Act, the next major change in the role of the federal government came more than 40 years later in the regulation of food and drugs. After 20 years of debate and much public pressure, Congress enacted the Federal Food and Drug Act in 1906 to regulate the adulteration and misbranding of food and drugs, a responsibility previously exercised exclusively by the states.

A number of other important developments in the early decades of the 20th century had a strong impact on health care and health policy. Among the most significant were reforms in medical education that transformed not only education but also professional licensing and, eventually, health care itself. The American Medical Association and the large private foundations (e.g., Carnegie and Rockefeller) played a major role in this process. Voluntary hospitals also grew in number, size, and importance. Medical research produced new treatments. Infant mortality declined as nutrition, sanitation, living conditions, and maternal and infant care improved. Health care changed in significant ways, but it was little affected by public policy.

The Evolution of Health Policy: From Dual Federalism to Cooperative Federalism (1935–1961)

The Great Depression brought action by the federal government to save banks, support small business, provide direct public employment, stimulate public works, regulate financial institutions and business, restore consumer confidence, and provide Social Security in old age. The role of the federal government was transformed in the span of a few years. Federalism evolved from a dual pattern, with a limited role in domestic affairs for the federal government, to a cooperative one, with a strong federal role.

The Social Security Act of 1935 was certainly the most significant domestic social legislation ever enacted by Congress. This marked the real beginning of what has been termed "cooperative federalism." The act established the principle of federal aid to the states for public health and welfare assistance. It provided federal grants to states for maternal and child health and crippled children's services (Title V) and for public health (Title VI). It also provided for cash assistance grants to the aged, the blind, and destitute families with dependent children. This cash assistance program provided the basis for the current federal-state program of medical care for the poor, initially as Medical Assistance for the Aged in 1960 and then as Medicaid (Title XIX of the Social Security Act) in 1965. Both later programs linked eligibility for medical care to eligibility for cash assistance. More important, however, the Social Security Act of 1935 established the Old Age, Survivors' and Disability Insurance (OASDI) programs that were to provide the philosophical and fiscal basis for Medicare, a program of federal health insurance for the aged, also enacted in 1965 (Title XVIII of the Social Security Act). Passage of the Social Security Act of 1935 was significant, for it provided the basis for direct federal income assistance to retired persons and established the basis for federal aid to the states in health and welfare; however, this legislation did not include a program of national health insurance. This was due principally to the opposition of the medical profession to any form of health insurance, particularly publicly funded insurance.

In 1938, after the death of a number of children due to the use of Elixir of Sulfonamide, consumer protection became an important issue for policy makers. This disaster resulted in the enactment of the Food, Drug and Cosmetic Act of 1938, which required manufacturers to demonstrate the safety of drugs before marketing. This law was a further extension of the federal role and was consistent with other major changes in that role that occurred during the 1930s. After the passage of this act, little change was made in drug regulation law until the thalidomide disaster in the early 1960s.

Growing attention to maternal and child health, particularly for the poor, was reflected in grants to the states and in a temporary program instituted during World War II to pay for maternity care of wives of Army and Navy enlisted men. This means-tested program successfully demonstrated the capacity of the federal government to administer a national health insurance program. With rapid demobilization after the war and opposition by organized medicine, the program was terminated; but it was often cited by advocates of national health insurance, particularly those who accorded first priority to mothers and infants.

Introduction of the scientific method into medical research at the turn of the century and its gradual acceptance had a profound effect on national health policy and health care. The first clear organizational impact of the growing importance of research was the transformation of the U.S. Public

Health Service Hygienic Laboratory, established in 1901 to conduct bacterio-logic research and public health studies, into the National Institutes of Health (NIH) in 1930, with broad authority to conduct basic research. This was followed by enactment of the National Cancer Act of 1937 and the es-tablishment of the National Cancer Institute within the framework of NIH. There followed multiple legislative enactments during and after World War II that created the present institutes, focused primarily on broad classes of disease, such as heart disease, cancer, arthritis, neurologic diseases, and blindness.

In addition to federal support for biomedical research, largely through medical schools and universities, and a limited program of grants to states for public health and maternal and child health programs, federal policy related to hospital planning and construction became of primary importance. After World War II, it was evident that many of America's hospitals were woefully inadequate, and the Hill-Burton federal-state program of hospital planning and construction was launched in response in 1942. Its initial purpose was to provide funds to states to survey hospital bed supply and develop plans to overcome the hospital shortage, particularly in rural areas.

By 1953, when the Department of Health, Education, and Welfare (DHEW) (now the Department of Health and Human Services), was created, the federal government's role in the nation's health care system, although limited, was firmly established. This role was designed primarily to support programs and services in the private sector. Biomedical research, research training, and hospital construction were the major pathways for federal sup-port. The Food and Drug Administration also became part of DHEW and was its primary regulatory agency. Traditional public health programs, such as those for venereal disease control, tuberculosis control, and maternal and child health, were supported at minimal levels through categorical grants to the states. Federal support for medical care was restricted to military person-nel, veterans, merchant seamen, and native Americans until 1960, when en-actment of the Kerr-Mills law authorized limited federal grants to states for medical assistance for the aged. This program proved short-lived, but it highlighted the need for a far broader federal effort in medical care for the poor and the aged.

The Transformation of Health Policies: The New Frontier, The Great Society, and Creative Federalism (1961–1969)

A number of major federal health policy developments took place between 1961 and 1969, during the presidencies of John F. Kennedy and Lyndon B. Johnson. Although federal support was extended directly to universities, hospitals, and nonprofit institutes conducting research, most federal aid in health was channeled through the states. The term *creative fed-eralism* was applied to policies developed during the Johnson administration that extended the traditional federal-state relationship to include direct federal support for local governments (cities and counties), nonprofit organizations, and private businesses and corporations to carry out health, education, training, social services, and community development programs. The primary means used to forward the goals of creative federalism were grants-in-aid. More than 200 grant programs were enacted during the five years of the Johnson administration.

The 1962 amendments to the Food, Drug and Cosmetic Act specified that a drug must be demonstrated to be effective, as well as safe, before it could be marketed. Advertising also was strictly regulated, and more effective provisions for removal of unsafe drugs from the market were included.

The categorical programs that developed during the period of creative federalism were numerous and varied. Some programs were based on disease (heart disease, cancer, stroke, and mental illness); some on public assistance eligibility (Medicaid); some on age (Medicare, crippled children); some on institutions (hospitals, nursing homes, neighborhood health centers); some on political jurisdiction (state or local departments of public health); some on geographic areas that did not follow traditional political boundaries (community mental health centers, catchment areas, the Appalachian Regional Commission); and some on activity (research, facility construction, health professionals training, and health care financing).

Among the more important new laws enacted during the Johnson administration were the Health Professions Educational Assistance Act of 1963, which authorized direct federal aid to medical, dental, pharmacy, and other professional schools, as well as to students in these schools; the Maternal and Child Health and Mental Retardation Planning Amendments of 1963, which initiated comprehensive maternal and infant care projects and centers serving the mentally retarded; the Civil Rights Act of 1964, which prohibited racial discrimination, including segregated schools and hospitals; the Economic Opportunity Act of 1964, which provided authority and funds to establish neighborhood health centers serving low-income populations; the Social Security Amendments of 1965, particularly Medicare and Medicaid, which financed medical care for the aged and the poor receiving cash assistance; the Heart Disease, Cancer and Stroke Act of 1965, which launched a national attack on these major killers through regional medical programs; and the Comprehensive Health Planning and Public Health Service Amendments of 1966 and the Partnership for Health Act of 1967, which reestablished the principle of block grants for state public health services (reversing a 30-year trend of categorical federal grants in health). This legislation also created the first nationwide health planning system, which was dramatically changed in the 1970s to focus on regulation of health care as well as health planning. It should be noted that not until the Nixon and Reagan administrations was the block grant concept widely applied to federal grants-in-aid to the states. Of the many new health programs initiated during the Johnson presidency, only Medicare was administered directly by the federal government.

The programs of the Johnson presidency had a profound effect on intergovernmental relationships, the concept of federalism, and federal expenditures for domestic social programs. Grant-in-aid programs alone (excluding Social Security and Medicare) grew from $7 billion at the beginning of the Kennedy and Johnson administrations in 1961 to $24 billion in 1970, at the end of that era. In the next decade, the impact was to be even more dramatic as federal grant-in-aid expenditures for these programs grew to $82.9 billion in 1980. "Grants-in-aid," note Reagan and Sanzone, "constitute a major social invention of our time and are the prototypical, although not statistically dominant [they now constitute over 20 percent of domestic federal outlays], form of federal domestic involvement."

Health Policy in an Era of Limited Resources: From Creative Federalism to New Federalism and a Return to Dependence on Competition and the Private Sector (1969–1993)

During the 1970s, President Nixon coined the term "New Federalism" to describe his efforts to move away from the categorical programs of the Johnson years toward general revenue sharing, through which federal revenues were transferred to state and local governments with as few federal strings as possible, and toward block grants, through which grants are allocated to state and local governments for broad general purposes. During the Nixon and Ford administrations (1969–1977), considerable conflict developed between the executive branch and the Congress with respect to domestic social policy, including the New Federalism strategy originally advocated by President Nixon. Congress strongly favored categorical grants, with their detailed provisions, and was opposed to both revenue sharing and block grants. This period also witnessed an erosion of trust between federal middle management and congressional committees and subcommittees.

President Nixon also differed sharply from President Johnson in his explicit support for private rather than public efforts to solve the nation's health problems.

Although categorical health programs proliferated in the 1960s and 1970s, the expansion of two programs—Medicare and Medicaid—dwarfed the others. While these programs contributed to medical inflation, their growth was due largely to the rising costs of medical care in the 1970s. Federal and state governments became third parties that underwrote the costs of a system that had few cost-constraining elements, and the staggering expenditures had profound effects on health policy.

The federal government's response to skyrocketing health care costs (and thus governmental expenditures) assumed a variety of forms. Federal subsidies of hospitals and other health facility construction were ended and replaced by planning and regulatory mechanisms designed to limit their growth. In the mid-1970s health personnel policies focused on specialty and geographic maldistribution of physicians rather than physician shortage and, by the late 1970s, concern was expressed about an oversupply of physicians and other health professionals. Direct subsidies to expand enrollment in health professions schools were cut back and then eliminated. Funding for biomedical research began to decline in real dollar terms when an abortive "war on cancer" launched by President Nixon appeared to produce few concrete results and when Medicare and Medicaid preempted most federal health dollars.

More important than the constraints placed on resources allocated for health care were regulations instituted to slow the growth of health care costs. Two direct actions were taken by the federal government: (1) a limit on federal and state payments to hospitals and physicians under Medicare and Medicaid (included in the 1972 Social Security Amendments), and (2) a period of wage and price control applied to the general economy when the Economic Stabilization Program was introduced to dampen increasing inflation. Wage and price controls on hospitals and physicians were continued after the general restrictions were removed. When controls were lifted in 1974, health care costs again began to climb.

Another regulatory initiative was designed to control costs through limiting the use of hospital care by Medicare and Medicaid beneficiaries. Although the original Medicare and Medicaid legislation required hospital utilization review committees, these appeared to have little effect on hospital use or costs. In 1972, amendments to the Social Security Act (PL 92-103) required the establishment of professional standards review organizations (PSROs) to review the quality and appropriateness of hospital services provided to beneficiaries of Medicare, Medicaid, maternal and child health, and crippled children programs (paid for under authority of Title V of the Social Security Act).

Although the New Federalism advocated by President Reagan was a dramatic departure from previous policies and trends because of the scope of his proposals, the roots of these policies were first evident in the comprehensive Health Planning and Public Health Service amendments enacted in 1966 during the presidency of Lyndon Johnson. They were increasingly evident in both the policy initiatives and the budgetary decisions of Presidents Nixon and Ford. The Nixon and Ford New Federalism policies were not only similar to those later advocated by President Reagan, but their fiscal and monetary policies also were designed to reduce the growth of federal spending and program responsibility.

The Reagan administration accelerated the degree of pace of change in policy that had been developing since the early Nixon years. The most prominent shifts in federal policy advanced by the Reagan administration that directly affected health care were (1) a significant reduction in federal expenditures for domestic social programs, including the elimination of the revenue-sharing program initiated by President Nixon; (2) decentralization of program authority and responsibility to the states, particularly through block grants; (3) deregulation and greater emphasis on market forces and competition to stimulate health care reform and more effective control of health care costs; (4) tax reductions, despite significant increases in the national debt, with a resulting decline in the fiscal capacity of the federal government to fund domestic social programs; and (5) Medicare cost containment through the implementation of a prospective payment system for hospitals based on costs per case, using diagnosis-related groups (DRGs) as the basis for payment.

An important consequence of the block grants enacted by Congress at the urging of the Reagan administration is that the wide discretion that these grants provide to the individual states fosters inequities in programs among the states. This, in turn, makes it impossible to ensure uniform benefits for target populations, such as the poor and the aged, across jurisdictions or to maintain accountability with so many varying state approaches. Because the most disadvantaged individuals are heavily dependent on state-determined benefits, they are especially vulnerable in this period of economic flux. These policies also have increased pressure on state and local governments to underwrite program costs at the same time that many states, cities, and counties are under mounting pressure to curb expenditures.

Although the Reagan administration strongly favored deregulation and stimulation of procompetitive market forces, this had little impact on federal health care policies except in the health planning area. The federal health planning legislation was not renewed in the 1980s, but a number of states continued to operate certificate-of-need programs in an attempt to control the proliferation of expensive technologies.

In contrast to eliminating health planning as a means of regulation, the Reagan and Bush administrations used regulations to limit hospital reimbursement and physician fees in the Medicare program.

At the state level, however, major changes are under way that respond to the growing influence of the free-market ideology. In California, major reforms were enacted in 1982 in an attempt to increase competition among hospitals and reduce the costs of Medicaid in that state. Private insurance companies were also authorized to contract directly with hospitals through preferred provider contracts in an attempt to stimulate price competition among hospitals.

Although recent federal procompetition-deregulation policies have attracted the greatest attention, it is the dramatic reduction in federal fiscal capacity due to tax cuts and the growing federal deficit that have had the most immediate effect on health services. While the federal government is debating cost-containment strategies, a number of states have moved to restrict expenditures for Medicaid beneficiaries because of the continued impact of high costs on Medicaid expenditures at the state and federal levels.

Several states, including California, have enacted dramatic policy changes, restricting patients' freedom to choose providers, reducing levels of hospital and physician reimbursement, and shifting the burden of large numbers of poor patients back to local government.

The politics of limited resources began to dominate the U.S. political scene in the 1970s, and this continued into the 1980s, with little prospect of change. The prolonged period of postwar economic growth, based on productivity gains, came to a halt in the early 1970s, and the additional resources needed in domestic social programs and defense have been more and more constrained as a result. Controlling the costs of health care has become a critical need at the federal and state levels.

The cost-containment strategies of the past decade, particularly those since 1981, combined with the effects of the recessions of 1981–1982 and 1990–1992 on unemployment and access to private health insurance; the growth of the undocumented alien, immigrant, and refugee populations; and the diminishing commitment to provide for the near poor and the working poor have led to a significant increase in the number of uninsured and underinsured. Census Bureau data for 1984 revealed that 17 percent of the population under age 65 years (35 million people) lacked any health insurance, an increase of more than 20 percent since 1979. These figures dipped slightly in the late 1980s with the country's economic recovery, but rose again with the recession of 1990–1992.

For two decades, health care spending in the United States has outpaced the growth of the rest of the economy, with consequences for workers (depressed wages), businesses (a growing share of profits to health care), families (rising out-of-pocket costs and rising taxes to pay for public programs), and government (increasing share of government expenditures for health care).

There is no justification for the fact that the United States is one of only two industrialized nations failing to provide its citizens with comprehensive health care protection. The other nation is South Africa.
—Health Care USA

One significant question for the 1990s is whether the United States will continue its unique approach to health care cost containment, which emphasizes competition and limited use of regulation, particularly in the Medicare and Medicaid programs, or adopt more comprehensive strategies pursued successfully in France, Germany, and Japan—three countries with systems that resemble our own.

There are signs of an emerging consensus amid all the conflicts and tensions engendered by the need to constrain the growth in the health care sector. Various forces will affect future policies: some, such as the aging of the population, are beyond the control of policymakers; others, such as the rapid increase in physician supply and the use of an increasing number of new technologies in health care, are amenable to more direct policy interventions. One of the keys will be to reach agreement on the nature and scope of universal health insurance. Another will be to modify reimbursement policies to achieve appropriate policy goals. Still another will be to deal realistically with the failure of the "free market" and unregulated competition to assure equity.

The regulatory approach to cost containment began to gather support again in the 1980s with Medicare's prospective payment system in hospitals in 1983, and the adoption of a Medicare fee schedule by Congress in 1989. In addition to the Medicare fee schedule, Congress adopted an expenditure target, called a *volume performance standard*, to limit the rate of increase in expenditures for physicians' services. Both the Medicare fee schedule and the volume performance standard drew on the experience of other countries, particularly Canada and Germany. The fact that other major industrialized nations had managed to provide universal health insurance and control costs was a lesson that was gradually beginning to be appreciated by U.S. policymakers.

In addition to this evident failure of U.S. health care cost containment efforts and the apparent success of countries that have provided universal coverage with effective cost containment, there has been a substantial change in public attitudes favoring health care financing reform. This change in public attitude and the growing dissatisfaction of Americans with the present system of health care financing and the rising costs of care may overwhelm the special interests (insurance companies, physicians, hospitals) that have long thwarted comprehensive reforms in health care financing and cost containment.

Health care became a major political issue in 1991 and is likely to remain so until the problems of health care cost containment and universal access to health insurance are solved in the United States. The next major chapter in national health policy may well be written before the elections of 1996.

❖ About the Authors

Philip R. Lee, M.D., was appointed by President Clinton as Assistant Secretary for Health, Department of Health and Human Services, in 1993. Prior to that he was Professor of Social Medicine, Institute for Health Policy Studies, School of Medicine, University of California, San Francisco, and was the founding director of the Institute.

A. E. Benjamin, PH.D., is Professor of Social Welfare, University of California, Los Angeles.

❖ Privatization, the Welfare State, and Aging: The Reagan-Bush Legacy

Carroll L. Estes

President Ronald Reagan successfully shifted the focus of discourse on social policy in the United States from activism and social improvement to crisis and budget cutting. This was accomplished with the support of an ideological revolution reinstating the primacy of the economy as the driving rationale for state action and a romanticized notion of individualism and the family as a justification for shifting social responsibility to the private sector. This paper explores the Reagan-Bush legacy, lays out the paradigm shift that has occurred, examines its symbolic and material consequences, and assesses the implications for old age in the U.S. welfare state, with particular attention to health care.

The theme of crisis was a central motif resonating throughout the Reagan presidency and preparing the way for action. Aging policy was a key element of the schema of crisis definition and the resulting outcomes. Understanding the contemporary welfare state requires theoretical and empirical attention to crisis construction and crisis management by the state. The "Reagan Revolution" was a product of the tensions among the state (government and its institutions), the corporate sector, and labor in working through the crisis tendencies associated with capitalism.

Under Reagan, economic crisis has been used to justify the imposition of cost containment policies in health care that shifted costs from the state to individuals (including the elderly) and the transfer of an increasing amount of funding from public and nonprofit health provider organizations to for-profit enterprise. Furthering a process that commenced with the passage of Medicare and Medicaid in 1965, Reagan administration policies fueled the growth of the for-profit components and the costs of the medical care system. Although 40 percent of the cost of U.S. health care spending is financed by the federal government, it supports a largely private sector medical-industrial complex. The state has limited its own activities in the health and social services to those that support and complement the market through limited public financing programs of health insurance, primarily for the aged (Medicare) and the poor who cannot afford to pay for private insurance (Medicaid).

Through the regulation and financing of medical care and social services, state policy under Reagan stimulated market investment opportuni-

138

ties for private capital in potentially profitable service arenas (e.g., hospital and home health services) that had been traditionally controlled by non-profit health care entities. State policy also provided productive opportunities for private capital through civil law and regulation protecting the market and proprietary health entities including the federal tax subsidy of the purchase of private health insurance. The combination of Reagan's deliberate strategies to increase privatization and competition through the promotion of medical and community care for profit and requirements for competitive contracting, and substantial public subsidies to the corporate sector through tax cuts in 1981, significantly exacerbated the fiscal problems of the state.

These state actions and policies contributed to (1) the deepening of divisions in the *de facto* rationing system of U.S. health care based on ability to pay, and (2) a largely unchecked rise in federal health care costs. Under Reagan, the state intensified the constraints on funding for social and community care services—areas of the greatest dependency by nonprofit service organizations on the government. The state-financed services that experienced the most severe cuts early in the Reagan administration were the social and supportive services that are least attractive to business investors because they tend to be less profitable due to their labor intensity, lower technological content, and general unpredictability. Each of these state actions has altered the terrain of health and aging policy, and each has generated consequences.

In the Reagan era, health and aging policy exemplify the contradictions facing the state as it is pressed to regulate and contain government costs in medical care, while simultaneously being required to deregulate and promote economic expansion and profit through a robust state-financed but privately run and extremely costly medical-industrial complex. At the same time, as the state and the private sector shift more of the costs onto the consumer, the poor and the uninsured grow, ultimately increasing welfare costs that must be borne by the state.

❖ The Reagan Legacy: An Ideological Revolution

All political regimes use ideology as the discourse with which to communicate and impose a reflection of economic and power relations. One of the most striking and significant features of the Reagan legacy is its phenomenal success in advancing neo-liberal and neo-conservative ideologies as strategies in the social construction of crisis, subsequent crisis management, and restructuring of the welfare state. The ideological legacy of the Reagan administration is profound.

As deeply held systems of beliefs, ideologies are generally unexamined as both evidential and moral truths. Ideologies frame the possible and the ethical, orienting us to what is ("reality"), who we are, and how we relate to the world. Ideologies influence what we conceive of as imaginable and as right and wrong. The production and uses of ideology are integral to three processes by which dominant power relations are sustained: (1) the successful creation of cultural images by policymakers, experts, and the media; (2) the appeal to the necessities of the economic system; and (3) the implementation of policy and the use of expertise in ways that focus attention on rational problem solving in familiar organizational structures and professions rather than the more fundamental questions and in ways that camouflage their class, gender, racial, and ethnic implications.

Reagan's ideological revolution simultaneously promoted the revival of the free market and the now-mythical patriarchal autonomous family. Two elements of the revolution are (1) neo-liberal ideology, which is distinctly oriented toward a "minimalist state" and hostile to anything that may impede the order of the market and its natural superiority; and (2) neo-conservative ideology, which appeals to authority, allegiance, tradition, and "nature." The allegiance of the citizen to the state is seen as transcendent. "A corollary . . . is that [a particular vision of] the family is central to maintaining the state." The attractiveness of this new right model is that it embraces two potentially disparate elements: "intellectual adherence to the free market and the emotional attachment to authority and imposed tradition." The New Right is committed to a view that the primary, if not only, justification for government intervention is maintaining the national defense and law and order. President Reagan successfully blurred the concepts of national security with the national economic interest.

Reagan was remarkably influential in using ideology to shape public consciousness by limiting a vision of the "possible" to inherently pro-market solutions. In health care, the vision was that the only route to universal health care is through competition and market strategies. Not surprisingly, this ideology bolstered the U.S. health care system as a pluralistically financed and essentially private delivery system dominated by a powerful medical profession and for-profit medical industries. The doubling of the cost of health care consonant with the dramatic decline in access to care for millions of Americans during the Reagan-Bush era is testimony to the inadequacy of market approaches to health care as a means either of controlling costs or ensuring access.

❖ The Health Legacy of Ronald Reagan: 1981–1988

Reagan's strategy in health care was to focus on cost containment and to advance market principles in health (competition, deregulation, and privatization). A companion strategy was to implement cuts in the Medicaid program for the poor. While Reagan's policies stimulated a revolution in the organization of health care and its corporatization and privatization, these efforts to stimulate the market had the opposite effect of what they promised for cost containment. Medical costs continued to rise at two to three times the rate of inflation.

The Reagan administration had reaffirmed the course of health policy embarked on by previous administrations. The structure of private provision and service delivery, the pluralistic methods of financing, and the orientation of the government-financed programs of Medicare and Medicaid remained essentially intact. Significantly, however, Reagan's approach also deepened and extended the nation's commitment to the commodification and "medicalization" of old age through state policy. Health care was reconceptualized as a commodity through the rhetoric and policies that established health care as a market good rather than a right. The medicalization is reflected in the construction of "aging as illness," the exclusive targeting of federal reimbursement through Medicare for medical treatment (not social supportive or even chronic illness care), the designation and slanting of federal research priorities toward biomedical problems, and the direction of medical education.

The most important effects of the Reagan legacy in health care for the aged are (1) the fueling of the commodification and medicalization of care for the aging in ways that are consistent with capitalist expansion of the medical-industrial complex; (2) the continuing refusal of the state to provide meaningful long-term care benefits to the elderly and disabled; (3) the accumulation of multiple pressures on a beleaguered network of traditionally nonprofit home and community-based health and social service providers thinly stretched by the demands of very sick and very old patients discharged from the hospital earlier than ever before; and (4) the use of policies to promote family responsibility and the informalization of care. These efforts to restore and regulate family life (and particularly the lives of women) are congruent with the deep concerns of both the state and corporate sectors to minimize state costs for the elderly, as well as the New Right for restoring patriarchal family arrangements in order to ensure a continuing supply of women's free labor for the reproduction and maintenance of the labor force.

The Reagan administration's resistance to a federal policy solution to the problem of long-term care and its unstated policy of informalization are part of a larger austerity strategy in the context of the state's need for women (regardless of their labor force participation) to continue to perform large (and increasing) amounts of unpaid servicing work, particularly in the care of the aged.

Health Care as a Market Good

The stated health policy goals of equity, access, and accountability that were hallmarks of the 1960s died in the Reagan White House. America's elders were caught between (1) the dual interests of the state and corporate sectors, each of which was attempting to constrain and reduce its own costs and neither of which was especially concerned about inequities in access to care; and (2) the tensions between the shared goals of the state and those segments of corporate capital that wanted to reduce medical care costs *versus* that part of the corporate sector in the medical-industrial complex (including hospitals and physicians) that were pressing for the expansion of a growing and profitable market in high technology medical care guaranteed by government subsidy. The result has been a more costly and deeply stratified health care system for all Americans.

❖ The Bush Legacy in Health

The Bush approach to health policy was a continuation of the Reagan strategy of privatization, competition, and deregulation, laced with the rhetoric of crisis and the urgency of cost containment. On the *ideological* front, the Bush and Reagan legacies are virtually indistinguishable: the unswerving commitment to market rhetoric, joined with images of the aborted fetus, reflect the far right's intimidation and capture of Bush and the Republican party. With it there were serious attacks on the rights of women and minorities, as well as (not so paradoxically) children. The difference between the two administrations was in the political acumen, the charisma, and media savvy of President Reagan in contrast to that of President Bush.

President Bush's capitulation to the extreme right wing was expressed in the regulation of medical practitioners through the imposition of a "gag" rule on health providers in family planning clinics and a ban on fetal tissue research that might result in a cure for such maladies as Parkinson's or Alzheimer's diseases. Family planning and "choice" with regard to pregnancy became dirty words.

The failure of both Reagan and Bush to control health costs over the 12 years of their administrations contributed to a three-fold increase, from $1,000 to $3,000 per person and from $250 to $870 billion in national health expenditures during their combined terms of office. The average health payments of families rose 169 percent between 1980 and 1992, while wages increased far less than that (54 percent). During the Bush presidency, an estimated 1.8 million Americans lost their jobs due to rising employer health costs.

In spite of significant reductions in hospital lengths of stay (in excess of 22 percent) and the shift of health work to informal careers with the extension of ambulatory day surgery and the shortened hospital visits, the escalation of health costs continues. Market competition and the massive restructuring of the health industry of the 1980s have not fulfilled their promise as "the solution" to the cost crisis. Physician expenditures galloped at more than 13 percent a year, two to three times the inflation rate. In 1991, health insurance premiums comprised 10.7 percent of corporate payroll and, based on current trends, premiums will consume 22.9 percent of payroll by the year 2000. Health care expenditures represent one seventh of the entire U.S. economy.

When examined over 28 months, the number of Americans presently without health care insurance coverage part or all of the time exceeds 63 million, or 28 percent of the U.S. population. Without a change in policy, the number of Americans uninsured for health care is projected to rise from the present 37 million to well above 52 million between 1991 and the year 2000. In spite of the enormous and growing coverage gap, the implications of failing to systematically control U.S. health spending are staggering. The proportion of the gross national product (GNP) will almost double in the next decade alone, rising from 12 percent to 20 percent of GNP.

The failure of policy makers either to stem costs or to improve access is due in no small part to the U.S. politics of health. Health industry contributions from political action committees (PACs) to politicians—the "mother's milk" of politics—increased 22 percent over the last four-year election cycle alone. Since Mr. Reagan's election in 1981, representatives of the medical-industrial complex have contributed in excess of $65 million to House and Senate races, and members of the last (102nd) Congress have received $48.5 million. Additional millions are spent on Washington lobbyists. Indeed, health industry political contributions are rising faster than health care costs. Researchers for *Public Citizen* have projected a 178 percent increase in PAC contributions between 1989 and 1992. Although some 300 health care proposals were introduced in the last (102nd) congressional session, the president of *Public Citizen*, Joan Claybrook, contends, "Most of these bills could have been written on the word processors of the health industry." The Health Insurance Association of America will spend $4 million to discredit reform proposals. The Canadian model is a favorite target in view of recent poll data indicating the public support of Americans for this system.

President Bush's health proposals during the 1992 election promised no structural health reform. They contained four elements: (1) a health insurance credit or tax deduction to provide up to $3,750 annually to cover the purchase of private coverage and health care costs. (Critics note that this is far less than the $4,700 average cost of private insurance now and the $10,000 projected as early as 1996. They note, further, that Bush had no plan to regulate insurance industry pricing); (2) medical malpractice reform; (3) coordinated or managed care (which has not yet been proven to be cost effective); and (4) electronic billing to reduce administrative costs.

The cost of Bush's proposed tax breaks for all Americans and the tax subsidies for the purchase of private health insurance for his second term of office, should he have been elected, was estimated at $1 trillion (including his promised deficit reductions and new programs). Bush's proposed balanced budget amendment would have required major, if not draconian, cuts in existing programs like Medicare and Social Security for the elderly. Democrats estimated results of the Bush plan would have meant the loss of between 2.2 and 6.4 million U.S. jobs.

Without a dramatic change in health policy, the elderly will be negatively affected on multiple counts: (1) the predictable continuing health care cost escalation that is eroding government's ability to afford to provide adequate Medicare and other benefits; (2) out-of-pocket health care costs for elders that are continuing to rise (now exceeding 18% of annual income and consuming 4.3 months of the average elder's annual Social Security payments); (3) the private Medi-gap insurance policies that most (80 percent) older Americans purchase to supplement Medicare, which are becoming increasingly unaffordable to more and more elders; and (4) the continuing reluctance of policymakers to adopt a national long-term care policy. Finally, with a growing deficit and ever-escalating Medicare costs, there is the persistent danger of the intensified politicization and significant erosion of other major social programs that are crucial to elders, such as Social Security.

Probably the most profound effect of the Reagan and Bush presidencies is the enormous and mushrooming federal deficit, now approximating $3 trillion. A deficit of this magnitude was achieved through massive tax cuts and huge military spending. The goal was not simply to reduce welfare benefits; it was nothing less than "the transformation of the very tax structure that generated the revenues necessary for the welfare benefits. . . . Thus, tax policy became social welfare policy." The size and magnitude of the deficit and interest on the debt had their intended salutary effects for the conservative agenda; *they staved off new state programs unless they can be paid for by trading off other programs within a zero-sum or fixed state budget.*

A key priority of President Bush was an amendment to the U.S. Constitution requiring Congress to balance the budget annually. Due to extreme pressure from the White House, such an amendment almost passed in the last full congressional session of President Bush's presidency. The effects of a balanced budget amendment, should it pass, on the social domestic budget would be profound. No less than 20 percent cuts would be necessitated in virtually all social programs. If there were a protection clause to exempt Social Security from contributing to the deficit reduction under a balanced budget amendment, the level of cuts across all other federally funded domestic programs is expected to exceed 30 percent.

Legitimacy of the U.S. State

Meanwhile, the legitimacy problems of the U.S. state continued as economic problems stubbornly resisted the usual pre-election presidential tinkering with interest rates, unemployment statistics, and other economic indicators.

During the Reagan and Bush presidencies, the state successfully played its "class role" by restructuring and redistributing state benefits from the worker and middle class to business and the upper class rather than dismantling the state. Rhetoric to the contrary, both state funding and regulation have been redirected rather than reduced.

Under Reagan and Bush, the rhetoric of fiscal crisis and the state's mythical and pathetic cost containment efforts obfuscated the massive transfer that was underway—the transfer of health care benefits from labor, the poor, minorities, women, and small business to an increasingly concentrated, unstable, and disorganized complex of medical and other corporations, fending for their lives within a restructured capitalist world order. Health programs for the poor and for women and children were hit the hardest and with the most lasting and deleterious effects. One fifth of all of America's children today are in poverty and one third in California are expected to be on public welfare sometime during their childhood. The redistribution of resources and growing inequities extend to the declining standard of living of working and middle class Americans.

The astounding three-fold growth in expenditures for the medical-industrial complex under Reagan and Bush demonstrates the ability of the U.S. state and the nation's health and aging policies to assist in attending to crises in the capitalist system, as the state subsidy for profit making in medical care and technology expand. The attack on the nonprofit sector in health care is part of the same phenomenon: new opportunities for corporate investment capital in health are needed and the opportunities for proprietaries in the health care market are enhanced with the weakening of the nonprofit sector and the erosion of its legitimacy.

An important question is whether the increasing personal difficulties ("troubles") with health care of what is becoming literally all but the richest 1 or 2 percent of Americans will generate the necessary political heat to ignite an effective movement for broad health policy change. The high unemployment (officially 7.6 percent, but estimated more accurately at 10 percent), as well as the rising number of part-time workers without health benefits augments the potential that this will occur. There is substantial and enduring public support for the major U.S. entitlement programs such as Social Security and Medicare that form the bedrock of the U.S. welfare state—this despite White House and media assaults of more than a decade. According to public opinion, the momentum for structural change in health policy is building. The majority (61 percent) of the U.S. public would prefer the Canadian system of health insurance to the U.S. system, in which "the government pays most of the cost of care for everyone out of taxes, and the government sets all fees charged by doctors and hospitals." Support is strongest (68 percent) among those in the middle class.

❖ Crisis, Social Struggles, and the Reagan Legacy

The Reagan-Bush legacy is contained in the social struggles that characterize the 1980s and 1990s. These include generational struggles, gender struggles, racial and ethnic struggles, and class struggles. First, questions of generational equity were socially constructed and fueled as public and political issues in the 1980s by demographers, economists, and politicians. They remain salient today. Pointed questions of fairness between different age cohorts and of the inevitability of rationing choices between generations penetrate and now threaten to dominate political discourse on income and health policy for the aged. The specter of this socially constructed "intergenerational war" continues to plague the progressive policy agenda in health and aging.

Second, Reagan and Bush rekindled old gender struggles. Neo-conservative ideology increased pressures for family responsibility laws and more private responsibility for posthospital and informal care. Pressures on women are sure to increase both with the demographic changes and the "baby dearth," and they will be exacerbated to the extent that we lack a comprehensive national long-term care policy in the United States that addresses issues of gender justice in the caregiving work in our society.

Supposedly we have the highest standard of living in any country in the world. Do we, though? It depends on what one means by high standards. Certainly nowhere does it cost more to live than here in America. The cost is not only in dollars and cents but in sweat and blood, in frustration, ennui, broken homes, smashed ideals, illness and insanity. We have the most wonderful hospitals, the most gorgeous insane asylums, the most fabulous prisons, the best equipped and the highest paid army and navy, the speediest bombers, the largest stockpile of atom bombs, yet never enough of any of these items to satisfy the demand. Our manual workers are the highest paid in the world; our poets the worst. There are more automobiles than one can count. And as for drugstores, where in the world will you find the like?
—Henry Miller

Indeed, the 1980s were a period of reassessment of women's place in society. Women are needed in the labor force for both public (to fulfill service roles including temporary low paid work without benefits) and private reasons (to maintain individual standards of living); yet, women are essential in filling the nation's growing need for long-term care given that women's work comprises the bulk of the nation's long-term care. The Reagan-Bush period was one in which the contradictions in women's lives became starkly apparent and their roles in the labor market and the home were simultaneously but differentially reinforced and expanded (but not necessarily supported).

Third, Reagan policies exacerbated class divisions both in the distribution of wealth and along the health care access dimension. Not only have privatization policies failed to stem the rising costs of medical care, but also they spurred reductions in coverage by public and private insurance and the exclusion of more and more of the U.S. population from access to that coverage. Since 1980, there has been a significant roll-back in early achievements in health care access following the passage of Medicare and Medic-aid. With the reemergence of a two-tier system of health care, the present class war in health is experienced in the declining access to care by the poor, rising infant mortality, and the erosion of health insurance benefits for the working population.

Another aspect of the deterioration of access is the reversal of decades of legitimacy and privileged state support for the nonprofit provision of health and social services. As the role of for-profit enterprise in health has flour-ished in the 1980s, nonprofits have found themselves in a beleaguered, un-certain, and highly competitive environment that is eroding their capacity to continue providing charity services. Nonprofit health and social services have themselves been part of the restructuring of delivery that has affected virtually all aspects of the formal and informal care system, including the nature and scope of services provided, the clientele served and their access to care, the composition of the labor force, and organizational financing. With changes in the structure, type of ownership, and control of these orga-nizations, there has been an increase in the fragmentation of service delivery and provider targeting to clients who can pay privately and to services that are profitable or reimbursable by the state or private insurance.

The Reagan-Bush legacy broke the labor, race, and gender accords that were reached between the 1940s and the 1970s. In addition to the resurgence of the ideology of patriarchy through the "family values" theme, there was a systematic attack with severe restrictions placed on the reproductive rights of women, particularly for poor women. Welfare rights and benefits also were eroded.

As Abramovitz observes, the support of the welfare state by both busi-ness and government prior to the 1980s was conditioned by the need to ad-dress and pacify the political movements that arose in labor in the 1930s and 1940s, in civil rights in the 1950s and 1960s, and in women's issues in the 1960s and 1970s.

The economic crisis of the 1970s changed the political scene, as "the wel-fare state became too competitive with capital accumulation and too sup-portive of empowered popular movements." What had to be achieved was the redistribution of income from the bottom to the top, the reduction of the costs of labor, and initiation of a new conservative social movement to counter the expansive welfare state. Reagan's accomplishments on all of these fronts accounts for the undoing of the labor, race, and gender accords.

❖ Conclusion

Aging and health policy represent a major battleground on which the social struggles presently engulfing the state are being fought as it attempts to address growing tensions between capitalism and democracy. The construction of the aging of the population in crisis terms has served dual ideological purposes. First, the "demographic imperative" has been a rallying point for those who argue that the elderly are living too long, consuming too many societal resources, and robbing the young—justifying rollbacks of state benefits for the aged. Additional antistatist sentiments have been expressed in the unfounded contention that state policy to provide formal care will encourage abdication of family responsibility for the aging, which, in turn, will bankrupt the state. This line of reasoning is consistent with the state's continuing refusal to provide long-term care and reinforcing the idea that such care is (and should remain) the responsibility of the informal sector and the unpaid labor of women.

Second, the projected chronic illness burden of pandemic proportions (another version of the crisis) has been used in ideological attacks on health care as a right for the elderly, particularly by those promoting the intergenerational war. The elderly are accused of crippling both the state and corporate sectors with unsupportable demands.

In anticipation of the continuation of crises in the face of the growing needs of an aging society and the difficulties manifest in the modern form of advanced capitalism in the United States, the nation appears to be set on a collision course. Two alternate scenarios are possible. The first is one in which the state takes actions that extend the direction and influence of the economic and ideological commitments of the Reagan-Bush presidencies. The second is one in which the contradictions and resulting potential for social struggles presently engaged (class, generation, gender, and race) are realized, exploding with a force and effect that cannot be turned aside. The issue ahead is whether President Clinton's proposals for health reform alter the direction and course on which the nation has been set by the Reagan-Bush legacy.

❖ About the Author

Carroll L. Estes, PH.D., is Director of the Institute for Health and Aging and Professor, Department of Social and Behaviorial Sciences, School of Nursing, University of California, San Francisco.

❖ The Brave New World of Health Care

Richard D. Lamm

❖ Health Care as Economic Cancer

Let me be blunt: Health care costs in the United States are making our economy sick. We have come to believe that everyone is entitled to unlimited health care regardless of how costly and without regard to a patient's prognosis for recovery. The mere suggestion to the contrary is looked upon as an act of callous insensitivity and prevents us from asking questions that desperately need to be asked.

More than 12 cents of every dollar spent in the United States is spent on health care, and costs continue to rise at more than double the rate of inflation. Carried to its most absurd conclusion, if current trends continue, our entire gross national product (GNP) will be spent on health care in about 70 years. This clearly will not happen, but it underscores the need to begin making hard choices and develop a system that provides the best possible health care to the greatest number of people at a price the nation can afford.

Our factories need modernization and refurbishing, our trade with other nations is unbalanced, our infrastructure is deteriorating, our classrooms are overcrowded, yet we continue to spend over $600 billion a year on health care in the United States—more than $2,400 for every man, woman, and child in this country. Ironically, for all the money we spend Americans are no healthier than people in many countries that spend considerably less than we do on health care; nor are we significantly healthier than we were 30 years ago when health care consumed only 6 percent of GNP. Most of our national drop in mortality occurred before our upsurge in spending on health care.

Health care costs do affect our international competitiveness. In an international economy, the amount of money a society spends on social programs, including health care, affects its overhead costs and thus its competitive ability. Skyrocketing health costs are an important intrinsic factor in making American goods uncompetitive on international markets.

Business health care costs have increased at an annual rate of 16 percent this past decade. American corporations have seen their health care costs go up from an amount equal to 14.4 percent of corporate profits in 1965 to a staggering 94.2 percent of corporate profits in 1987. Health care costs are the single biggest cause of individual bankruptcy and of industrial unrest. Most recent labor disputes involve health care. Not only have current and imme-

149

diate health care costs risen, but U.S. businesses have enormous unaccounted liability for future health care costs. The unfunded post-employment health care obligations for the Fortune 500 companies are almost $2 trillion. A proposed regulation by the Financial Accounting Standards Board seeks to incorporate by 1992 these liabilities into corporations' income statements and balance sheets. Though mitigated by Medicare coverage, this accounting item could wreak havoc with reported profits, book values, and stock market valuations.

Health care is among the fastest growing items in governments' budgets. Tax funds provide 42 percent of our nation's health bills, up from 26 percent in 1965. Publicly funded health programs claim $0.15 of every government tax dollar, as opposed to only $0.06 in 1965. Every sector of our society is being pinched by exploding health care costs.

❖ What Drives Health Care Costs?

Whole books have been written about what drives health care costs. Most agree that the principal causes are:

1. The aging of America's population
2. Advances in medical technology
3. The expectations of the American public as to the kind of health care it deserves
4. The fact that most health care is paid for by third party payers (users of the system feel little economic pain)
5. The tax system which allows an employee to receive health benefits tax free and thus reduces economic incentives for health care
6. Medical malpractice insurance premiums

But I would add one more:

7. The refusal to recognize that infinite needs have run into finite resources

I believe there is an additional, less recognized, reason for our exploding health care costs: the medical model that assumes we can deliver to every patient all possible health care. America must eventually admit to its collective self that some limits must be set. Our medical genius has outpaced our ability to pay for all we are capable of doing. Once we admit to this, we will, at last, be able to address the issue of buying the most health care with our limited resources. Any other alternative to facing the new reality of exploding technology will be fiscal suicide. The key to other industrialized societies being able to stabilize their health care spending was their ability to prioritize their spending. They recognized that there were infinite medical procedures that could be "beneficial" at the margin. American doctors are trained to deliver to patients all the medicine that is remotely "beneficial" to patients. Very little medicine does not meet the current standard of "beneficial"—so we are currently using a yardstick that is bound to bankrupt us. We shall, inevitably, have to decide what is "appropriate"—not what merely could be "beneficial."

There is an "invisible hand" in the American health care delivery system that generates expenditures beyond what our society can afford. Adam Smith spoke first of the "invisible hand," whereby every person seeking his own self-interest created an "invisible hand" which built the economy. The sum total of every individual seeking his economic goals was a prosperous economy.

There is likewise an "invisible hand" in the health care system. It is the hand of the doctor who is sworn to deliver all the health care that he considers "beneficial" to the patient. . . . The implicit assumption is that the nation can afford to fund the total health care needs (as defined by doctors and the health care providers) of all the individuals within the society.

It is also tacitly assumed that "the system" will allocate the correct proportion of society's resources into health care vis-à-vis other social needs like education, infrastructure, social services, etc. Increasingly, we are coming to understand that these assumptions are incorrect. Health care providers have developed more beneficial medicine than society can afford. Our medical genius has outpaced our economic abilities.

Health care, for all its technical genius, has become an economic cancer that is eating into other necessary public functions. The best building in almost every town in America is the hospital (35 percent vacant) and the worst building is usually the school (overcrowded). The highest paid professionals in America are the doctors; the worst paid are school teachers. We will not remain a great nation by overtreating our sick and undereducating our children. Our health care industry is draining resources desperately needed elsewhere to keep America a competitive nation.

The individual doctor's "invisible hand," which delivers to a patient all the health care deemed beneficial, is guided also by the presence of the "invisible lawyer" at his/her side. If America's health care delivery system runs to excess, our legal system runs amok. With 5 percent of the world's population we have almost 70 percent of the world's lawyers and this "legalflation" sits astride America, compounding the risks and costs of almost everything we do as a society. The reality of medical malpractice is bad enough, but the myth is even greater.

The "invisible lawyer" advises every doctor to leave no alternative unexplored—no matter how cost inefficient. Careers must be protected. The combination of real worries about malpractice suits and unreasonable worries (but no less real to the individual doctor) hangs like a black cloud over the health care delivery system—pushing it beyond reason to deliver to each patient all health care available, no matter how unlikely it is to be worthwhile. We have built a system without brakes which threatens to undercut our economic prosperity.

Our "invisible hand," guided and influenced by our "invisible lawyer," has created an "invisible foot" which is kicking apart our economy. At the rate that health care costs have exploded over the last 30 years, by 2057 100 percent of our GNP will be spent on health care. This "invisible foot" thus threatens to kick apart everything our forefathers have built for us.

American goods and services can only carry so much health care before they become totally priced out of the international marketplace. America must develop a way to set priorities. The "invisible hand" that guides the doctor also cannot consider alternative uses of those resources. Doctors cannot be "double agents." Doctors consider a patient's health, but a society must consider the total health of its citizens. A doctor does not ask, "How do we keep our society healthy?" They are, properly, so busy with individual patients that they too often cannot see the impact on the total society.

We thus move 90-year-olds to intensive care units and restart their hearts 20 or 30 times before they die, but don't give health insurance to 31 million people. We pay for transplants under Medicare yet we do not vaccinate all children or give prenatal care to pregnant women. Our system urges a doctor to give chemotherapy to an 85-year-old with metastatic cancer, while our society tolerates 600,000 women giving birth each year with inadequate prenatal care.

Inevitably someone in America must stay the relentless movement of the "invisible hand" and ask, "How do we take limited resources and buy the most health care for our society?" Every dollar we spend has an "opportunity cost" and too often our current system allocates that dollar in the least efficient way.

America is not allocating its health care resources in a way that maximizes the nation's health. We have built a system that maximizes the delivery of health resources to individuals but not to the society. We have too many "invisible hands," too many "invisible lawyers," and too many "invisible feet" kicking at our system.

❖ How Do You Keep a Society Healthy?

It is timely, then, to explore what options a society has to keep its citizens healthy. Certain public policies clearly buy more health than others. The American Medical Association often brags that the United States has "the best health care system in the world." We clearly have the most expensive, but is it the best? Technologically it is superb, filled with dedicated health care providers and a surfeit of ingenious machines and innovators. Yet America does not keep its people as healthy as our other industrial competitors: an American male is 15th in the world in life expectancy and American females are eighth; we are 20th in infant mortality; 12 nations have lower rates of cancer and 25 nations have better cardiovascular health. For all our spending, we do not keep our people as healthy as the Japanese, the Canadians, or the Europeans.

The reasons for this are both complicated and hotly debated. Some physicians will tell you that it is our "heterogeneous" society. And this is partly true. African-American women, even adjusted for income, have proportionately more low-birthweight babies. That drags our infant mortality rate down; but Asian-American women have fewer low-birthweight babies which partly offsets the low-birthweight numbers among African-Americans. A heterogeneous society does have special challenges, but our public policy, culture, and the way we practice medicine also misdirect massive resources in health care spending.

There seem to be some obvious reasons why other nations have more health for less money.

The century of specialization has collected vast information about each and every organ of the body. The data available through modern research methods is beyond the wildest dreams of the medical scientist of even fifty years ago. But this information has been derived from, and applies to, isolated bits of human tissue. . . . This is, of course, the basic dilemma of the analytic method. In spite of the rich harvest of information we have reaped, the fact remains that people are still complaining of their aches, their pains and their inadequacies.
—Ida Rolf

Public Policy and Public Health

The great enemies of death and disease over the years have been the public health people. We are too easily led to believe that doctors and hospitals translate directly into health. Not true. Human health has improved and life expectancy increased mainly because of improved standards of living, particularly improved nutrition, decisions about family size and birth control, and public health measures: sanitation, refrigeration, chlorination, and vaccination have saved far more people than doctors and hospitals. Soap is probably one of the most powerful health weapons of all time. We are healthier primarily because we are more educated, more sanitary, eat better, exercise more, and have a higher standard of living.

The United States has a number of public policy options available to it to reinforce its medical care system. A cigarette tax of $1 per pack would be a health care measure that would gain—not cost—the government money. The U.S. has much lower tax rates on cigarettes and alcohol than do most industrial nations. Mandatory seat belt laws throughout America would save more lives than all our expensive computerized tomography (CT) scanners. Screening for hypertension would likely save more lives than all our intensive care units.

Public policy can save more lives more cheaply than many of the fancy technologies with which we fill our hospitals. We need a larger vision of the concept of health care. A drunk driving bill is health care. Gun control is health care. One has to ask whether it makes sense to pour billions of dollars into a health care delivery system that is often effective only at the margin while foregoing these other much more effective policies that clearly save more lives and health.

Societies That Give Basic Health Care to All Their People Are Healthy Societies

A second reason why other nations are healthier is that they provide basic health care for all their citizens, while the U.S. allows 37 million people to go uninsured. In addition, the Robert Wood Johnson Foundation has found, in a recent one-year period, that as many as 1 million American families had one or more members denied some basic health care.

Approximately one quarter of our population is uninsured or underinsured. Twenty-one percent of our children under 15 have no health insurance. Similarly, 26 percent of women of reproductive age are not covered by maternity benefits. Our "social safety nets" are full of holes. Only 41 percent of Americans with incomes below the federal poverty levels are covered by Medicaid.

American physicians often point with horror at Great Britain where kidney dialysis is denied people over 55, but Great Britain gives all its people basic health care. They may not have as many fancy neonatal care units, but a visiting nurse twice calls upon new mothers to make sure the mother is recovering and the baby thriving. Visiting nurses for everyone are better health investments than neonatal units.

Basic health care is cost-effective health care.

The U.S. Misdirects Too Many Health Care Dollars

A third reason why we spend more for poorer results is that we drain off incredible numbers of health care dollars into the legal system and bureaucracy. It is hard to quantify what these two factors cost our society, but we do know it is immense. Our legal system hangs over the health care system like a sword of Damocles, urging doctors to do everything remotely beneficial to each patient. With professional reputations on the line, and with self-interest also urging a maximum of care, it is no wonder that our health resources are overcommitted to those "in the system," while many outside the system cannot get even basic medical care. Similarly, our system of myriad individual insurance companies plus the paperwork demands of Medicare and Medicaid cost as much as 24 cents out of every health dollar according to some estimates. No other health care system creates as many pieces of paper

per treatment or comes close to draining as much from direct patient care as does the United States. We spend more on health care bureaucracy than many nations spend on their whole health care system.

A fourth inefficiency in our health care delivery system is an excess supply of doctors, hospitals, and technology. While some thoughtful people dispute a physician surplus, The Graduate Medical Education National Advisory Committee, the official body which estimates physician need for Health and Human Services, believes that we currently have a surplus of 40,000 physicians and that, by the year 2000, we will have 140,000 surplus physicians. The estimates of surplus hospital beds range between 200,000 and 400,000 and there is strong evidence that many of the people in a hospital bed do not really need to be there. The American Hospital Association will admit that the occupancy ratio of American hospitals is only 64 percent, but they vociferously claim that the marginal cost of an empty bed is small. For an individual hospital that may be true, but for the nation the unused capacity translates to approximately 1,000 unnecessary hospitals, which is a phenomenal expense and a wasteful allocation of limited resources.

Then there is the tremendous duplication of expensive medical technology. Almost every hospital strives to be a "full service" hospital. This is partly driven by institutional chauvinism and partly due to the need to attract physicians to that hospital.

A fifth reason we misdirect our health resources lies in the strengths and weaknesses of American culture. Culture is a powerful and little discussed factor underlying various countries' health delivery systems. Rudolph Klein, an English health economist, observed that Great Britain has an "original sin" society where people are much more ready to accept sickness as part of life. When their doctor says, "There is nothing I can do," they are accepting of that judgment. He contrasts Americans who have a "perfectibility of man" society wherein we are much less accepting and will spend considerable resources to explore even small chances of recovery. Seldom do American doctors say, "There is nothing I can do."

Related to this is our cultural taboo of death and dying. No other health care system spends as disproportionately on the elderly or on the dying process. Every day, at multiple hospitals across America, people are brought back from death by miracle machines—so they can die again later, after days of horribly expensive and degrading "living." The often-cited fact that 30 percent of Medicare goes into the last year of life is dramatic, but somewhat overblown. Physicians point out correctly that we never know when the last year of life will begin.

This leads us to the sixth, and most important, reason we do not get value from our health policies: no one sets priorities. There is no system of comparing alternate strategies. We spend incredible sums in an intensive care unit on someone whom we did not bother to screen for hypertension. We fly premature babies in helicopters to expensive neonatal care units—

born to women who could not get even one prenatal exam. Ten percent of the population yearly accounts for 70 percent of the total health expenditure.

There is an illusion in America that we can pay for everything and that to deny some level of health care would be to "ration medicine." Yet every day it becomes clearer that we cannot cover everyone with all the health care our ingenious society has invented. The miracles of medicine are multiplying faster than our economy, yet we refuse to admit that we shall have to set limits and compare one health care alternative with another. We have not admitted to ourselves that we cannot (as Victor Fuchs puts it) give "presidential health care to all Americans." Once we admit to ourselves that we cannot give everything to everybody we will painfully start to prioritize our health care spending: we will start asking "How do we buy the most health for our limited dollars?"

❖ The Brave New World of Health Care

We are careening rapidly into a brave new world of health care. The basic defining characteristic of this brave new world of health care is that we have invented more beneficial medicine than we as a society can afford to pay for. Infinite medical needs have run smack into finite resources.

We are thus left, in this new and strange world, with the task of deciding not what is "beneficial" to a patient (which is a medical decision) but what is "appropriate" or "cost effective" (which is partly a socioeconomic and a fairness decision). We shall have to balance quality of life with quantity of life, costs and benefits, preventive medicine versus curative medicine. We are, unfortunately but realistically, into prioritizing medicine. Medicine will never be the same.

Tonsils, vermiform, appendices, uvulas, even ovaries are sacrificed because it is the fashion to get them cut out, and because the operations are highly profitable.
—George Bernard Shaw

Once we admit that we cannot pay for everything, we must ask ourselves not what does a patient need, but how do we spend our resources to buy the maximum health for the largest number of citizens. This will inevitably impinge on a physician's judgment on what is the best medical treatment for an individual patient; when and where to admit patients to hospitals and when to discharge; under what conditions and symptoms are certain diagnostic or therapeutic procedures appropriate; what prescriptions are appropriate under certain circumstances. It is the world of DRG writ large.

❖ Solutions

The often-cited "solutions" to the health care cost crisis are valid and important to accomplish. They will not of themselves bring spending under control, but they are part of the answer.

1. We must reform the tort law to give more protection to physicians, hospitals, and other health providers. We can develop no-fault compensation systems and limit pain and suffering damages.
2. We must, as a society, stop training so many doctors and lawyers. Similarly, we must stop training so many medical specialists. We should bring in fewer immigrant doctors.
3. We must close some of our redundant, overbuilt hospitals; we should close surplus beds within other hospitals. We should close some cost-inefficient intensive care units and regionalize some high technology medicine.
4. We can forbid doctors from owning their diagnostic facilities; we can maximize generic drugs. We can initiate health data commissions so that consumers have adequate information and data on the past performance of individual hospitals and physicians.
5. We can pass living will legislation and promote its use, use "no code," and form hospices.
6. We can push for a "smoke free" society. We can tax cigarettes and alcohol, not at luxury tax rates but at rates appropriate for killer drugs.
7. We can push for alternative delivery systems; move more to "managed care"; license para-professionals; and more fully develop pre-admission screening.
8. We can promote immunization.
9. Most important of all, we can and must recognize that our medical destiny lies mainly in our own hands. We can encourage health education and health promotion. We can move from health care to self-care. We can teach and encourage patients to be more efficient consumers.
10. We can educate Americans to be more realistic about their expectations as to the kind of care they deserve.
11. Employers and health care purchasers can join together and develop cost management systems that define a health-care package and judge its quality. They can use their combined purchasing power to get the lowest costs from producers. Similarly, states and the federal government can use their buying power to purchase health care efficiently. We can stop mandating by law so many services in our health insurance benefits.
12. But all this is not enough. After we do all these things, and more unmentioned, we must ultimately develop a concept of "appropri-

ate care" or some sort of "cost effective" medicine. As Dan
Callahan has said:

> the problem lies in our success rather than in our failures,
> our goals rather than our means, our ideals rather than our
> defects.

How do we move from a yardstick that delivers all health care that may
be remotely "beneficial" to the new realistic world of "appropriate care?"

❖ Appropriate Health Care

We must develop new yardsticks, new methods of delivering
health care which is caring and just, but will in certain instances be less than is
technically available. This will be difficult in the abstract and even more difficult in the real world of media and public policy. It will require a new level of
understanding on the part of the American public (and the media).

Death and Dying

I think it is desperately important to discuss much more can-
didly and openly the subject of death and dying. We treat death as if it were
optional. People talk about the right to die, as if we have the right to refuse
to die. Shakespeare says, "We all owe God a death." Once we stop treating
death as an enemy and recognize it as an inevitability, we can save massive
resources. Today patients with massive strokes are saved from death but live
for years in a comatose state. Others with metastatic cancer are subject to
myriad studies and therapies that add little to their longevity. I think we
must look rationally at the phenomenal amount of resources we spend on
the last few weeks of people's lives only to prolong suffering.

Age as a Consideration in the Delivery of Health Care

I suggest America doesn't need any more age-based benefit
programs. Our programs should be based on need rather than age, which
leads me into Medicare, an ultimate sacred cow. But when Medicare was
passed in 1965, the elderly were disproportionately poor. There was every
good reason for Congress to vote for Medicare then. But the elderly are no
longer disproportionately poor. In 1970, 23 percent of the elderly were poor
and 12 percent of the kids were poor. Today, 12 percent of the elderly are
poor and 23 percent of the kids are poor. You no longer have those same reasons. And yet we give 600,000 millionaires Medicare and we are closing
well-baby clinics. We have socialized much of the cost of health care to the
elderly while ignoring needy kids.

I believe that we shall inevitably have to recognize age as a valid ethical
consideration in the delivery of medical care. Is it not only fair, but desirable,

to have a different level of care for a 10-year-old than for someone who is 100? Should not public policy recognize that some people have far more statistical years ahead of them than others? In rationing scarce resources, age is an ethical and valid consideration.

We Must Better Evaluate and Control Our Technologies

Public policy defines medical technology to connote a drug, device, or medical or surgical procedure used in medical care. This is an admittedly broad definition, but includes the detection, prevention, and treatment of disease. It includes both drugs and medical devices. Let us examine three categories of medical technology.

1. *There are wasteful technologies and wasteful uses of technologies.*

There are some medical technologies that have been judged useless—but not many. The Wasserman test for syphilis was used 40 years before it was discovered to identify unaffected people as carriers 50 percent of the time. This, then, was an ineffective technology, though it was one that was widely used. Another example would be gastric freezing to treat peptic ulcers; it was largely used in the late 1950s and early 1960s, until a study showed that there was no real effectiveness to it.

I would put the artificial heart program in this first category; that even if it is a technological success it will be a public policy failure. The artificial heart will not replace any other treatment that could be dropped once the artificial heart is developed. There is no conceivable way it could meet the test of "cost effectiveness."

We simply cannot continue with the illusion that we can spend any amount of money as long as a life is at stake. It is corrupting our perspective and focusing too much on the individual and not enough on the total societal needs.

2. *There are other technologies that are cost effective, but we have too many of them in too many places.*

Heart transplants will serve as a good example. A study published in the *Journal of the American Medical Association* estimated that only between 19 and 48 transplant programs are needed to perform an optimum number of heart transplants. By those figures, America already has three or four times the number of heart transplant centers as are needed. Duplicating the capacity of existing facilities clearly does not optimize the use of limited health dollars. It also doesn't maximize the delivery of health to our patients: the evidence is very clear that the more cases a facility handles, the better it gets at it, and the lower the risk of mortality.

3. *The toughest question, however, is: Most technologies have some benefit; do they have enough benefit to meet what Victor Fuchs calls the "flat of the curve" medicine? In this, he points out that almost all medical procedures have some benefit, but at some point we get into an area where the benefit is*

only marginal. In other words, he argues that some of our health dollars buy a lot of health, but in other areas, when our health care dollars are spent in the "flat of the curve," they only buy marginal amounts of health. The real question is: "How do we develop ways to be cost effective?"

It isn't that these technologies are not beneficial. The problem is that they cause a "blockage function," that is, they fail to meet the test of relative value: how much good for how many. Too many dollars that could buy much more health in the basic health care area are being drained off by high-technology medicine.

Prioritizing Health Care

If our publicly funded programs can't pay for everything that health care providers can deliver, we have to decide what to pay for and what not to pay for. I suggest that one of the major issues of the 1990s will be defining what is an "adequate level of health care." We will not be able to deliver all "beneficial care"; we must start to ask when are the marginal benefits equal to the marginal costs.

Oregon gave us a glimpse of the future when it decided not to fund transplants under its Medicaid program, but to spend the money instead on basic health care for the people currently outside the health care system.

Oregon, like every other state, previously rationed people by excluding them from the system. Anyone in Oregon who made more than $7,800 a year for a family of four wasn't eligible for Medicaid. Oregon became the first state to cover 100 percent of people under the poverty line and the price they paid for this was to refuse to fund a select number of high-cost, high-technology procedures. They shifted from rationing people out of the system to prioritizing procedures but covering all of the poor.

Oregon has set up a health services commission made up of providers and consumers which sets priorities in services and procedures, based on the respective procedures' benefit to the population. The commission is charged with looking at all the information available and prioritizing all health care, starting with the most important and moving down to less important ones. It is better, Oregon argues, to ration some limited list of high-technology procedures rather than rationing people out of the system. The debate is shifted from who is covered to what is covered.

1. *How do we prioritize medicine?*

   ❖ Reform tort law.
   ❖ Move from health care to self-care.
   ❖ Teach and encourage patients to be effective consumers.
   ❖ Educate Americans to be realistic about their expectations.
   ❖ Admit that we can't do everything to everybody.
   ❖ Stop training too many doctors and lawyers.

- ❖ Close hospitals, close beds in other hospitals, close some intensive care units, and regionalize high technology.
- ❖ Maximize generic drugs.
- ❖ Tax cigarettes and alcohol, form hospices, and promote immunizations.
- ❖ Push for a smoke-free society. Pass living will legislation, use no code.
- ❖ License paraprofessionals.
- ❖ Push for alternative delivery systems.
- ❖ Develop a one-payer system.
- ❖ Develop an ethic of restraint and a concept of "appropriate care" and "cost-effective medicine."

As we move into prioritizing health care, we, like every other country, will inevitably decide that the first priority is basic health care for all our citizens. Other countries wrestling with these priorities have emphasized public health, preventive care, and basic health care.

After this, the going gets tougher. Generally in prioritizing health care, there are two general yardsticks: increased life expectancy and improved quality of life.

This is the easy part. Like so many other things, the devil is in the detail. Oregon has started down the road, in a rare and unusual display of political courage. Scholars are starting to think seriously about how these decisions are made. We have started down the painful road of health-care prioritization and I suggest there will be no turning back.

2. Role of physicians

Society cannot set priorities and maximize limited dollars without the help of doctors.

Physicians correctly ask, "Does this turn me into a double agent?" Does it interfere with their sworn duty to their patient?

It must be understood that doctors wear more than one hat. A doctor at a patient's bedside must be 100 percent the patient's advocate. But that bedside/patient advocate role does not preclude doctors in different circumstances from helping society to set general priorities. They can serve a different role in a committee of the medical society advising on priorities than they serve when they have an actual patient.

Priorities must be set and we must have the expertise and experience of physicians to help accomplish this task.

3. Two-tiered system

Such a proposal will give us a two-tiered system. True. But we already have a two-tiered system. Every European system of health care has a two-tiered system. If you have money in Great Britain and don't want the National Health Service, you go to Harley Street. Wealthy Europeans go to England or the United States.

The ethical test of a fair and just health-care system cannot be that it has only one tier. We have a two-tier system in this country (and all others) for every social good. We pay for public schools but not for private schools. We give people food stamps but not unlimited food. We give people public housing but don't buy them a house. We provide police protection but not burglar alarms or security guards.

It is reflective of America's strong belief in egalitarianism that we worry about a "two-tiered system." But it presently is counterproductive to the true interest of poor people. The immediate challenge of our nation ought to be to get good primary health care to all its citizens. We should push to ensure that this basic health package is as generous as possible. But, inevitably, it will be a two- or three-tiered system.

❖ Summary

We are rapidly entering into a brave new world of health care. Infinite medical demands have run smack into finite resources. We can't pay for everything but we can spend our limited resources in a much more health-effective way.

We have no other alternative but to devise systems that give maximum health to our society with our limited resources.

It is time to begin this process.

❖ About the Author

Richard D. Lamm, L.L.B., directs the Center for Public Policy and Contemporary Issues at the University of Denver; he was Governor of Colorado 1975–1987.

❖ Chapter 4
The Critical Role
of Nurses

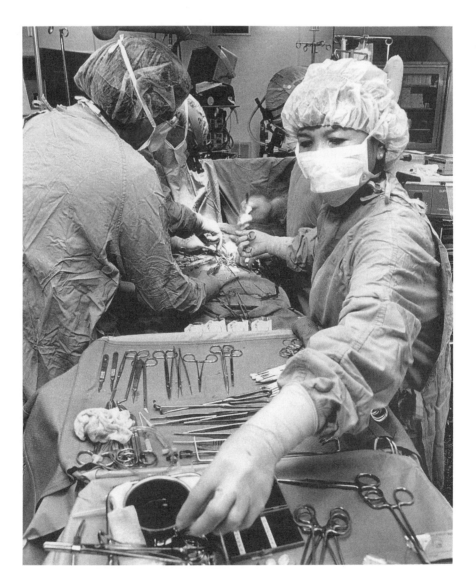

Nurses outnumber doctors, dentists, and every other group of health professionals in the United States. They are responsible for a major proportion of patient care, and the issues that surround this profession have important implications for every health care delivery setting in the nation and for national health policy as well.

In the past 15 years, nursing has undergone a major transition. Some call it a revolution. Enormous changes in modes of patient care have brought the nurse into direct application of complex health care technologies. Nursing responsibilities have also been affected by policy changes in the hospital setting, which have led to a greater proportion of acutely and severely ill patients and of surgical patients in the hospital. The aging of the population, with a greater need for long-term care, has also affected nursing. New nurse specialists have increased in number; among them are nurse practitioners, who have obtained advanced clinical training for treating patients with common health problems in ambulatory settings, and clinical nurse specialists who may be placed in a variety of inpatient settings, including intensive care units. Other areas of expanded opportunities and responsibilities for nurses include long-term care nursing, home care nursing, nursing anesthesia, and nurse midwifery. While these changes mean increased emotional and physical demands on nurses, they have also opened new doors.

Despite many positive developments, there is another side to current trends. Nurses' salaries have not kept pace with the increased skills required for the added responsibilities. Also, working conditions are some of the most stressful anywhere, with everyday exposure to illness; long, inconvenient hours; inflexibility of schedules; and inadequate support staff. Nurses continue to experience a lack of autonomy, with many key decisions affecting their work made by doctors and hospital administrators. They have responded to these pressures in different ways. For the first time, many are becoming active in the health policy arena, and they are working to widen the scope of control over work and career mobility.

A persistent problem related to the nursing work force is the issue of a "nursing shortage." Despite the fact that there are more nurses today per capita than ever before, the demand has risen steadily in relation to population—one employed nurse for every 142 Americans. There are over 2 million registered nurses in the United States today; approximately 80 percent are employed at any one time, and approximately 66 percent of these nurses work in hospitals. Nurses' salaries make up approximately one-third of a hospital's expenses.

Nursing schools, of which there are 1,451 in the nation, report difficulty in attracting sufficient qualified applicants. Many nurses opt to leave their profession for family reasons or because they want to seek higher paid employment. Employers complain that the current pool of nurses is not adequate for their needs, and the policy literature on the nursing profession has continued to focus on this issue for the past 25 years.

Charlene Harrington and her colleagues on the Commission on Health Care Policy of the American Academy of Nursing present recommendations for a comprehensive national health program that would help to ensure universal access to health care, improved quality of care, and greater cost control. They identify a number of agenda items that policymakers must address in the near future: a shortage of primary care practitioners, including primary care nurses; maldistribution of health care providers; discrimination against nurses; inadequate reimbursement levels; lack of cultural diversity among nurses; and many others. The authors contend that health care services will not be adequate in quantity or quality in the United States until these critical issues are addressed.

In "Charting the Future of Hospital Nursing," Linda H. Aiken, a leading health policy analyst, examines the question of supply and demand. She tackles a number of enigmas. For example, with nursing a growing field and with the ratio of nurses to patients continuing to increase, why is enrollment in nursing schools down, job turnover high, and job dissatisfaction a major factor? This is happening, she points out, at a time when hospitals are undertaking elaborate restructuring of their labor mix, including downsizing of support staff, and when patient length of stay is being cut drastically. For these and other reasons, hospital nurses spend a great deal of time on administrative, clerical, and housekeeping tasks. Dr. Aiken offers a perceptive analysis of the changing role of nurses and sorts out a number of the seeming contradictions experienced by the profession. She discusses the flaws in hospital business and management practices that may interfere with the nurse-patient relationship, and she makes recommendations for restructuring the profession with specialized career tracks to better meet the clinical challenges nurses face in today's hospital settings.

Claire M. Fagin addresses a problem that has long been identified by nurses as a barrier to full realization of their potential to contribute to patient care. This is the lack of collaborative working relationships between physicians and nurses. A long-time participant in the effort to forge a more effective role for nurses in all health care settings, Dr. Fagin contends that in today's world of high technology and complex health care regimens, institutions that educate and employ nurses and doctors must reevaluate the doctor-nurse relationship and assess the value of making it a more collaborative one. She addresses the compelling reasons to promote collaboration as well as the barriers to more effective interdependence, and she cites pertinent research on the subject.

❖ Health Care Access: Problems and Policy Recommendations

Charlene Harrington, Suzanne Lee Feetham,
Patricia A. Moccia, and Gloria R. Smith

❖ Access Problems Related to Health Personnel

Access to needed health care personnel is a critical concern that needs to be resolved through public policy changes. In the United States, the education and training of health professionals and other health personnel is largely a private function carried out by universities and colleges in an unplanned and unregulated fashion. Standards for the education and training of health personnel are largely established by professional organizations and influenced by private accrediting organizations. The distribution and practice of health personnel are functions of private market supply and demand.

In spite of the largely private system for health professionals, the U.S. government is playing an increasingly important monitoring role. State governments establish licensing procedures for health professionals and personnel based on provider standards and monitor the behavior of professionals relative to these licenses. State governments certify provider participation in the Medicaid program and also establish Medicaid reimbursement rates for health professionals. The federal government certifies participation of health professionals in Medicare and establishes reimbursement rates for the program. Private insurers and health maintenance organizations (HMOs) are also active in monitoring quality and utilization patterns and using the information for selecting providers to participate in their programs.

Shortages of Primary Care Practitioners

The United States is in a unique position relative to the supply of health personnel. The supply of physicians has grown from 1.6 per 1,000 population in 1970 to 2.4 per 1,000 in 1990. Projections are for 2.6 physicians per 1,000 population by the year 2000. As noted above, the increases in overall physician supply and the number of specialists are fueling the overall increases in health care costs.

At the same time the United States is reporting an oversupply of physician specialists, there is a shortage of primary care practitioners. General practitioners (GPs), family physicians (FPs), general pediatricians, obstetricians, and general internists are frequently referred to as primary care practitioners. Nurse practitioners, physicians' assistants, and nurse midwives also are important primary care practitioners. Access to primary care practitioners is believed to be associated with improved health care outcomes, reduced use of emergency rooms, and reduced morbidity. Other studies show that patients losing access to primary care decline in health status and those without care have higher risk for hypertension and other problems.

With a suddeness that surprised even long-time observers of cyclic shortages of nurses, the demand for registered nurses is outstripping the supply, and the factors that add up to this shortage suggest that there is no quick solution to the problem.
—John K. Iglehart

GPs and FPs represented only 19 percent of all professionally active physicians in 1970 and only 13 percent in 1988. The supply of GPs declined from 73,000 in 1963 to 25,000 in 1986, and 60 percent were over the age of 55. The proportion of physicians serving the geriatric population is not expected to keep pace with demand. An estimated 40,000 to 47,000 primary care practitioner full-time equivalents (or 160,000 to 188,000 individuals) will be needed in 2020 to meet the demand for the care of the aged population. These trends raise concern about the adequacy of the future supply of key primary care providers.

The nurse practitioner (NP) specialty developed in the 1960s in response to the shortage of physicians, as did the nurse midwife specialty in the 1920s (as part of the Frontier Nursing Service). Numerous studies show the value of NPs and certified nurse midwives (CNMs) as providers of primary care. Clinical nurse specialists (CNSs), as the newest providers, assess health status and illness conditions and assist clients through direct care or coordination of care involving other health care professionals. Gerontological nurse practitioners (GNPs) and gerontological clinical nurse specialists (GCNSs) are trained to care for the aged population. Certified registered nurse anesthetists (CRNAs) are critical providers for anesthesia services throughout the country, where they provide 65 percent of all anesthetics. CRNAs are the sole anesthesia providers in 85 percent of rural hospitals, and they ensure access to obstetrical, surgical, and trauma services and clinical education programs. All these nurses in advanced practice play valuable roles in providing care to the general population as well as to underserved population groups.

The projected growth in the number of elderly people will double by the year 2000, exacerbating the shortages of primary care providers. There is a paucity of NPs and CNSs in nursing homes and long-term care. Current projections indicate a slow growth in the supply of nurses and an increasing inability to meet the health care needs of the elderly and disabled populations. The provision of physician services to nursing home patients is often noted as a major problem in long-term care. Especially in inner cities, physicians willing to visit nursing home patients are difficult to find. Primary care physicians, even in communities with high physician-to-population ratios, are no more likely to participate in nursing home care than those in undersupplied areas. These facts suggest that an increase in the physician supply is unlikely to solve the physician shortage problem in long-term care.

A high priority should be given to the training of nurses in advanced practice as primary care practitioners. These practitioners require less training time than physicians (two years in a master's degree program compared with five years for medical school and internship and additional residency training). Although the training costs for nurses in advanced practice are high, the training costs are significantly less than for physicians. Expanding the number of nurses in advanced practice is the most efficient strategy for ensuring enough primary care practitioners to match the demand for basic services for all Americans. In fact, the current utilization of nurses in advanced practice in the United States is estimated to cost between $6.4 and $8.75 billion in 1991 dollars. Efforts to shift the number of physician specialists to general practice, family practice, pediatrics, and obstetrics are also needed.

❖ **Recommendation:** Match supply and demand for access to basic health care services by expanding the number of nurses in advanced practice, general practitioners, and other primary care practitioners.

Maldistribution of Practitioners in Rural and Inner City Areas   Physicians, nurses, and other health professionals are not evenly distributed across the states. The national ratio of nonfederal physicians is 2.3 per 1,000 population. Ratios in individual states, however, range from a low of 1.4 in Mississippi to a high of 3.5 in Maryland. Because of these shortages, 16 million people live in 1,944 primary-care health manpower shortage areas (HMSAs) in both urban and rural areas. An estimated additional 4,104 primary care providers are needed to remove these designations.

The supply of physicians, nurses, and other health providers in rural areas is increasing but still inadequate. Rural areas have 50 percent fewer physicians providing patient care than urban areas (0.9 to 2.2 per 1,000 residents in 1985). In counties with fewer than 10,000 residents, there are only 0.5 physicians for every 1,000 persons. Over 100 U.S. counties have no practicing physicians at all. Of all rural residents, 29 percent live in HMSAs compared with 9 percent of urban residents. The future supply of primary care physicians is in jeopardy and the projected shortages are expected to occur disproportionately in small rural areas. The shortages can be expected to continue because medical school graduates are increasingly expressing a reluctance to choose rural practice and primary care.

Nurses in advanced practice improve the accessibility of basic primary care services, especially for inner city and rural populations. About 67 percent of NPs practice in communities of 50,000 or more. In addition, 49 percent of CNSs provide services to inner city racial and ethnic minority groups, and 47 percent provide services to groups in poverty. Significant percentages of NPs and CNSs practice in ambulatory, community, and public health centers where poor and elderly persons from minority groups often receive health care. About 30 percent of NPs and 15 percent of CNSs are employed in ambulatory settings. Community and public health clinics make up 30 percent of employment sites for NPs and 11 percent for CNSs.

Nurses in advanced practice are credited with improving the geographic distribution of primary care because many of them are willing to locate in underserved rural areas. Approximately 31 percent of NPs practice in areas with populations of 1,000 to 50,000 and 2 percent in areas with populations of less than 1,000. Of CNSs, 27 percent work with rural groups and 57 percent with the elderly. NPs and physician assistants (PAs) are more likely than physicians to locate outside metropolitan areas and to view their location choices as permanent. Thus, nurses in advanced practice reduce inequities in primary care distribution and geographic location. Efforts to increase the number of nurses in advanced practice can substantially improve access to people in rural areas.

The shortage of nurses in rural areas is growing. The proportion of NPs in rural areas decreased slightly (from 18 percent to 15.8 percent) between 1984 and 1988. The number of CNMs practicing in communities of fewer than 50,000 residents also decreased by over 10 percent between 1982 and 1987. Furthermore, the Office of Technology Assessment (OTA) reports that the overall number of registered nurses (RNs) working in rural areas declined from 20 percent in 1980 to 17 percent in 1988. The OTA predicts that the current national shortages of primary care practitioners (including RNs, NPs, and PAs) will have a disproportionately negative effect on small rural communities.

❖ **Recommendation:** Develop public policies to stimulate professional service and expand the supply of primary care practitioners in underserved areas.

Appropriate High Quality Services

There is growing evidence that primary care practitioner services, and particularly nurses in advanced practice, can result in less costly utilization patterns and overall costs as well as improved quality of care. Nurse midwives provide lower cost deliveries with fewer caesarean sections. If more primary care practitioners were available for obstetrical care, the caesarean section rate could be reduced. Improved primary care management could also prevent and manage some of the problems that lead to other unnecessary procedures and surgeries.

Individuals, families, and communities increasingly require primary care services including health maintenance, personal assistance, chronic disease management, recognition of acute or exacerbating chronic conditions, ongoing accurate and comprehensive health assessment, appropriate referral to various team members, medication management and review, coordination of daily services, family and patient education, and counseling. Primary care practitioners, particularly nurses in advanced practice, are trained to provide these services as well as health promotion and disease prevention. For example, midwives are oriented toward childbirth as a natural process; and midwives and nurse anesthetists are oriented to care, comfort, use of low-technology interventions, and effective communication. Fagin recently confirmed that the evidence on the effectiveness of nurses in advanced practice is excellent in terms of quality of care. OTA concluded that primary care NPs could satisfy 50 to 90 percent of the ambulatory care needs of the population. Thus, the number of primary care practitioners should be expanded to provide the types of services most needed by the population, to reduce the overall cost of health services, and to improve the quality of care.

Nurses in advanced practice can also address the poor quality of care received by the 1.5 million residents in 16,000 nursing homes, where as many as 33 percent of homes operate at substandard levels. Higher staffing levels in nursing homes are associated with higher quality of nursing care and reduced hospitalization. General nurse practitioners in nursing homes also reduce the use of hospital services. Expanded geriatric services are needed for nursing home patients. Several teaching nursing home projects show the positive relationship between the education and training of nurses and high quality of care. Recognizing this need, Congress passed legislation to expand the role of advanced practice nurses in nursing homes in 1989 and 1990. Greater financial support for professional and primary care services is needed to ensure high quality long-term care. The quality-of-care goal is to improve health outcomes for individuals and families and especially for people in underserved groups.

❖ **Recommendation:** Expand the number of primary care practitioners to provide the types of services that reduce the overall cost of health care and improve the quality of care.

Barriers to Practice

Barriers to primary care practice for primary care practitioners including nurses, PAs, therapists, and others must be removed if shortages and maldistribution problems are to be solved. For example, some states have adopted restrictions to practice that limit nurses in advanced practice and other health care providers in terms of the allowed scope of practice and professional autonomy. These restrictive practices are promoted by professional organizations that want to protect the economic interests of their members.

State rules that mandate the supervision of health professionals by physicians should be changed to encourage the collaboration of physicians with all other health personnel.

❖ **Recommendation:** Identify and eliminate barriers to practice for nurses in advanced practice and other health professionals at the state and federal levels through legislative action.

Discrimination

Facilities and providers of Medicare and Medicaid services must meet federal Conditions of Participation. These Conditions give hospitals and other facilities discretion in staff membership and clinical privileges for physicians and other practitioners as well. Many hospitals discriminate against nurses in advanced practice in terms of staff membership and clinical privileges because nonphysicians are viewed as competitors of physicians. A good example of an anticompetitive practice clause was adopted by the Council of the District of Columbia in their licensure act in 1983. The Federal Conditions of Participation should be changed to prohibit facility discrimination against nurses in advanced practice as a class. This would ensure greater access to care, particularly for NPs, CNSs, CNMs, and CRNAs in rural and inner city areas.

Several policy changes have been made recently to encourage the use of nurses in advanced practice, but many of these policies still have clauses that limit access to nursing services. In the Omnibus Budget Reconciliation Act (OBRA) 1989, the services of NPs were authorized for payment under Medicare in nursing homes when performed within the scope of state law and in collaboration with a physician. NPs and CNSs are allowed to certify and recertify the medical necessity for skilled nursing services under Medicare and to supervise the medical care of nursing home residents. Unfortunately, OBRA 1990 requires that a physician admit a resident to a nursing home even though care may be provided by NPs or CNSs. Similar hospital rules that require that a physician conduct admitting histories and physicals are barriers that can affect patient outcomes. These requirements are outmoded because nurses in advanced practice are trained to conduct admitting histories and physicals. Medicare and Medicaid rules should be revised not only to allow admitting privileges for nurses in advanced practice in all institutional settings, but also to allow advanced practice nurses to conduct the admitting history and physical. The rules should state that practitioners (not physicians) with admitting and clinical privileges may carry out all admitting activities.

❖ **Recommendation:** Prohibit discrimination against primary care practitioners by institutional and ambulatory care providers and institute monitoring of such practices on a regular basis.

Reimbursement Reform

The greatest barrier to primary care practice is that of inadequate reimbursement levels. Historically, physicians in primary care practice have received lower payment levels than specialty physicians. The imbalance in reimbursement rates across types of physicians and nonphysicians is a concern of policymakers. The Physician Payment Review Commission was established by Congress in 1986 to address the issues of payment reform. Major changes in Medicare reimbursement rate structures and the institution of a schedule were recommended by the Commission and passed by Congress.

The OTA states that reimbursement reform would dramatically increase the number of nurses in advanced practice by allowing them to establish fee-for-service practices. With greater autonomy, nurses in advanced practice could provide the full range of services for which they are trained and licensed. Other goals to be sought are access to continuing education and improved acceptance by physicians.

Reimbursement reform must provide adequate payment levels for services provided in nursing homes. Many reasons are given for staff shortages in nursing homes, including the lack of advancement opportunity and professional isolation. The greatest problem, however, is the artificially and inequitably low wage and benefit structure. Reimbursement reform is also important as a stimulus to increase the numbers of NPs and CNSs in gerontological subspecialties.

One important federal policy change needed is to allow direct reimbursement for services delivered by nurses in advanced practice from both Medicare and Medicaid. Current policies are confusing and restrictive. Although the role of NPs and CNSs has been expanded and clarified, they are not authorized to receive direct Medicare reimbursement unless practicing in rural settings. The limited direct reimbursement policy creates inequities for different types of nurses in advanced practice in various settings. These limitations should be removed from the Medicare program for all nurses in advanced practice in all types of health care settings.

Federal Medicaid program guidelines mandate the coverage and payment of nurse midwives, certified pediatric nurse practitioners, and certified family nurse practitioners, but does not mandate the coverage of all NPs, CNSs, and CRNA services. Several states have already changed their Medicaid payment and coverage policies for nurses in advanced practice, as in New Hampshire, particularly to utilize NPs in well child care, prenatal care clinics, and family planning clinics. Washington has established NP and CNM providers in maternal service clinics and increased the deliveries by these clinics. The fact that other states have not made such changes creates substantial inequities in access across states. If Medicaid mandated coverage for all nurses in advanced practice and direct payment, this change would result in improved access to needed primary care practitioners.

Reimbursement reform should include adoption of the principle of reimbursement based on services delivered rather than on which provider delivers the services. The Physician Payment Review Commission (PPRC) recently reviewed payment levels for nonphysician practitioners and recommended that for the same services they should receive the same reimbursement as physicians minus the differential costs of malpractice and overhead. These recommendations are now being considered by Congress and should be given priority for passage. Similar policies are needed for the Medicaid program. States should set reimbursement rates on the basis of the services provided rather than on the type of practitioner providing the services. Medicaid programs vary in how they establish rates, but this policy should be established as a general principle at the federal level. Currently, 19 states pay NPs at 100 percent of the physician rate. In Washington, where this policy was recently adopted, practitioners were recruited from the program and access to prenatal care and deliveries of infants was expanded. Differential fees based on the type of provider create disincentives for employers to utilize some types of providers, particularly nurses who primarily practice as employees of health facilities. Lower payment rates can discourage nurses in advanced practice from providing services to underserved population groups.

❖ **Recommendation:** Adopt reimbursement reforms that ensure standard fees for specific procedures regardless of provider type and that mandate payment for primary care practitioner services by public and private programs in all health care settings.

Incentives to Train Primary Care Practitioners

The Medicare program currently provides funding to hospitals for graduate medical education programs. These funds have been utilized by hospitals to develop residency programs. Unfortunately, many residency programs train specialists in subspecialty areas that are oversupplied with physicians. One approach would be to target Medicare funds to programs that train specified primary care practitioners. Another alternative is to alter the payment formula to give greater resources to programs that train primary care specialists. Preference should also be given to programs that emphasize the preparation of practitioners who are from low-income and minority groups and are willing to work in underserved areas and with vulnerable population groups.

Legislation should be passed to implement mandated requirements or incentive payments for Medicare graduate education training funds for primary care. In addition, Medicare training funds should be broadened to include all types of primary care practitioners rather than physicians alone. Medicare should include support for the training of nurses in advanced practice, physical therapists, psychologists, social workers, and other health personnel who provide primary and basic services to Medicare beneficiaries. Currently, Medicare is not allowed to fund such programs in hospitals, but a demonstration program was established by Congress to test this approach. Five projects were funded by Health Care Financing Administration (HCFA) and Health Resources Services Administration (HRSA) in 1989 to conduct clinical training for master's or doctoral nursing students. The outcomes of these projects show increased recruitment rates and lower turnover rates. This demonstration program should be made a regular component of Medicare graduate education funding for the training of primary care nurse practitioners.

❖ **Recommendation:** Redirect Medicare training funds from specialty training to focus on the training of primary care practitioners, including nurses in advanced practice.

Incentives for Practice in Underserved Service Areas

Other public policy changes have been made to improve the supply of primary care workers. The recent Medicare payment changes recommended by the PPRC and adopted by Congress will increase payments to primary health care physicians, and Medicare bonuses for physicians delivering primary care in rural HMSAs can ease the financial burden for practitioners. The PPRC recommends that nurses practicing in rural areas also receive the bonus payment. The question is whether the current 10 percent bonus rate is adequate to retain rural practitioners. The OTA recommends a study of this question and adjustments as necessary to ensure that the rural practice payment incentive is adequate.

In addition to the bonuses provided by Medicare, state Medicaid programs should offer special reimbursement bonuses for practitioners working in underserved rural and urban areas. Tying state Medicaid practitioner reimbursement rates to the new Medicare payment system would also improve access to care for underserved populations. Medicaid programs should continue to provide bonus payments for providers that have a "disproportionate share" of Medicaid and uninsured clients. Studies of innovative approaches to encouraging more practitioners and providers to offer services to Medicaid recipients and low-income clients are needed and must be supported by federal and state funds.

The National Health Service Corps is a public program designed to address the problems of maldistribution of health professionals in HMSAs. This program recruits and places health care professionals in federally designated shortage areas throughout the United States and its territories. The program needs about 4,400 primary care practitioners (physicians, nurse practitioners, physician assistants, and certified nurse midwives) and about 3,600 dentists, and mental health professionals should be expanded particularly for nurses in advanced practice, mental health professionals, and physician assistants. Priority should be given to health professional students from low-income, minority, and rural backgrounds.

Other new approaches are needed to assist primary care practitioners, particularly those who are from minority groups, in establishing practices and community centers in underserved areas. For example, programs by the U.S. Small Business Administration could assist with technical support and funding (either loans or start-up funds) for establishing practices and community centers in underserved areas. Funds for start-up health maintenance organizations and innovative community-based programs in underserved areas would also be valuable. Special reimbursement from Medicaid and Medicare and tax incentives for such programs in underserved areas would encourage practitioners.

❖ **Recommendation:** Develop financial incentives that encourage higher payment rates for practitioners in underserved areas and establish new practices and community programs for underserved population groups (such as aged, disabled, AIDS/HIV, and minority groups).

Training Programs for Minority Groups and Special Areas

Members of minority groups, particularly African-American, Hispanic, and native American populations, are seriously underrepresented among health professionals. Among physician graduates in 1989, only 5 percent were African-American, 5.5 percent were Hispanic, and 8.3 percent were Asian. Minority group members are particularly underrepresented in the nursing profession. Major efforts are needed to recruit and train students from all racial, ethnic, and cultural minority groups in all health professions. These students often have greater financial need for loans and support than white students. Special federal and state financial support programs are needed for minority students.

Historically, efforts to expand nurse supply have had negative effects on wages and resulted in cyclical shortages. In spite of this concern, federal support for nurse training programs is needed in three areas: (1) for nurses in advanced practice, (2) for students from minority and low-income groups, and (3) for students who will practice in underserved areas. The need for nurses in advanced practice has been outlined above not only to supply primary health services to underserved populations and geographical areas but also to provide cost-effective services. Federal grants and loans continue to be needed because nursing students are often from low-income families and are likely to work while in school.

Graduate training funds for students in special areas should be encouraged. The training program in aging sponsored by the National Institute on Aging is needed to increase the number of geriatricians and nurses in gerontology, and the Division of Nursing training programs to increase personnel in primary care. Other special training programs for students from minority groups are needed. Special programs for loan forgiveness should be developed for graduates who work with underserved population groups.

❖ **Recommendation:** Make financial scholarship and loan programs more widely available to expand the number of students from all racial, ethnic, and cultural minority groups in all types of health profession education programs.

❖ Conclusion

The Commission on Health Care Policy of the American Academy of Nursing recommends that a comprehensive national health program be adopted to ensure universal access, comprehensive benefits, improved service delivery, greater cost control, and improved quality of care. Most important, the financial costs can be spread across the entire population and financed through progressive taxes from a combination of sources. Beyond this, many changes are needed in the financing and delivery of care. Such changes would enhance access, improve quality, and control costs.

This policy paper attempts to identify a public policy agenda for change. Specific changes in both the financing and delivery systems are identified to improve access to care for vulnerable population groups and to improve the overall health status of the nation. Public policies are needed to develop the appropriate type and mix of health care personnel, with a particular emphasis on developing primary care practitioners who will provide services to underserved population groups.

Research is of critical importance to making changes in public policy, particularly studies that examine the delivery system and personnel and their relationship to improving health outcomes. The effectiveness of the health system must be evaluated on the basis of access to care and health outcomes for the entire population, especially for underserved groups. Recommendations were made throughout this paper that federal research funding should be directed toward studies of (1) health promoting behaviors particularly for vulnerable populations; (2) health and health care outcomes; and (3) cost effectiveness of health services, procedures, and technologies. The research required to address the complex health care concerns must be both interdisciplinary and intradisciplinary and designed to inform policy makers of alternatives for change in the health care system.

Although not all of the recommended changes can be made immediately, a plan is needed with short-term and long-term objectives. This country has the resources to provide better health care for its population and the responsibility to develop a reasonable system of health care services. The public supports this approach. Health and human service professionals and public policymakers need the courage to implement such a system.

❖ About the Authors

Charlene Harrington, PH.D., is Professor of Social and Behavioral Sciences and Chair, Department of Social and Behavioral Sciences, School of Nursing, University of California, San Francisco. Dr. Harrington also chaired the Commission on Health Care Policy, American Academy of Nursing from 1991–1993.

Drs. Suzanne Lee Feetham, Patricia A. Moccia, and Gloria R. Smith are all members of the Commission of Health Care Policy of the American Academy of Nursing.

❖ Charting the Future of Hospital Nursing

LINDA H. AIKEN

Modern nursing has been characterized by a symbiotic relationship with physicians and hospitals. The legitimacy and authority of
nurses derive to a substantial degree from their close collaboration with physicians and their central roles in the life-saving care provided in technologically sophisticated hospitals. One of nursing's greatest challenges for the
future will be attaining a more balanced relationship with physicians and
hospitals—a relationship that encompasses shared values and common objectives for the well-being of those under their care but also gives nurses
opportunities for personal and professional growth and for independent
achievement and recognition. But hospitals are complex, bureaucratic, intractable institutions. The title of a recent survey report aptly captures
nurses' perceptions of hospital practice: "I Love My Work, I Hate My Job."

❖ Hospital Nursing in the Future

Motivated by the lack of responsiveness to the concerns of
nurses over many years, an increasing number of nursing leaders appear to
have "written off" hospitals, choosing instead to focus on the expansion of
other practice options. The rationale often cited is the prediction that in future decades the hospital sector will be significantly smaller and recede in
importance. Support for such a prediction is found in the annual decline of
more than 50 million inpatient days and the closing of 10 percent of community hospitals, accounting for more than 500 hospitals since the early 1980s.

Often overlooked in forecasts of future practice patterns of nurses is the
reality that, even though there are fewer patients, hospitals employ more
nurses than ever before. Paradoxically, as inpatient utilization declined, the
demand for nurses increased, leading to the perception of a national nursing shortage.

Long-standing trends often are the best predictors of the future. The number of nurses employed in hospitals and the ratio of nurses to patients have
been increasing steadily for 50 years and show no sign of slowing. In fact, the
ratio of nurses to patients has increased sharply over the decade of the 1980s.

Nowhere in the hospital sector has the decline in patient population been
greater than in public psychiatric hospitals over the past several decades. The
changes in nurse staffing are illustrative of what could happen in general hospitals. In 1974, almost 16,000 nurses cared for approximately 366,000 patients

in public psychiatric hospitals—a ratio of 1 nurse to 23 patients (on a 24-hour basis). In 1988, approximately 19,300 nurses cared for only 123,500 patients— a ratio of 1 nurse for every 6 patients. The actual number of nurses employed in public psychiatric hospitals increased by more than 20 percent despite a 66 percent decline in the number of inpatient beds.

Nurses are by far the largest group of health care professionals....
They are often the professionals with whom patients have the most
sustained contact. And because of the profession's perceived
tradition of holism and "care more than cure," nursing is often
upheld as a hopeful paradigm for the future. But the paradigm is
changing.
—Gerald R. Winslow

At present, two thirds of employed nurses practice in hospital settings. Thus, today and probably well into the future, the general welfare of the majority of nurses is dependent on conditions of professional practice in hospitals. Moreover, some 20 million Americans spent an average of 7.2 days in a hospital last year and paid $260 billion for the privilege. Nurses are of critical importance in determining the quality of hospital care and the nature of patient outcomes. Giving up on hospitals is simply not an option.

❖ Nursing Outcomes

Every major multihospital study on mortality has demonstrated substantial variation across hospitals. For the past several years, the federal government has published hospital-specific mortality statistics for Medicare patients demonstrating higher than expected mortality in some hospitals and lower than expected mortalilty in others, renewing interest in outcome studies to determine the factors responsible for variation.

A consistent finding across these studies is that nursing is among the important factors that explain variation in death rates between hospitals. One of the first comprehensive studies of community hospitals documented the importance of the ratio of nurses to patients in predicting patient outcomes, including mortality.

Scott et al. conducted an extensive survey of factors affecting postoperative mortality and morbidity in 17 hospitals and found that the higher the ratio of registered nurses to licensed practical nurses and the better the qualifications of registered nurses, the lower the death and morbidity rates. Moreover, better outcomes were related significantly to the organization of the nursing unit including (a) decentralization of nursing decisions at the unit level rather than at the level of central nursing administration, (b) standardization of nursing procedures, and (c) use of higher ratios of clerks and secretaries on the wards. The researchers concluded that registered nurses have their impact on quality of care not only through direct patient care but also through the medium of the ward organizations that they create.

Probably the single most compelling study of how the organization of nursing affects hospital mortality was Knaus, Draper, Wagner, and Zimmerman's multihospital study on outcomes of intensive care. Important differences between predicted and observed death rates in intensive care were found for nonoperative and operative patients as well as differences within specific diagnostic categories. These differences in outcome appeared to be related to the process of care, particularly the interaction and communication between physicians and nurses, and led to the conclusion that involvement and interaction of critical care personnel can influence directly the outcome of intensive care.

All of these studies contradict the popular belief that nursing care is important to the comfort and satisfaction of patients but has little to do with who lives and who dies. The observations and clinical judgment of experienced nurses—the only professionals at the bedside around the clock—are critical in anticipating and intervening to prevent potentially fatal complications from advancing to stages that cannot be reversed by the best medical and technological interventions available.

Hospital executives appear to understand the contributions that nurses make in maintaining the quality of care in hospitals. A recent national survey of hospital chief executive officers revealed that almost all believe nurses to be one of the most important factors in maintaining the quality of hospital care. Chief executive officers were more likely to identify nurses as being the key to quality than they were the technical expertise of the medical staff.

Yet despite the recommendations of three blue ribbon panels convened during the 1980s to identify solutions to the nursing shortage, hospitals have been slow to adopt management practices and policies that show promise for reducing nurse vacancy and turnover rates. There is increasing evidence that the reforms advocated by these panels result in improved nurse recruitment and retention. The "magnet hospitals" identified by the American Academy of Nursing during the early 1980s as institutions that were successful in attracting and retaining nurses despite shortages in their local labor markets had implemented reforms comparable to those proposed by the blue ribbon panels. A recent follow-up study of a sample of the same hospitals showed that they were able to sustain their low vacancy and turnover rates during the most recent nursing shortage as well. Many of the dimensions that characterized the magnet hospitals, and appeared to explain their success attracting and retaining nurses, were the same dimensions of organizational structure found to be associated with lower than predicted mortality and morbidity in the study of Scott et al. on postoperative patient outcomes and the research of Knaus et al. on outcomes of intensive care.

The purpose of this discussion has been to make the case that nursing cannot afford to turn a deaf ear to the persistent problems that undermine innovation and creativity in hospital nursing practice. As important as the broad agenda of nursing is to expanding community-based nursing practice, it is essential to the majority of nurses and to the public we serve to persevere in our attempts to reform hospital nursing practice.

The time is ideal to chart a new course for hospital nursing because (a) there is a perception that the present nursing shortage will be long lasting; (b) there is increasing concern about the potential adverse consequences of cost-containment initiatives on quality of care and increased appreciation of the role of nurses in maintaining quality of care; and (c) more nurses than ever before work in hospitals, thus giving nurses more power and influence to bring about change. Two steps are required. First, a broader consensus needs to be developed on the underlying causes of the present nursing shortage. Second, promising models must be designed that fully utilize what is already known to work, and they must be implemented and systematically evaluated. Information on those that prove to be successful needs to be more widely disseminated.

❖ Developing a Consensus on Causes of the Shortage

The intuitive solution to the nation's cyclical nursing shortages—increasing the supply of nurses—has not worked thus far to eliminate the persistent shortages that have disrupted hospital care on and off since World War II. Nurse to population ratios have grown by more than 100 percent over the past 30 years. In the last decade alone, the number of *employed* nurses grew by 50 percent while the population grew by only 10 percent. The supply of nurses in the United States now exceeds 2 million—one employed nurse for about every 142 Americans, most of whom are well most of the time.

Despite the failure of increased supply to solve nursing shortages, most proposed solutions still focus primarily on supply. These proposed solutions include importing foreign trained nurses, increasing nursing school enrollments, and training new categories of workers to supplement nurses as in the American Medical Association's proposal for registered care technologists. One possible explanation for continuing shortages in the face of large increases in the supply of nurses is that the United States has not yet produced a sufficient number of nurses to meet demand. However, an examination of the data from other developed countries raises major doubts about the viability of such an explanation. Nurse to population ratios vary more than 50-fold across the countries of the world, but all countries report persistent or cyclical shortages of nurses. Trends over many years in the United States and other Western countries suggest that increasing the supply of nurses in the absence of efforts to moderate demand will not be successful in eliminating nursing shortages.

Myths about the Nursing Shortage

Several unfounded but popular notions about the causes of persistent nursing shortages obfuscate potential solutions. While it is true that enrollments in nursing schools have fallen by some 25 percent since 1984, the number of graduates is still significantly greater than is the number of nurses retiring, and thus the pool of nurses is continuing to increase at a substantial rate. Declining enrollments, should they persist, will not affect the size of the pool of nurses until the next century, and they do not provide an explanation for the current shortage.

Contrary to popular opinion, nurses are not leaving the profession in large numbers. A remarkably low proportion of registered nurses—some 5 percent—elect to leave health care for other careers. Moreover, nurses have a very high employment rate for a predominantly female occupation. Slightly more than 80 percent of registered nurses are currently employed, which is as high as might be expected. While many new jobs for nurses have been created, hospitals continue to employ two thirds of a growing pool of nurses.

There is a high turnover in hospital nursing positions, reflecting the widespread dissatisfaction of nurses with hospital employment. Yet the vast majority of nurses who resign their positions in hospitals take a job in another hospital so that nurse resignations, while contributing to vacancy rates in individual hospitals, do not provide an explanation for the aggregate national shortage of nurses.

Explanations

Where have all the nurses gone? More nurses than ever before are working in hospitals even though hospitals have substantially fewer inpatients. Hospitals, since 1980, have increased their employment of nurses by more than 140,000 full-time nurses, even though inpatient days fell by 51 million annually over the same period.

One explanation for the increased ratio of nurses to patients was the change in patient mix resulting from substantially altered admission patterns, shorter length of stay, and increased use of nurse intensive technologies (exemplified by an increase in intensive care unit (ICU) days as a percentage of all inpatient days). The Prospective Payment Assessment Commission estimated that the cumulative increase in real case mix from 1981 to 1988 was 14.2 percent. However, nurse to patient ratios increased by twice that magnitude over the period, on the order of about 28 percent, suggesting that changing case mix was not the only factor affecting the increased employment of nurses in hospitals.

During the period of the most recent nursing shortage, hospitals restructured significantly their labor mix. Almost 70,000 licensed practical nurses were moved out of hospital employment between 1980 and 1988 and were replaced by registered nurses. In addition, the nonnursing service infrastructure of hospitals was also downsized over the same period, resulting in fewer personnel in support departments such as pharmacy, central supply, housekeeping, patient transport, and administrative and clerical services. Many of these support departments have minimal staff available on nights and weekends.

A number of studies have documented that a substantial proportion of hospital nurses' time is spent in nonclinical activities—a long-standing problem but one exacerbated by the downsizing of the support infrastructure in recent years. A direct observation study in five Boston hospitals in the mid-1970s found that tasks were performed by personnel who happened to be available, with little regard for the training, certification, or degree of competence of the individuals involved. In a similar study conducted in the early 1980s, it was found that only 25 percent of nursing time was in direct care with 60 percent in indirect activities and 15 percent unavailable for care. Communicating, charting, clerical work, and administrative functions accounted for almost 50 percent of the indirect care time. Registered nurses spent 25 percent of their time charting and doing clerical work, while ward clerks spent only 43 percent of their time on those activities. A 1989 study by the Hay Group estimated that, on average, registered nurses spend only 26 percent of their time in professional nursing, which includes physical assessments, care and treatments, monitoring patients' conditions, and planning and documenting care. The greatest portion of time—52 percent—was consumed in housekeeping details, answering phones, and ordering supplies, all activities clearly outside the sphere of nursing. Hence the restructuring of the labor mix in hospitals with greater dependence on nurses appears to be an additional explanation of how a nursing shortage could have occurred in the context of dramatic reductions in the national inpatient census.

Substituting nurses for lower level personnel seems an unusual choice during a period of increasingly constrained hospital budgets. Yet a closer examination of the context in which the shift to a higher ratio of nurses occurred reveals some possible explanations. From a strictly economic point of view, the shift to more nurses was not as costly to hospitals as most might assume. The real incomes of nurses were seriously eroded throughout the 1970s when their annual wage increases did not keep up with inflation. Nurses' real incomes did not return to their 1972 value until 1989. Moreover, the initial impact of the Medicare Prospective Payment System in the 1980s was also to hold the growth of nurses' wages below those of other comparable occupations. Between 1983 and 1985, nurses' real wages fell an average of 0.03 percent annually. Despite perceptions of an acute national nursing shortage, their real incomes increased by an average of only 1.45 percent annually over the period from 1986 to 1989.

Over a 25-year period, hospital cost containment initiatives have had the possibly unintended consequence of holding increases in the wages of nurses below those of other workers. Since nurses are such versatile workers in the hospital context and require very little supervision, they become an increasingly economical source of labor when their wages decline relative to those of alternative workers. Hence, from an economic point of view, the substitution of nurses for licensed practical nurses, aides, and others has not been particularly costly at prevailing wage rates. Additionally, nurses influence length of stay, a factor of increasing importance to the financial position of hospitals under the Prospective Payment System. And, in an era when a substantial number of hospitals have low patient census, having sufficient numbers of qualified nurses is considered to give hospitals a competitive edge in attracting physicians and their patients.

❖ Results from More Nurses in Hospital Practice

For the most part, nurses have been advocates for the employment of additional nurses. Many hospitals adopted the concept of the "all-RN" staff, and nurse researchers provided the evidence that all-RN staffs were not more costly than alternatives at the prevailing wage rates. It was expected that with more nurses, work loads would be more reasonable, nurses would have more time to spend with patients, the continuity of care would improve, and collaboration with physicians would be enhanced.

The results of the experiment to date are less than satisfactory. The increased number of nurses employed by hospitals has not resolved persistently high vacancy and turnover rates, nor has it resulted in more manageable work loads. Nurses still perceive staffing to be dangerously inadequate in many institutions, and levels of dissatisfaction are high.

Nurses are particularly dissatisfied that they must fulfill many nonnursing functions—a result of the downsizing of the support services infrastructure—and the increasingly problematic issues concerning the need for more nurses during unpopular hours because of inadequate support services. The downsizing of the support services infrastructure must be recognized as the price nursing has paid to increase the additional positions for nurses.

Most observers of the hospital scene would also admit that having more nurses has not improved substantially the relationships between physicians and nurses and that both groups continue to harbor resentment against and/or disappointment in each other. There has not been a noticeable improvement in continuity and accountability for nursing care, exemplified by the perceptions of most patients that no single nurse is responsible or accountable for their care.

The increased number of nurses employed in hospitals also exacerbates long-standing problems including wage compression. Ginzberg argues that there is something contradictory in a policy that both advocates expanding the supply of nurses and insists on raising the salaries. Nurses' wages have recently shown some responsiveness to the nursing shortage in some local labor markets. Should this trend continue nationally and become more widespread, the increased ratio of nurses to patients could become very expensive to maintain. Nurses themselves should give careful consideration to whether or not such investment is really in the best interest of professional nursing practice in hospitals.

Also, hospitals have not been successful in the development of career trajectories for nurses in positions of increasing *clinical* responsibility. Most advancement still requires movement into management and away from direct patient care. With so many more nurses seeking professional growth and advancement opportunities in hospitals, most will ultimately be disappointed unless more opportunities for advancement in clinical positions are developed. On this note, it is particularly worrisome that, as their fiscal pressures increase, hospitals appear to be eliminating positions for clinical nurse specialists.

What should be done at this point? What should be done to chart a future for hospital nursing where the supply and demand for nurses is in better balance, where nurses are more satisfied with hospital practice, where nurses and physicians collaborate more effectively to achieve the best possible patient outcomes at a cost affordable to the health care system? I suggest that the organization of nursing within hospitals needs to be restructured substantially and that other hospital services must be reorganized to provide more efficient support for nurses and physicians in their care for patients. The objective would be a system with fewer nurses but appropriately compensated nurses with greater opportunities to use their special expertise in the care of patients and better support services to help them use their time appropriately.

❖ A Proposed New Course for Hospital Nursing

This proposal calls for the development of additional career tracks in hospital nursing, the majority of which are predominantly clinical. The clinical career trajectories should be designed to approximate more closely the organization of medical care in hospitals and have the explicit goal of closer collaboration between medicine and nursing. These trajectories must include nurses with varying levels of education and expertise and acknowledge explicitly that the 2.1 million nurses in the United States vary in their career aspirations and/or commitment to professional roles that require ongoing accountability. The following is a brief outline of four possible career trajectories that if successfully implemented hold promise for improving hospital nursing.

Attending Nurses

Currently, most nurses in hospitals are assigned responsibility based on a specific unit of the hospital. Physicians, however, are organized into clinical services that often admit or care for patients across hospital units. Thus nurses on a given unit deal routinely with many different physicians and numerous types of illnesses. This basic difference in organization of responsibilities in medicine and nursing is at the heart of much of the miscommunication and difficulties in establishing joint practice. Under current arrangements, it is an accident when a physician responsible for a patient encounters the nurse who knows the patient best. Even in most primary nursing models, physicians have difficulty identifying easily the primary nurse for a given patient. Moreover, nurses and physicians often do not know each other well and thus cannot be expected to have an accurate appreciation of each other's clinical judgment. The most extreme example of this phenomenon is general medicine and general surgery. It is important to note that these are the very units for which recruitment and retention of nurses is uniformly difficult.

Despite the dedication of literally millions of talented health care professionals, our health care is too uncertain and too expensive, too bureaucratic and too wasteful. It has too much fraud and too much greed.
—President Bill Clinton

An important exception is specialty units where a single group of physicians admits patients, usually with a common problem or problems, to a single unit (except for overflow), thus creating a setting in which a group of physicians and a group of nurses share the responsibility for a panel of patients with common needs. In general, nurses practicing in specialty units are more satisfied with their jobs, and vacancy and turnover rates are lower than they are on general or multispecialty units. Higher job satisfaction is found even in specialty units in which nurses experience substantial stress inherent in the care of special populations, including intensive care, oncology, and AIDS.

I propose reorganizing the senior nurse clinicians into attending nurse services and integrating them into the existing medical staff organization so that each clinical service would consist essentially of a nurse/physician group practice. Attending nurses would have 24-hour responsibility for patients on their service and would make clinical decisions about nursing care for all patients on the service, whatever their location in the hospital. The attending nursing staff members on each service could devise suitable procedures for sharing on-call responsibilities just as medical staff members do. Staff nurses would continue to cover each hospital unit on a shift basis to respond to unanticipated needs and problems and to implement the plan of care developed by the attending nurses and physicians. Attending nurses would be involved centrally in direct care as well as working through other staff nurses.

Specialty units essentially have such a system in place now, although, if necessary, it could be more formalized. The attending nurse concept is a way to create on general medicine and surgery units the context for practice that often exists in specialty units without dividing units structurally.

Intensivists

In clinical areas such as trauma and emergency care, surgery, and recovery and intensive care, career trajectories should be developed for the most expert and knowledgeable nurses in acute, high-technology care. In these highly specialized clinical areas, attending nurses would delegate responsibility to nurse intensivists for the patient's stay in the specialized area, retaining a presence with the patient and family but relying on the nurse intensivist to make clinical decisions. Nurse intensivists would work closely with the physicians responsible for the patients in a joint practice model.

Subspecialist Consulting Nurses

A cadre of nurse subspecialist consultants should be available to consult across clinical specialties and units of the hospital. Psychiatric nurses specializing in psychiatric manifestations of acute illness or the care of psychiatrically impaired persons with acute medical or surgical problems exemplify this role. The nurse subspecialists would hold an appointment on the clinical service of their specialty (psychiatry in the above example) but would be available to consult with nurses, physicians, or patients/families on any service.

Nurse Manager

The responsibility of the nurse manager would be to ensure that the necessary staff nurse coverage and other services were available for the safety and well-being of patients around the clock and to support the efficient delivery of care by nurses and physicians. The nurse manager would be responsible for communicating the needs of nurse clinicians to hospital management and for helping clinicians adapt to institutional priorities. The nurse manager would be responsible for supervising all nursing personnel at the staff nurse level or below, and for sharing responsibility with the attending nurses for mentoring young nurses.

❖ Restructuring Support Services

It will not be possible to reduce the number of nurses needed to provide hospital care unless substantial changes are made in the organization and delivery of nonnursing services in hospitals. The formal organizational charts of most hospitals do not have lines of authority and accountability to the patient unit level except for the department of nursing. This has to be changed to reduce the inappropriate utilization of nurses.

There will never be a sufficient number of nurses to cover for departments that perform inadequately or that are understaffed during unpopular hours. Ideally, a nonnurse administrator would be held responsible and accountable for the delivery of support services at the unit level. However, since these services are necessary for nursing and medical care, nurses and physicians must have a reasonable way to influence the delivery of these support services without taking direct responsibility themselves.

Second, the number of nurses could be reduced without affecting adversely the care of patients if additional administrative, secretarial, and clerical personnel were available to nurses. Nurses spend far more time than is necessary in organizing care, coordinating services, transcribing orders, recording treatments, and charting. The best nurse extenders would be competent secretarial assistants and improved clinical computer systems. In addition, greater creativity could be used in developing safe and effective roles for assistants to whom nurses could delegate the myriad of functions that need to be done in hospitals but do not require the time of a professional.

❖ Some Concluding Thoughts

Health care in America clearly meets any definition of "big business," with expenditures exceeding a billion dollars a day. However, I continue to be skeptical that the business and management models that have been promulgated in hospitals and embraced enthusiastically by nursing are ideally applicable to an enterprise primarily devoted to the care and cure of sick people. Clearly, hospitals must be financially viable to exist. However, the financing of hospitals should not be nursing's main concern. Overidentification with the concerns of management and preoccupation with the day-to-day operation of the institution divert nurses' time, attention, and perhaps even loyalties away from patients and away from the clinical challenges and common interests they share with physicians.

Although the interests of medicine and nursing diverge in some areas, there is a considerable mutual interest in the central aspects of patient care. An essential aspect of restructuring hospitals to better meet the challenges of the future will be the forging of closer ties between nursing and medicine.

❖ About the Author

Linda H. Aiken, R.N., PH.D., is Trustee Professor of Nursing and Sociology and Director, Center for Health Services and Policy Research, School of Nursing, University of Pennsylvania, Philadelphia.

❖ Collaboration between Nurses and Physicians: No Longer a Choice

CLAIRE M. FAGIN

Rapid social, economic, and technical changes are having profound effects on health care. Demographic shifts, the rise in the numbers of people of all ages who need chronic and maintenance care, the interest of consumers in self-care, cost restraints that influence the use of medical technology, changes in the ways that medical care is paid for, pressures for a greater focus on care rather than cure, and questions of who needs what at what cost are some of the factors having important impacts on how our society heals its sick and injured and keeps them well.

These factors are forcing many of us in the health professions and academic medicine to reexamine the health care paradigm. In this essay, I present my own and others' views and findings on an old and crucial element of that paradigm, one that an increasing number of institutions and individuals are seriously reexamining: the nature of the relationship between nurses and physicians and how much it should be one of *collaboration*. That is, how much should the relationship be an interdependent one, where nurses and physicians have complementary roles, rather than a hierarchical one, where one partner is subordinate to the other?

Since most nurses are women, feminist ideology has affected the professional and personal lives of nurses. It influences how nurses see themselves, their patients, and the health care system. Indeed, feminist ideology has legitimatized nurses' interest in developing and using power and politics to reshape society's definitions of health and roles for nurses in developing programs for health and illness.
—Connie Vance, Susan W. Talbot, Angela Barron McBride, and Diana J. Mason

---

Most readers will not be surprised when I report that physicians and nurses often have opposing answers to that question. Surveys and anecdotal evidence make clear that physicians, more often than not, do not value or demonstrate collaboration in their work with nurses; nurses, on the other hand, more often seek a collaborative relationship. Because I am a nurse, I probably have the nurses' bias. However, my knowledge of the literature on collaboration and my own rewarding experiences in collaborative relationships with physicians have strengthened my conviction that collaboration is the preferable relationship and will be even more essential for good health care in the future (which is upon us).

The following pages present both my own observations and those of physicians on the most important issues concerning collaboration. In addition, I summarize the research literature on the reasons to promote collaboration and the barriers to developing it. Finally, I discuss possible strategies for the future to help increase understanding between nurses and physicians and hopefully foster collaboration in their work.

❖ The Changing Doctor-Nurse Game

In 1967, Stein described what he called the *doctor-nurse game*. In brief, this arrangement stipulated that the hierarchical relationship between doctors and nurses would be managed so that nurses' recommendations and initiatives would be couched in such a way as to maintain the hierarchy and allow the attribution of decisions to physicians. Each would play a role that would preserve the physicians' aura of omniscience.

Feminist women and nurses have frequently experienced an uneasy relationship. Much of the energy in the women's movement has been directed toward moving into nontraditional fields of study and work. Nursing has been seen, therefore, as one of the ultimate female ghettos from which women should be encouraged to escape.
—Connie Vance, Susan W. Talbot, Angela Barron McBride, and Diana J. Mason

---

Stein and others later revisited the scene, and in a 1990 report they comment on the changes affecting the doctor-nurse game since 1976. In particular they note that public esteem for physicians has deteriorated and that "the concept of physicians' omnipotence has given way to broader recognition of their fallibility." Stein and colleagues acknowledge that nurses have unilaterally decided to stop playing the game for several reasons, such as nurses' interest in autonomy, the changes in women's status, the realization that the nursing shortage is caused more by conditions of work than by supply problems, and nurses' increased confidence. They believe that the role of "stubborn rebel" has replaced, more often than not, "willing supplicant."

Stein and colleagues go on to say that many physicians are puzzled and confused by nurses' behavior and feel betrayed and angry. While nurses reacted with some dismay to many of Stein's comments, his overall assessment of the situation should not give any nurse a problem: "Physicians' ability to remain technically expert while maintaining a humane attitude toward patients may depend in large part on the arrangements they work out with other professionals, especially nurses. When a subordinate becomes liberated, there is the potential for the dominant one to become liberated too."

Makadon and Gibbons indicate similar views when they say that "sincere efforts will enable nurses and physicians to work together in positive ways to accomplish the difficult task of providing the highest quality of care in the most economical way." They believe that decreased length of stay, increased severity of illness in hospitals, and decreased resources mandate the need for collaboration in management. It is expected that nurses have the clinical competence and creativity necessary to make physicians' work easier.

The NJPC

In 1971, the American Nurses Association (ANA) and the American Medical Association (AMA) jointly supported the development of the National Joint Practice Commission (NJPC). The concerns they identified were the constraints on nurses in hospitals, for which they blamed physicians, and the excessive demands on both groups because of increased patient loads and cost constraints. The physicians and nurses involved in the NJPC, with mutual concern for patients and families, agreed that roles and responsibilities should be predicated on a clear definition of patients' various needs. They recognized that divisiveness and conflict had high cost for each discipline but had even higher costs for society in duplication of effort, unnecessary conflict, energy-depleting discord, and the potential for greater risks to patients.

The NJPC studied four hospitals that had attempted to alter nurse-physician relationships. Funding for the project came from the participating hospitals; the leadership staff was funded by the Kellogg Foundation. Subjective and objective evaluations of this project indicated extraordinary success on all measures, including economics. Forty-eight physicians, 74 nurses, and 109 discharged patients were interviewed by telephone. The report of the survey states that "once established, the demonstration units resulted in *everyone* (doctor, nurse, and patient) being better off."

The four hospitals showed no cost difference between the demonstration units and other units despite the introduction of primary nursing. Several showed cost reductions in indirect savings, and all four hospitals reported that length of patient stay and organizational redundancy were reduced.

In 1981, the AMA withdrew support from the NJPC. The issues that precipitated the withdrawal were the expanding of nurses' roles and the raising of their salaries to be commensurate with their professional services. Thus, while the work of the commission was valuable, it was never completed.

Collaborative Nursing Models

More recently, in an AMA Board of Trustees report on independent nursing models, Ring describes some nursing models as collaborative and meritorious "because they are patient-centered and incorporate medical protocols through the cooperative efforts of physicians and nurses." He adds that collaborative models promote moral autonomy for both professions and advocates educational programs to prepare physicians for collaborative case management with nurses. At the same time, he cautions monitoring federal and state legislation for direct reimbursement of non-physicians so that physician supervision for reimbursement can be maintained. During the 1980s the issues of independence and payment assumed even more importance for nurses and, apparently, they have elicited a continued negative stance from organized medicine.

❖ Reasons for Collaboration

Despite the premature termination of the NJPC's work, it made an important and lasting contribution by introducing a research basis into discussions of collaboration. New research has allowed us to learn even more about the value of collaboration: investigators are examining a variety of factors that both professionals and patients perceive to be diminishing the quality of care, such as cost constraints, early discharge, the nursing shortage, competition among providers, poor communication, managed care, and the privatization of care. Some of the data that are available deal specifically or inferentially with nurse-physician relationships.

To summarize: compelling evidence—both in the literature and anecdotal—reveals the value of collaboration and the need to promote it. The evidence includes improved patient outcomes and, in many cases, cost savings. This evidence is valid despite the fact that in some studies, quality of care and cost efficiency were increased because several factors, including collaborative care, were involved, which could be interpreted to mean that there is no way to show that collaborative care had a significant helpful effect. My response to this criticism is that when one looks at all the studies as a group, the importance of collaborative care "hits you over the head" and that it would be much harder to show that collaborative care was not important. In fact, the problems that can emerge and affect patients and the system because doctors and nurses are miscommunicating and sometimes creating an emotional tone of negativeness and hostility are, to some observers (including me), sufficient cause to promote collaboration between them. But are the barriers to promoting collaboration equally strong?

In a recent study of hospitalized patients, those queried mentioned the following as nursing functions: taking doctors' orders, giving medications, serving meals, giving shots, and providing bedpans. The nurse's role has frequently been viewed as being analogous to that of the traditional wife and mother in a household.
—J. L. Muyskens

❖ Barriers to Collaboration

Education

The late 1940s signified the end of an established order between nursing and medicine. Medical science and medical education were transformed and nursing education advanced through federal financing and accreditation programs. The changes produced by these advances are still far from complete as we near the 21st century. Had nursing education been completely transformed during the same time period as was medical education, a natural progression in the relationships between the two disciplines might have occurred. As it was, a huge gap formed that affected several generations and is still responsible for unusual, antiquated attitudes not made less noxious by the fact that they are perpetuated by many nurses. As a way to narrow the gap, some nursing leaders now are proposing that the doctorate be the entry-level credential for professional nursing. At least part of the reason for this recommendation is the parity this would provide with medicine. Clearly the difference in education is one of the barriers, both real and perceived, in achieving collaboration.

Jurisdiction

Jurisdiction issues loom large as a barrier. Nursing and medicine share an occupational kinship that is unique and anomalous. This kinship gives rise to many of the problems (as well as the satisfactions) experienced by the two groups. It engenders a sense of closeness and understanding that tends to obfuscate the differences between the two professions in structure and priorities.

Nurses' Dissatisfactions

Nurses' dissatisfactions are frequently expressed in indirect and covert behavior, such as the modern versions of the doctor-nurse game, rather than through organized aggressive and vocal action, which is seen as disloyal and might put their jobs at risk. Physicians and administrators take the view that open expression of such dissatisfactions will surely shake the boat. Thus, an informal conspiracy keeps these dissatisfactions, their causes, and their possible remedies from the public. Unfortunately, all these factors make for situations as well as relationships that are dishonest and demeaning and prevent many physicians from seeing clearly the role of the nurse.

Sex-Role Stereotypes

Two aspects of sex-role stereotypes need to be taken into consideration as barriers to collaboration. One is the gender difference between nurses and doctors that existed until recent years. For some reason, the women's movement did not penetrate into hospitals to homogenize role expectations and behaviors. A question often raised is "will the increased number of women in medicine make a positive difference in nurse-physician relationships?" A recent survey of over 1,000 nurse readers of the journal *Nursing 91* indicated that more than 55% found their working relationships with women physicians to be no better, or worse, than those with men physicians.

Women physicians often do not want to be linked with nurses, for several reasons, especially because of the assumption that they will be seen as subordinate to men and because nurses are seen as behaving in maternal ways, that is, being nurturing, caring, comforting, etc. (This is the other sex-role stereotype.)

Hands-On versus Intellectual Activities

The latter factor, coupled with the "hands-on" aspect of nursing, contributes to nursing's invisibility as a major player in the hospital scene. This is because such behaviors are seen as essentially mundane and not worth noticing, even though they are expressed through highly visible acts. Nurses as people may be highly visible in a vast variety of forums. But *nursing*, the professional practice, remains arcane to many observers.

Medicine, on the other hand, is seen as highly intellectual, technological, and scientific as it focuses on diagnoses and strategies for treatment and cure—activities that are looked up to and respected. The intellectual operations can be said to be invisible from the standpoint of the patient's understanding what is going on—therefore they are seen as almost a kind of magic, which is awe-inspiring and worth noticing.

Social Class

Class differences between nurses and physicians are real. It is important to recognize that a social status gap exists between career aspirants. While students from all social classes are represented in the large nursing student group, for the most part nursing students have been drawn from the middle class and working class. To the contrary, medicine has drawn the majority of its students from the upper middle and upper classes. Education is the major force for social mobility in our culture and nursing has been a wonderful field for social mobility. When nurses have entered the college route rather than the substandard routes many have chosen, the social status gap is ameliorated or removed. It would be foolish to ignore the power of social status on professional interactions and on the parity and equality implied in a collaborative relationship.

Education Reforms

There is no question that the focus on collaboration is a focus on clinical practice. Yet many experts believe that a most important strategy for change must be in the educational setting. Medical and nursing curricula, for the most part, are totally separated. . . . It is clear that major change in nursing and medical education is essential as a strategy to develop collaborative behaviors, and that the notion of cooperation should be seen as the first step in this learning strategy.

Nursing education is a major problem in and of itself in developing the basis for colleagueship and collaboration. The difference between the educational preparation of nurses and that of physicians and the differences between the educational preparation among nurses themselves perpetuate communication problems. It should be clear that upgrading basic nursing education to a single, clear, and respected level (e.g., at least the B.S. degree) will help nurse-physician relationships become more reciprocal. Further, master's-level preparation for all clinical specialists, with certification recognizing their educational and experiential qualifications, will inform physicians and others, at the start of an interaction, of the uniform qualifications of these nurses.

Faculty Initiatives

Faculty involvements in patient care and in research are other strategies for improving nurse-physician relationships.

It may be that starting from the top of the nursing and medical professions is at least as effective a strategy as starting from the bottom. It is interesting to note in this regard that one approach to influence the profession of nursing has been to design programs that aim to increase the entry-level population or change it in some way. Another approach is to reach for the top rather than the bottom, i.e., entry level.

Practice Arena

Clearly, the area of practice is the most important and most likely arena for change. Hospitals are using a variety of approaches to improving relationships between physicians and nurses. New methods of issue resolution, comprehensive redesign of nurses' roles, sensitivity training, special educational programs, joint practice committees, and the establishment of a corporate culture that supports nurse-physician collaboration are all reported.

Organizations

It *does not* go without saying that the primary organizations affecting nurses and physicians must endorse change and must be willing to have open dialogues about strategies to which they are equally committed. The AMA has shown unwillingness to confront these issues and maintain a lasting presence in any discussions. While speaking for collaboration, they remain obsessed with competition and the threats from nurse practitioners and nurse midwives. It is quite possible that the Association of American Medical Colleges and the various associations dealing with medical specialties would be more interested in constructive action.

❖ Conclusion

If we envision the knowledge and activities of nurses and the knowledge and activities of physicians as occupying two partly intersecting spheres, we can see that much is shared. The more discrete and separate knowledge and activities of each profession are in the parts of the spheres that do not intersect, with a predominance of health maintenance, preventive, and caring functions in the nursing sphere and a predominance of curative, diagnostic, and prescriptive functions in the medical one.

The present and future are placing great pressures upon the ways these spheres intersect. Changes are already occurring—but if we are to control and fashion these changes so that society is served best, physicians, nurses, and the institutions that educate and employ them will have to rethink and refashion the ways that doctors and nurses have been brought up to think about themselves and their roles in the health care delivery system—that is, their powers, their authority, and their domains.

I have hope that when today's medical students become physicians, they will be predisposed to participate with nurses and others to constructively reshape and redefine health care delivery in the coming decades. For these students have decided to enter medicine at a time when they know that the rewards for medical practice, both financial and otherwise, will not be as immediate and uncomplicated as they were for their predecessors. Therefore, I assume that their commitment to the practice of medicine is very deep and that they are willing to confront the different and difficult future creatively.

One of the hardest tasks will be to reevaluate the traditional way that physicians view the broad, complex health care field. Until recently, this long-ingrained viewpoint, which has been single-discipline-centered and thus one of the chief barriers to more collaborative behavior of the health care team, has not gotten in the way of the individual physician. However, the new complexities and constraints of the health care system are making this traditional approach dysfunctional for all players. The extent to which physicians are able to move to a broader, more shared perspective will directly contribute to the satisfaction that they and their patients experience. The fact that must guide them is that physicians and nurses are both (even if not jointly) engaged in the business of getting sick people well and keeping them well. Neither profession can function without the other.

The challenge for physicians and nurses to work together to address the very real health care problems of our present and future has never been greater. A single-discipline, self-centered view of the future will be destructive to both professions, to the newly emerging health care system, and, most of all, to those who must be healed.

❖ About the Author

Claire M. Fagin, Ph.D., R.N. is a Professor in the School of Nursing, University of Pennsylvania. She is the former Margaret Bond Simon Dean at that school and is President of the National League for Nursing.

❖ Part III

Health Care Reform in the 1990s

❖ Chapter 5
Initiatives for Reform

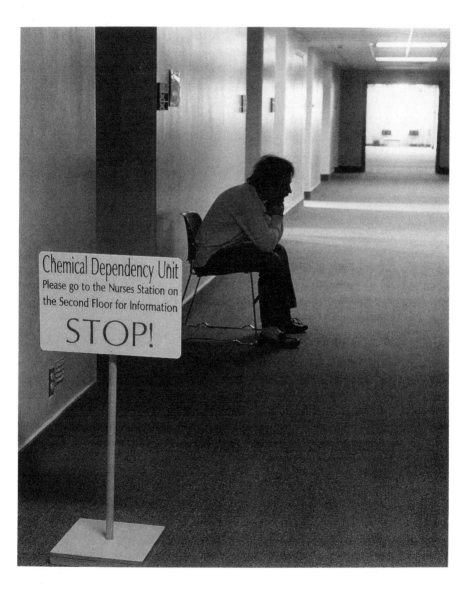

Although at one time Americans believed that theirs was the best health care system in the world, this is no longer true. In fact, a 1989 Louis Harris and Associates survey reported that Americans are more dissatisfied with their health system than either Canadians or Britons, despite the higher levels of health care spending by Americans. The poll reported that 89 percent of U.S. residents called for fundamental changes in the delivery of health services, and 61 percent would be pleased to trade the U.S. system for a model like that in Canada.

More recent polls indicate continuing discontent with the present system. A 1991 Time and Cable News Network poll found that the number of those who called for fundamental reform in the health care system was as high as 91 percent. A *Wall Street Journal* poll in March 1993 also found that a significant majority of Americans believe the U.S. health care system "needs major change." In a November 1991 poll, Pennsylvanians were asked what they thought was the biggest problem with health care, and 77 percent responded that the biggest problem for themselves and their families was cost. A Roper survey estimated support for extending Medicare coverage to everyone to be as high as 69 percent. An analysis of U.S. polls taken between 1989 and 1991 by Blendon and Donehue concluded that support for a national health plan was supported by well over half of the nation. This new climate of public opinion reflects dissatisfaction with a number of aspects of the current system, including limitations on access to services, high costs, complex technologies, fragmentation of services, uneven quality, and many others.

Some say this is but another expression of the basic American wish to have our cake and eat it, too. We want miracle cures, but we don't want prices to go up. Although the system is meeting the personal needs of many people, collectively there are failures. These failures reflect the tradeoffs that are necessary under the current payment system. For example, over 37 million low-income people have no insurance coverage and thus no means of payment for health care, and these are often the people who most desperately need care.

In addition, the great expense of many advanced technologies forces health care providers to weigh individual circumstances of patients against economic constraints in making therapeutic decisions. Thus, providers find they must limit resources and withhold treatment from patients who could benefit from the care. A recent report that infant mortality was higher in the United States than in Singapore and that the United States ranked twenty-second in infant mortality worldwide raised many questions about the lack of availability of prenatal care to certain groups in this country, which experts say could prevent needless deaths. African-American infants are more than twice as likely to die in their first year as are white infants. Most alarmingly, the ratio of African-American to white infant mortality has increased in recent years, from 1.8 in the early 1970s to 2.2 in 1990. Life expectancy in the U.S. at birth ranks twentieth for men and fifteenth for women worldwide. A 1991 study found the in-hospital death rate of uninsured patients to be 1.2 to 3.2 times higher than the rate for insured patients. African-American women have been found to show higher rates of invasive cervical cancer, and this has been connected to their lower access to Pap tests. There is no disputing that under the current system one's health status and access to services are statistically tied to one's income and race.

Though the problems are apparent to everyone, there is by no means a consensus about how to reform the system. In recent years, proposals for health care reform have proliferated. During the 1992 presidential election campaign, millions of voters called for fundamental change in the health care system. Candidates Bush and Clinton presented positions on reform, both calling for increased access to health services and cost containment, with Clinton advocating managed competition and universal coverage.

Most policymakers and analysts recognize the fact that Americans cannot have it all. It is understood that there will be serious tradeoffs in any major health care reform package. The question is how much each of us will have to sacrifice in order to usher in the necessary changes.

Currently, there is a hot debate about changes in financing and organization that may or may not address the problems faced by the health care industry and may or may not address some sources of dissatisfaction reflected in recent polls. In the 1980s, the trend toward for-profit medicine emerged in the form of privately owned proprietary hospitals and other health services. This was coupled with an increase in centralized ownership and investor-owned national chains, which tend to seek out affluent, well-insured markets. The policies under Presidents Reagan and Bush favored employment of market principles in allocating health resources, thus progressing toward greater competition in health care and away from strict regulation of the industry and universal coverage.

Health economist Alain C. Enthoven took an optimistic view of fair competition as a means to address the underlying causes of uncontrolled cost increases and to result in the survival of health plans that offer good value to their customers. Out of this grew an approach he labeled "managed competition," the goal of which he described as "to divide the providers in each community into competing economic units and to use market forces to motivate them to develop efficient delivery systems." This policy was adopted by President Clinton and woven into his plan presented to Congress in 1993. In describing it, the president said the plan would "give groups of consumers and small businesses the same market bargaining power that large corporations and large groups of public employees have now." He said it would allow plans to compete on the basis of price and quality rather than by excluding sick people.

The plan proposed by President Clinton would provide universal coverage to all Americans and guarantee a comprehensive basic benefit package. It included an employer mandate that would require employers to pay at least 80 percent of employee health care coverage, and it proposed creation of purchasing groups or "health alliances," which would include both regional and corporate networks to provide coverage to large consumer groups. The plan also called for a national health board whose members would be appointed by the president to oversee and monitor various aspects of the plan, including administration of the plan within the states, which would be given considerable responsibility and flexibility if the plan were adopted. Part of the strategy was to make both providers and consumers more cost conscious by offering everyone a choice of plans. This would foster competition among the provider networks, all of whom would have to offer a guaranteed benefit package.

Other proposals introduced in Congress deviate in various ways from the president's plan. One prominent theme that has taken a variety of forms during the past 25 years is the call for a national health plan, often referred to as the single-payer option. The model favored by many is the one adopted by Canada, where the government is the single payer, everyone is covered, and people freely select their providers. Considerable savings would be realized through elimination of the insurance industry. Proponents predict that such a government-run program could be financed by money that is already in the system.

Republicans in Congress have introduced a number of proposed health plans, all of which favor less government intervention than the president has called for. Although some of these more conservative plans have similarities to the one proposed by President Clinton, in general they would not include an employer mandate; they call for gradually achieving universal coverage, and they do not favor sweeping restructuring of the nation's health care system. Many policymakers who hesitate to embark on uncharted waters support the concept of providing tax credits or other means to make insurance more affordable for the unemployed and others who are uninsured in order to provide easier access to benefits, but many of them consider universal coverage to be an unrealistic first step. Much of the debate centers on how much reform will cost and how to pay for it. No one expects it to come cheaply.

We open this chapter with an overview of health care reform by policy analysts Philip R. Lee, Denise Soffel, and Harold S. Luft. The authors provide an insight into the root causes of the current crisis: rising costs and the growing ranks of uninsured. This is followed by a discussion of factors contributing to rising health care costs, including market failure, high technology, administrative costs, unnecessary care and defensive medicine, patient complexity, excess capacity, and low productivity. Lee and associates also assess attempts to control costs by the federal government and the private sector, which have been largely unsuccessful.

Eli Ginzberg, a veteran health policy analyst, provides us with a capsule summary of the positions the various interest groups have carved out for themselves on the subject of reform. Despite the intransigence of most of these groups, he predicts that some means of reform will be undertaken soon because of the simple fact that the nation cannot possibly afford to continue on its present path through the rest of the 1990s. He follows with a discussion of the urgent need for global budgeting, which would place a cap on annual expenditures in order to limit health care spending.

While he echoes many of Dr. Ginzberg's concerns about the urgent need for reform, David Blumenthal is less optimistic about the prospect for policymakers to "brave the adverse consequences" endemic in any attempt at sweeping reform. In "The Timing and Course of Health Care Reform," he predicts that any package implemented in the near future "will perpetuate at least some of the current system's inequities and inefficiencies." Thus the crisis atmosphere surrounding health care will continue to build until its catastrophic effects are experienced first hand by a greater proportion of the electorate and the national economy is threatened.

John K. Iglehart writes regularly for *The New England Journal of Medicine* concerning the nation's health care system. His articles are always a great contribution to the dialogue because they include clear, articulate analyses of some of our most complex concepts and issues. This fourth edition of *The Nation's Health* includes analyses by Mr. Iglehart of two of the most important concepts that are part of the current debate on health care reform. The first of these is on the subject of managed competition and the second is on managed care. Both terms are likely to be with us for a long time, and having an understanding of their roots and their range of implications is essential to students of the health care system.

The first principle, managed competition, is embraced at least in part by a number of health care reform plans that have been considered by Congress in recent years, and it is a central factor in the president's plan. The second concept, managed care, is already a reality for many Americans, and we can expect that more and more of us will come to experience it in the coming years. Mr. Iglehart provides a valuable analysis of the trend toward "plans that integrate the delivery and financing of care and that apply new constraints on encounters between physicians and patients," which have proliferated in the past decade. The author provides a historical overview of such plans, which have been evolving for many years, and he describes the different features of various forms managed care can take and how the plans function to reduce physician spending. In summarizing the potential role of managed care plans, Iglehart cautions that players in the system must accept the fact that the current system is no longer considered viable. Thus in evaluating managed care, we must compare it to the alternatives, one of the most obvious being centralized government regulation.

This chapter would not be complete without a statement that reflects the point of view of physicians. In this role is one of medicine's most articulate and important spokesmen, George D. Lundberg, editor of the *Journal of the American Medical Association*. In his article "National Health Care Reform: The Aura of Inevitability Intensifies," Dr. Lundberg begins by outlining five national and world events that brought the health care reform debate to the political forefront of the nation. He then describes the necessary characteristics of what he views as a successful reform package, including specific steps to control costs, and he closes with a call for compromise among all players in the system in order to prevent "the 1990s health care system meltdown."

We close the chapter with a list of highlights from the health care plan introduced to the nation in 1993 by President Bill Clinton.

❖ Costs and Coverage: Pressures toward Health Care Reform

PHILIP R. LEE, DENISE SOFFEL,
AND HAROLD S. LUFT

A survey conducted by Louis Harris and Associates in 1988 found that 89% of Americans wanted to see a dramatic change in the health care system: 29% thought that the health care system needs to be completely rebuilt, and an additional 60% thought that the system needs fundamental changes. A poll conducted by *Time* and the Cable News Network found that 91% of Americans thought that the health care system needs fundamental change, and 75% of those surveyed said that costs are much higher than they should be. A poll in 1990 found only 10% of Americans satisfied with the current health care system, in contrast to 56% in Canada, 41% in West Germany, and 22% in Great Britain.

Clearly the public perceives a problem that stems from the high cost of health care, and they call for the federal government to engineer major reforms. Research by the Public Agenda Foundation, in association with the Gallup organization and the Employee Benefit Research Institute, suggests that the public is particularly concerned about out-of-pocket costs. According to the Public Agenda Foundation, people attribute high costs to "unnecessary tests, overpaid doctors, wasteful hospitals, profiteering drug companies, and greedy malpractice lawyers." Surveys have found that the great majority of the public thinks that spending on physician services is too high and that physicians are too interested in financial reward.

The general public concern is that physician fees are too high, and, in fact, physicians' real earnings have increased considerably in the past decade. Average inflation-adjusted physician income grew by 24% from 1982 to 1989. This increase was not spread equally across all specialties, however, with some experiencing only modest gains as others reaped dramatic increases. In areas like family practice and internal medicine, income levels have been relatively flat.

Although Medicare policy changes to control costs have been enacted by Congress since 1983, little interest has been shown for systemic reforms until recently. Only in the past year has the notion of a major federal role in cost containment for the private sector begun to attract serious attention. In recent years, more than 40 bills have been introduced in Congress, ranging from incremental changes in health insurance and malpractice reform to sweeping "top-down" reform. The three basic approaches before Congress are a market approach, a single-payer approach, and a "play or pay" approach.

At the state level, discontent is also evident, particularly with reduced state revenues and climbing Medicaid expenditures. Minnesota recently enacted a plan to cover the uninsured, and more than 30 states are considering major health care reforms.

Physicians agree that there is a problem, although they tend to focus on the uninsured rather than on rising costs. Health care reform issues are beginning to attract attention within medicine. The American Medical Association, the American College of Physicians, and the American Academy of Family Practice all supported the Medicare fee schedule included as part of the 1989 Medicare physician payment reforms enacted by Congress. The landmark May 15, 1991, issue of the *Journal of the American Medical Association* and now a second special issue dedicated to health care reform proposals illustrate a broad, open approach, in contrast to the past when most proposals suggesting government intervention were rejected out of hand by physician organizations. Indeed, the American Medical Association has endorsed the idea of government-mandated private insurance coverage and has hinted that it might support some form of overall cost containment. The California Medical Association qualified a proposition for the November 1992 ballot called Affordable Basic Care that would require employers to provide health insurance for their employees. In September 1992 the American College of Physicians published their plan for systemwide reform in the organization and financing of health care.

❖ Factors Driving Reform: Rising Costs and the Uninsured

Growing calls for health care reform in the United States are largely the result of two factors: the continued increase in health care costs, which have been well above increases in gross national product (GNP) for most of the past 20 years, and the large number of uninsured and underinsured. In addition, as costs increase, employer coverage is deteriorating. Millions of people will not change jobs for fear of losing their employment-based private health insurance. This is due in part to the erosion of risk-pooling and the increasing use of experience rating, the practice of pegging a group's insurance premiums to its historical use patterns. This practice is in contrast to community rating, which charges insurance premiums based on the experience of an entire community rather than a small group. Insecurity about changing health plans is further exacerbated by preexisting condition clauses that exclude or impose restrictions on coverage for health problems documented at the time of enrollment. Finally, it is a matter of increasing concern that the United States does not compare well with other industrial democracies in universal coverage, cost containment, and health status.

Rising Health Care Costs

The most important factor propelling health care reform in the United States is the cost of health care, both in absolute terms and in the rate of cost increases. A few figures tell the story. Measured in current dollars, health care spending in the United States between 1970 and 1990 rose at an annual rate of 11.6%, whereas national income, as measured by the GNP, increased at an average annual rate of 8.8%. As a result, the share of the GNP devoted to health care grew by more than half in 20 years: from 7.3% to 12.3%. The Commerce Department predicts that the share of the GNP devoted to health care will rise to 14% very soon. The Health Care Financing Administration (HCFA) projects that health care will absorb more than 16% of the GNP by the year 2000.

The pluralistic nature of health care financing means that persons, families, insurers, employers, and government at all levels (federal, state, and local) are affected by high costs.

In the end, it is families and individuals who bear the financial burden. Steuerle analyzes the cost to families in a manner that reveals the true cost of health care. He estimates that the average expenditure per household is $8,000 per year. Of this, only about a third is paid directly by household members. The largest costs are indirect, particularly through taxes that finance public programs and reduced wages that are siphoned into insurance premiums paid by employers.

Spiraling costs are also endured by Medicare beneficiaries. Although Medicare is a major source of financial security for older Americans, the proportion of their income spent on health care is increasing. In 1972, they spent 10.6% of their income on health care. This rose to 16.2% in 1984 and 17.1% in 1991. The bulk of the increase has been in Medi-Gap premiums and direct out-of-pocket costs—deductibles and coinsurance for private health insurance and Medicare Part A and Part B; balance bills and uncovered services, such as prescription drugs; and nursing home costs.

Health care is also taking a growing portion of federal funds. In 1970, spending on health constituted 7.1% of the federal budget, a share that rose to 13.4% in 1990. The Congressional Budget Office projects that health care will account for more than 20% of the federal budget by 1996. Although federal health expenditures are projected to rise by 7.0% annually, Social Security expenditures are expected to rise by 2.2%, net interest on the debt 1.4%, and the percentages devoted to all other federal expenditures are expected to decline.

Uninsured Americans

The second major factor stimulating a host of health care reform proposals is the growing population of uninsured persons. Most estimates place the number of Americans without public or private health insurance between 31 and 36 million. The 1987 National Medical Care Expenditure Survey found that 18.5% of the population (47.8 million Americans) lacked health insurance for all or part of 1987. On any given day, between 34 and 36 million were uninsured, and 24.5 million were uninsured throughout the year. Analysis of the March 1990 Current Population Survey found that 33.4 million people (13.6% of the population) had no health insurance (public or private) throughout 1989. Thus, millions of people in this country lack access to even the most basic health services.

The 1987 survey found that of the uninsured population, 70% were employed or dependents of employed persons. Approximately 10% are unemployed persons and their dependents, and the remainder are nonworkers, such as students.

The number of uninsured increased rapidly between 1979 and 1984, from 28.8 million in 1979 to 37.3 million in 1984. The most notable factor in the rising number of uninsured Americans was the recession of the early 1980s. From 1984 though 1989 the number of uninsured seems to have stabilized. It is not yet clear what effect the current recession has had on the number of uninsured persons. Unemployment is currently more than 7% nationwide, and it is even higher in some regions, such as California, where it is 9.5%. Signs of an economic recovery are still faint.

The continuing realignment of the economy, with changes in the mix of industries and occupations, is also contributing to the rise in the number of uninsured. The volume of jobs in the manufacturing sector is declining as the service sector is growing. The manufacturing sector has a strong union tradition with generous employee benefits. Whereas 90% of persons working in manufacturing had health insurance in 1990, employees in most other sectors of the economy did not receive health benefits at this level. Of those employed in agriculture 30% did not have health insurance, and of those in service sector jobs 25% did not. Also, the erosion of Medicaid in many states has resulted in a growing number of poor without Medicaid eligibility. Where 65% of the poor were once eligible for Medicaid, the program now covers less than 40% of the population below poverty.

Good health is a basic part of a large dream of opportunity.
—Edward M. Kennedy

Lack of public or private insurance coverage ranges from less than 10% in 13 states, including Hawaii, Massachusetts, Connecticut, Michigan, Wisconsin, and Iowa, to more than 20% in Texas, Louisiana, and New Mexico. California has the largest number of uninsured, a figure that has climbed to 6 million. Uninsured persons are found in disproportionate numbers among those 18 to 28 years of age, Hispanics and African Americans, those with low incomes, and those living in rural areas.

A lack of insurance has several important consequences. It places a substantial financial burden on persons and families with relatively low incomes. High costs reduce access to care for appropriate services. Poor access to primary care is associated with increased health care costs and decreased health status.

❖ Factors Contributing to Rising Health Care Costs

As problems related to costs and the uninsured motivate policymakers to explore ways to improve or revamp the medical care system, assessments of various proposals must consider how they address these twin issues. Most of the current crop of proposals offer some detail on how they will address the problem of insurance coverage. Specifics on how costs will be contained are less often available. To assess the plausibility of various approaches, it is helpful to examine first the causes of spiraling health care costs.

The rise in personal health care expenditures can be broken into four components: general inflation, as measured by the consumer price index; population growth; medical care price inflation above general inflation; and all other factors, including increases in volume and intensity of services. Whereas the components that are not controllable within the health care system—general inflation and population growth—accounted for about 55% of the increase in the past 20 years, medical care price inflation has accounted for 17% of the increase and the volume and intensity of services for approximately 28%.

It is difficult to differentiate the effects of medical care inflation, quality improvements, and increased volume and intensity. This collection of components, however, is affected by a variety of factors, including

- ❖ Market failure
- ❖ Technology
- ❖ Administrative costs
- ❖ Unnecessary care and defensive medicine
- ❖ Patient complexity
- ❖ Excess capacity
- ❖ Productivity

Market Failure

Market failure is an economic term describing a situation in which normal marketplace behavior cannot be assumed to lead automatically to an efficient allocation of resources. In this context, "failure" is a technical explanation of the common observation that medical care is different from other goods and services. Five factors contribute to market failure in the United States: suppliers may influence demand, consumers are usually cost "unconscious" when using medical care, workers are shielded from the true costs of insurance, uncertainty in the services needed for treating individual patients leads to the predominance of fee-for-service reimbursement, and information is lacking on what works.

An inherent aspect of medical care, regardless of the organizational and economic system, is uncertainty at the outset concerning the need for and efficacy of specific treatments. Arrow's classic article on this issue laid the groundwork for the field of health economics.

In the United States, the consumers' desire to insure against the risk of costly medical care led to the growth of private health insurance, both employment-based and self-purchased. The number of companies providing group health insurance has grown from only 37 such companies in 1942 to more than 1,500 companies today. Although about 100 companies provide coverage to 90% of the covered population, and an additional 250 companies provide most of the rest, hundreds of other companies provide some type of health coverage.

Fragmentation of the insurance market has several deleterious effects. First, because providers are reimbursed by many insurers, each company represents a small fraction of a physician's caseload. Thus, it is impossible for an individual carrier to collect valid information about a provider's quality and practice style. It also becomes infeasible to negotiate average payment rates for episodes of care as an alternative to fee-for-service reimbursement while protecting physicians from costs associated with treating patients with unusually complicated conditions. Second, competition among insurers for enrollees leads to fragmentation of the risk pool (those being insured) because of the voluntary nature of health insurance and the fact that more and more insurers use experience rating. Voluntary enrollment means that a given premium will be most attractive to those most in need of treatment. Because of this, insurers will seek to avoid high-risk enrollees.

Technology

Developments in technology—new drugs, devices, and procedures—play an important role in improving the quality and effectiveness of health care and in escalating costs. After pharmaceuticals are developed and approved as safe and effective for specific indications, their application may be broadened, and they may be used when they are only marginally effective or even ineffective. Diagnostic technologies such as endoscopy, computed tomographic scan, and magnetic resonance imaging may also be used initially for a limited number of indications, but gradually the application is broadened, and there may be misuse, overuse, and underuse.

Administrative Costs

Administrative costs have been the focus of considerable interest and complaint but not a large amount of careful research. These include the costs of claims processing to pay physician and hospital bills, marketing, enrollment, and eligibility determination, including risk profiling. A particularly difficult problem is posed for small businesses: health insurance premiums are higher because of administrative costs that can be as much as 35% greater than those for large employers with the same coverage. In addition, in their effort to contain costs through constraining use, payers have developed extensive review and authorization programs, further adding to administrative costs. Not only are administrative costs high for third-party payers, but costs of administration must be borne by hospitals, nursing homes, physicians, and consumers.

It has been estimated that administrative costs account for about 25% of the $738 billion health care expenditures in 1991. Estimated savings in administrative costs for various health care reform proposals range from $31 billion to $67 billion or even $100 billion for single-payer systems.

Unnecessary Care and Defensive Medicine

Growing attention in recent years has been focused on the potential importance of unnecessary care, including defensive medicine, in rising health care costs. Whereas some care may be deemed unnecessary or inappropriate on retrospective review, it is difficult to make such a judgment at the time the care is provided. The existence of uncertainty in clinical decision making has always been recognized, but it has long been thought to be a random occurrence with few economic or policy implications. A major factor, in Wennberg's view, has been uncertainty about outcomes of care and the fact that practice styles and patterns of practice vary idiosyncratically from one community to another. Additional evidence regarding inappropriate or unnecessary care has come from the work of Chassin and associates. Their studies suggest that for some procedures the application to specific clinical situations may be inappropriate as much as a third of the time.

It is difficult to estimate the effect of malpractice on defensive medicine and the cost of health care. . . . A 1991 study estimated that between 1982 and 1989, about 1% per year has been added to expenditures for physician services as a result of the professional liability system. The authors concluded that 30% of professional liability costs went to the direct payment of malpractice premiums, whereas 70% was attributable to practicing defensive medicine.

Patient Complexity

Patient complexity is recognized as a factor of importance in the cost of care, particularly for low-birth-weight infants; older persons with multiple chronic diseases and disabilities; patients infected with the human immunodeficiency virus (HIV) or acquired immunodeficiency syndrome (AIDS), particularly those with numerous infections, including drug-resistant tuberculosis; trauma patients with multiple injuries associated with the growing wave of violence; and patients requiring such major procedures as heart, lung, and liver transplants. It is evident to most clinicians that because of the rapid increase in ambulatory and hospital outpatient services, patients are coming to the hospital with more complex and difficult problems. Although these factors are important clinically and affect increases in hospital costs, they are not a major factor in overall cost increases because the less complicated segment of patients is being treated in less costly settings.

Excess Capacity

The issue of excess capacity is yet to be seriously addressed by policymakers, but it is likely to become more and more important. Excess capacity is evident in some areas, such as in the number of hospital beds and the availability of medical technologies. Statewide hospital occupancy rates in 1988 were as low as 49% in Alaska, 52% in Wyoming, and 55% in Louisiana, Nebraska, and Texas. Nationwide, one in three hospital beds has been empty since 1985, as hospital occupancy rates have dropped below 65%. Recent work by Fisher and associates, using the techniques of small area analysis, estimated savings in Oregon of as much as $50 million if the hospital bed supply were reduced.

The current supply of physicians is also in excess of what is needed, and there is certainly a maldistribution by specialty and geographic area. Most of the imbalance by medical specialty has resulted from a rapid growth in surgical specialties and medical subspecialties. A projection of the supply of physicians by specialty for 1990 showed shortages in the five specialties of child psychiatry, physical medicine, emergency medicine, preventive medicine, and psychiatry and an oversupply in 16, with cardiology, endocrinology, neurosurgery, and pulmonary showing the greatest surpluses. More recently, both the Council of Graduate Medical Education and the Bureau of Health Professions reported a physician surplus, although persistent problems of maldistribution, both by specialty and by geography, continue to leave some areas underserved.

Physician supply has increased rapidly since the mid-1960s when federal and state policies were implemented to increase medical student enrollments and expand physician supply. Total nonfederal patient care physicians per 100,000 population increased from 125 in 1965 to 193 in 1989. The United States now has more physicians per capita than almost all other nations.

Productivity

Assessing productivity in medical care is important, but conventional measures of productivity are inherently limited. Productivity is usually defined in terms of output per labor hour, and industry typically attempts to increase productivity by substituting new machinery for workers. The service and cognitive aspects of medical care make it difficult to achieve productivity increases in this manner, although some opportunities do exist. Changes ranging from laparoscopic surgical procedures to computerized billing systems can reduce labor input.

From a population perspective, the greatest productivity improvements are likely to come from two areas: increased prevention of illness and reduced use of marginally effective interventions.

❖ Health Care Reforms: Setting the Stage

During the past 20 years, and particularly in the past decade, actions have been taken by the private and public sectors to slow the rate of increase in health care costs. Considerably less has been done to expand health insurance coverage to uninsured persons. Beginning in 1984, however, Congress has mandated incremental changes in Medicaid eligibility. This legislation, culminating with the Omnibus Budget Reconciliation acts of 1989 and 1990, required all states to establish minimum Medicaid income eligibility thresholds at 133% of the poverty level for children younger than 6 and then to phase in coverage, one year at a time, for children ages 18 and younger. Several states have taken limited additional actions in an attempt to increase access for the uninsured. Minnesota recently enacted a major reform proposal to cover uninsured persons, and Vermont passed legislation to set in motion a plan for statewide health care coverage by 1995. Several other states are likely to enact reform proposals soon.

The first major federal attempt to contain Medicare costs was the "prospective payment system" for hospitals, passed in 1983 and implemented in the mid-1980s. It had two important effects, one intended and one unintended. As intended, expenditures for Part A (hospital services) slowed notably relative to previous trends. An unintended consequence of the fixed payments, however, was that hospitals were no longer able to cross-subsidize uninsured patients through cost reimbursement with paying patients. This difficulty was exacerbated by the growth of contracting with hospitals by Medicaid programs, particularly Medi-Cal in California, and preferred provider organizations and insurers. The spread of fixed-payment arrangements and contracts by payers unwilling to cross-subsidize led to rapid increases in charges (list prices) paid by the shrinking pool of conventionally insured. This, in turn, has forced up the premiums for small group enrollees—large groups typically have the power to negotiate discounts— and often to a loss of coverage. It has also deprived hospitals of implicit subsidies, which had been used for uncompensated care, adding to hospitals' financial stress and an increasing reliance on public facilities to provide care for uninsured persons.

The second major step by the federal government to curtail Medicare expenditures began in 1984, when Congress froze physician payments in the Medicare program. Congress followed by reducing payments for overvalued procedures, including many surgical and imaging procedures, limiting charges by physicians above the Medicare allowed charge—the Maximum Actual Allowable Charge program—and establishing the participating physician and provider program. These efforts culminated in 1989 with the enactment of the comprehensive Medicare physician payment reforms, including establishment of the Medicare fee schedule, limits on balance billing, and volume performance standards.

Following implementation of the Medicare fee schedule on January 1, 1992, many private payers began to consider applying a fee schedule based on the Medicare relative value scale but with a different conversion factor. How widespread this will become remains to be seen.

In the private sector, actions have been taken by self-insured employers and by commercial and nonprofit insurance companies. In their attempt to control costs, employers have emphasized competitive market-based strategies. These include shifting costs to employees through co-payments, deductibles, and increased premium costs; reducing benefits, sometimes eliminating coverage for dependents; cost management, including utilization review, concurrent review, preadmission or preprocedure certification, and case management; managed competition; and selective contracting. Many of these approaches have affected practicing physicians, adding to what has been called the "hassle factor."

In response, physician groups, including the California Medical Association, have proposed major initiatives to extend health insurance coverage universally. Many of these proposals have called for employer-mandated health insurance and an expansion of Medicaid to cover the unemployed and unemployable younger than 65. The Physicians for a National Health Program proposal suggests a more basic restructuring of the way health care is financed, proposing a single, comprehensive public insurance program.

The problems of the health care system arise from a combination of social, legal, historical, political, and technologic factors. Simple solutions are unlikely to work, but the prospect of important changes has energized the policy debate.

❖ About the Authors

Philip R. Lee, M.D., was appointed by President Clinton as Assistant Secretary for Health, Department of Health and Human Services, in 1993. Prior to that he was Professor of Social Medicine, Institute for Health Policy Studies, School of Medicine, University of California, San Francisco, and was the founding director of the Institute.

Denise Soffel, PH.D., was a postdoctoral fellow in the Pew Health Policy Program, Institute for Health Policy Studies and Institute for Health and Aging, University of California, San Francisco, 1991–1993.

Harold S. Luft, PH.D., is Professor of Health Economics and Acting Director of the Institute for Health Policy Studies, School of Medicine, University of California, San Francisco.

❖ Health Care Reform: Where Are We and Where Should We Be Going?

Eli Ginzberg

My intention here is to explore where the nation stands on health care reform and to assess when the issue may move beyond rhetoric and preliminary skirmishing to substantive political engagement.

A good place to begin is to identify the principal parties whose action or inaction will determine when health care reform will rise to the top of the nation's agenda. Much of the answer will depend on the direction taken by the four principal payers: the federal government, employers, state governments, and households.

The federal government, faced with a prospective annual deficit of $400 billion, is poorly positioned to take any initiative that would require substantial new outlays.

Matters of resources aside, it would be out of harmony with U.S. political tradition to expect Congress to act on major health care reform in the face of disagreement and lack of agreement among the principal pressure groups about the direction reform should take.

Employers, the second major payer, are deeply divided. Some would welcome the opportunity to end their commitment to provide health insurance benefits to their employees, active and retired, but many others believe that the prospect of unloading this task on the public sector is doomed to failure. No government plan would match in breadth and depth the benefits that large employers currently provide, which means they would be forced to offer their employees supplemental health benefits.

Furthermore, many employers are disinclined to see their freedom restricted by a possible modification of the Employee Retirement Income Security Act (ERISA), the federal statute governing employee benefits, which has protected them since 1974 from numerous state taxes and regulations. Moreover, they will avoid any action that might expand the jurisdiction of the federal government over employee benefits. True, employers are disturbed by the large annual increases in the cost of health benefits, but not to the point of taking the initiative to broaden federal involvement.

State governments have been protesting to the administration and Congress since the late 1980s over continuing congressional mandates to extend eligibility and broaden benefits under their Medicaid programs. In 1989, the National Governors Association officially requested that such mandates cease, and when Congress turned a deaf ear to their pleas, the states resorted to various financial schemes to enrich federal matching grants for their Medicaid programs. These were of such dubious propriety that the administration and Congress outlawed many of them. Even with additional federal matching money, steeply rising expenditures for Medicaid will inhibit most states from initiating substantial health care reforms. It is therefore noteworth that a few—namely, Oregon, Minnesota, and Vermont—are moving ahead with efforts aimed explicitly at providing universal coverage.

Households—the fourth source of payment—are concerned about deficiencies in insurance coverage and increases in out-of-pocket costs. The number of people with private health insurance has been dropping since 1989, and people with a history of serious medical problems often find that if they lose their coverage they are unable to replace it at an affordable price. The same is true of people in good health who work in high-risk industries or for a small employer; health insurance, if obtainable at all, comes at a cost that is frequently beyond the reach of employers and employees alike. The failure of Medicare to cover long-term care, either in a nursing home or at home, is a cause of anxiety for large numbers of older people, who are disturbed by their growing personal outlays.

In sum, the principal payers—the federal government, employers, state governments, and households—are poorly positioned to assume the leadership in health care reform. The four could provide coverage for the uninsured and make at least limited benefits available for long-term care, but not until U.S. taxpayers change their formidable resistance to higher taxes.

Let us now shift focus to the principal provider groups—physicians, hospitals, pharmaceutical and medical-supply companies, and various types of managed-care organizations. Physicians, the key provider group, generating about 75 percent of all health care costs, are frustrated by the steady erosion of their clinical autonomy, the avalanche of paper with which they must contend, and the latest assault on their earnings by the Health Care Financing Administration, which under the current resource-based relative-value scale is capping both their fees and the volume of services they provide to Medicare patients. The disruptions caused by malpractice litigation continue, though recent years have seen some reduction on this front. Despite these threats to their professional integrity and career satisfaction, physicians are not in the vanguard of health care reform. Most of them continue to prefer their current fee-for-service arrangements, which yield a mean annual income of about $165,000, to prospective reforms that hold uncertain promise of reducing or eliminating the drawbacks in their current practice environment.

In the late 1970s, the hospitals were able to prevent the Carter administration from introducing new federal regulations aimed at capping their expenditures; since then, they have directed their political efforts at protecting their freedom of decision making as regards new investments and current operations. More recently, governmental payers have reduced their reimbursements for inpatient care, and private-sector payers have applied increasing pressure to obtain price discounts, often in exchange for a guaranteed number of admissions. Although their margins for patient care and their total margins have been declining, most hospitals continue to operate in the black. With an average occupancy rate of slightly more than 60 percent, many are uncertain about the future, but for now hospital trustees and chief executive officers generally prefer the status quo to any alternative they see on the horizon.

The pharmaceutical and medical-supply companies have had few if any reasons to complain in the free-wheeling financing environment of recent decades because of the insatiable appetite of hospitals, physicians, and households for the latest innovations spawned by research and technology. Although a few warning shots have been fired—namely, the requirement by the Health Care Financing Administration that the cost effectiveness of selected new forms of technology be assessed before payment is approved and recent legislation by Congress requiring maximal discounts to the federal government on the purchase of drugs—the large, for-profit manufacturers of health care products have much to gain from the continuation of the status quo. This perception still guides their behavior.

The last of the principal providers are the many for-profit and nonprofit organizations, small and large, that continue to develop new financing and delivery mechanisms, including health maintenance organizations, preferred-provider organizations, and risk-sharing arrangements between large employers and insurance companies. These entities have grown considerably since the early 1980s, from about 10 million enrollees to close to 40 million, but their future remains uncertain for a variety of reasons: physicians prefer to practice in a fee-for-service system, large numbers of the insured prefer to retain total freedom in their choice of providers, and new risk-sharing systems for the delivery of managed care are difficult to organize. Exacerbating this uncertainty about the future is the limited success these innovations have had in braking costs—their *raison d'être*. A reasonable assumption is that the new entities will continue to expand, but not at a rate that will substantially alter the established patterns of health care financing and delivery in the United States. In short, providers, like payers, do not appear to have any strong drive to assume leadership in the reform of the health care system.

Can one conclude from the foregoing that reform is a mirage, a subject for discussion but not for action? To remain on the present trajectory, the United States would have to find another trillion dollars between the mid-1990s and the end of the decade. It is my contention that at recent and projected rates of economic growth, a second trillion dollars to support the nation's health care system will not be forthcoming in the last half of the 1990s. Such a level of expenditure would imply an average yearly health care cost of $320,000 per family of four, more than that family will be paying for food, clothing, housing, and transportation combined. Even if the dollars could be found, it would make no sense.

What are the implications of this spending projection for health care reform? First and foremost, the current health care system, more attractive to most payers and providers than the alternatives they can anticipate, is likely to be derailed later in this decade. The derailment of the current system will mean the loss of private health insurance for many people; it will place many small and large hospitals at serious risk of bankruptcy; both the federal and state governments will be forced to appropriate emergency funds to ensure the maintenance of critical health care services; and all the other concerned parties, particularly physicians and patients, will be seriously disrupted. When that happens, reform will of necessity command attention; inaction and drift will no longer be possible.

The U.S. has one of the most inefficient health care systems in the world, as well as one of the most expensive.
—Richard D. Lamm, Governor of Colorado, 1975–1987

In April 1991, Charles Bowsher, the comptroller general of the United States, testified before the House Ways and Means Committee and offered the following agenda for reform: universal coverage, global budgeting, and administrative simplification. Congress listened and did nothing, taking its lead from interest groups and the public at large, which continue to complain vociferously about the current system but are not willing to pay the price of reforming it. A first challenge is therefore to impress on the concerned parties and the public that time is running out and that unless a reform effort begins now, the long-term costs will be horrendous.

In terms of priorities, I believe we should immediately address the comptroller general's second proposal, global budgeting, which holds the greatest promise of stabilizing our increasingly unstable health care system. If successful, it will give us time to introduce the many other reforms that are needed to ensure the system's viability. Since the federal government pays for 30 percent of all health care expenditures, covers more than half of all Medicaid costs, and undergirds private health insurance through its tax subsidy, it should be able to elicit the cooperation of the key parties—employers, private health insurers, and state governments—in implementing global budgeting. Annual expenditures would be capped at the previous year's total plus a sum that did not outstrip by much the growth rate of the gross national product.

The critical step in implementing global budgeting is broad public support for action now, rather than temporizing until we have the chaos that is inevitable if we delay. What are the steps that must be taken promptly? Since the states will have the task of allocating their share of the global funding to the health care providers within their jurisdictions, they will need to elaborate and strengthen their statistical reporting systems. They will also need to design and implement the bargaining mechanisms that will guide their payments to providers. These new mechanisms will require a period of experimentation, ongoing assessment of their early operating results, and subsequent refinement and adjustment.

We are not starting from scratch, however. A number of states have considerable experience as sole payers for hospital care. Having put in place a radically revised fee system under Medicare, the federal government is accumulating experience in physician reimbursement within budgetary constraints. Implementing a system of global budgeting will obviously not be easy, but given the alternative of financial chaos and institutional disintegration, the difficulties encountered in its implementation should not be insurmountable. With so much to lose, the key parties should be willing to cooperate in the development and institution of global budgeting. It alone offers them the prospect of protecting their current interests and providing the stability they will need to advance those interests in the future.

❖ About the Author

Eli Ginzberg, PH.D., is Director of the Eisenhower Center for the Conservation of Human Resources, Columbia University, New York City.

❖ The Timing and Course of Health Care Reform

DAVID BLUMENTHAL

The conventional wisdom among health policy makers now holds (as it did 20 years ago) that major federal reform in our health system is just a matter of time. This view originates in the extraordinary economic, social, and ethical tensions created by a system that consumes 12 percent of our gross national product while failing to provide any insurance coverage to over 31 million citizens. Business, it is argued, will soon rebel against the cost of health care. The public at large, scandalized by the plight of the uninsured and insecure about eroding private health care coverage, will support a guaranteed federal entitlement to health care insurance.

Like all conventional wisdom, the view that major reform is upon us is plausible but potentially misleading. The current politics and past experience of health care reform suggest the need for caution in predicting wholesale change before the late 1990s.

Our message is simple and it's straightforward. The hospital field in the United States today is in fragile condition.... Congress can no longer balance the budget with cuts in the public Medicare and Medicaid expenditures without damage to all who rely on a sound health care delivery system.
—Carol McCarthy, President, American Hospital Association

Two basic observations underlie this assertion. First, for a variety of reasons the political requirements for substantial health care reform are not yet in place. Second, American political institutions favor incremental over revolutionary change, making it likely that any reformed system will perpetuate at least some of the current system's inequities and inefficiencies.

❖ The Politics of Health Care Reform
The Role of Business

The concern of business leaders about the rising cost of health care is increasingly clear and obviously justified. Between 1989 and 1990, average health care premiums increased by more than 17 percent, and between 1965 and 1987 health care increased from 2 percent to 6 percent of the average company's payroll expenses.

Business can play an important part in stimulating health care reform. The political importance of business's changing views on health care should not be overestimated, however. Substantial segments of the business community, including the drug, equipment, hospital, and nursing home industries, benefit from the continued growth of health care expenditures and are unlikely to support aggressive new cost-control measures. There is also no consensus among business leaders about how to achieve the critical goal of controlling costs: whether to support regulation or the as yet unproved strategy of competition.

Similarly, there is no consensus in the business community about how to provide health insurance for the nation's uninsured. Some large companies are relatively receptive to the concept of mandating that all employers provide some kind of coverage for employees and their dependents. The reason is that 99 percent of companies with more than 100 employees already insure their workers. Small businesses, however, vigorously oppose this approach, since substantial numbers of them do not currently cover their employees.

The American Public

As Blendon and Donelan have demonstrated, public opinion concerning health care reform is a minefield of contradictory views. More Americans (73 percent) now favor a federally financed national health care program than at any time since 1965. But only 14 percent consider it one of the two most important problems facing our country, and only 22 percent would pay more than $200 a year in new taxes to support a national health care program. As for cost control, two thirds of Americans report that as a nation we spend too little on health care.

In response to these conflicting findings, Blendon and Donelan propose a series of principles that may very well form the basis for the compromise that eventually enacts health care reform. But a key question is: Where is the political impetus for risk-averse politicians to set foot in this minefield to begin with?

Both cost control and expanded access carry major political risks. Cost control is not inherently popular with the public at large, and it has the potential to reduce the availability of services as providers cut back in the face of lower reimbursement. Expanding access to care for the uninsured will require higher taxes on middle-class Americans (if it is funded by government) or increase the financial burdens of small businesses (if it is achieved through mandating that employers provide health care insurance).

To brave these adverse consequences in health care reform, political leaders will have to be convinced that the voting public, including a substantial segment of the middle class, is deeply discontented with the health care system. That level of discontent does not yet seem to exist.

Most Americans, especially those who are employed, still enjoy reasonable access to services. In 1988, a full 87 percent of Americans (211 million of 243 million) had some public or private insurance against the cost of illness. Out-of-pocket expenditures for health care in 1988, including health insurance premiums, averaged only 5 percent of after-tax income, as compared with 6.1 percent in 1965.

This helps to explain why Senator John D. Rockefeller IV (D-W.Va.), chairman of the Pepper commission, has concluded that "politicians see more to lose than to gain in taking a stand" on major health care change. Despite the recent introduction of major Democratic health care legislation by Senators Kennedy, Riegle, Mitchell, and Rockefeller, support for such proposals is by no means universal among Democrats, and most Republicans are opposed.

Difficult as the problems of our health care system currently are, they will probably have to get worse before discontent becomes widespread among voters. This is most likely to occur through the erosion of workplace health care benefits, as businesses transfer increasing costs to their employees in the form of larger copayments or reduced coverage. That process is less advanced than many observers may have surmised. Employees' share of their health insurance premiums was unchanged between 1986 and 1988 and increased only 4 percent on average between 1988 and 1989.

❖ The Implications of Incrementalism

The history of federal health care reform further suggests that the government is likely to undertake change in limited incremental steps rather than great leaps. Important as the enactment of Medicare was, it actually constituted an incremental expansion of a preexisting program of social insurance—the social security system. Similarly, Medicaid represented an extension and revision of the preexisting Kerr–Mills program, a cooperative state and federal initiative providing health care coverage to the elderly poor.

The tendency toward incremental reform in health care suggests that any federal initiative will preserve and build on important features of the current health care system, including the following.

First, employment-based insurance. In 1988, 153 million Americans, 73 percent of the insured, obtained health insurance in association with their employment. Although the employment-based system of health insurance is under pressure, it has by no means collapsed, and it would be uncharacteristic of Congress to reject it completely.

Second, the private health insurance industry. Politicians are reluctant to eviscerate industries, however cogent the policy rationale, and the private health insurance industry is unlikely to prove an exception to this rule. The industry employs tens of thousands of workers. Some of the 1,500 private health insurance companies can also claim respectable records of performance. The Traveler's Insurance Company, for example, uses only 10 cents of every dollar of health care premiums to cover its expenses, as compared with as much as 33 cents for some competitors. Even though public programs such as Medicare are more efficient in processing claims than any private company, putting companies such as Traveler's out of business is likely to be viewed as unjust.

Third, a pluralistic delivery system, including the fee-for-service practice of medicine. Americans remain committed to freedom of choice in selecting providers of health care. As Blendon and Donelan note, only 30 percent of Americans support a national health plan if it will limit their choice of physicians.

Fourth, a strong role for state government. The retreat of the federal government from support of domestic programs over the past decade has resulted in an increased state role in health policy. States are now in the forefront of experimentation with expanded access (Massachusetts and Hawaii) and cost containment (Maryland, New Jersey, Massachusetts, New York, and Oregon). Any broad federal proposal for health care reform seems likely to retain this strong state role, if only to limit the federal government's financial burden in providing health care protection to the uninsured.

If incrementalist tendencies in American health policy result in the preservation of these aspects of our current health care system, then any first federal attempt at health care reform may take the following shape: workplace-based private health insurance will be expanded to cover all or most employed Americans and their dependents; the free choice of providers will be preserved, as well as a strong role for the fee-for-service practice of medicine; and the states will be relied on to administer important aspects of the new system, including the regulation of private insurers and the provision of publicly sponsored insurance for those who are unemployed and uninsured, perhaps through an expanded Medicaid program. At least initially, states may also have some discretion in designing and implementing cost-control measures, although the federal government seems likely to impose standards of performance.

It is difficult enough to speculate on the characteristics of a new federal health insurance plan, let alone its likely effects on costs and access, but a few additional points are in order. First, continued reliance on private health insurance to provide coverage to most Americans could limit the hoped-for administrative savings that would result from creating a single source of payment for all health care expenditures.

Second, the preservation of fee-for-service practice may limit the success of cost-control efforts, since economic incentives to perform more services will persist. The record of Medicare's recent physician-payment reforms in affecting physician and other health care costs will be instructive in this regard.

Third, a strong state role in the administration of any national plan could mean that both the generosity of health care coverage for the nation's poor and the effectiveness of new cost-control efforts will continue to vary from state to state.

❖ The Importance of Time

The amount of time it takes to develop the necessary consensus and political will to reform our health system is a matter of no small importance. As our national debate goes on, uninsured Americans continue to encounter financial barriers to health care that affect both the quantity and the type of services they receive. Also, our commitment of economic resources to the health care sector continues to grow.

The implications of this growing commitment of resources are substantial. Fuchs has noted that from 1977 to 1987 health care expenditures rose relentlessly, at an average annual rate of 3 percent in real terms. If this 3 percent rate of increase persists, we shall be spending approximately 15 percent of our gross national product on health care by the year 2000. Once committed, these resources are unlikely to be withdrawn from the health care sector, regardless of the cost-control measures that any reforms put in place.

The full consequences of this long-term allocation of our national productive power to health care remain to be explored, but some likely effects are apparent. Each year, larger proportions of American industry and labor depend on health care for their livelihood. Between 1989 and 1990, the number of Americans employed in the health care industry grew 7.7 percent, to 8.4 million. As this trend continues, groups likely to oppose major federal cost-control programs will become progressively more powerful, and political consensus concerning federal legislation will become more difficult to achieve.

It is hard to avoid the conclusion that the growing crisis in American health care will have to reach unprecedented proportions if comprehensive national reform is to be successful. Health insurance will have to become unaffordable to substantial numbers of middle-class Americans. Costs will have to constitute a palpable, threat to the economic well-being of the nation. Whatever the timing of ultimate change, it is unlikely to occur before we have committed at least 15 percent of our national wealth to this single economic sector.

❖ About the Author

David Blumenthal, M.D., M.P.P., is on the staff of the Brigham and Women's Hospital, Boston.

❖ Managed Competition

JOHN K. IGLEHART

What is "managed competition," the blueprint for reforming the health care system that has been endorsed by President Bill Clinton and key elements of which former president George Bush incorporated into the scheme he introduced? As applied to practitioners, its central idea is to divide physicians and hospitals into competing economic units, called "accountable health partnerships," that would contract with insurance-purchasing cooperatives to provide standardized packages of medical benefits for fixed per capita rates. Thus, managed competition would hasten the demise of fee-for-service payment, require providers to bundle their care into defined benefit plans, and by remunerating providers at fixed rates, place them at financial risk for their performance. Taken together with other proposed reforms—presumably some form of global limit on expenditures—managed competition would lead to a restructuring of the health care system unprecedented in the U.S. experience.

Managed competition is based on a belief that economic incentives are the principal determinant of how patients, payers, and providers behave when they seek, finance, or render medical care. According to its proponents, if the incentives are changed and people are made to bear the economic consequences of their choices more directly, systemic reform will follow. But the model does not leave this prospect to the unpredictable ways of a free marketplace. Instead, it prescribes in detail the changes its architects deem necessary to transform the system through market-oriented principles. Moreover, recognizing that possible savings from managed competition may take years to realize, President Clinton has said that he would combine the plan with an annual global limit on expenditures.

Already, many physicians are no longer being reimbursed on a fee-for-service basis, and hospitals and medical groups are experimenting with offering packages of services. But physicians have been uneasy about moving to alternative payment schemes, such as capitation, because they fear for their clinical autonomy and their control over their incomes. Until now, policy makers, too, have been reluctant to endorse fixed, per capita payments as a systemwide approach because they encourage the provision of too few medical services—the opposite effect from that of the fee-for-service system. Medicare and Medicaid, for example, have lagged well behind private payers in their promotion of per capita payments for medical services. But in the administration's pursuit of more predictable trends in spending for medical services, its stewards are attracted to alternatives to fee-for-service medical care.

This report has two objectives: to sketch the broad outlines of managed competition and how it may change the current system, and to underscore the formidable challenge that looms for President Clinton as he seeks to sell his reform proposal. Persuading his fellow Democrats to embrace managed competition alone, with its emphasis on decentralized, private markets, may provoke a major struggle, since many party members favor direct government controls on payments to physicians and hospitals as the key to cost containment. Taking no chances, the President offers both approaches.

❖ Context

Clinton is the first president to invest substantial political capital on behalf of reforming America's troubled system of financing and providing health care. He also is the first chief executive to become truly conversant with the complex issues surrounding such reform and to commit himself strongly to reining in health care costs as an important social goal. Straying from his prepared text for the State of the Union address to Congress on February 17, 1993, President Clinton said:

> All of our efforts to strengthen the economy will fail—let me say this again, I feel so strongly about it—all our efforts to strengthen the economy will fail unless we also take this year—not next year, not five years from now, but this year—bold steps to reform our health care system.

The President further tied his political fortunes to achieving success with health reform by naming his wife, Hillary Rodham Clinton, chair of the White House–based task force that he created to design his health care plan. Public opinion surveys have repeatedly suggested that many Americans share President Clinton's view that fundamental reform is necessary. In the most recent survey of a national sample of the adult population, conducted for a newspaper and a television network, pollsters Robert Teeter, a Republican, and Peter Hart, a Democrat, reported that by a margin of 74 percent to 22 percent, the 1503 respondents agreed that it would be impossible to control health costs and provide insurance to all citizens unless the system was completely overhauled. According to Teeter and Hart, Americans believe the system "needs major change, not just tinkering or work around the edges."

❖ Evolution

Bill Clinton advanced managed competition as an option for reform during his campaign for the presidency. Midway through it, when Republican George Bush was sharply criticizing Clinton's call for a "play or pay" plan—under which employers would be required to provide health insurance to their employees either privately or through a tax that would finance care through a public program—the Democratic nominee shifted his position and announced his support for managed "competition within a budget" and "universal coverage. . . privately provided, publicly guaranteed." This deft shift neutralized Bush's attacks, but Clinton never precisely spelled out during the campaign what he had in mind.

Managed competition is intended to reorganize the health care market by recasting both the relations among patients, payers, and providers and their respective roles. Its chief architect is Alain C. Enthoven, an economics professor at Stanford University who has offered variations on this theme for 15 years. Clinton, however, is the first president to become personally involved in promoting this set of ideas. Enthoven's early thinking was influenced by Dr. Paul M. Ellwood, Jr., and Scott Fleming, a lawyer who for many years served in executive positions with the Kaiser Permanente Medical Care Program, for which Enthoven has long acted as a consultant.

In 1970, Ellwood proposed a national "health maintenance strategy" to the Nixon administration, and his proposal led to the enactment of the Health Maintenance Organization Act of 1973. This law authorized federal grants and loans to finance the creation of nonprofit health maintenance organizations (HMOs) and required employers of more than 25 workers to offer HMO coverage if such plans were available and met federal requirements. HMOs integrate the financing and delivery functions of medical care—the same approach that is called for in the creation of accountable health partnerships. The HMO act represented the government's first real effort to develop an alternative to fee-for-service medicine.

Fleming, while serving under Richard Nixon in 1972 and 1973, developed a national health insurance proposal that he called "structured competition within the private sector." The proposal recommended ways of extending the Federal Employees Health Benefits Program to the entire population. This program resembles a health insurance purchasing cooperative (HIPC), the mechanism through which small businesses and self-employed persons would secure their coverage under managed competition. The federal program contracts with a variety of health plans that offer benefits packages to eligible workers for a fixed annual premium. In 1977, Enthoven developed the Consumer Choice Health Plan, described as "a national health insurance proposal based on regulated competition in the private sector." The Carter administration rejected it flatly, opting instead for a hospital cost-containment plan that, after two years of consideration, Congress ultimately killed in 1979 as too regulatory. Enthoven wrote recently:

> Experience has shown that Fleming's "structured competition" and my "regulated competition" did not quite describe what we had in mind . . . The intent of both of our terms was interpreted as structuring the market by a set of rules laid down once and for all, with purchasing by individual consumers and a passive regulatory agency. As critics identified actual or hypothetical problems, I would often reply, "I think that problem could be managed using the following tools . . . ." This led me

to believe that a more accurate characterization of what actually works would be managed competition.

❖ Structure

Managed competition is price competition, but the price it focuses on is the annual premium for comprehensive health care services, not the price for each service. The competition occurs among integrated financing and delivery plans, which offer similar benefits packages to consumers. Minneapolis, perhaps more than any other city, has done the most to transform its health care delivery system along the lines of managed competition. Advocates of managed competition anticipate that independent physicians, medical groups, hospitals, and other health care entities will form accountable health partnerships for one overriding reason: HIPCs, or sponsors, as they are also commonly called, would contract only with partnerships, not with individual providers. HIPCs were characterized as "the central innovation" of managed competition by two staff members of Mrs. Clinton's task force. However, the administration proposes the regulation of all health insurance, not just coverage purchased through an HIPC.

HIPCs would ensure that each eligible beneficiary received health care at a reasonable price, but they would not actually deliver medical care, pay individual providers, or assume financial risk. Instead, they would act as purchasing agents. In a sharp departure from the current insurance market, managed competition calls for a federally established, uniform benefits package that must be offered by health plans competing for approval by the HIPCs. This requirement would not bar supplementary insurance benefits provided by employers that already provide more generous coverage, although such benefits would probably no longer be nontaxable. But it would mean that plans competing for enrollees through HIPCs would have to compete on the same benefits package regardless of whether the plans were organized as group-model or independent-model HMOs, preferred-provider organizations, or other health care delivery arrangements that allowed patients some flexibility in choosing a physician.

HIPCs would prohibit health plans from barring enrollees because of a preexisting medical condition or using other screening techniques such as medical underwriting, the process insurers use to determine whether, and on what basis, they will accept an applicant for coverage. HIPCs would also set other rules of participation, manage the enrollment process, collect premium contributions from employers and employees, pay premiums to health plans, and administer cross-subsidies among beneficiaries on the basis of their respective medical-risk profiles. These functions are performed haphazardly and inequitably now by payers and providers who freely shift costs.

HIPCs could be set up in a variety of ways, from a comprehensive tax-financed model favored by California's insurance commissioner, John

Garamendi, that would arrange insurance for all employees in a region, except those working for large, self-insured employers, to the initiative put forward by the Jackson Hole Group, which, to start, would require participation only for employers with 100 or fewer workers, about 45 percent of the work force. Whether the HIPCs would be private, cooperative associations of purchasers, governmental bodies, or organizations of some intermediate type such as public corporations is an issue that Congress will undoubtedly debate when it considers President Clinton's plan. The Bush health care reform proposal also called for the creation of entities similar to HIPCs. But the "health insurance networks" proposed by Bush would have encouraged rather than required small businesses to purchase insurance through such collective arrangements. Most advocates of collective purchasing cooperatives believe that they should be accountable to boards composed exclusively of employers and consumers. Paul Starr, a staff member of Mrs. Clinton's task force, has written: "Strict conflict-of-interest rules should bar any provider or insurer from serving on the cooperatives' policymaking boards."

An example of an organization that resembles an HIPC is the California Public Employees Retirement System (CalPERS), which offers a choice of plans to state employees and their dependents (a total of 875,000 people) of some 800 participating local government agencies, some of which have only two employees. For a fee of 0.5 percent of health premiums, which totaled $1.3 billion last year, CalPERS handled all the administrative functions normally performed by an employer. Almost 80 percent of its insured beneficiaries were enrolled last year in HMOs, all of which offered the same benefits package. The package, like most such plans, limits coverage for mental health care and the treatment of chemical dependency.

❖ Advocates and Opponents

In recent years, the managed-competition model has attracted supporters from academic institutions, private business, publishing, and the health care industry. Because some of its adherents gather periodically in Ellwood's home at the foot of the Grand Teton mountain range in Wyoming to discuss their favored approach, they have become known as the Jackson Hole Group. The ideas of the Jackson Hole Group began to take on greater national importance. Members of the Conservative Democratic Forum, a group of 60 legislators, introduced the Managed Competition Act of 1992; Clinton promoted the concept; and *The New York Times*, among other periodicals, endorsed the approach.

Managed competition also has its detractors, not the least of whom are some of the Democratic legislators who will ultimately pass judgment on this model of health care reform. Advocacy groups representing the poor, organized labor, and some medical organizations also take a dim view of managed competition. Two of the most outspoken critics are Representative

Pete Stark (D-Calif.), chairman of the House Ways and Means Subcommittee on Health, one of the panels that has jurisdiction over health reform proposals, and Senator Howard Metzenbaum (D-Ohio). Stark believes managed competition will increase administrative costs, bolster the interests of for-profit enterprises, and do little to help cover the millions of uninsured U.S. citizens quickly. In a statement on the Senate floor on March 3, Metzenbaum criticized the powerful interests that have embraced managed competition, although most of them did not endorse the concept until they recognized that enactment of a more radical reform approach was a distinct possibility.

A critical question that proponents of managed competition must address is its potential for slowing current trends in health care spending. Among the key respondents to that question will be the Congressional Budget Office, which is charged, along with the President's Office of Management and Budget, with estimating the potential cost or savings entailed in any plan introduced by the Clinton administration.

During the past 12 years of Republican administrations, the government paid virtually no attention to the nature and size of the physician work force, but that will certainly change as the debate unfolds. If managed competition emerges as the main vehicle of health care reform, the health plans it fosters would be far more dependent on generalist physicians than is currently the case in nonmanaged delivery settings. In internal medicine in particular, however, the generalist is becoming an endangered species. In an effort to correct the imbalance between medical generalists and specialists, the Clinton administration may attempt to intervene directly in the process of medical education. Dr. Fitzhugh Mullan, director of the Bureau of Health Professions in the Department of Health and Human Services and chair of the working group on health care work-force development of the President's health reform task force, recently suggested the creation of a government-sponsored commission on the physician work force.

❖ Private Interests

The exercise of power by private groups has perhaps been the most characteristic feature of American democracy. During the administration's development of its health care reform proposal, however, representatives of private interest groups were prohibited from participating in its deliberative processes. The work groups created to help President Clinton develop his reform plan were staffed by 511 government analysts and bureaucrats, congressional staff members, and independent consultants not deemed to represent a particular private interest. Their ranks include very few people with medical degrees and virtually no practicing physicians.

Despite the absence of direct involvement by private interests in the administration's deliberative processes, these groups are nevertheless active in offering proposals that represent a compromise between the status quo and President Clinton's ambitious designs. The pharmaceutical industry, in an effort to preclude mandatory price controls, has proposed a voluntary program under which each company's annual average price increase for drugs would be limited to the rate of inflation. In another important break with the past, commercial health insurers have proposed the enactment of a federal law that would require coverage for all Americans and a limitation on tax breaks for the purchase of insurance. The American College of Physicians proposed a universal system of insurance that would operate within a national health care budget—"a ceiling on total health expenditures, sometimes referred to as a global budget." The American Academy of Family Physicians has endorsed a similar approach.

At the winter meeting of the American Medical Association (AMA) in December, 1992, the position of the American College of Physicians sparked strong oposition from the House of Delegates. But more recently, under different circumstances, the AMA has signaled its willingness to accept spending limits and the creation of a national health board that would oversee the system.

The debate on reforming the U.S. health care system will be protracted. Past reform efforts during this century have failed, but President Clinton's efforts may well represent the most ambitious attempt yet, given his energy, his promise to take the issue to the public through an election-like campaign, and the unsustainable rate at which health care spending is rising. No matter what the outcome, it seems reasonable to predict that the United States is moving away from an open-ended health care system to one that places limits on the resources available for health care. In this context, the interests of physicians may be well served if they can somehow accommodate themselves to this new reality, while insisting on retaining the responsibility to allocate resources according to their best clinical judgment rather than the demands of a distant third party.

❖ About the Author

John K. Iglehart is Editor of *Health Affairs*, Project HOPE, Chevy Chase, Maryland, and a special correspondent to the *New England Journal of Medicine*.

❖ The American Health Care System: Managed Care

JOHN K. IGLEHART

America's private and public third-party payers, squeezed by health care costs that continue to soar at rates well above inflation, are persuaded that "managed care" plans will produce demonstrable savings as compared with the current cost trends of traditional fee-for-service medicine. They are accelerating their efforts to promote plans that integrate the delivery and financing of care and that apply new constraints on encounters between physicians and patients. The key constraint for doctors is the limitation placed on the autonomy of their clinical decisions. The constraint for patients is the requirement that they see only physicians who are members of a plan's closed or partially open panel or who are selected as "preferred" practitioners. In general, these doctors have agreed to deliver only "necessary" medical services in return for prescribed fees.

Most definitions characterize managed care as a system that integrates the financing and delivery of appropriate medical care by means of the following features: contracts with selected physicians and hospitals that furnish a comprehensive set of health care services to enrolled members, usually for a predetermined monthly premium; utilization and quality controls that contracting providers agree to accept; financial incentives for patients to use the providers and facilities associated with the plan; and the assumption of some financial risk by doctors, thus fundamentally altering their role from serving as agent for the patient's welfare to balancing the patient's needs against the need for cost control—or, as Mechanic put it succinctly, moving "from advocacy to allocation."

Because these features circumscribe the freedom of physicians to practice medicine autonomously, they receive decidedly mixed reviews from doctors. Nevertheless, at least half of all practicing physicians have become involved in at least one managed care arrangement, and they have accepted the trade-off of lower fees for a guaranteed flow of patients. The reality is that this new model has rapidly emerged as a dominant one in the American health care system. At the same time as these new networks are developing, some existing large multispecialty group practices that previously treated patients only on a traditional fee-for-service basis are offering benefit packages directly to payers for a prepaid, fixed premium.

The emergence of managed care is the subject of this report. It represents the latest stage in a long struggle that has pitted the priorities of practicing physicians against management structures that have sought to gain firmer control over what doctors do. The traditional autonomy that physicians have enjoyed as ministers to the sick and as recipients of a state grant of monopoly power in medical practice—what Freidson calls "professional dominance"—is being threatened by these new arrangements. The new constraints, along with other economic and social pressures, are encouraging physicians to aggregate in larger professional groups that offer them greater protection against external assaults on their autonomy, as well as more regular working conditions.

Most organizations that provide managed care are called either health maintenance organizations (HMOs) or preferred-provider organizations (PPOs). Within these categories, there are variations on the basic theme, reflecting the fact that the organization of managed care is evolving rapidly. Although still largely a regional phenomenon, far more prevalent on the East and West coasts and in the Midwest, managed care is clearly a phenomenon that, in one form or another, is here to stay, despite the misgivings of many doctors. The states with the largest numbers of people enrolled in HMOs and the highest percentages of their population enrolled in such plans are California (33.4 percent), Massachusetts (30.9 percent), Minnesota (28.3 percent), Oregon (26.4 percent) Arizona (24.2 percent), Hawaii (22.9 percent), Wisconsin (22.5 percent), Maryland (22.3 percent), Colorado (21.9 percent), and Connecticut (20.7 percent).

Most of the legislative proposals to reform the health care system, regardless of the ideological stripe of their sponsors, promote expansion of managed care. Private business—the community of interests that, if it ever really extended itself on behalf of health care reform, could propel it forward—views managed care as its best current hope to control costs and preserve the dominance of the health system by private providers and payers. Recently, even the American Medical Association, in the form of a speech delivered on June 8, by executive vice-president Dr. James S. Todd, conceded that it has been "slow in recognizing and accepting the legitimacy, the benefits, of these modes of practice"; Todd acknowledged the positive contributions made by HMOs and other members of the Group Health Association of America.

❖ Evolution

The current managed care plans are based on concepts that have been evolving for more than 50 years. The earliest entrants were prepaid group practice plans like Group Health of Puget Sound, the Kaiser-Permanente Medical Care Program, and the Health Insurance Plan of New York, in which groups of physicians that served plan members provided comprehensive health services for a fixed monthly premium. Because premiums were the same for all members, the healthy subsidized the sick. Spawned by the consumer and labor movements and by the interest of industrialist Henry J. Kaiser, such plans faced strong opposition from organized medicine for decades and operated as aberrations within the fee-for-service system.

In 1971, to the dismay of most of the medical profession, President Richard Nixon's administration embraced the concept of prepaid group practice as its favored policy for slowing the rate of increase in health care expenditures. The Nixon administration renamed the prepaid group-practice plans "health maintenance organizations" and worked with Democratic legislators to enact the Health Maintenance Organization Act of 1973. To increase the number of plans, the government awarded subsidies of more than $200 million to nonprofit groups during the 1970s under this act. Although the government fell far short of its ambitious goal of creating 1,700 HMOs that could serve 40 million members by 1976, it sent a signal to organized medicine that Washington was prepared to enact laws intended to reform the health care delivery system.

The government has not been nearly as successful as the private sector in enrolling people who are eligible to receive publicly financed health services in managed care plans. In 1991, of Medicare's 33.6 million beneficiaries, only about 2.1 million were receiving health care through managed care arrangements, predominantly HMOs in California, Colorado, Minnesota, Nevada, and Oregon. Of Medicaid's 24 million beneficiaries, only 2.6 million were enrolled in managed care plans last year, although a number of large states, searching for ways to stem the rapid growth of the Medicaid program, have announced plans to increase enrollment substantially.

Only in the 1980s, when employers became more concerned about soaring health costs, when commercial carriers began to recognize that the future of indemnity insurance was in jeopardy, and when traditional fee-for-service practitioners responded by becoming associated with health plans, did managed care expand substantially. In the past decade, enrollment in HMOs increased from 10.2 million to almost 39 million at the end of 1991. Growth in the population covered by PPOs was also substantial. Only 1.3 million households were enrolled in PPOs in 1984, as compared with more than 18 million by 1989. In addition, data on the growth of managed care arrangements between 1987 and 1990 indicate that virtually all health insurance packages are now subject to various forms of utilization review.

❖ Types of Managed Care Plans

Managed care programs seem endlessly varied, but there are essentially two types of HMO: the group or staff model, in which groups of physicians contract to provide services, and the independent practice association (IPA), in which doctors remain in their own offices but agree to treat patients enrolled in a health plan. The IPA model was the fastest-growing of the HMO variants in the past decade. In an IPA, a health plan contracts with individual practitioners or groups to provide care at a negotiated rate per capita, for a flat retainer, or for a negotiated fee-for-service rate. The physicians maintain their own offices and continue to see patients on a fee-for-service basis, as well, while contracting with one or more HMOs.

In a group-model HMO, physicians usually aggregate in independent medical groups (like the 12 such groups that provide services within the Kaiser-Permanente Medical Care Program). In a staff-model plan, physicians are employees and are not organized in separate medical groups.

Given the increasing management of the details of fee-for-service practice by third parties, group- and staff-model HMOs feature two important characteristics: first, physicians accept the responsibility to provide comprehensive care for a fixed fee in exchange for autonomy in the practice of medicine; any oversight is carried out by peers, not external managers. Many of the most successful IPAs, seeking more constructive and permanent relations with physicians, are employing doctors as medical directors to perform the peer-review function, thus hoping to buffer the practitioners' relation with management. Second, in return for this freedom, group- and staff-model HMOs tightly control the kind and amount of care received by enrolled patients by carefully selecting the numbers and types of doctors in their panels in relation to the needs of the population served. Primary care doctors act as gatekeepers—generalists who serve as the entry point to a plan. Each enrolled member can be referred to specialists only by his or her primary care doctor. HMOs thereby ensure adequate access to primary care and maintain full patient schedules for their specialists.

Many plans incorporate financial incentives into their agreements with physicians in an attempt to influence the frequency with which primary care doctors refer patients, order tests or procedures, and admit patients to the hospital. Physicians often assume this gatekeeping role with some reluctance because of the potential conflicts it creates with patients and specialists. Nevertheless, the key role of primary care doctors in HMOs places them in positions of greater authority in relation to specialists than is the case in the traditional system. Ironically, managed care plans find it increasingly difficult to recruit primary care doctors because training programs continue to emphasize the medical specialties, despite the strong need for generalists in the HMO market.

Other forms of managed care include the PPO and the latest variant of managed care—the point-of-service plan. Under such a plan, a PPO contracts with networks or panels of physicians who agree to provide medical services and be paid according to a discounted fee schedule. Enrollees are offered better coverage if they agree to see physicians on the preferred list, which is generally assembled by either insurers or employers, but the plan makes no provision to couple a patient with a primary care doctor as gatekeeper. A point-of-service plan does encourage such a coupling by offering employees incentives (usually more benefits or lower copayments) to channel their care through a primary care doctor to other selected practitioners. This option, offered to employees by a growing number of Fortune 500 companies, including AT&T, Marriott, Chevron, and Sears Roebuck,

strengthens the role of the primary care physician. An enrollee has the freedom to seek care from a physician not affiliated with the plan, but he or she
pays substantially more out of pocket for such care.

❖ Costs

The evidence regarding whether managed care plans save
money is mixed.

Average costs do not reflect the fact that HMO coverage is generally
more comprehensive and members' out-of-pocket costs are usually substantially lower than is the case with indemnity benefits; however, the average
costs per employee to employers also included care for older retirees, who
frequently opt for indemnity coverage or are offered no other plan. In general, these different modes of delivery attract employees with different
health risks. Although conventional wisdom has long held that HMOs attract younger and healthier people, research does not provide definitive data
on this question. Biased patient selection does occur, but as these plans ma-
ture there will also be cases in which HMOs attract sicker people.

The situation is further complicated by the fact that, in most instances,
when large employers offer their workers a choice of plans, they cover the
cost of both the lower-priced and the higher-priced insurance package. This
approach amounts to a subsidy of the more expensive health insurance options. Enthoven and Kronick, the main architects of the managed-competition model, have argued that their model has never been properly tested,
and thus the modest record of managed care organizations in controlling
premium increases is not necessarily valid. No one is suggesting, however,
that managed care alone, without other structural changes, will adequately
stem the rising tide of national health expenditures.

❖ Selecting Physicians and
Influencing Their Behavior

The success of managed care will probably depend on the abil-
ity of these organizations to influence physicians' choices in the direction of
increased value. Managed care organizations therefore seek physicians with
appropriate professional credentials and practice characteristics, and a willingness to accept their philosophy. Finding and training physicians who believe that "more may not be better" is difficult in a society in which teaching
institutions accept it as given that new forms of technology should be incorporated into standard care. Methods of selecting providers are evolving rapidly, and the plans characterized as trendsetters in one recent report were
the most assiduous in their approaches to the process. Intensely competitive
local markets are one key factor driving payers in the direction of greater
selectivity in recruiting physicians.

Once plans contract with a physician, they use two basic mechanisms, which have been characterized as clinical "rules and incentives," to influence physician practice patterns. Clinical rules have been given various names and take various forms: quality assurance, treatment protocols or algorithms, regulations, administrative constraints, practice guidelines or parameters, or utilization review. The process by which such rules are designed, implemented, monitored, and evaluated is new, and there is little conclusive evidence about its efficacy with respect to the cost and quality of medical care.

❖ The Future

Before physicians reject managed care as too interventionist, they should consider the probable alternatives. In the future they are likely to face a choice between centralized government regulatory mechanisms, including global budgets, and individual incentives for cost control that operate in a pluralistic, privately dominated system. The status quo is not a viable option.

Disaffected doctors do not make for a successful enterprise. Thus, the basic challenge of managed care plans is to create systems in which physicians are delegated the responsibility for managing care and then held accountable for their performance. Finding formulas to bridge the different "cultures" of management and medicine is a particular challenge for traditional insurers, because employers, rather than doctors, have long been regarded as the key to these insurers' success in controlling costs. Reflecting this priority, many of the current utilization-management techniques are, as one physician recently observed, "marginally effective, follow-the-leader, regulatory interventions that are concerned more with restricting benefits and hassling providers than with developing cost-effective programs." The nation's largest commercial carriers (Aetna Life and Casualty, CIGNA, Metropolitan Life, Prudential, and Travelers), all of which are pursuing managed care aggressively, are developing new approaches that strike a better balance between the interests of payers and those of physicians. The 73 Blue Cross and Blue Shield plans, which have already enrolled 20 million people in their managed care packages and anticipate a tripling of that number by the end of the century, also recognize the importance of reaching a rapprochement with physicians, moving beyond case-by-case micromanagement, and substituting profiles of physicians and other tools that measure doctors' overall performance.

Given the unsustainable rate at which medical spending continues to escalate, serious efforts to make further structural changes in the health care system are inevitable. At this point, well-run managed care schemes have considerable potential for allowing physicians to use their clinical skills as full partners in the quest to allocate scarce health care resources effectively. But the transformation of American medicine along these lines will take at least a generation to accomplish. And without substantial support from the medical community, the likelihood of success will diminish commensurately. Even if managed care prevails, more than a few physicians and patients will remain with fee-for-service medicine, believing that it serves the interests of both doctors and patients better than managed care plans that attempt to make the uneasy transition "from advocacy to allocation."

❖ About the Author

John K. Iglehart is Editor of *Health Affairs*, Project HOPE, Chevy Chase, Maryland, and a special correspondent to the *New England Journal of Medicine*.

❖ National Health Care Reform: The Aura of Inevitability Intensifies

GEORGE D. LUNDBERG

Major political change in a democratic republic such as ours comes about when a cluster of forces temporarily coalesces to form a critical political mass of sufficient strength to power that change. Sometimes, tangential, seemingly unrelated events create that coalescence although the need for such change, people wanting it, and the resources necessary to produce it were long present. So it is with national health care reform in this country.

In my opinion, five salient events have brought health care reform to the forefront of the U.S. national agenda:

1. The nasty recession that began in 1990 and has lingered, causing large numbers of politically active voters without adequate health insurance to join the politically impotent poor in insisting on reform.
2. The expanding tragedy of the acquired immunodeficiency syndrome (AIDS) epidemic, which created a large new group of highly educated and financially secure individuals who became economic paupers on their way to death as a result of underinsurance for their catastrophic illness.
3. The publication by the Scientific Publications group of the American Medical Association (AMA), representing the medical establishment, of nearly 100 articles in our 10 journals in May 1991, giving ample reason for demanding significant health care reform. Most of the articles were written by physicians; no longer could the Washington political establishment blame the doctors for preventing reform.
4. The disintegration of the Union of Soviet Socialist Republics following collapse of the Warsaw Pact, the Iron Curtain, and the Berlin Wall. These cataclysmic events, of almost biblical proportions, pre-empted, at least for now, our nation's long-term preoccupation with massive defense attention and expenditure.
5. The sudden death of Senator John Heinz of Pennsylvania in an airplane crash in 1991. President George Bush hand-picked then-Attorney General Richard Thornburgh to run for that senatorial position. The Democratic candidate, Harris Wofford, who had never held political office, was elected, largely on the basis of his outspoken advocacy for a national health care plan. Shortly thereafter, White House Chief of Staff John Sununu departed and, in February 1992,

the Bush administration joined the national health care reform debate one week before the first presidential primary.

Many other things have happened, involving many other people, but I believe these are the five keys that unlocked the debate on health care reform.

❖ Value for Money

Since the year 1900, we Americans have added 7 hours to the average life expectancy at birth for every 24 hours lived—an incredible modern achievement. Of this, we as a civilization should be extremely proud. But the major gains were in the first several decades when expenditures were low, while in the middle and latter portions of the century, the slope has been much more gradual. Whether or not there is cause and effect, there seems to be little relationship between the percentage of gross national product spent on medical and health care and the extent of improvements in expected life span. Is there any wonder why many doubt that we are providing value for money?

❖ The Characteristics of Successful Health Reform

What is the grid on which all proposed programs must be stretched and tested (see table)?

Providing Access to Basic Medical Care for All of Our People

An accepted definition of *basic medical care* has been difficult to establish. The term is subject to everyone's personal value judgment. Two widely differing but excellent frames of reference are the basic benefits package approved as policy by the AMA House of Delegates and the Oregon Health Decisions list of 709 treatment plans. The AMA plan has the benefit of clarity, simplicity, and broad support. The Oregon plan has the advantage of a stepwise prioritization of services, created by professionals and grass roots individuals based upon the judgment of benefit vs. costs.

As long as we are in a free society with medical pluralism, providing access means that there must be insurance coverage for all, either paid for by individuals (or families), by employers, by government, or by some combination thereof. But, insurance alone is not enough. There must also be education regarding the availability of care, attempts to remove cultural and language barriers that would prevent adequate care, provision of local resources (or transportation to appropriate facilities), and the abolition of racial discrimination as it manifests itself in health care provision. If we retain a system of private health insurance, such insurance must be community-rated and not risk-rated, must be available to all without consideration of preexisting conditions, must be transportable by the insured, available to all

The Grid upon Which to Test Health Care Reform Proposals
_____
Does the proposal achieve the following:

> Provide access to basic medical care for all of our people?

> Produce real cost-control?

> Promote continuing quality?

> Limit professional liability?

> Reduce administrative hassle?

> Retain necessary patient and physician autonomy?

> Consider long-term care?

> Encourage primary care?

> Enhance disease prevention?

> Possess staying power after 5, 10, or 20 years?
_____

U.S. inhabitants (or covered by government), and affordable. If all of these conditions cannot be met, then private insurance for the general populace should cease to exist for basic medical care and should be confined to individually purchased "boutique" care.

Payment for providing access for all can be made available by promptly effecting cost controls that slow the anticipated increase in expenditures for health care.

Producing Real Cost Control

Without real cost control, successful health care reform cannot happen. The slope of costs for medical and health care in this country, as expressed in the percentage of gross national product expended on medical and health care, has changed from asymptotic to the horizontal to nearly asymptotic to the vertical in the course of my lifetime. Obviously, this extreme is unacceptable. During the burgeoning scientific revolution of the 20th century, to increase the amount and percentage of resources spent on medical and health care was entirely valid. But now health care costs have reached a doubling time of less than 5 years. Earlier articles have itemized the reasons for these out-of-control costs and proposed many solutions. A mixture of several solutions is probably the best answer. I believe that the following steps should be taken to control costs:

- ❖ Clearly futile care should cease.
- ❖ Unnecessary and inappropriate care should stop.
- ❖ Self-referral to physician-owned facilities should be eliminated.
- ❖ The tort system of liability should be reformed.
- ❖ Managed care and managed competition should be drastically expanded.

❖ All Americans should have a primary care physician to function as caregiver, patient advocate, adviser, and medical manager-gatekeeper for access to specialty care.

❖ We should retain a private-public mix of payers and the health care industry.

Even if all of this is done, I agree with Ginzberg that we still must have some form of global budget that curtails the flow of new money from government and insurers. Excess capacity and utilization must be limited and a ceiling established no matter how distasteful or politically dangerous that may seem to be. To fairly set such global budgets (by state or nationally) it will be necessary to legislate a national health expenditure board, with independent authority to effect such decisions.

Promoting Continuing Quality

Quality is best defined as the totality of features and characteristics of a product or a service that plays on its ability to satisfy given needs. For those intelligent and literate individuals with strong comprehensive health care insurance, our quality of care is as good as the best in the world. Preserving this quality in an era of harsh economic constraints will provide a major challenge. Active use of practice guidelines/parameters and outcome measurements should allow us to preserve quality. Government and the people will rely on the professionalism of physicians to defend the quality of care given those for whom they have specific responsibility.

Limiting Professional Liability

The costs of malpractice coverage and defensive medicine are unknown but very large—perhaps in excess of $20 billion per year. Defensive medicine probably benefits no one except those with the health care jobs that are generated by this practice. Only about half of the total fiscal resources placed into the malpractice insurance pool ever find their way to truly injured patients. The remainder is consumed by "friction costs" of investigators, administrators, insurance companies, expert witnesses, lawyers, and courts. This grossly unfair and inefficient situation must be solved as part of health care reform.

Reducing Administrative Hassle

Everyone admits that the current system is rife with administrative waste, inefficiency, and a ubiquitous "hassle factor." Physicians and their office staffs could be greatly benefited by elimination or at least serious diminution of unnecessary hassles. Such absurdities as billing Medicaid several times to receive a single minuscule payment months later or forcing a competent physician to call a nonphysician somewhere to authorize a needed routine service for an ill patient must be replaced.

Retaining Necessary Physician and Patient Autonomy

Who is in charge? The patient, whose life it is? The physician, whose profession it is? Or the payer, whose money it is? They all are, and it is at this interface of values that the medical ethicist of the future will be most active. Patients and physicians must both retain substantial autonomy. Each health care reform proposal must be scrutinized to assess the extent to which all parties' essential rights are compromised, and value judgments must be deliberately and openly debated so that informed decisions can be made in advance.

Considering Long-Term Care

Aside from access for all and real cost control, the most vexing element in this whole conundrum probably is long-term care. Since we are, in effect, victims of our own success, the very old (those over 85 years old or even over the age of 100) comprise the most rapidly growing segment of our population. Many need long-term care. And if the Boston study, which documented a 47% incidence of Alzheimer's disease in our population over age 85, is validated by other studies, we are really in trouble economically. Medicaid costs are stressing virtually every state's budget, and long-term care is a major element of that expense. The private health insurance sector has barely scratched the surface on providing comprehensive long-term care coverage for a significant proportion of our population. It may be in this area that the most wrenching, end-of-life ethical policy decisions await us.

Encouraging Primary Care

Our system of allowing individual physicians freely to choose the field they will enter has been terrific for individual physicians but a mass catastrophe for the country. The incentive/disincentive of paying much for procedures (whether or not they are needed or effective) and little for primary care has discombobulated supply and demand. We now have about 615,000 physicians; 65% are in specialty care and 35% in primary care. The principles other developed countries practice are that the proportion of primary care physicians and specialists should be about 50-50, and all individuals should have a primary care doctor whom they see first. We need to retain about 100,000 specialist physicians as competent primary care physicians and have them practice as such. Only financial incentives and disincentives will likely be strong enough to motivate that profound shift. Obviously, trained specialists will not be clamoring to become primary care physicians, at least not soon.

Enhancing Disease Prevention

The massive funding now going toward futile care or care for those with preventable full-blown disease should be redirected to prevention. We should begin paying doctors more for preventing diseases and less for treating them. No restrictive copayments or deductibles should be applied to retard use of proven preventive measures such as Papanicolaou tests, mammograms, vaccinations, and prenatal care.

Possessing Staying Power after 5, 10, or 20 Years

Our last major national health care reform occurred 27 years ago, with enactment of Medicare and Medicaid legislation. We must be prepared to live with the next set of major reforms for a substantial number of years—but not forever. We should strive to enact legislation with a successful use-life of at least 10 years. Analyses that realistically project the effects of proposed legislation at 5, 10, or even 20 years from enactment are an absolutely essential component of this debate and these deliberations. And methods for continuing evaluation and mid-course adjustments should be put into place with initial legislation.

Of course, maintaining our tradition of great strengths in medical education and research is also crucial during and after reform.

❖ Preventing the 1990s Health Care System Meltdown

During the greedy 1980s, we as a society experienced, in addition to all-time record federal budget and international trade deficits, an embarrassing savings-and-loan debacle, and a Wall Street junk bond collapse. Each was predictable and preventable, and each, because it was not prevented, has had massive long-term economic federal budget implications.

We are now poised near the brink of what I call the 1990s health care system meltdown. Our doubling time for health care expenditures is now less than 5 years. We are looking at potential health care expenditures in 1992 dollars of $1.4 trillion by 1996. I do not believe our economy can tolerate these costs. If business continues as usual without major change, I predict meltdown by 1996. At that point, in a worst-case scenario, the Congress would panic and nationalize the entire health care industry; they can do that. The physicians, nurses, pharmacists, and other health care workers would be conscripted as government employees; hospitals would be taken over and run by the government; health insurance companies would be abolished; the pharmaceutical and medical device industries would be nationalized. I believe that such an event would be tragic, catastrophic, and certain to fail over time. I cannot imagine a government monopoly of that size succeeding.

But I believe that medicine is different from the savings-and-loan and Wall Street businesses. I believe that physicians are professionals. We know that true professionalism means self-governance, self-determination, and ethical behavior in the public interest. To merit still being called professionals, we physicians will have to prevent the anticipated meltdown in advance, by proper preventive, scientific, educational, and political action—now.

❖ Benefits for Physicians

In successful health care reform, all players and all stakeholders will have to compromise—the patients, the physicians, the insurance companies, the hospitals, the government, the politicians, and all the special interest groups. But the essence of compromise means that the major players all give up something and get something. The current U.S. health care reform movement, if successfully negotiated, can benefit physicians through (1) malpractice tort reform, (2) decreased hassle factor, (3) elimination of uncompensated care, (4) ability to practice medicine of high quality, (5) improved public image, and (6) pride in their professionalism.

❖ Physicians—The Champions of Change

American physicians are champions of change. There has been more change since the year 1900 than in the entire preceding course of human history. Much of that change has been in medical and surgical information and clinical actions. Little of the technology now routinely used by physicians was invented, or even conceptualized, when I was in medical school in the 1950s.

This past decade manifested enormous change in medical practice patterns, in social economics, and in government decisions. The implementation of diagnosis-related groups, managed care in many segments, the resource-based relative value scale, and the impending Clinical Laboratory Improvement Amendments are examples. We as a profession have encountered, participated in, and succeeded in each of these revolutions. But these changes, momentous though they may have seemed at the time, were mere pilot tests—warm-up exercises—for the changes that lie ahead of us.

Most physicians are concerned about the future, many are apprehensive, some are afraid. But, as a group, we are very smart, very well educated, very highly motivated, very well organized and led, and ready for any challenge. With all of these positive characteristics and outstanding ongoing communications, as long as we continue to place the interests of patients and the public first, we shall prevail.

❖ About the Author

George D. Lundberg, M.D., is Editor of the *Journal of the American Medical Association*, Chicago.

❖ Major Features of the Health Care Plan President Clinton Introduced to the Nation September 22, 1993

❖ Universal Coverage for All Citizens and Legal Residents

This would include:

- ❖ a guaranteed comprehensive benefit package with hospital and physician services, prescription drugs, laboratory tests, and a variety of other services
- ❖ a long-term care program for the disabled and expanded home care services
- ❖ a limited extension of coverage for dental, mental health, and vision services with later expansion of coverage for these services
- ❖ prevention care such as prenatal and well baby care, immunizations, annual examinations, cholesterol screenings, and Pap smears and mammograms according to a preset schedule

❖ Managed Competition

In the Clinton plan this concept involves large groups of consumers paying a fixed price per month for health coverage to large alliances or purchasing cooperatives that would offer a selection of plans (made up of networks of providers) at varying prices. Because the plans would compete for subscribers through their quality and price, this could be expected to curb inflation. Regulation of the plan calls for the government to impose mandatory limits if the competitive process does not succeed in curbing the growth of premiums.

❖ Health Alliances

These would be giant purchasing groups that negotiate the price of coverage for thousands of consumers and offer them a selection of health plans. There would be both regional and corporate alliances (very large employers). The health plans, networks of providers, in turn negotiate contracts with the alliances, which would be required to offer a range of plans, including fee-for-service, HMOs, and preferred provider organizations. This process would be overseen by a seven-member government panel, the National Health Board, that would monitor compliance and set the budget.

❖ Employer Mandate

Employers would be required to pay 80 percent of their workers' premiums, and employees would be required to pay the balance. Employers could opt to pay more than 80 percent, however. A ceiling of 7.9 percent of payroll would be imposed and special provisions and requirements are included relating to small businesses and the self-employed. Subsidies to the unemployed and the poor would allow them to receive full benefit coverage.

❖ National Health Security Card

All U.S. citizens and legal residents would receive this identification card, which would be their entrée into the system and serve as proof of their eligibility to register for a benefit plan.

❖ Chapter 6
Health Care Cost Containment

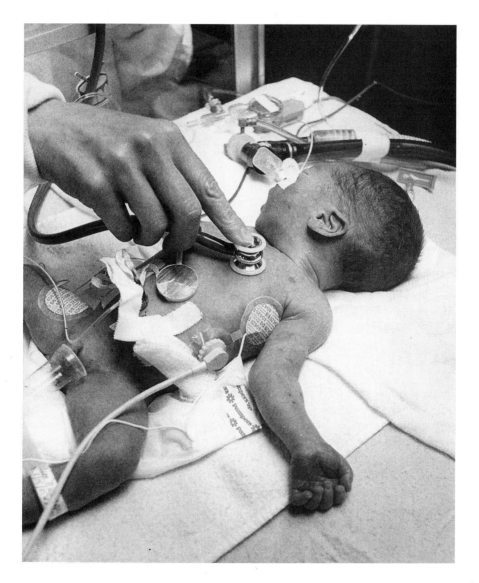

Issues relating to health care costs are raised in each section of this book. They underlie all aspects of the health care system, and they influence all policy questions. It is not unreasonable for us to ask why it is that the United States spends three times as much per person for health care as many other Western nations with little or nothing to show for this extra expense, or why it has been possible for six large industrial European countries to reduce the proportion of the gross domestic product spent on health care and for others to maintain a proportion that is unchanged, while in the United States health care spending between 1970 and 1990 rose at an annual rate of 11.6 percent and its share of the gross national product (GNP) grew by more than half from 7.3 percent to 12.3 percent, a problem that continues to this day.

There are three fundamental forces behind the tremendous upward spiral of health care expenditures: rising prices per unit of service; an increasing volume of services per capita; and growth in the population, particularly the growing number of elderly. The most obvious causes are related to inflation, including inflation in the price of medical services above the consumer price index; improved and costly techniques and technologies; an increase in the practice of defensive medicine by physicians to avoid malpractice suits; a greater number of people who use the services, which is partly a function of the nation's aging population; and the structure of the system itself, particularly the way doctors and hospitals are paid.

Health care costs increased by over 51 percent between 1984 and 1989, nearly three times the period's rate of inflation. Health care expenses in 1992 were approximately $800 billion, compared to those in 1965, when costs were over 500 percent lower for health services. At the same time, the percentage of health care costs paid by the government and by private insurance companies increased considerably. These costs have overwhelmed third-party payers, who have then dramatically reduced the coverage they provide resulting in 15 percent of the nation's population having no health care benefits. The government has drastically tightened the health benefits covered by Medicare and Medicaid through hospital and physician payment reforms, and employers have developed strategies to reduce their costs by providing incentives for workers to contain their use of medical services or to change the type of plan they utilize. Many employers, particularly those in the growing service and nonmanufacturing industries, provide no health insurance coverage. Insurance companies have in some cases begun to require prior approval for hospital admissions and concurrent review of lengths of stay, and there is a clear trend among insurers to refuse coverage and terminate coverage of patients who are very sick or advanced in age and therefore the poorest risks. Employers also have undertaken a variety of new approaches to underwriting benefits, including cost sharing and financial incentives.

The health care market no longer reflects the traditional dichotomy between fee-for-service and prepaid care. Pure fee-for-service plans that include first dollar coverage declined from 90 percent in 1984 to 28 percent in

1989, as monthly premiums, deductibles, and copayments increased for most plans and as a variety of managed care plans entered the picture. Health maintenance organizations (HMOs) and preferred-provider organizations (PPOs), which offer care with selected hospitals and doctors, have vastly increased in popularity with employers. Also, new alternative delivery systems have developed that utilize different reimbursement models, including risk sharing, case management, utilization review, and premium pricing. In addition to the great variety of HMOs and PPOs, some alternative delivery systems on the medical marketplace today include state-licensed prepaid plans, competitive medical plans, exclusive provider plans, and primary care networks.

The system is fluctuating rapidly. Costs continue to rise. At the same time, government and corporate payers are reconsidering what levels of health coverage they will provide and in what structures care will be available. Clearly, they would like to see individuals use greater measures of prevention and exercise restraint in their utilization of services. They would also like to see physicians and hospitals contribute to efforts toward cost containment at the same time that patients begin to shoulder a greater portion of the cost burden.

Because these measures were not undertaken voluntarily, the federal government instituted systems of its own that have had a drastic effect on the manner in which care is administered and have compromised physician autonomy and patient choice in a manner heretofore considered unacceptable. In 1983, Medicare, which insures over 30 million elderly and disabled people, instituted a prospective payment system for hospitals that fixed payments for admissions based on diagnosis-related groups (DRGs), to slow the rate of increase in hospital costs through decreasing admissions and lengths of stay. In 1984, Congress applied a two-year fee freeze for Medicare physicians' charges and, in 1989, a comprehensive reform of physician payment was adopted in the Medicare program.

Those who pay health care bills, principally the federal and state governments, insurance companies, and corporate employers continue to seek reductions in their expenditures for health services or at least to slow the rapid rate of increase in those expenditures. Although the government has been the leader in the move toward cost containment, private industry has also begun to play a major role, as providing employee health care coverage has become a major expense that cuts into profits. The targets of the government's cost containment efforts have largely been the elderly and the poor, beneficiaries of Medicare and Medicaid; while private industry has taken aim at employed middle-income recipients. In both cases, people are discovering that their access to health care services has been altered and, through constraints imposed by payers, they feel the pressure to conform to new cost containment measures.

Cost containment strategies include a wide range of activities, some of which have already been employed by the government, such as preadmission screening for hospitalization, placing a ceiling on hospital and physician charges, reducing waste in such areas as laboratory tests and unnecessary hospital admissions, raising the amount of out-of-pocket payment required, deductibles, copayments, regionalization and centralization of selected major services, setting payments according to diagnostic categories, and decreasing the availability of health care services, especially to those who receive government coverage and those who have no coverage.

Other measures are designed to get either the recipient or the provider to submit voluntarily to cost containment through such means as stressing behaviors to reduce the risk of disease. In some cases, the approach has been to stimulate competitive markets and price competition; in others, it has been through increased regulation of providers. The results of such measures thus far include a vast increase in the gap between the kind of services available to the poor and the rest of the population and a rise in dissatisfaction and even alarm among members of the middle class over the financial costs and quality of services available to them. There has also been discussion of taxing both health insurance contributions and health insurance benefits.

This chapter includes an outline of patterns of spending for health services during 1991 drawn up by the Division of National Cost Estimates, Office of the Actuary, Health Care Financing Administration. Spending for health care rose to $751.8 billion in 1991, an increase of 11.4 percent over the 1990 level. National health expenditures as a share of the gross domestic product increased to 13.2 percent, up from 12.2 percent in 1990, representing the largest increase in the share of the U.S. output consumed by health care in the past 30 years. This article also examines reasons for the unusually large growth in Medicaid expenditures and discusses issues related to third-party payers.

In the next article, Uwe E. Reinhardt, one of the nation's most distinguished health economists, compares the U.S. health care system with those of 23 other Western nations, with particular emphasis on costs of care and access to services. The greatest contrast is that most of these nations provide comprehensive, universal, first-dollar coverage for most major services. Another sharp contrast is that most consumers in these countries are much more satisfied with their health care systems than are consumers in the United States. Included in this article are a number of suppositions about how the European and Canadian systems and the U.S. system might be influenced in the coming years by economic events and public attitudes so that our system might begin to look more and more like theirs, while theirs begins to take on more of the characteristics of our market approach.

The subject of Bruce C. Vladeck's article, "Old Snake Oil in New Bottles," is managed competition. Dr. Vladeck contends that this new version of "voodoo economics" would put patients at risk of "underservice," while attempting to address what the system's proponents label "overuse." He sees a number of other pitfalls to the proposal, including its failure to provide mechanisms to address the two most critical problems we face today: soaring costs and limited access.

Alain C. Enthoven and Richard Kronick make an important contribution to the dialogue with their article, "Universal Health Insurance through Incentives Reform." Dr. Enthoven, a founder of the principles encompassed in the managed competition model, is a key theorist in the health care reform debate. In this analysis, he and Dr. Kronick propose "comprehensive reform of the economic incentives that drive the system." They include a diagnosis of the problem as well as a clear and detailed discussion of the basic principles embraced by managed competition and a defense of these principles based on anticipated criticisms and alternative proposals.

❖ National Health Expenditures, 1991

Suzanne W. Letsch, Helen C. Lazenby,
Katherine R. Levit, and Cathy A. Cowan

The question is to decide whether health or economic growth should have priority in determining the type of environment in which we live.
—René Dubos

❖ Highlights

The nation spent $751.8 billion, or $2,868 per person, for health care in 1991. Total health expenditures exceeded the aggregate amount spent in 1990 by 11.4 percent. Health spending continued to increase at a rapid rate, despite the slowdown in the general economy. Highlights from the 1991 update to the national health accounts include

- ❖ Americans spent 13.2 percent of the nation's gross domestic product (GDP) on health care, up from 12.2 percent one year earlier. Slow growth in GDP was largely responsible for the 1.0 percentage point increase in the share of the nation's resources going for health care.
- ❖ Almost 88 percent of all health expenditures go for the purchase of medical care services or products (Figure 1). In 1991, these purchases of personal health care (PHC) amounted to $660.2 billion, 11.6 percent higher than in 1990.
- ❖ Expenditures for hospital services of $288.6 billion in 1991 are the largest single component of PHC expenditures, 43.7 percent. Consumers funded only 3.4 percent of these purchases from out-of-pocket sources, down from 4.0 percent in 1990.
- ❖ The Health Care Financing Administration's (HCFA) Medicare and Medicaid programs paid for 33.8 percent of all personal health care benefits in 1991, up from 30.5 percent in 1990. Most of the increase came from Medicaid.
- ❖ In 1991, federal and state/local expenditures for Medicaid benefits amounted to $96.5 billion, an increase of 34.4 percent from the 1990 level. Recent expansions in recipient eligibility, expanded outreach efforts by states to establish eligibility for qualified poor persons, and

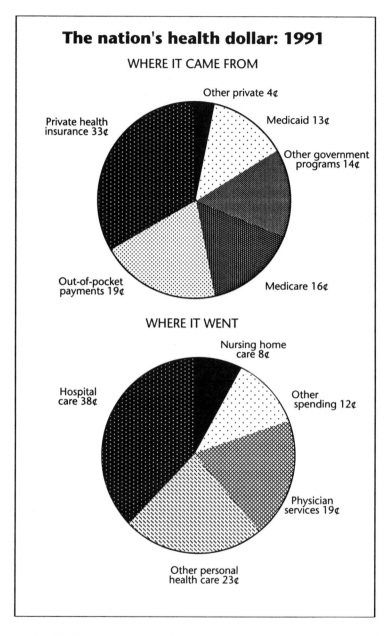

The nation's health dollar: 1991

WHERE IT CAME FROM

Other private 4¢
Private health insurance 33¢
Medicaid 13¢
Other government programs 14¢
Out-of-pocket payments 19¢
Medicare 16¢

WHERE IT WENT

Nursing home care 8¢
Hospital care 38¢
Other spending 12¢
Physician services 19¢
Other personal health care 23¢

Notes: "Other private" includes industrial in-plant health services, nonpatient revenues, and privately financed construction. "Other personal health" care includes dental, other professional services, home health care, drugs and other nondurable medical products, vision products and other durable medical products and other miscellaneous health care services. "Other spending" covers program administration and the net cost of private health insurance, government public health, and other research and construction.
Source: Health Care Financing Administration, Office of Actuary: Data from the Office of National Health Statistics.

Figure 1. The nation's health dollar: 1991.

the recession caused increases in the number of persons with coverage under the Medicaid program.

❖ Of all benefits paid by Medicaid, hospital expenditures grew the most, up 49.9 percent from the 1990 level. Creative financing by state governments, using provider tax and donation programs and payments to hospitals serving a disproportionate share of Medicaid recipients and other poor persons, contributed to these large increases in Medicaid spending for hospital services.

❖ The Medicare program spent $120.2 billion on health care benefits in 1991, an increase of 10.9 percent from the 1990 levels. Medicare funded 18.2 percent of all personal health care services in 1991.

In 1990 and 1991, health's share of GDP grew 0.7 and 1.0 percentage points, respectively. On average, the share of GDP going for health care increased 0.2 percentage points each year since 1960. The rapid growth experienced over the past 2 years signals the dramatic change in pressure health care costs are exerting on the nation's resources, which have been growing at an abnormally slow rate for the past two years.

Changes in state financing over the past few years illustrate the type of response to which financers of health care are turning when confronting continually rising costs and limited resources. Faced with slower growth in tax revenue and increases in Medicaid responsibilities through rising prices, federal mandates, and the recession, states resorted to alternative financing methods to extend the purchasing power of their limited resources.

❖ National Health Expenditures

The national health accounts (NHA) are a means for systematically describing the expenditures of health services and products purchased in the United States and the sources of payment for them. The NHA provide a comprehensive picture of health care spending and financing, consistently defined over time. They are coherent, in that the two-dimensional (source of funds and type of service) matrix design of NHA provides internal cross checks of aggregate expenditure estimates with their sources of funding.

In 1991, national health expenditures amounted to $751.8 billion, an increase of 11.4 percent since 1990. This is the fourth consecutive year in which nominal growth exceeded 10 percent. In 1991, the gross domestic product increased only 2.8 percent, while health care expenditures increased 11.4 percent, causing the share of gross domestic product going for health care spending to jump, from 12.2 percent in 1990 to 13.2 percent in 1991 (Figure 2).

National health expenditures contain two major components: health services and supplies (HSS) (those services and products that are currently consumed) and research and construction (those services and products whose benefits accrue now and in the future). Expenditures for the current con-

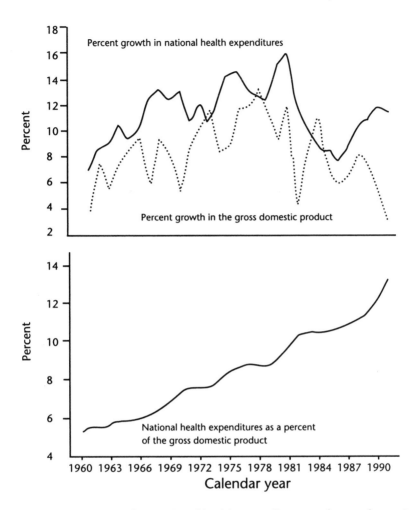

Figure 2. Percent growth in national health expenditures and gross domestic product, and national health expenditures as a percent of gross domestic product: Calendar years 1960–91. SOURCE: Health care Financing Administration Office of the Actuary: Data from the Office of NAtional Health Statistics.

sumption of health services and products amounted to $728.6 billion in 1991. Research and construction expenditures, representing investment in future health care resources, amounted to $23.1 billion, increasing only 2.1 percent over the 1990 level. This slow growth is attributable to absolute declines in expenditures for construction of health facilities, which in 1991 were 2.2 percent lower than the 1990 level. HSS is further disaggregated into personal health care, administration of public programs and the net cost of health insurance, and government public health activities.

Personal Health Care Expenditures

Personal health care expenditures grew to $660.2 billion in 1991, 11.6 percent higher than the 1990 level. Each American spent, on average, $2,518 in purchasing PHC services and products. Personal health care expenditures include all services and products purchased that are associated with individual health care, such as hospital services, physician services, drugs, and nursing home care.

Private funds paid for 57.1 percent of all PHC expenditures, mostly through out-of-pocket expenditures of individuals (21.9 percent) and private health insurance (31.7 percent). A small amount of PHC expenditures (3.6 percent) was funded through private non-patient sources, such as philanthropy and hospital revenues from cafeteria sales and educational programs.

Public funds picked up 42.9 percent of PHC expenditures in 1991, with most of those funds (76.5 percent) coming from the Medicare and Medicaid programs. Public funds grew 16.9 percent in 1991, significantly faster than overall PHC spending. The unusually fast growth was caused by Medicaid program expenditures, which increased 34.4 percent in 1991.

Spending for *hospital care* totaled $288.6 billion in 1991, accounting for 43.7 percent of personal health care expenditures. Hospital care includes expenditures for both inpatient and outpatient care. Spending for drugs and other services and supplies associated with hospital care, including services of hospital-salaried physicians, are also included in the hospital care category. Hospital output is valued as revenues received by the facility, which are discussed in more detail later in this article. In 1991, hospital revenues grew 11.8 percent over the 1990 level, marking the fifth year of accelerated growth. Growth rates this high have not been experienced since 1982, just prior to the implementation of the Medicare prospective payment system (PPS). Unusually large growth in Medicaid payments to hospitals (a 49.9-percent increase in 1991) contributed to this rapid growth. The causes for the tremendous growth in Medicaid payments are addressed in a later section of this article.

Short-term, acute care community hospitals delivered 86 percent of all hospital care in 1991, a share which has remained relatively stable over the past decade. While the majority of community hospital revenues comes from inpatient services, this share has been falling over the past 8 years, as more care is being delivered on an outpatient basis.

The remaining 14 percent of hospital revenues is split almost evenly between non-federal non-community hospitals ($19.5 billion) and federal hospitals ($19.7 billion).

Nearly all hospital care is financed by third parties, with only 3.4 percent paid for by consumers directly out-of-pocket. Private health insurance financed 35.2 percent, more than any other payer. Public funding, primarily the Medicare and Medicaid programs, financed 56.3 percent. The remaining 5.1 percent of hospital revenues comes from philanthropic and non-patient sources, such as hospital gift shops, cafeterias, or parking facilities.

In 1991, expenditures for *physician services* reached $142.0 billion, a growth of 10.2 percent from the previous year. These expenditures include care provided in offices and clinics of physicians, independent medical laboratory costs, and salaries for physicians employed by staff-model health maintenance organizations (HMOs). Excluded from these expenditures are professional fees received by physicians from hospitals, which are paid from hospital revenues and counted under the hospital sector in NHA.

Physicians' services accounted for 21.5 percent of PHC expenditures, and are funded primarily by private sources. Out-of-pocket payments accounted for $25.7 billion and private health insurance for $66.8 billion, a total of 65.1 percent of physician service expenditures. Public funds, the remaining 34.8 percent of physician services, consisted primarily of payments from Medicare and Medicaid, and amounted to $39.7 billion in 1991.

Dental service expenditures grew 8.8 percent from 1990 to 1991, from $34.1 billion to $37.1 billion. The NHA definition of dental services includes the business receipts of private dental offices (including dental laboratory costs) and salaries of dentists in staff-model HMOs.

Spending for dental services is generally more sensitive to changes in the overall economic environment than are other health sectors. This was reflected in slower growth in dental expenditures during 1989 and 1990, while the economy slowed down. However, in 1991 when the economy lapsed into a recession, a rise in dental prices as measured by the consumer price index caused dental expenditures to rise at a faster rate than before. One explanation for the rising prices may be the concern with acquired immune deficiency syndrome and the cost that was incurred purchasing supplies to ensure that patients and dental office personnel are protected from the spread of this disease. These increased costs are reflected in higher dental fees.

Private funds paid for the majority of dental services, 97.1 percent in 1991, with out-of-pocket expenditures accounting for 53.7 percent and private health insurance for 43.4 percent.

Other professional services include expenditures for licensed health practitioners, such as chiropractors, podiatrists and psychologists, services rendered in freestanding outpatient clinics, and ambulance services reimbursed under Medicare. A total of $35.8 billion was spent for all of these services in 1991, an increase of 16.7 percent from 1990. Private funds financed 76.6 percent: 27.0 percent was paid by out-of-pocket expenditures, 37.2 percent was paid by private health insurance, and 12.4 percent was paid by non-patient revenues (primarily philanthropic funds). Public sources paid 23.4 percent of expenditures for other professional services.

Home health care includes spending for services and supplies furnished by non-facility-based home health agencies (HHAs). It is the smallest but fastest growing component of PHC spending. In 1991, expenditures for home health care reached $9.8 billion, 29.0 percent higher than spending in 1990. Home health care furnished by facility-based HHAs is included with hospital care in this report. Including the hospital share of home health ($2.3 billion), $12.0 billion was spent for home health care in 1991.

Almost three-fourths of the expenditures for non-facility-based home health care was financed from public sources, predominately through the Medicare and Medicaid programs. In 1991, Medicare funded 44.7 percent, and Medicaid 27.1 percent. Out-of-pocket payments accounted for 12.7 percent and the residual funding was from private health insurance (7.6 percent) and non-patient revenues (7.5 percent) sources.

Recently available data from the 1987 National Medical Expenditure Survey (NMES) provide an indication of spending for a much broader definition of home health care than that included in the NHA. According to a forthcoming report, 5.9 million non-institutionalized people received care furnished in the home in 1987, spending $11.6 billion, as compared with NHA expenditures for facility- and non-facility-based home health care of $5.0 billion. NMES includes visits to the non-institutionalized population furnished by physicians, nurses, therapists, or other medical persons under the auspices of a home health agency. In addition to care provided by medical professionals, the NMES data include services provided by paid homemakers associated with or independent of a home health agency. Most homemaker services are currently beyond the scope of medical care in the NHAs.

Retail purchases of *drugs and other medical non-durables* reached $60.7 billion in 1991, an increase of 9.0 percent from the previous year. Prescription drugs accounted for 60.0 percent of these purchases, amounting to $36.4 billion. The remaining $24.3 billion is mainly over-the-counter (OTC) drug purchases, but also includes purchases of other drug sundries such as contraceptive and first-aid products.

For the past several years, expenditures for prescription drugs have been growing more rapidly than expenditures for non-prescription drugs and other medical non-durables. Since 1985, the prescription drugs as a share of the total category have grown from 55.9 percent to 60.0 percent in 1991.

In 1991, expenditures for *vision products and other medical durables* amounted to $12.4 billion, a growth of 5.4 percent over 1990. This category includes purchases of eyeglasses and contact lenses, and the purchase or rental of other durable medical products such as wheelchairs, crutches, hearing aids, and artificial limbs. Third parties paid for less than half of these purchases. Private insurance paid for only 9.6 percent; government payments, mostly Medicare, accounted for 28.5 percent. The remaining 61.9 percent of purchases were funded by out-of-pocket payments.

Expenditures for *nursing home care* reached $59.9 billion in 1991, 12.4 percent higher than in 1990. The growth of these expenditures in 1991 would have been slower without the influence of the rapidly growing Medicaid expenditures. The reasons for Medicaid's accelerated spending are discussed later in this report. Public funding for nursing home care, mainly from Medicaid, accounted for $32.3 billion in 1991. Medicaid's share of total spending increased from 45.1 percent in 1990 to 47.4 percent in 1991, the highest this share has been since 1981. Between 1990 and 1991, the out-of-pocket share declined from 45.3 percent to 43.1 percent, amounting to $25.8 billion in 1991.

Administration and Net Cost of Insurance

Third-party payers incur administrative costs in reimbursing providers for health care. These expenditures exclude any costs incurred by providers in meeting billing requirements of payers or in meeting standards for public program participation. For example, the cost incurred by a physician's office in tracking patient charges and in billing third-party payers is included under physician services, rather than administration or net cost of insurance.

The administration of public programs that finance PHC services and products amounted to $8.1 billion in 1991, 9.8 percent higher than the 1990 level. In 1991, public administration accounted for 4.0 percent of Medicaid, and 2.1 percent of Medicare total program costs.

A small amount of private administration costs are recorded for the administrative activities of philanthropic health organizations. These funds are estimated at $0.6 billion in 1991.

The net cost of private health insurance amounted to $35.1 billion in 1991, up 13.4 percent since 1990. Net costs are the difference between the premiums earned and the benefits incurred, and exclude any rate dividends or credits returned to policyholders. These expenditures of private insurers include the administrative costs associated with processing and paying insurance claims, marketing and advertising costs, commission paid to salespersons, state premium taxes, expenses associated with meeting licensing and reserve requirements, profits or dividends paid to owners or stockholders, and rate credits and dividends paid to policyholders. In 1991, the net cost of private health insurance accounted for 14.4 percent of all private health insurance expenditures.

Government Public Health Activities

Various levels of government spent $24.5 billion in public health activities in 1991. Almost nine-tenths of these expenditures, amounting to $21.8 billion, came through state and local health departments. Most of the federal expenditures are concentrated in the U.S. Public Health Services' Centers for Disease Control and the monitoring activities of the Food and Drug Administration.

Research and Construction

The nation spent $12.6 billion on non-commercial research activities in 1991, 6.1 percent more than in 1990. Only a small proportion of non-commercial research is financed through private philanthropic sources, 7.2 percent in 1991. The remainder came from federal funds (80.8 percent), mostly through the National Institutes of Health, and from state and local governments (12.0 percent). These figures exclude spending by drug companies in the United States on research and development, estimated by the Pharmaceutical Manufacturers Association as $7.3 billion in 1991.

Expenditures for the construction of medical facilities declined from 1990 to 1991, from $10.8 billion to $10.6 billion. Private business expenditures, which declined 2.8 percent in 1991, financed 72.7 percent of all construction. The remaining funds came from philanthropy (4.9 percent of construction expenditures), federal government (6.8 percent), and state and local governments (15.6 percent).

❖ Sources of Funds

Medical care in the United States is funded through a variety of private payers and public programs. Since 1979, private funds—including private health insurance, out-of-pocket expenditures, and non-patient revenues such as philanthropy—paid for approximately 58 percent of all health care expenditures. In 1991, that share dropped to 56.1 percent. The change in funding share between public and private financing was due primarily to dramatic growth in Medicaid program expenditures that began in 1990 and accelerated in 1991. The causes of this acceleration will be discussed later in this article.

Out-of-Pocket Expenditures

In 1991, Americans spent $144.23 billion out of pocket for personal health care services, increasing a modest 5.7 percent from 1990. Out-of-pocket purchases amounted to 21.9 percent of all PHC expenditures—the smallest share ever. Almost every service category in PHC experienced declines in share of out-of-pocket spending over the past three decades. These declines were fairly small in the beginning of the 1980s, but have become more exaggerated in the past four years.

Direct out-of-pocket payments consist of copayment and deductible amounts required by many third-party payers and direct payments for services and medical products not covered by third parties. These payments are limited to those out-of-pocket expenditures that result from specific decisions to purchase health care services or products. They exclude periodic consumer out-of-pocket private and/or public insurance premium payments made regardless of health care purchases.

Third-Party Financing

Unlike most other markets, the health care market is dominated by funding from third-party sources. For the elderly, the primary third-party payer is Medicare; for the non-elderly population, the primary third-party source of health care financing is private health insurance; other public programs such as Medicaid provide primary third-party funding of health care for the poor. The prevalence of third-party payers diminishes the role price plays in determining the quantity of medical services and products demanded and/or supplied. Without the equilibrating effects of price in the marketplace, quantity (including intensity) of medical care grows faster than it would otherwise. Consumers are less likely to limit the quantity of medical purchases based on price because the total price is not paid by the consumer. Price inflation also increases because providers and product producers are less likely to gain market share by lowering prices. This is because consumers, who ultimately make the decision to purchase services or products, pay such a small proportion of the total cost that it does not influence the consumer's choice of provider or product to the same extent as in other markets. During the 1980s, medical-specific price inflation played a more significant role in health cost growth than it had in the 1960s and 1970s.

In the national health accounts, private third-party payers are grouped into two sectors: private health insurance accounting for 32.5 percent of all NHA in 1991 and other private revenues accounting for 4.4 percent. In 1991, private health insurance premiums of $244.4 billion increased at a rate of 10.0 percent from the 1990 level, only slightly slower than the overall growth in national health expenditures. Private health insurance premiums include premiums paid by employers or unions, employee share of employer or union sponsored premiums, and premiums paid entirely by persons purchasing policies independently or through associations. Persons covered by private health insurance incurred $209.3 billion in benefits, 9.4 percent more than one year earlier. The difference between insurance premiums paid and benefits incurred is defined as the net cost of private health insurance, discussed in a previous section. The net cost includes expenses incurred in administering insurance, net additions to reserves, rate credits and dividends, premium taxes, and profits or losses of commercial insurers. In 1991, net cost amounted to $35.1 billion, an increase of 13.4 percent above 1990 levels.

Other private revenues include philanthropic giving, industrial in-plant health care services, and privately financed construction. They also include other non-patient revenue sources of hospitals, nursing homes, and home health agencies, such as revenues from educational programs, gift shops, parking lots, and other sources not associated with patient care. In 1991, other private revenues of $33.2 billion experienced a marked deceleration in growth—up only 6.0 percent from 1990. Absolute declines in funding for privately funded construction was the biggest identifiable factor in deceleration of aggregate other private revenues, although growth in non-patient revenues funding health care benefits and in industrial in-plant services also slowed.

All health care financing from the public sector is considered to be third-party payers. Broadly, public payers consist of two groups in the NHA: federal government, and state and local governments. In 1991, federal expenditures of $222.9 billion financed 29.6 percent of all national health spending while state and local expenditures of $107.1 billion paid for 14.2 percent. In both cases, growth in government expenditures exceeded those in the private sector by a wide margin, with federal expenditures increasing 14.6 percent and state and local expenditures up 18.3 percent.

For both the federal and state and local sectors, health spending jumped as a share of overall government spending in 1991. For the federal sector, health spending climbed to 16.7 percent of all federal expenditures in 1991, up from 15.3 percent in 1990. This is the single largest annual increase in share since 1967, just following the introduction of Medicare and Medicaid. For state and local governments, health spending as a share of all expenditures rose to 14.1 percent, up from 12.9 percent in 1990.

Programs administered by the U.S. Health Care Financing Administration—Medicare and Medicaid—are responsible for funding two-thirds of all publicly financed health care in 1991. Together, they spent $216.7 billion in providing health care benefits to aged, disabled, and poor Americans, and another $6.6 billion in administering the two programs. In 1991, the Medicaid program provided services to 28.3 million recipients, while the Medicare program covered 34.9 million enrollees.

Medicare expenditures increased 11.4 percent on average each year from 1980 to 1991; for 1991 alone, spending increased 10.9 percent, only slightly slower than the average growth over the past 11 years. For Medicaid, spending increased 10.1 percent annually from 1980 through 1989. In 1990 and 1991, however, expenditures increased rapidly, growing 21.3 percent and 33.2 percent, respectively. Recent expansions in recipient eligibility, increased efforts to reach eligible persons who are not currently covered, and the recession caused additional persons to qualify for coverage under the program. Creative financing by state governments, using provider tax and donation (T&D) programs and payments to hospitals servicing a disproportionate share of Medicaid recipients and other poor persons, contributed to large increases in Medicaid spending, particularly for hospital services. This dramatic acceleration in total Medicaid program expenditures dominated spending patterns in the public sector in 1991.

Other public financing of national health expenditures comes through state and local public health activities conducted by public health departments within those jurisdictions; through the U.S. Department of Defense and U.S. Department of Veterans Affairs expenditures in their own medical facilities, in the Civilian Health and Medical Program for the Uniformed Services and the Civilian Health and Medical Programs of the Veterans Administration, and in direct payments to community providers; through federally funded research; through state and local subsidies of hospitals; and through state and local workers' compensation programs. Each of these programs accounts for between 1 and 3 percent of all national health expenditures in 1991. All remaining public funding sources account for less than 1 percent each of all health spending.

❖ About the Authors

Suzanne W. Letsch, Helen C. Lazenby, Katharine R. Levit, and Cathy A. Cowan are on the staff of the Office of National Care Expenditures, Office of the Actuary, Health Care Financing Administration, Department of Health and Human Services.

❖ Providing Access to Health Care and Controlling Costs: The Universal Dilemma

Uwe E. Reinhardt

The human condition surrounding the delivery of health care is everywhere on the globe the same:

> The providers of health care seek to give their patients the maximum feasible degree of physical relief, but overall (if not for every patient they treat) they also seek a goodly slice of the gross national product (GNP), in the form of money-vouchers, as a reward for their efforts.

> Patients seek from the providers of care the maximum feasible degree of physical relief, but collectively (if not in each and every case) they also seek to minimize the amount of GNP that must be granted the providers as a reward for their efforts.

In other words, while there typically is a meeting of the minds between patients and providers on the *clinical* side of the health care transaction, there very often is conflict on the *economic* front. It has always been so, since time immemorial, and it will always be so, from here to kingdom come. It is part of the human condition.

Health insurance does not lessen this perennial economic conflict; it merely transfers it from the patient's bedside to the desk of some private or public bureaucrat charged with guarding a collective insurance treasury.

But health insurance does realign the parties to the economic fray. Because insurance shields patients from the cost of their medical treatments at point of service, it tends to move them squarely into the providers' corner when they are sick. Usually, in that corner, they rail against the heartless bureaucrats who refuse to surrender the key to the collective insurance treasuries they are there to guard. When patients are healthy and faced with mounting taxes or insurance premiums, however, they are typically found in the bureaucrats' corner. In that corner, they rail against the voracious financial appetite of health care providers.

Such is the intellectual purview from which the proverbial man and woman in the street beholds the health care sector. That, too, is part of the human condition.

In this essay, we shall explore how different nations approach the universal twin problems of modern health care: the provision of access to health care on equitable terms and the control of the cost of health care. It will be seen that there is a rich variety of alternative approaches to this twin problem, but there is no single *ideal* solution.

❖ Controlling the Transfer of GNP to Providers

Society can control the total annual transfer of GNP to the providers of health care through the demand side of the health care market, through its supply side, or through both. Nations differ substantially in the mix of approaches used to this end. Their choice of cost-control policies hinges crucially on the social role that is ascribed to health care. The two extremes of the spectrum of views one may have on this issue are

1. Health care is essentially a *private consumption good* whose financing is the responsibility of its individual recipient.
2. Health care is a *social good* that should be collectively financed and available to all citizens who need health care, regardless of the individual recipient's ability to pay for that care.

Canadians and Europeans long ago reached a broad social consensus that health care is a *social good*. Although their health systems exhibit distinct, national idiosyncrasies, these systems share in common their obedience to that over-arching ethical precept.

Americans have never been able to reach a similarly broad, political consensus on just where on the ideological spectrum defined by these two extreme views they would like their health care system to sit. Instead, American health policy has meandered back and forth between the two views, in step with the ideological temper of the time. During the 1960s and 1970s, the American health system moved toward the *social good* end of the spectrum. During the 1980s, however, a concerted effort was made to move the system in the opposite direction. This meandering between distinct ethical precepts has produced contradictions between professed principles and manifest practice that amuse the foreigner and that confuse and frustrate even the initiated at home. For example, at this time in the nation's history, poor, uninsured Americans often find it difficult to gain access to health care resources of which the nation has too many.

Table 1 presents a menu of alternative approaches to financing and organizing health care. That display distinguishes explicitly between the ownership of the *health insurance* mechanism and the *production* of health care. Almost all health care systems in the world can be fit into this grid.

The health systems of the United Kingdom and of Sweden, for example, occupy primarily box A in Table 1, although private medical practices in the United Kingdom occupy box C. One may think of box A as *socialized medicine* in its purest sense because the *production* of health care is substantially owned by the government. Clearly, the health system of the U.S. Department of Veterans Affairs resides in box A as well, as does the bulk of the

TABLE 1 Alternative Mixes of Health Insurance and Health Care Delivery

Production and Delivery	Collectivized (Socialized) Financing of Health Care			Direct Financing:
	Government Financed Insurance	Private Health Insurance*		Out of Pocket by Patients at Point of Service
		within a Statutory Framework	within an Unregulated Market	
Purely Governement Owned	A	D	G	J
Private Not-for-Profit Entities	B	E	H	K
Private For-Profit Entities	C	F	I	L
	The Canadian health system	The West German health system	The private portion of the Amercian health system	

* *Note:* Technically, whenever the receipt of health care is paid for by a third party rather than by the recipient at point of service, it is financed out of a *collective* pool and is thus "socialized" financing. In this sense, private health insurance is just as much "collectivist" or "socialized" as is government-provided health insurance. Both forms of financing destroy the normal working of a market because both eliminate the individual benefit-cost calculus that is the sine qua non of a proper market.

health care system for the U.S. armed forces. It has been said that President Eisenhower, a staunch opponent to *socialized medicine*, actually spent the bulk of his adult life in just such a system.

The Canadian health system occupies primarily boxes A, B, and C, as do the bulk of the American Medicare and Medicaid programs. These systems represent *public health insurance*, but not *socialized medicine*.

West Germany's health system is best described by boxes D, E, and F. It also does not represent *socialized medicine*. As noted above, the American health system is likely to slide toward that sort of arrangement before too long. At this time, the bulk of that system continues to reside in boxes G to L.

The Approaches Used in Canada and Europe

As noted, Canadians and Europeans typically view health care as a *social good*. In these countries it is anathema to link an individual household's contribution to the financing of health care to the health status of that household's members. Health care in these countries is collectively financed, with taxes or premiums based on the individual household's ability to pay. Only a small well-to-do minority—so far less than 10 percent of the population—tends to opt out of collective, social insurance in favor of privately insured or privately financed health care. Over 90 percent of the population in these countries typically shares in common one level of quality and amenities in health care.

Control over health care costs in these countries is exercised primarily by controlling the capacity of the *supply side*. The chief instrument for this purpose is formal regional health planning. Planning enables policymakers to limit the number of hospital beds, big-ticket technology such as computerized tomography scanners or lithotripters, and, sometimes, even the number of physicians issued billing numbers under these nations' health-insurance systems.

Regulatory limits on the capacity of the health system inevitably create monopolies on the supply side. To make sure that these artificially created monopolies do not exploit their economic power, these countries always couple health planning with stiff price and budgetary controls. Where the intent of price controls has been thwarted through rapid increases in the volume of health services rendered, for example, these countries eventually impose strictly limited global budgets on hospitals and doctors. Thus, Canada has long compensated its hospitals through pre-set global budgets. Similarly, West Germany now operates strict, statewide expenditure caps for all physicians practicing within a state under the nation's Statutory Health Insurance system. The United Kingdom and the Nordic countries budget virtually their entire health systems.

Figure 1 illustrates this three-pronged approach to health care cost control: (1) limits on physical capacity, (2) limits on fees and prices, and (3) limits on overall expenditures.

To effect their price and budget controls, Canada and the European countries tend to structure their health-insurance systems so that money

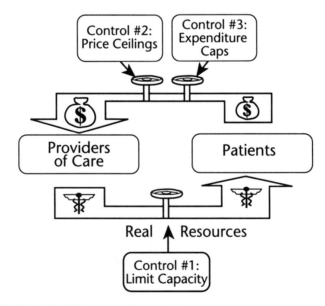

Figure 1. The Canadian/European Approach.

flows from third-party payers to the providers of care only through one or a few large money pipes whose money throughput is then controlled through formal negotiations between regional or national associations of third-party payers and associations of providers. As already noted, usually the negotiated prices in these countries are binding upon providers, who may not bill patients extra charges above these prices. Although France permits extra billing within limits, most of these countries see unrestrained extra billing as a violation of the spirit of health insurance.

The extreme version of this payment policy is illustrated in the bottom panel of Figure 2. It is the approach used in the typical Canadian province, where the provincial government administers both the hospital-insurance and the physician-service insurance plans.

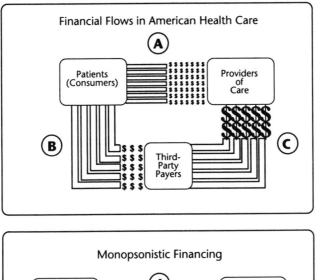

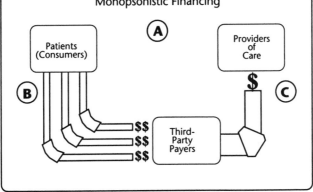

Figure 2. Alternative Financial Arrangements among Patients, Providers, and Third-Party Payers.

Remarkably, and in sharp contrast to the United States, Canada and Europe typically do not look to the individual patient as an agent of cost control; usually there is not a significant flow of money from patient to provider at the time health services are received. Instead, most of these countries provide patients with comprehensive, universal, *first-dollar* coverage for a wide range of services, typically including drugs (although Canada covers these only for the poor). France does have some copayments at point of service, but usually not for serious illnesses. Furthermore, many French patients have supplemental private insurance to cover any copayments.

One should not assume that Canada and the European nations eclipse patients from the chore of cost control because these nations' health-policy analysts and policymakers lack the savvy of their American colleagues who, in their debates on health policy, tend to style patients as "consumers" who are expected to shop around for cost-effective health care. Rather, one suspects that Canadians and Europeans are inclined to perceive patients as, for the most part, "sick persons" who should be treated thus. Table 1 suggests why that perception may be a valid one.

As Table 2 illustrates, the distribution of health expenditures across a population tends to be highly skewed. In the United States, for example, only about 5 percent of the population accounts for as much as half of all national health expenditures in any given year, and 10 percent account for as much as 70 percent to 80 percent of all health spending (see Table 2). The distribution of health expenditures in other countries is apt to trace out a similar pattern.

One must wonder whether the few individuals who account for the bulk of health care expenditures in any given year actually *can* act as regular "consumers" who shop around for cost-effective health care. Although cost sharing by patients can be shown to have some constraining effect on utili-

Table 2 Distribution of Health Expenditures over the U.S. Population (Selected Years)

Percentage of U.S. Population	Percentage of Total Health Expenditures Accounted for by That Percentile of the U.S. Population		
	1970	1977	1980
Top 1 percent	26	27	29
Top 2 percent	35	38	39
Top 5 percent	50	55	55
Top 10 percent	66	70	70
Top 30 percent	88	90	90
Top 50 percent	96	97	96

Source: Berk, Monheit and Hagan (1988).

zation for mild to semi-serious illness, it is unlikely to play a major role in the serious cases that appear to account for the bulk of national health care expenditures.

Where price and ability to pay cannot ration health care, something else must. Usually, in Canada and in Europe, that non-price rationing device is a queue for elective medical procedures. At the extreme, some high-technology medical interventions—for example, renal dialysis or certain organ transplantations—are simply unavailable to particular patients if the likely benefits from the intervention are judged by the attending physician to be low.

More generally, high-technology innovations are introduced rather cautiously in these nations, and only after intensive benefit-cost analysis. At any given point in time, these nations' health systems are therefore likely to lag behind the United States in the degree to which a new medical technology has been adopted.

Finally, the tight control on overall outlays for health care tends to preclude the often luxurious settings in which health care is dispensed to well-insured patients in the United States. Atriums and gourmet dining in hospitals, or physicians' offices with plush, deep carpets, are not common in Canada or in Europe.

The Entrepreneurial, American Approach

Americans have traditionally looked askance at regulation. To be sure, some regulatory controls of the supply side of health care have been attempted at various times in a number of states (through so-called Certificate-of-Need laws) and there have also been occasional flirtations with price controls (e.g., under Richard Nixon's presidency or in states that regulate hospital rates).

For the most part, however, Americans have always viewed the supply side of their health sector as an open economic frontier in which any and all profit-seeking entrepreneurs may seek their economic fortunes. Indeed, traditionally Americans have seen the very openness of their health system to profit-seeking entrepreneurship as the key driving force that has made the American health system, in their own eyes, "the very best health-care system in the world."

Health, as a vast societal enterprise, is too important to be solely the concern of the providers of services.
—William L. Kissick

American physicians, for example, have always prided themselves on their status as staunch "free-enterprisers" and they have vigorously, although not entirely successfully, defended that status against inroads by

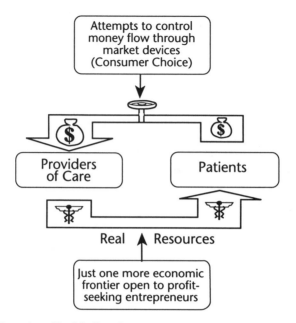

Figure 3. The American Health Care Sector.

third-party payers. Furthermore, as historian Rosemary Stevens has shown convincingly in her recent *In Sickness and in Wealth: A History of the American Hospital in the Twentieth Century* (1988), even the nation's so-called not-for-profit hospitals have typically run their enterprises very much on business lines, and they normally have booked profits, although they do not distribute them to any outside owners.

In contrast to Canada and Europe, who tightly control the supply side of their health sector, Americans have generally freely opened theirs to the seekers of fortune in the belief that the transfer of GNP the providers of care can extract from the rest of society can easily be controlled through the demand side of the sector—primarily by forcing patients to behave like regular consumers. Figure 3 illustrates that so-called market approach to health care in its purest form.

The traditional instrument of demand-side cost control in the United States has been cost sharing by patients. *On average*, American patients are not nearly as well insured as is sometimes supposed—not even in the heyday of the Great Society—although there is a wide dispersion around this average. Some Americans have no health insurance at all, others have very shallow insurance, and some receive from their employers relatively generous coverage that approximates the comprehensive, first-dollar coverage available to Canadians and Europeans. Typical among the latter insured are unionized workers in the Northern rust belt.

Even the relatively high degree of cost sharing by American patients, however, has not appeared to be able to constrain the growth of national health care expenditures. As Table 2 suggests, perhaps that particular donkey is just too weak to carry much of a cost-containment load. For that reason, additional forms of demand-side controls have been deployed in recent years, to wit, (1) ex post utilization control, (2) prospective and concurrent utilization review by third-party payers (otherwise known as "managed care"), and (3) the so-called preferred-provider organizations (PPOs). These PPOs are networks of fee-for-service providers who have agreed to grant large third-party payers price discounts in return for insurance contracts that steer the insured toward these "preferred" providers through specially tailored forms of cost sharing.

A uniquely American form of cost control, aimed more at the supply side of the health care market, is the health maintenance organization (HMO). Basically, the HMO is an insurance contract under which a network of providers is prepaid an annual lump sum capitation per insured, in return for the obligation to furnish the insured all medically necessary care during the contract period. The contract is designed to make providers hold to the medically necessary minimum in their use of resources in treating patients. Usually, the HMO contract leads to lower rates of hospitalization, other things being equal, and to relatively lower average per-capita health costs. Their drawback, in the eyes of patients, is that they limit choice of providers, and that they may underserve patients.

❖ The Economic Footprints of These Approaches

It is generally agreed, both here and abroad, that the American, entrepreneurial approach to health care has begotten one of the most luxurious, dynamic, clinically and organizationally innovative, and technically sophisticated health systems in the world. At its best, that system has few rivals anywhere, although many health systems abroad also do have facets of genuine excellence.

The Cost of Health Care

Unfortunately, but perfectly predictably, the open-ended American health system is plagued by perennial excess capacity in most parts of the country, and by large and rapidly growing costs. With the exception of New York City—where capacity *has* been tightly controlled through health planning—the average hospital occupancy ratio in the United States is now in the mid 60 percent range. It is below 50 percent in many regions. American physicians, for their part, have for years deplored a growing physician surplus.

This enormous capacity and excess capacity comes at a stiff price. No other country now operates as expensive a health system as does the United States and therein lies a major ethical problem:

So expensive has American health care become that the nation's middle- and upper-income classes now seem increasingly unwilling to share the blessings of their health system with their millions of low-income, uninsured fellow citizens. The gentleness and kindness for which Americans had come to be known after World War II has, thus, literally been priced out of the nation's soul. By international standards, American health policy toward the poor—particularly toward poor children—now appears rather callous.

The Uninsured

At this time, some 35 million Americans, about three quarters of them full-time employees and their dependents, and about one third of them children, have no health insurance coverage of any form. Most of these American families have incomes below $20,000 per year, yet for such families, if they are healthy, an individually purchased commercial insurance policy with considerable cost sharing would now cost anywhere between $3,000 and $4,000 per year, and some insurance companies have ceased to offer such policies even at these prices because they are unprofitable. If such families have chronically ill members, however, a private health-insurance policy may not be available to them at all.

Such enormous gaps in health-insurance coverage are not known anywhere else in the industrialized world. As noted above, without exception, the other member-nations in the Organization for Economic Cooperation and Development (OECD) offer their citizenry *universal* health-insurance coverage for a comprehensive set of health services and supplies, typically including dental care and prescription drugs (with the exception of Canada, where these items are covered only for low-income families).

Traditionally, the American health system has dealt with the uninsured thus: for mild to semi-serious illness, care to the uninsured has been effectively rationed on the basis of price and ability to pay. For critically serious illness, however, care was generally made available through the emergency rooms of hospitals who then shifted the cost of that charity care (including needed inpatient care) to paying patients, notably those insured by the business sector.

Unfortunately, in recent years this source of charity care has begun to dry up as the profit margins of hospitals have come to be squeezed by a combination of excess capacity and downward price pressure on the part of both the public- and private-sector payers. On average, an uninsured, low-income American now receives only about 50 percent to 60 percent of the health care received by an identical, regularly insured American. Thus, the myth that, unlike other nations, America does not ration health care is just that, a myth. Americans do ration health care by price and ability to pay, sometimes in rather disturbing ways.

Styles of Rationing

The preceding observation suggests that nations differ from one another not by whether they ration health care—all of them do somehow and to varying degrees—but in their style of rationing.

One style is to limit physical capacity and then to use triage based on medical judgment and the queue to determine the allocation of artificially scarce resources among the populace. That style of rationing is sometimes referred to as *implicit rationing*.

The other style is to ration *explicitly* by price and ability to pay. It is the natural by-product of the so-called market approach to health care.

Implicit rationing predominates outside the United States. In principle, the approach is thought to allocate health care strictly on the basis of medical *need*, as perceived and ranked by physicians. It is not known whether other variables, such as the patient's social status, ultimately do enter the allocation decision as well. For example, one wonders whether a gas station attendant in the United Kingdom has quite the same degree of access to limited resources as does, say, a barrister or university professor who may be able to use social connections in attempts to jump the queue.

As noted, many Americans believe that health care is not now rationed in the United States. That belief seems warranted for well-insured patients who are covered by traditional, open-ended indemnity insurance, and who are living in areas with excess capacity. For many such patients, there seems to be virtually no limit, other than nature, to the use of real resources in attempts to preserve life or to gain certainty in diagnosis. However, persons who are less well insured, who are uninsured, or who are covered by managed-care plans (including HMOs) do on occasion experience the withholding of health care resources strictly for economic reasons. In fact, in a recent cross-national survey, some 7.5 percent of the respondents (the equivalent of 18 million Americans) claimed that they had been denied health care in the previous year for financial reasons. In Canada and the United Kingdom, much fewer than 1 percent of the respondents made that claim.

The American public has been warned that medical care may soon have to be rationed. . . .The truth is that medical care is already rationed and it always has been. One of the disgraces of national policy is that the poor and unemployed who cannot afford to pay for medical care or have no medical insurance must often accept inferior treatment, if they can get it at all.
—John P. Bunker, Stanford University

Remarkably, it seems easier to implement the *implicit*, supply-side rationing practiced in most other countries than it is to use the *explicit* American approach to rationing. In the previously cited survey, Americans appeared much less satisfied with their health care system now than were Canadians and British respondents reacting to the identical set of questions on the subject.

For some reason, both physicians and patients appear to accept with greater equanimity the verdict that needed capacity is simply not available than they do the verdict that available, idle capacity will not be made available because some budget has run out. Thus, while the American approach to rationing does work after a fashion, it tends to create greater rancor among both patients and physicians than does the *implicit* rationing practiced elsewhere in the world. No one likes to see monetary factors enter medical decisions quite so blatantly at the patient's bedside as *explicit* rationing requires. Yet, a nation bent on using the market approach to health care ultimately cannot escape those troubling acts.

Summary on the Economic Footsteps

To sum up at this point: There appears to be a trade-off in the organization of health care that simply cannot be avoided; it is a trade-off among three distinct *desiderata* in health care, namely, (1) the freedom granted the providers of health care to organize the production of health care as they see fit and to price their products and services as they see fit, (2) the degree of control over total health care expenditures, and (3) the degree of equity attained in the distribution of health care.

❖ The Convergence of Health Systems

If one wished to paint with a very broad brush the evolution of health policy during the past four decades in the industrialized world, one might describe it as a gradual *shift from expenditure-driven financing of health care toward budget-driven delivery of health care.*

Under *expenditure-driven financing*, the providers of health care were allowed to do for patients whatever they saw fit and to send the rest of society a bill at prices that seemed "reasonable." Typically, those presented with that bill paid without reservations or, if they had reservations, they paid the bill nevertheless because they lacked the countervailing power present in normal markets without third-party payment. Naturally, under this open-ended approach the supply side of the health sector became a rich economic frontier that attracted both the genius of private entrepreneurship and its relentless search for revenues. Technological innovation flourished under this approach as the health sector stood an old adage on its head: instead of necessity being the mother of invention, invention became the mother of necessity. Once a technical innovation was at hand, its application was quickly deemed a "medical necessity" as long as it promised any additional benefits at all to the patient. Benefit-cost ratios played no role in this world because the denominator of that ratio—cost—was deemed irrelevant. Indeed, even to consider cost was deemed ethically unacceptable because that consideration might lead to the "rationing" of health care, which was deemed unacceptable on its face.

Under the second approach, *budget-driven health care delivery*, society establishes some sort of prospective budget for health care and tells providers to do the best they can with that budget. Typically, the establishment of the overall budget has been rather arbitrary in practice, in that the budget is tied to some arbitrary criterion, such as a fixed percentage of the GNP or a fixed annual growth rate. Ideally, of course, this approach should lead the budgeters to explore what additional benefits might be had by incremental expansions of the budget and to set the ultimate budget limits in that way. In any event, the application of new medical technologies in this world will typically be subjected to rigorous benefit-cost analysis before payment for such technologies will be made out of the fixed budget. Merely demonstrating promised benefits is no longer sufficient and will not be accepted by those who would stand to lose from applications of novel technology within the given budget constraint.

As noted earlier in this essay, most of the industrialized world has already gone a long way toward *budget-driven health care delivery*, some (England and Sweden, for example) completely. The United States is the odd one out because it is only just beginning to move in that direction. For the most part, both the government and private-sector payers in the United States are able to figure out what they have spent on health care in any given year only with a lag of a year or so. In fact, the announcement of total national health spending in recent years has lagged actual spending by close to two years. That announcement is eagerly anticipated by all concerned, and the actual numbers always come as a complete surprise (and, typically, as a complete shock as well).

There seems little doubt, however, that the 1980s were the last decade of the completely open economic health care frontier in the United States. There is now wide agreement in both government and the private sector that health spending in the United States is out of control and needs to be reigned in by means other than just the free market.

Several recent health-reform proposals—including the proposal put forth by President Clinton during his campaign and one put forth by the prestigious American College of Physicians—have called for a global national health care budget. That budget is to be determined by a national board of stakeholders, somewhat akin to Germany's *Konzertierte Aktion*. At this time, of course, the United States lacks the organizational infrastructure for setting such a budget and for apportioning it to the local level. Establishing that infrastructure alone will take over half a decade.

Furthermore, there is as yet widespread and open hostility toward the very idea of global budgets in the United States, and not only among those who define health care spending as health care income. Opponents to global budgeting in the United States offer as an alternative the strategy of *managed competition and managed care.* Some proponents of that approach market it as the Last Hurrah of the free market although, in fact, the approach is inherently regulatory.

"Managed competition" is frequently confused with "managed care," although these terms refer to entirely different concepts.

Managed care means the external monitoring and co-managing of an *ongoing* doctor-patient relationship, to make certain that the attending physician prescribes only "appropriate" interventions, where the term *appropriate* certainly excludes procedures without any proven medical benefit, but may also eventually exclude beneficial procedures with a low benefit-cost ratio.

Managed competition, on the other hand, is a highly structured and highly regulated framework that forces vertically integrated, income-seeking *managed care* systems to compete for patients on the basis of prepaid capitation premiums and quality, where the latter is to be measured by both clinical outcomes and the satisfaction of patients. In other words, the central idea is to put competing *managed care* systems each into transparent, statistical medico-fishbowls that can be compared both by patients and by those who pay on behalf of patients—for example, government agencies or business firms procuring health-insurance coverage for their employees.

At this time, the contrast between the current Canadian/European approach to resource allocation in health care and this newly emerging American approach is stark.

Canadians and Europeans still appear to believe that the best way to control overall health spending is to (1) constrain the *physical* capacity of the health system, (2) control prices, and, for good measure, (3) impose something as close as possible to global monetary budgets on the entire system. Within these constraints, however, they allow doctors and their patients considerable clinical freedom, on the thought that in this way the system will tend to maximize the benefits that are wrung out of the constrained set of real and financial resources. In other words, there is (as yet) considerable trust in the medical establishment's willingness and ability to use the resources made available to it properly, without the need for day-to-day supervision. Direct co-managing of an *ongoing* patient-doctor relationship on the American model is still rather rare in Canada and in Europe.

By contrast, the American proponents of *managed competition* believe— and the proper word is *believe*—that, by paying for everything that *is* beneficial, but denying payment for everything else, the nation can avoid setting an arbitrary global budget and will, in the end, devote the "right" percentage of the GNP to health care. These proponents have considerable faith in the ability of ordinary consumers to choose wisely among the alternative cost-quality combinations offered to them by competing *managed-care* systems in the health care market. However, they have little faith in the ability or willingness of the individual physician to use scarce resources wisely in the treatment of patients and, therefore, would subject each doctor to constant statistical monitoring and hands-on supervision.

A huge health-services research industry already has been busily working on constructing the statistical fishbowls this enterprise will require, and an even larger effort along this line will pour forth in the coming decade. Whether the American automobile industry will grow in the 1990s is an open question. That the health-services research industry will grow by leaps and bounds seems assured. By the end of the decade, clinical freedom, as older American physicians once knew it and loved it, will be all but dead. The physicians' daily activities, their successes, and their failures will become highly visible blips on sundry computer screens.

And what of the twenty-first century? How will the health systems of Canada and Europe then compare with the American health system?

It is my thesis that the current differences between the systems will vanish over time. Americans most likely will learn that a *managed-care–managed-competition* approach will do many wondrous things, but it will not be able to stop the medical arms race that characterizes the American health system. The proponents of managed competition probably oversell the importance of price in consumers' choices concerning health care. To be sure, price does matter among low-income households. But it is a safe bet that the competing managed-care systems will beckon higher-income households not chiefly with lower premiums, but with promises of ever new and abundant medical technology that these more elevated economic classes will find hard to resist. To deny the well-to-do such novel technology in the American context is very difficult. In the end, those who would be forced to deny it will seek comfortable refuge behind some larger constraint—something like a global national or regional budget. Sooner or later the United States health system will therefore envelop the competing medico-fishbowls by a global national budget imposed from the top.

At the same time, however, one must wonder whether countries that could not resist Elvis Presley, McDonalds hamburgers, and Apple computers will be able to resist the magnificent statistical medico-fishbowls now being manufactured all over the United States. There will continue to be top-down budgeting in these countries, but there is apt to be less faith in ability or willingness of the delivery system to use these budgets wisely, without hands-on supervision. Would it not be nice, and eminently proper, to inquire just what the little medico-fish in the health system actually do with all of the dollars, francs, marks, and pounds poured into these health systems, particularly when such information is easily retrieved and structured? Should there not be better accountability by *individual* doctors and hospitals for their spending, their clinical outcomes, and the satisfaction they achieve among patients? Thus, it is my bet that, around the year 2005, the health systems of Canada and Europe, too, will be a combination of budgets and statistical medico-fishbowls and that there will be a brisk commerce of ideas among health-services researchers and health care managers across the globe on how best to construct these medico-fishbowls, how best to behold them, and how best to direct the busy medico-fish within them toward desirable ends.

In short, our health systems will converge substantially, bound together by the imperative to constrain the share of GNP allocated to health care, on the one hand, and by the awesome capacity of ever new information technology to extract accountability even from the hitherto impenetrable health care delivery system on the other.

❖ About the Author

Uwe E. Reinhardt, PH.D., is James Madison Professor of Political Economy, Woodrow Wilson School of Public and International Affairs, Princeton University, Princeton, New Jersey.

❖ Old Snake Oil in New Bottles

BRUCE C. VLADECK

For those who missed the publicity blitz, managed competition is a system under which

consumers would be combined into large groups and represented by sophisticated sponsors. The sponsors would negotiate with doctors and hospitals, forcing them to provide high-quality treatment at reasonable cost. Sponsors would pay providers a fixed fee for each patient, independent of how much care the patient turned out to need, thus encouraging doctors to keep patients healthy and provide the most efficient care when they are sick.

It sounds too good to be true.

In fact, managed competition is a grand design for the complete reorganization of the American health care system, but it speaks only tangentially to the most important problem in health care in the United States today—the fact that one in seven Americans lacks the financial means to get the health care he or she needs—and offers only untested theory (most of it contrary to actual experience) as a solution for the other central problem, the continuing upwards spiral in the costs of health care. Indeed, one has to be only moderately cynical to suspect that much of the appeal of managed competition lies in the recognition of its capacity to divert attention from these more important, and thus more contentious, issues.

With its promise of unmitigated benefit, managed competition may be this decade's intellectual and moral equivalent of the Laffer Curve, the construct which purported to demonstrate that cutting federal taxes would increase federal government revenues, inspiring George Bush to coin the phrase "voodoo economics." Of course, most responsible economists now agree that the Laffer Curve never had much empirical basis and that the public policy developed by its advocates is a major source of the unmanageable, continuing federal budget deficit. In a similar attempt to find a painless solution to a difficult policy problem, the advocates of managed competition propose to create a "market" in health care coverage though an extraordinarily complex regulatory scheme.

❖ Blaming the Victim

Proposals for managed competition in health care, such as those advanced by Professor Alain Enthoven of Stanford University or the "Jackson Hole Group" led by Dr. Paul Ellwood, are rooted in two basic propositions, which purport to explain much of what is wrong with the American health care system. The first proposition—widely accepted although largely inaccurate—is that health care in the United States costs so much because Americans use too much health care. According to the proponents of managed competition, Americans are overinsured, at least in part because the value of employer-provided health insurance benefits is exempted from taxable income. Because people have so much health insurance, the argument then goes, they are inadequately "sensitive" to the price of health care at the point of service, and thus use more than they otherwise would.

This "excess" demand for health care, according to the proponents of managed competition, is the major source of the extraordinary, continuing inflation in health care costs. Thus, most full-fledged managed competition proposals start with the abolition or limitation of tax exemption for employer-provided health insurance. The most comprehensive managed competition proposals then use the new tax revenues derived from reducing the benefits available to most of the population to finance coverage for some of the uninsured.

It certainly is true that the tax exemption for fringe benefits is one of the more regressive features of the Internal Revenue Code: not only are such exemptions worth more to people in higher tax brackets, but higher paid employees tend to get more generous health insurance coverage. But the significant cuts in income taxes in the early 1980s (remember the Laffer Curve) did not reduce demand for health insurance, as this theory would seem to predict. Nor is there any actual experience that demonstrates that real people, with the exception of a few highly paid employees, pay any attention at all to the relatively minor tax implications when thinking about health insurance coverage. More to the point, the sorts of health insurance coverage to which advocates of managed competition most strenuously object—first-dollar coverage for an unlimited range of services at the consumer's option—largely disappeared from the private sector during the latter half of the 1980s, not because of any changes in the tax code, but because, in real life, employers couldn't afford them any more.

Still more pernicious is the underlying assumption that cost inflation in health care is largely a problem of excessive discretionary utilization by consumers. Again, the facts do not support this interpretation. During the 1980s, a period in which real health care costs grew faster than at any time in history, the average American used considerably fewer health services than in the decade before. Total hospital days fell 15 percent, and physician visits per capita, the service over which consumers exercise the most discretion, also fell. To be sure, consumers received more services, especially high-technology services, per hospital day or physician visit in the 1980s than they had in the past, but they paid for a greater share of them out of pocket. And those services are largely initiated by providers, not consumers. A trip to the doctor is not like a trip to Cape Cod, a colonoscopy is not like a haircut, and a lens procedure is not like getting a new TV.

International comparisons are always dangerous, as anyone watching the current policy debates will quickly conclude, but it is not inappropriate to point out that in the other Western nations that have both universal health insurance coverage and lower costs than we do—that is to say, all other Western nations—consumers use more health care than we do. They go to the doctor more often, are hospitalized more often, and stay much longer once they are hospitalized. (They also live longer, which may or may not be related.) It's also worth noting that the absence of copayments and other out-of-pocket liabilities for health care consumers in those nations is the principal reason that the administrative overhead in their health care systems is so much less than ours.

❖ Reforming the Market

The other proposition underlying arguments for managed competition is more soundly based, even if its implications are not necessarily those managed competition advocates would identify. Put most simply, the current "market" for health services doesn't work because of the fundamental imbalance in power between buyers and sellers. Most consumers don't want to worry about the price when they need, or think they need, health care for themselves or their children; that's why they have insurance. Indeed, most of the time people seek health care, they don't even know what they need; they are paying health professionals to tell them and are rarely in a position to evaluate independently what they are told. Indeed, most Americans think there is something faintly immoral about forcing people who are acutely ill or in serious pain or experiencing a life-threatening illness to weigh financial considerations when deciding what to do.

The way to redress this fundamental imbalance in the health care marketplace is, indeed, as the advocates of managed competition contend, to aggregate the buying power of consumers and to employ sophisticated organizations with the consumers' best interests at heart to work as their agents. It doesn't necessarily follow, however, that those agents should be big insurance companies or big health maintenance organizations or similar "sponsors."

There are many ways to redress the absence of consumer market power without forcing all consumers into a small number of self-appointed, unaccountable insurance plans. One could imagine, for example, a public or quasi-public price-setting mechanism, as we now have for electric and gas service and are about to recreate for that most vital of all public services, cable television. In fact, prices for more than a third of health services—those rendered to Medicaid and Medicare patients—are already set by government. Proponents of managed competition oppose such price-setting mechanisms: the academic economists believe that government will set the prices too high, while the provider groups think they will be too low.

Given our national distaste for government, other alternatives should also be considered. One possibility might be to create a narrowly drawn exemption to antitrust law permitting private insurers to bargain collectively about prices with organized providers—as is, in effect, now done in Germany and the Netherlands. Or one could pursue the proposal already floating around in the Congress to permit, but not require, private insurers to pay physicians and hospitals the same prices Medicare pays. Or one could develop some sort of arbitration strategy in which, for example, a neutral third party heard claims from payers and providers and then made a binding decision, not that such a strategy has worked terribly well in controlling the prices paid for major league shortstops.

But the reason proponents of managed competition have rejected these options is because they are after more than prices. They want to reform medical care at the same time. This is where their first proposition reappears—and with a considerable tinge of moralism, as demonstrated by the *New York Times*'s choice of such locutions as "consumers would be combined" and "forcing" doctors and hospitals. Proponents of managed competition—pursuing a theoretically efficient system at the expense of theoretically wasteful patients and health care providers—would limit the kinds of insurance people could choose, require them to participate in "managed care" arrangements that would severely restrict their choices of doctors and hospitals and put them at enormous risk of underservice, and impose extraordinarily detailed oversight of professional practice in order to "force" high quality care, all in the name of eliminating the overuse of service and making the health care system more "efficient."

❖ First Principles

In other words, while much of the current discussion of health care reform is driven by the need to find a way to get the uninsured and underinsured into the health care system, proponents of managed competition insist on a thoroughgoing reshaping of that system first. Of course, we can't afford to cover the uninsured unless we can control costs; we can't even continue to cover those who currently have insurance unless we can control costs. But neither can we afford to wait a generation or so to rebuild the system, particularly when what the proponents of managed competition are seeking to fix may not be broken.

One cannot simultaneously control health care costs, protect the economic interests of all health care providers, and extend universal health insurance coverage. If managed competition really controlled costs, providers (as well as consumers) would be substantially worse off; the reason so many providers support managed competition is because they don't believe its cost containment mechanisms will really work, and they're afraid the mechanisms in other proposals for health care reform would. In this way, the debate on managed competition becomes a smokescreen for the most important issues, distracting us from what should be the first priority: coverage for everyone.

One way or another, we're going to have to figure out how to control the costs of health care—by taking away revenue from providers, taking away freedom to choose from consumers, or quite possibly both. But that's only an economic problem. The fact that American citizens who are sick can't get health care because they don't have health insurance is also, I would suggest, a moral problem. In fact, it's a disgrace.

There are many ways to get health insurance coverage to those who don't now have it. The president has proposed a plan to do so. So have lots of other people. I have my preferences, but that's almost beside the point. Let's get everybody covered, now. After that, we can fight about money. Indeed, we might even find that insuring everyone could be the impetus for solving the cost problem.

❖ About the Author

Bruce C. Vladeck, PH.D., is Administrator of the Health Care Financing Administration, Department of Health and Human Services, and is past President of The United Hospital Fund of New York.

❖ Universal Health Insurance through Incentives Reform

ALAIN C. ENTHOVEN AND RICHARD KRONICK

❖ The Paradox of Excess and Deprivation

American national health expenditures are now about 13% of the gross national product, up from 9.1% in 1980, and they are projected to reach 15% by 2000, far more than in any other country. These expenditures are straining public finances at all levels of government. At the same time, roughly 35 million Americans have no health care coverage at all, public or private, and the number appears to be rising. Millions more have inadequate insurance that leaves them vulnerable to large expenses, that excludes care of preexisting conditions, or that may be lost if they become seriously ill. The American health care financing and delivery system is becoming increasingly unsatisfactory and cannot be sustained. Comprehensive reform is urgently needed.

❖ Diagnosis

The etiology of this worsening paradox is extremely complex; many factors enter in. Some factors we would not change if we could (e.g., advancing medical technology, people living longer). We emphasize factors that are important and correctable.

First, our health care financing and delivery system contains more incentives to spend than to not spend. It is based on *cost-unconscious demand*. Key decision makers have little or no incentive to seek value for money in health care purchases. The dominant open-ended fee-for-service (FFS) system pays providers more for doing more, whether or not more is appropriate.

Contrary to a widespread impression, America has not yet tried *competition* of alternative health care financing and delivery plans, using the term in the normal economic sense; i.e., *price* competition to serve cost-conscious purchasers. When there is price competition, the purchaser who chooses the more expensive product pays the full difference in price and is thus moti-

---

Health care is as much a component of American goods and products and services as are raw materials. The U.S. spends eight times more than many of its international competitors on health care.
—Richard D. Lamm, Governor of Colorado, 1975–1987

---

vated to seek value for money. However, in offering health care coverage to employees, most employers provide a larger subsidy to the FFS system than to health maintenance organizations (HMOs) thereby destroying the incentive for consumers and providers to choose the economical alternative. Many employers offer no choice but FFS coverage. Others offer choices but pay the whole premium, whichever choice the employee makes. In such a case, the HMO has no incentive to hold down its premium; it is better off to charge more and use the money to improve service. In many other cases, employers offer a choice of plan, but the employer pays 80% or 90% of the premium or all but some fixed amount, whichever plan the employee chooses. In all these cases, the effect is that the employer pays more on behalf of the more costly system and deprives the efficient alternatives of the opportunity to attract more customers by cutting cost and price.

The rational policy from an economic point of view would be for employers to structure health plan offerings to employees so that those who choose the less costly plans get to keep the full savings.

The second major problem is that our present health care financing and delivery system is not organized for quality and economy. One of the main drives in the present system is for each specialist to exercise his or her specialty, not to produce desired outcomes at reasonable cost. In a system designed for quality and economy, managed care organizations would attract the responsible participation of physicians who would understand that, ultimately, their patients bear the costs of care, and they would accept the need for an economical practice style. Data would be gathered on outcomes, treatments, and resource use, and providers would base clinical decisions on such data.

There are too many beds and too many specialists in relation to the number of primary care physicians. A high-quality cost-effective system would carefully match the numbers and types of physicians retained and other resources to the needs of the population served so that each specialist and subspecialist would be busy seeing just the type of patient she or he was trained to treat. We have a proliferation of costly specialized services that are underutilized.

The third major problem area is "market failure." The market for health insurance does not naturally produce results that are fair or efficient. It is plagued by problems of biased risk selection, market segmentation, inadequate information, "free riders," and the like. Insurers profit most by avoiding coverage of those who need it most. The insurance market for small employment groups is breaking down as small employers find insurance unavailable or unaffordable, especially if a group member has a costly medical condition.

Fourth, public funds are not distributed equitably or effectively to motivate widespread coverage. The unlimited exclusion of employer health benefit contributions from the taxable incomes of employees is the second-largest federal government health care "expenditure," trailing only expenditures for the Medicare program. While providing incentives for the well-covered well-to-do to choose even more generous coverage, this provision does little or nothing for those (mainly lower-income) people without employer-provided coverage.

In brief, powerful *incentives* that shape behavior in the health care system and that influence the distribution of services point the system in the wrong direction: services too costly for those who are covered, and the exclusion of millions from any coverage at all.

❖ Our Proposal

We propose a set of public policies and institutions designed to give everyone access to a subsidized but responsible choice of efficient, managed care (HMO, preferred provider insurance plans, etc.). *We propose comprehensive reform of the economic incentives* that drive the system. We propose cost-conscious informed consumer and employer (or other sponsor) choice of managed care so that plans competing to serve such purchasers will have strong incentives to give value for money. We also propose a strategy of *managed competition* to be executed by large employers and public sponsors (explained below), designed to reward with more subscribers those health care financing and delivery plans that offer high-quality care at relatively low cost. The goal of these policies would be the gradual transformation of the health care financing and delivery system, through voluntary private action, into an array of managed care plans, each competing to attract providers and subscribers by finding ways to improve the quality of care and service while cutting costs. We propose restructuring the tax subsidies to create incentives to cover the uninsured and to encourage the insured to be cost conscious in their choice of plan. We propose the creation of public institutions to broker and market subsidized coverage for all who do not obtain it through large employers. We favor substantial public investments in outcomes and effectiveness research to improve the information base for medical practice and consumer/employer choice.

The rise and growth of competition is surely one of the most significant developments in the health care sector in the last decade.
—Lawrence D. Brown, University of Michigan

Public Sponsor Agencies

The Public Sponsor, a quasi-public agency (like the Federal Reserve) in each state, would contract with a number of private-sector health care financing and delivery plans typical of those offered to the employed population and would offer subsidized enrollment to all those who do not have employment-based coverage. Except in the case of the poor, the Public Sponsor would contribute a fixed amount equal to 80% of the cost of the average plan that just meets federal standards. The enrollee would pay the rest. (The 80% level was chosen to balance two incentives. First, we wanted the subsidy level to be low enough so that there would be room for efficient plans to compete by lowering prices and taking subscribers away from inefficient plans. Second, we wanted the subsidy to be high enough so that the purchase of health insurance would appear very attractive even to those who expect to have no medical expenses.) To the enrollee, the Public Sponsor would look like the employee benefits office.

In the case of the poor, we propose additional subsidies. People at or below the poverty line would be able to choose any health plan with a premium at or below the average and have it fully paid. For people with incomes between 100% and 150% of the poverty line, we propose public sharing of the premium contribution on a sliding scale related to income.

Public Sponsors would also act as collective purchasing agents for small employers who wished to take advantage of economies of scale and of the ability of Public Sponsors to spread and manage risk. Small employers could obtain coverage for their groups by payment of a maximum of 8% of their payroll.

Today, a substantial part of the money required to pay for care of the uninsured comes from more or less broadly based state and local sources, including employers' payments to private hospitals for bad debt or free care and direct appropriations from state and local governments to acute-care hospitals. In our proposal, federal funds (the sources of which are described below) would be the main source of support for the Public Sponsors. These funds would be supplemented by funds from state and local sources.

Mandated Employer-Provided Health Insurance

For better or worse, we have an employment-based system of health insurance for most people under age 65 years. It can be modified gradually but not replaced overnight. Most employers and employees agree that health care will be included in the compensation package. This is responsible behavior; if one of the group gets sick, the group pays the cost. Some employers and employees do not include health care in the package. The effect is irresponsible behavior; if an employee becomes seriously ill, these employers and employees count on someone else to pay. They are taking a "free ride." It is hard to justify raising taxes on the insured to pay for coverage for the employed uninsured unless those uninsured are required to contribute their fair share.

The existence of Public Sponsors would give all employers access to large-scale efficient health care coverage arrangements. However, in the absence of corrective action, the availability of subsidized coverage for uninsured individuals would create an incentive for employers to drop coverage of their employees. This would create additional expense for the Public Sponsor without compensating revenue. To prevent this, our proposal requires employers to cover their full-time employees (employers would make a defined contribution equal to 80% of the cost of an average plan meeting federal standards and would offer a choice of health plans meeting federal standards).

Premium Contributions from all Employers and Employees

Many people who are self-employed, who have part-time or seasonal work, or who are retired and under age 65 years do not have enough attachment to one employer to justify requiring the employer to provide coverage.

We propose that employers be required to pay an 8% payroll tax on the first $22,500 of the wages and salaries of part-time and seasonal employees, unless the employer covered the employee with a health insurance plan meeting federal standards. Self-employed persons, early retirees, and everyone else not covered through employment would be required to contribute through the income tax system. An 8% tax would apply to adjusted gross income up to an income ceiling related to the size of the household. The ceiling would be calculated to ensure that households with sufficient income paid for approximately the total subsidy that would be made available to them through the Public Sponsor.

The proceeds of these taxes would be paid by the federal government to the states, on a per-person-covered basis, for use by Public Sponsors in offering subsidized coverage to persons without employment-based coverage.

This tax would be at the federal level because individual states might be deterred from levying such a tax by employer threats to move to a state without the tax.

Limit on Tax-Free Employer Contributions

We propose that Congress change the income and payroll tax laws to limit the tax-free employer contribution to 80% of the average price of a comprehensive plan meeting federal standards. The average price of a qualified health plan in 1991 might be roughly $290 per family per month. As a condition of tax exemption, employer health plans would be required to use fixed-dollar defined contributions, independent of employee choice of plan, not to exceed the limit, so that people who choose more costly health care plans must do so with their *own* money, not with that of the taxpayer or employer.

The purposes of this measure are two-fold. First, it would save the federal budget some $11.2 billion in 1988 dollars. This money could be used to help finance subsidies for the uninsured comparable to those received by the employed insured. Second, making people cost conscious would help enlist all employed Americans in a search for value for money in health care, would stimulate the development of cost-effective care, and would create a market for cost-effective managed care. Thus, this tax reform is defensible on grounds of both equity and efficiency.

Budget Neutrality

The Congressional Budget Office has estimated the effects of our proposal on coverage, costs, and the federal budget and has found that our proposed new revenues would equal the added outlays. We have not done a state-by-state analysis, but, in the aggregate, required state and local contributions appear to approximately equal outlays for care of the uninsured.

Managed Competition

The market for health insurance does not naturally produce results that are fair or efficient. It is plagued by problems of biased risk selection, market segmentation, inadequate information, etc. In fact, the market for health insurance cannot work at the individual level. To counteract these problems, large employers and Public Sponsors must structure and manage the demand side of this market. They must act as intelligent, active, collective purchasing agents and manage a process of informed cost-conscious consumer choice of "managed care" plans to reward providers of high-quality economical care. Tools of effectively managed competition include the annual open-enrollment process; full employee consciousness of premium differences; a standardized benefit package within each sponsored group; risk-adjusted sponsor contributions, so that a plan that attracts predictably sicker people is compensated; monitoring; surveillance; ongoing quality measurement; and improved consumer information.

Outcomes Management and Effectiveness Research

As Ellwood and Roper et al. have pointed out, there is a poverty of relevant data linking outcomes, treatments, and resource use. Although such data are costly to gather, they constitute a public good, and their production ought to be publicly mandated and supported. Combined with the incentives built into our proposal, such data could be of great value to providers and patients seeking more effective and less costly treatments. Without incentives for efficiency, such data are likely to have little impact on health care costs.

Mutually Supportive Components

We recognize the propensity of the American political system to seek minimal, incremental change. Some components of our proposal would be viable and helpful on their own. However, we believe that effective solution of the problems of access and cost requires a comprehensive strategy, and the merits of the combined package exceed the merits of the individual components.

❖ Will It Work?

Our confidence that a reasonably well-managed comprehensive reform plan along these lines can be made to work rests on two propositions.

First, efficiently managed care does exist. It is possible to improve economic performance substantially over the non-selective FFS, solo practice, third-party intermediary model.

Second, people do choose value for money. Our limited experience with even attenuated price competition in employment groups such as federal employees, California state employees, and Stanford University suggests that, over time, people do migrate to cost-effective systems.

In recent years, the main inhibitor of the growth of HMOs has been the employer contribution policies we have discussed; that is, most employers do not structure their health plan offerings in such a way that the employee who chooses the most economical plan gets to keep the savings. Nevertheless, some nonprofit HMOs have been growing rapidly through the 1980s.

❖ Comprehensive Reform That Relies on Incentives Is Preferable to Direct Government Controls

One alternative to the system we have proposed is a system like Canada's, in which the government is the sole payer for physician and hospital services. While Canada's system has evident strengths, there would be major difficulties in successfully adopting or implementing it in the United States. First, it would require a political sea change to adopt such a system here. . . . Second, government regulatory processes tend to freeze industries and often penalize efficiency. The Canadian system is not as frozen as it might be because proximity to the United States exposes Canadians to our innovations. If American medical care were also entirely financed and regulated by the government, the negative effects of regulation would likely loom larger.

A second alternative would be to leave the financing of health insurance for the employed population in the private sector but to have the government regulate physician and hospital prices for all payers. It is possible to imagine a political compromise in which such a system could be adopted—in the midst of a recession, providers might agree to accept all payer price controls in exchange for an employer mandate, and employers might acquiesce to a mandate in exchange for price controls—but it is hard to imagine that such a regulatory structure could be effective over time in promoting quality or economy.

Finally, administrative costs in the present system are high and increasing. We believe administrative costs would be greatly reduced under our proposal. After a competitive shakedown, there would be relatively few managed care organizations in each geographic area. Everyone would get coverage through large group arrangements. Eligibility determination would be simple in a system of universal coverage. Today, the best managed care organizations do not bill patients for services. Providers are paid by health plans in simplified ways using prospective payments for global units of care. In a system with relatively few managed care organizations competing to serve competent sponsors and cost-conscious consumers, payers would not have to attempt to micromanage the delivery of care because providers would be at risk. Administrative costs and the "hassle factor" would be much lower than they are today. However, the most important economies would be in the effective organization of the process of care itself.

Over time, we would expect slowed growth in the price of the average health plan and continuing improvements in efficiency comparable to those in other competitive industries.

❖ About the Authors

Alain C. Enthoven, PH.D., is Marriner S. Eccles Professor of Public and Private Management in the Graduate School of Business, Stanford University.

Richard Kronick, PH.D., is in the Department of Community and Family Medicine, University of California, San Diego.

❖ Chapter 7
Inequities in Access
to Health Services

As national health expenditures have skyrocketed, millions of people in the United States still lack access to adequate health services. The common belief that health services are—and ought to be—available to every U.S. citizen is countered by the experience of individuals who receive infrequent health services of inadequate quality because of poverty, lack of insurance, preexisting conditions, unemployment, race, class, age, gender, geographic location, or health beliefs.

Many poor persons receive no benefits despite government-financed medical coverage through Medicare and Medicaid. More than 37 million Americans are without health insurance of any kind, and many of the insured fail to obtain services because they cannot afford required deductibles and copayments. Access is tangled in a complex knot of quality and cost, cost being the easiest aspect to measure and manipulate. Cost containment policy, which has had limited success in controlling costs, threatens to jeopardize access and quality. Improvements in the latter areas might in turn fan health cost inflation.

In addition to insurance status, race and place of residence are significant determinants of ability to obtain health services. Individuals least able to bear the cost of poor health are most likely to be ill and uninsured. The uninsured are unlikely to have a regular source of care and must travel further and wait longer for services than insured persons do. Deaths have resulted from the transfer for financial reasons of uninsured patients from one hospital to another. Even though the poor are experiencing more ill health than others, they receive fewer hospital and physician services.

Uncompensated hospital care is a growing problem facing federal and state policymakers, health providers, and society at large. Public hospitals bear an increasingly large share of the uncompensated care burden. In the past, cost shifting to other payer sources permitted community hospitals to care for nonpaying patients. As competition increased and third parties limited cost shifting within community hospitals, the burden was transferred to public hospitals. Thus, in the wake of market-driven price competition, teaching and public hospitals are left with a disproportionate share of unpaid cases.

The concept of access includes process and outcome indices, but can be simply defined as a match of service, need, and affordable cost. Such a match depends on many elements—perception and identification of need; availability of the required service; knowledge of the service; a referral mechanism; common understanding of service usefulness; transportation; physically accessible location; information, motivation, and assistance to sustain treatment; and ability to cover costs. Although these are only some of the steps involved in gaining access to health services, they indicate the complexity of the issue.

Significant barriers to access are the lack of continuity among fragmented and complex health services and the inability of the present system to adapt services to varying ethnic, class, age, and gender requirements. Emergency and acute care continue to be more accessible than basic care and chronic and preventive services, which, if provided, might delay or prevent acute needs. Health-related nonmedical services are particularly difficult to obtain. Availability of health services varies by geographic region, with prosperous states and urban areas providing a wider array of services than poor and rural areas offer. Differences in Medicaid coverage from state to state also create inequities.

This chapter examines the access question through the perspectives of demographic characteristics, provider and financing influences, and alternative policy solutions.

Karen Davis provides a historical overview of issues related to access to health care over the past 25 years. She points out that gains in health status in the United States have not been obtained uniformly throughout the nation, and she cautions that efforts in recent years by the government and other third-party payers, as well as providers, to contain costs have begun to reverse some positive trends of previous decades. One of the most destructive characteristics has been to limit availability of health insurance.

In "The Uninsured: From Dilemma to Crisis," Emily Friedman examines the uninsured: who they are, where they are, and how they got that way. She also introduces issues related to underinsured people with the startling figure that as many as 26 percent of the nonelderly population is inadequately protected from the advent of large medical bills. Ms. Friedman explores factors behind the erosion of employer-subsidized health insurance in recent years and how this has resulted in a large group of working uninsured, which is comprised both of low- and middle-class people. She outlines five reasons that she believes indicate that issues of the uninsured and underinsured have reached crisis proportions. She also brings up the larger issue that the rest of the population is paying for medical indigence "one way or another."

This chapter closes with the abiding theme of the unmet needs of children in our society. In the age of plenty, too many children are forced to settle for very little. What this implies about their future is worrisome both for them and for the nation. The poverty of their environment is the most significant determinant of their health and often dooms them to a lifetime of ill health. This destiny is not promised just for crack babies, the homeless, and infants born with acquired immunodeficiency syndrome (AIDS); it is a consequence of the environment itself.

Drs. Robert F. St. Peter, Paul W. Newacheck, and Neal Halfon describe a study they undertook to determine how coverage of Medicaid affects the use of preventive care, as well as the location and continuity of care for poor children. They found that poor children with Medicaid coverage were more likely than those without Medicaid to receive appropriate routine care, but these same children were less likely than middle-class children to receive routine care in a physician's office, and they had a greater likelihood of receiving fragmented care in community clinics and emergency departments. The authors conclude that, while Medicaid does improve access to care for poor children, it does not ensure continuity of care.

❖ Availability of Medical Care and Its Financing

KAREN DAVIS

Advances in modern medicine in the last 100 years have greatly improved our ability to prevent disease and injury, lengthen life expectancy, and improve the quality of life for people throughout the world. The benefits of modern medicine are so well demonstrated that nearly all industrialized nations intervene to ensure access to health care for those who need it.

As the United States nears the beginning of the next century, it is an important time of reassessment for national health policy. Either a basic societal commitment will be made to ensure access to health care for all or we risk a nation that is increasingly divided into the cared for and the neglected—with the consequent toll on human suffering, loss of life and economic productivity, and diminished social solidarity.

❖ The Great Society and Expanded Health Insurance Coverage

The passage of Medicare and Medicaid in 1965 brought in a new era of federal government commitment to improving the health of the poor and elderly and to increasing their access to health care services. Together with other Great Society programs, such as the comprehensive health center program and an expanded maternal and child health program, the poor, the aged, and the disabled were to enjoy the benefits of modern medicine along with other members of society.

The accumulated evidence suggests that this investment has been a contributing factor to major gains in health in the last 25 years. These gains have been especially noteworthy for the aged and for minorities.

Longer life expectancy at birth reflects lower infant mortality and lower death rates in middle age. However, a substantial portion of the improvement in life expectancy is accounted for by improvements in health of the aged. Life expectancy at age 65 increased 2.6 years between 1960 and 1987. Leading the gains in improved life expectancy among the aged were white women, who upon reaching the age of 65 in 1987 live an average of 18.7 more years, three years longer than in 1960. The Medicare program deserves at least a portion of the credit for the increased life expectancy experienced by those 65 and above.

Gains in health status have been especially rapid for those causes of death amenable to medical care intervention and which historically have been higher among the poor. Age-adjusted death rates for the entire population declined 29 percent from 1960 to 1986. Deaths from strokes dropped by 61 percent over this period—reflecting both the lower rate of uncontrolled hypertension in the population and improved health services. Deaths from pneumonia and influenza were cut in half between 1960 and 1986; historically, the poor have died from these causes at a greater rate than higher-income individuals. Heart disease death rates fell by 39 percent and, while the exact reasons for this decline are uncertain, better availability of sophisticated health services and emergency medical care may be an important factor. Death from diabetes declined moderately over the period, as did accidental deaths. Upward trends were evident in deaths from cancer, especially respiratory cancer; suicide; and homicide. These increases are more related to smoking, stress, and crime levels and could not be expected to be especially sensitive to the availability of improved health services.

Infant health has also improved over the last 25 years. Infant mortality has dropped by 62 percent between 1960 and 1987, dropping from 26 deaths per 1,000 live births in 1960 to 10 deaths per 1,000 live births in 1987. This is especially significant because infant mortality rates were virtually unchanged in the 10 years preceding passage of Medicaid and other Great Society health programs for the poor. Rates for both whites and African Americans have declined at similar rates—with African-American infant mortality rates continuing to be about twice as high as those of whites throughout the period. Some progress has also been made in reducing the proportion of low birth weight infants. The percentage of infants weighing less than 2,500 grams has declined from 7.9 percent in 1970 to 6.8 percent in 1986.

More women are obtaining care early in pregnancy. Studies have shown that receiving prenatal care in the first trimester is important in reducing infant mortality and low birth weight by identifying high-risk mothers and controlling chronic health problems such as diabetes and anemia, which can have an adverse effect on birth outcomes. The proportion of white women receiving prenatal care in the first trimester increased from 72.4 percent in 1970 to 79.2 percent in 1986. For African-American women, the gains were even more striking. The proportion of African-American women receiving prenatal care in the first trimester increased from 44.4 percent in 1970 to 61.6 percent in 1986.

Perhaps the most compelling evidence on the success of the Great Society programs for the poor has been the improved access to physician services. The poor, now as in the past, are much more likely than high-income persons to have fair or poor health and to suffer from chronic health conditions. Despite their poorer health status, low-income persons in 1964 were twice as likely *not* to have seen a physician in the previous two years as high-income persons. By 1987 the proportion of the low-income population not seeing a physician in the last two years was only 20 percent greater than that of the high-income population.

Hospital utilization among the general population has declined over the period since the introduction of the Great Society. In 1964, hospital discharges per 1,000 population averaged 109.1; by 1987 this had dropped to 96.5. With shortening hospital stays over this period, days of hospital care dropped even more rapidly. Important increases in hospital utilization did occur, however, for the poor and for the aged. Hospital discharges for the aged increased from 190 per 1,000 in 1964 to 256 per 1,000 in 1987. Studies have demonstrated that much of this gain in hospital use reflects an improved quality of life for the elderly—with major increases in cataract surgery and hip replacements. Medicare has made this use of modern medical technology associated with acute hospital care affordable for most elderly people without placing undue financial burdens on their families.

❖ Retrenchment in the Reagan Era

In 1981, the Reagan administration ushered in a major shift in health policy. Unlike previous administrations, it did not propose expanded coverage through a national health insurance plan. Rather, it called for major cutbacks in Medicare and Medicaid, and in direct primary care delivery programs.

Congress responded by attempting to protect the poor and elderly from harmful cuts in health programs. Medicare deductibles for hospital and physician services were increased, but Reagan budget proposals to institute a 10 percent hospital copayment and to increase the Part B premium to cover 30 percent of outlays were not enacted. Similarly, coverage of the working poor under Medicaid was restricted in 1981, but the Congress subsequently expanded coverage for poor pregnant women, children, elderly, and disabled. Reagan administration proposals for New Federalism to set a cap on federal payments for Medicaid or to turn the program over to state governments were defeated. Reagan administration proposals to reduce funding for primary care delivery programs by 25 percent and fold into state block grants were similarly rejected. Instead, Congress increased funding for primary care centers moderately and explicitly exempted them from Gramm-Rudmann automatic budget cuts. However, the need to find budgetary savings to counter Reagan administration proposals led to a number of legislative changes to tighten hospital and physician payment rates under Medicare and to give states greater flexibility to set payment limits under Medicaid.

The preoccupation with cutting Medicare, Medicaid, and primary care and the absence of any presidential leadership in support of national health insurance, however, have stymied serious efforts to make further progress in improving access to health care. The result has been a marked slowdown in further improvements in improving the health of the poor and mounting evidence of a deterioration in access to health care services.

The number of uninsured increased steadily throughout the 1980s. The proportion of the population under age 65 without health insurance coverage from either a private plan or a public program increased from 12.5 percent in 1980 to 15.3 percent in 1986—or from about 29 million people in 1980 to 37 million people in 1986.

About one third of the uninsured are children under age 18. Half of the uninsured are parents or other adults between the ages of 17 and 45. The remaining 16 percent of the uninsured are split equally between older adults between the ages of 45 and 54 and between the ages of 55 and 64. Many of these older adults are widows or spouses of retired persons who do not yet qualify for Medicare.

Every society creates its own casualties.
    —J. N. Morris

Although Medicaid provides a safety net for many low-income families, it fails to cover the majority of the poor. Absence of Medicaid coverage among the poor occurs because states set income eligibility levels well below the federal poverty level and because categorical restrictions limit coverage largely to one-parent families—excluding two-parent poor families, childless couples, and single individuals.

To a considerable extent, health insurance coverage in this country is a matter of luck. Those fortunate enough to be employed by large, unionized, manufacturing firms are also likely to be fortunate enough to have good health insurance coverage. Those who have modest incomes, live in the South and West or in rural areas, and those who are African American or other minority group members are more likely to bear the personal and economic effects of lack of insurance and the consequent financial barriers to health care.

Several factors account for the deterioration in health insurance coverage in the 1980s:

- ❖ The growth of jobs in the service sector, which tend not to have health insurance coverage
- ❖ The growth of jobs in smaller firms
- ❖ The increasing tendency for employers to require employee contributions to health insurance premiums, including paying the full cost of dependent coverage
- ❖ The growth in one-parent families, who are less likely to have health insurance coverage than are two-parent families
- ❖ The growth in the number of adults between the ages of 17 and 45 who are less likely to have health insurance coverage than are adults in other age groups

While considerable further analysis and research will be required to sort out the independent contribution of these and other factors, it is clear that gaps in employer-provided health insurance are responsible for a large portion of the uninsured population.

The reversal of trends in health insurance coverage has important implications for trends in improving the health of disadvantaged people and their access to health care services. A close examination of the trends in health status reveals that most of the gains in improved health occurred in the period from 1960 to 1980, with relatively little further progress during the 1980s. Life expectancy at birth and at age 65 have increased only moderately since 1980. Age-adjusted deaths from pneumonia and influenza are up slightly in the 1980s, although further improvements have occurred in death rates from diseases of the heart and cerebrovascular diseases. Infant mortality rates declined slowly in the 1980s. However, the percentage of African-American babies weighing less than 2,500 grams is up slightly, and the percentage of African-American women receiving care in the first trimester of pregnancy is down somewhat. These data suggest that progress in improving the health of poor and minority groups has certainly slowed or halted, if not actually reversed.

❖ Looking Forward to the Twenty-First Century

The United States moves toward the twenty-first century with several major problems in its system of financing health care for its citizens. Over 35 million Americans have no health insurance coverage—and evidence of the failure to get needed medical care as a result is a national embarrassment. The private health insurance market is becoming increasingly selective—with insurers declining to cover or restricting benefits for individuals viewed to be poor health risks. Acquired immunodeficiency syndrome and biomedical advances in genetic screening that make it possible to identify individuals at risk for a wide range of health conditions will exacerbate this trend. In addition, as the U.S. population ages markedly in the next several decades, the inadequacy of financing long-term care will become more serious.

The United States spends 11 percent of its gross national product (GNP) on health care—more than 40 percent more than the next closest country. Further, health expenditure as a percentage of GNP increased steadily throughout the 1980s, while it has stabilized at about 7 to 8 percent of GNP in most other industrialized nations. Medicare and Medicaid represent the most rapidly increasing segments of federal and state government budgets.

To further complicate matters, Medicare will enter the next century on the brink of insolvency. The hospital portion of Medicare is financed by a payroll tax set at 2.9 percent of earnings (including both the employer and employee shares). By 1995, outlays under the hospital portion of Medicare will exceed payroll tax revenues flowing into the Hospital Insurance Trust Fund—beginning the depletion of accumulated reserves. By the year 2006, under the most realistic economic assumptions, the Trust Fund will be bankrupt. This is just before the impact of the post-World War II baby boom bulge begins to affect retirement and growth in Medicare enrollment.

The magnitude of the problem we face as a nation of people growing older and living longer should mobilize us to begin now to undertake a fundamental reform of our health care financing system. Deliberation among alternatives should sort out the relative responsibility of the public and private sectors for both acute and long-term care financing; the desired distribution of the financial burden of health and long-term care expenses across the age spectrum and across income classes; and tradeoffs among cost, quality, and access to health care, which we as a nation desire to make.

At a minimum, this comprehensive look at the way in which we as a nation finance health care should accomplish the following:

- ❖ Ensure universal health insurance coverage, including coverage for the over 35 million currently uninsured individuals.
- ❖ Ensure that individuals are not denied health insurance coverage because of income or because they are considered to be poor health risks.
- ❖ Ensure adequate access to long-term care services for impaired elderly and disabled individuals—including home care as well as nursing home care.
- ❖ Create a mechanism for negotiating or setting hospital budgets and physician fees applicable to the care of all patients. Provider payment methods should create automatic incentives for efficiency and weighing the benefits of medical interventions against their costs.
- ❖ Encourage prevention wherever possible, including the use of preventive health services and adoption of healthier life-styles.
- ❖ Commitment of the necessary financial resources to assure the adequacy and quality of health care provided to our people.

The turn of the century promises to usher in new policy challenges. We would be best served by beginning now to build a strong health care financing system that ensures quality health care accessible to the entire population—with incentives for efficiency and a mechanism for making policy choices based on a social consensus regarding cost-quality-access tradeoffs. The United States cannot afford to continue on its present course—with a costly health system that lets many of its most vulnerable citizens fall through the safety net. Our problems will only be compounded as we experience an aging population, with growing needs for both acute and long-term care. We clearly have the economic and intellectual resources to meet this challenge. What we need is a national commitment to do so.

❖ About the Author

Karen Davis, PH.D., is Executive Vice President of the Commonwealth Foundation, New York City. She is former Professor and Chair, Department of Health Policy and Management, School of Hygiene and Public Health, The Johns Hopkins University, Baltimore.

❖ The Uninsured: From Dilemma to Crisis

Emily Friedman

Some health policy issues are like bad pennies; despite re-peated efforts to resolve them, they keep coming back. Probably no health policy issue of this century has proven as intractable as access to acute care for Americans who lack coverage for the cost of that care. It was a problem for most Americans at one time; after the introduction of private insurance early in the 20th century, it became a problem more of specific groups, nota-bly the elderly and the poor. Coverage of those who were uninsured was a policy centerpiece (largely unrealized) of President Harry S. Truman's ad-ministration. With the passage of Medicaid and Medicare in 1965, it was thought the issue was largely resolved.

The uninsured, however, like the proverbial poor, seem always to be with us. In fact, their numbers have grown significantly in the past 15 years. Proposals for solutions are rife, but consensus on how to attack the problem has proven, to say the least, elusive. Nevertheless, the dilemma of the unin-sured has become a crisis, affecting all aspects of the health care system and many aspects of society.

❖ Who Is Uninsured?

Most estimates place the number of Americans lacking public or private coverage between 31 and 36 million. The 1987 National Medical Expenditure Survey found that 47.8 million people lacked insurance for all or part of 1987, with between 34 and 36 million uninsured on any given day and 24.5 million uninsured throughout that year.

The U.S. Bureau of the Census found that, from the first quarter of 1986 to the last quarter of 1988, 63.6 million people lacked coverage for at least 1 month and 31.5 million lacked it in the final quarter of 1988. The Employee Benefit Research Institute reported that, in 1988, 33.3 million Americans had no private insurance and were ineligible for public coverage. Even the more conservative figures represent a significant increase over the 26.6 million uninsured reported in the 1977 National Health Care Expenditures Study.

When examined further, the statistics provide a troubling picture. Al-though most figures discussed herein are from the 1987 National Medical Expenditure Survey, virtually all other studies have found substantially the same patterns.

In terms of age, those who are 19 to 24 years old are most likely to be uninsured; 20.3% of this group were uninsured for all of 1987, and another

18.2% were uninsured for part of the year. Children younger than 18 years were the next most likely to lack coverage, with nearly one in four uninsured either all or part of the year. The National Center for Health Statistics reports that, in 1988, 17% of children under 18 years had neither private insurance nor Medicaid coverage. Given the importance of preventive and early intervention care to the health of the young, these rates are a cause of concern.

Of those aged 25 to 54 years, 19.8% were uninsured all or part of the year, as were 13.6% of those aged 55 to 64 years. (Medicare covers virtually all Americans 65 years or older.) The fact that more than one in eight Americans who are 55 to 64 years old lack coverage at least part of the year is disturbing, in that this group faces a much higher risk of serious health problems than do younger Americans.

Our retrograde health care system reserves its greatest hardships for the following groups: the poor and near-poor, workers (including those in agriculture), the unemployed, the disabled, displaced, homemakers, the elderly, and children.
—Health Care USA

Racial and ethnic differences affect rates of coverage. Of non-Hispanic whites, 18.6% were uninsured for all or part of 1987, as were 29.8% of African Americans and 41.4% of Hispanic Americans. Studies using differing methodologies going back as far as 1978 have shown that Hispanic Americans are the most likely to be uninsured of any ethnic group. As Hispanics represent the fastest-growing ethnic population group in the nation, their consistently low rate of coverage is a potential warning of worse yet to come.

Men are slightly more likely to be uninsured than women; 23.8% of men were uninsured for at least part of 1987 as opposed to 21% of women. This undoubtedly reflects the fact that virtually all men, regardless of their income, are excluded from eligibility for Medicaid. Also, Medicaid now covers low-income pregnant women with incomes up to 185% of the poverty line, as well as many mothers with dependent children. Furthermore, women are disproportionately represented in the poverty population, so, to the extent that Medicaid covers that population, more women than men are likely to be protected.

Income level is also associated with lack of coverage. The uninsured represented 47.5% of those with incomes below the poverty line in 1987, 45% of those with incomes between poverty and 125% of poverty, 36.7% of those with incomes from 125% to 200% of poverty, 17.8% of those with incomes 200% to 400% of poverty, and 8.8% of those with incomes above 400% of poverty.

The proportion of uninsured varies by state, depending on several factors, including the level of Medicaid coverage in the state, the demographics of the population, insurance practices, overall income, the nature of employment, and state health policy.

❖ Many Underinsured as Well

If the policy debate is to be framed accurately in terms of issues of coverage and access, a second group, the underinsured, must also be mentioned. This population is more difficult to define because it faces risks that are more specific. That is, a patient's diagnosis can determine whether coverage is sufficient or not, and surveys of whether a person has coverage at all are unlikely to reveal such gaps in protection. Where a person receives care, how long the person is a patient, what types of treatment are required, and whether there is a dollar or time limit to coverage all affect the sufficiency of insurance. Nevertheless, a 1985 estimate, based on data projected from the 1977 National Health Care Expenditures Study, was that 26% of the nonelderly population, or approximately 56 million people in 1984, were "inadequately protected against the possibility of large medical bills."

To this population, whose major problem is insufficient overall coverage, could be added those whose insurance precludes coverage of a given condition or imposes a waiting period before such coverage becomes operative (which is often the case with pregnancy). Also included are those who are covered by Medicaid but lack access to physician care because of physician reluctance to treat Medicaid clients and those who, insured or not, face difficulty in obtaining obstetric care because of the decreasing number of obstetricians willing to accept new patients.

Physician resistance to treating such patients has been ascribed to many causes, including low and delayed Medicaid payments, fears of malpractice litigation, paperwork, cultural or language problems, noncompliance, and other factors, including racial discrimination. Certainly, the prospect of low or nonexistent payment is a disincentive to most providers.

The total number of uninsured and underinsured, even if the latter group has not been sufficiently identified, could easily represent one in every four Americans on any given day.

❖ Erosion of Medicaid

How such a large number of Americans came to be at risk, through lack of coverage or lack of access or both, is a challenging question. Theoretically, coverage of health care costs is available to virtually all Americans through one of four routes: Medicare for the elderly and disabled, Medicaid for low-income women and children (and some men) and those with certain disabilities, employer-subsidized coverage at the workplace, or self-purchased coverage for those ineligible for the previous three. However, as many as 10 million more Americans were uninsured at least part of the year in 1987 than in 1977. What happened?

Of the four routes to coverage, Medicare has aged best. A universal enfranchisement that is neither means tested nor related to the workplace, Medicare each year covers more Americans for most acute care. Beneficiaries' out-of-pocket costs remain high, however, and coverage for long-term care remains skimpy, especially with the repeal of Medicare catastrophic care coverage.

Medicaid, however, has suffered a more equivocal fate. Although passed by Congress, Medicaid is a state-level program, with each state defining income levels and other standards of eligibility and the federal government subsidizing a certain portion of expenses, depending on the state's overall wealth. Thus, coverage has always varied from state to state, with Northern states and some Western states offering more generous benefits than Southern and other states.

In the early 1980s, both the federal and state governments sought to control or reduce Medicaid expenditures in the face of tax cuts, growing costs, and reduced federal funds for the program. This led to freezes and reductions in both eligibility and provider payments. The result was a basically stable number of beneficiaries despite an increase in the poverty population.

As a result of the rather tangled path it has traveled, Medicaid never covered the entire poverty population and was estimated to cover only 38.7% of that group in 1983. By 1989, it was estimated that only 40% of the poverty population was covered by the program. Although congressional mandates may boost that figure somewhat, the majority of the poor remain unprotected by the program that was designed to cover them.

❖ The Workplace Connection

The third route to coverage—employer-subsidized insurance for workers and often for dependents—has also seen serious erosion in recent years. This was the cornerstone of health insurance in the past—appropriate for a nation steeped in the Puritan work ethic and even more appropriate in an age in which labor shortages of many types are looming. The unspoken agreement was that, if a person was employed, he or she would receive health insurance benefits, subsidized to some degree by the employer or at least priced lower than individual coverage to reflect the fact that the subscriber belonged to an employee group.

However, the workplace is no longer a guarantor of coverage, if it ever was. The National Medical Expenditure Survey found that, in 1987, of the uninsured population, 46.4% were working adults, 6.8% were nonworking spouses of working adults, and 23.6% were children of working adults. In other words, 76.8% of the uninsured either were employed or were nuclear-family dependents of the employed. The Employee Benefits Research Institute found that, in 1988, 85% of the uninsured were either workers or family members of workers.

The employed uninsured are unevenly distributed. The National Medical Expenditure Survey found that they were more likely to work part time or to be self-employed and to work in settings with fewer than 100 workers, especially in settings with fewer than 25 workers. In settings with fewer than 10 employees, 26.3% of workers were uninsured.

Employers are not necessarily the villains. Insurance products for small business are both limited and expensive. According to the General Accounting Office, small businesses have little ability to spread risk over a large number of employees, which results in higher premiums, should an employee incur large costs.

Small businesses also face a far greater likelihood of premiums being based on experience rating rather than on community rating. Small employee groups are also seen by insurers as a higher risk, which means that, compared with larger employee groups, they are subject to more exclusions, medical testing of applicants, and denials of coverage because of health status and are less able to absorb the significant increases in premium prices that have been the pattern of the past two decades. . . .

If small businesses face problems in offering and retaining coverage, the individual insurance market faces collapse. This is the population that insurers characterize as the highest risk, requiring disproportionate administrative costs and usually proving unprofitable.

Medical underwriting, experience rating, refusal to cover those deemed "uninsurable," cancellation of policies on short notice, and high premiums are common if not almost universal barriers for those seeking individual coverage. As a result, for an individual unable to qualify for group or public coverage, obtaining affordable insurance is dependent on having a sufficiently high income and very good health status. This, needless to say, eliminates many of those who are most likely to need coverage, that is, those who are poor, sick, and/or unable to acquire workplace-based insurance.

The working uninsured are a complex population, and even data-based generalities are dangerous. Despite the small-business focus, many of the uninsured work for large firms, as is the case with agricultural and seasonal workers. Some of the uninsured simply choose not to acquire coverage, although they represent a small minority of this population. Some are eligible for either public or private coverage but are unaware of this and thus have never sought it. Although most of the uninsured are poor or near poor, some are middle-class people denied coverage by virtue of poor health status or "risky" jobs. It is a highly heterogeneous population, with multiple reasons for being at risk.

❖ Why a Crisis Now?

Most crises are born of a series of small events that one day reach critical mass. So it has been with the uninsured. The framers of Public Law No. 89-97, which brought Medicare and Medicaid into being in 1965, believed that universal health insurance was just around the corner, yet it failed to materialize. When it was reported in 1980 that 26.6 million Americans lacked coverage, a response might have been expected but was not forthcoming. A large number of efforts—expansion of Medicaid; coverage of children by Blue Cross and Blue Shield plans; state insurance pools for the "uninsurable"; and coverage experiments funded by states, localities, and private sources—have attempted to address at least part of the problem, yet it continues unabated.

Has the issue reached critical mass? If not, it is well on the way to doing so, for at least five reasons.

1. Although coverage is not the sole determinant of health status, it is a key factor in improved health, as Medicaid data have demonstrated.

2. The health care system is suffering damage as a result of being asked (implicitly) to provide care for the uninsured who cannot pay.

Care is often theoretically available through public or private clinics and other settings, both funded and voluntary. However, these are often so overloaded that access is illusory. Thus, a minority of U.S. hospitals carry the majority of the burden of the uninsured, and that burden is growing.

As a result, serious questions are being asked about the level of charity care that hospitals, clinics, physicians, and other providers should be expected to provide.

3. Another factor contributing to calls for action on the uninsured is the increasingly uncomfortable situation of employers. The number of employers who do offer coverage is dropping, which is not surprising in view of the increasing cost of insurance and the voluntary nature of the arrangement.

Employer discomfiture is being exacerbated by calls for mandated employer coverage of all workers and even of dependents. Only the state of Hawaii has succeeded in legally requiring that most people working more than 19 hours per week be covered by employer-subsidized insurance.

4. Another force for a solution is the interrelationship of the uninsured and health care costs. It can be argued that, if health care for the more than 200 million Americans who have at least some coverage is so expensive, we cannot afford to cover the 31 to 37 million who have no coverage.

The larger economic issue is that most of us pay the hidden costs of medical indigence, one way or another. Every insurance premium includes some of the costs of care of the uninsured. Even self-insured employers pay part of that cost. Paying patients subsidize nonpaying patients. The society as a whole pays the price of prenatal care that is not given, immunizations that are not provided, cancers that are not detected, diabetes that is not monitored, mental illness that is not discovered. The uninsured can be very expensive.

5. The last factor driving the need for action may appear secondary in a health care economy that has become hard edged. Nevertheless, issues of ethics and equity are as important and powerful as the economic or logistical issues. Foremost among these is whether a democracy that thinks of itself as the moral hope of the world can justify grave inequalities in access to health care, which in most countries is considered an essential human need.

It is often pointed out that, among developed nations, only the United States and South Africa have not implemented universal access to care. This is overstated; there are holes in every safety net. However, the holes in our net are more numerous and yawn deeper and wider than in many less-wealthy nations.

We claim that other nations ration care because the insured must wait sometimes; however, in our nation, the uninsured can wait forever. We claim that ours is the best health care system in the world; however, if tens of millions of Americans have little or no access to care, the claim rings hollow.

In addition, a health care system that has become too selective in terms of whom it treats carries with it the seeds of its own destruction. Our system has been built—properly, in my opinion—on a tradition of pluralism, public guarantees and private largesse, and both institutionalized and voluntary giving; a tradition of faith, hope, and charity.

Should the public lose faith in that arrangement (and in recent years we have seen evidence of such a loss of confidence), the very basis of the health care system is in jeopardy. Health care providers can hold themselves out as morally superior, but if they are not seen as such by the populace, voluntarism and autonomy can easily be replaced by fiat.

Many of our health status indicators are lagging or beginning to lag behind those in the rest of the developed world—and, indeed, in some of the Third World. Pressure is building to give up on our current system and develop another, based on the Canadian or some other centralized model. The moral standing of American health care is on the line. We must produce a workable answer to the crisis of the uninsured, or all of us—health care providers and the society alike—could suffer the terrible and long-term consequences of inaction.

❖ About the Author

Emily Friedman is a contributing editor for *Hospitals, Medical World News,* and *The Healthcare Forum Journal* and is a contributing writer for *Health Business, Health Progress,* and *The Journal of the American Medical Association.*

❖ Access to Care for Poor Children: Separate and Unequal?

ROBERT F. ST. PETER, PAUL W. NEWACHECK, AND NEAL HALFON

Government-sponsored health programs, especially Medicaid and the community health center system, have improved poor children's access to medical care. However, the number of children living in poverty and those without insurance has increased dramatically in recent years and outstripped the resources of available programs. In response, the Congress recently expanded the Medicaid program to phase in coverage for all poor children under 19 years of age by the year 2002. This will dramatically increase the number of children eligible for Medicaid. However, there is little information by which to anticipate whether these changes will improve access to basic preventive care for the nation's poor children or whether the care they receive will be comparable to that received by other children.

While a number of investigators have examined the role of Medicaid in improving access to care for poor children, few have focused on the impact of Medicaid on the use of routine, preventive services. While having a usual source of care is an important factor in influencing the use of preventive services, the effect of Medicaid on improving access to usual sources of preventive care is unknown.

Similarly, little is known about the locations where children receive routine care or the timeliness and continuity of the care they receive. Features of the Medicaid program may actually make it difficult for poor children to gain access to physicians' offices and to receive timely and continuous care. These are especially important issues because poor children are at increased risk for many adverse health outcomes and may be especially likely to benefit from timely preventive care.

Good health to the poor is the lifeline to all else.
—Philip R. Lee

This study uses recently released data from the 1988 National Health Interview Survey to examine the effect of Medicaid on having a usual source of routine care, the location and timeliness of preventive care, and continuity of care. This information may be helpful in anticipating some of the effects of recent Medicaid expansions on improving access to care for more than 10 million children living in poverty.

❖ Comment

Despite improvements since the implementation of Medicaid, significant barriers in access to medical care for children still exist. Results from this 1988 national survey indicate that more than 6 million children lacked a usual source of routine care, and over 12 million children had not made a timely visit for routine, preventive care. Limited access is especially a problem among poor children, who were less likely to have a usual source of routine or sick care, to receive care in a physician's office, to receive timely routine care, and to have continuity between their usual sources of care. Among poor children not covered by Medicaid, more than one in five lacked a usual source of routine care, and nearly one in three had not received timely routine care.

Medicaid coverage was associated with improvements in only some measures of access to care for poor children. Poor children with Medicaid were more likely than those without Medicaid to have usual sources of care and to receive routine care within an appropriate time interval. In fact, poor children with Medicaid compared favorably with children not living in poverty in these measures. However, poor children, even those with Medicaid, were much less likely than other children to receive routine care in a physician's office. They were more likely to receive routine care in community clinics and hospital clinics. Children who received routine care in community clinics compared with physicians' offices were more likely to lack continuity and to use an emergency department as their usual source of sick care. Surprisingly, Medicaid coverage was not associated with an improvement in continuity. Thus, while Medicaid does improve access to care for poor children, it does not ensure that they have access to the same locations and continuity as other children. These findings show that access to care for many poor children remains in some ways separate and unequal.

Our findings support previous analyses of national surveys showing differences in access to usual sources of care among children. These studies, however, did not distinguish between having a usual source of routine care and a usual source of sick care. With the growing recognition of the benefits of prevention and early intervention, improved access to usual sources of routine, preventive care will be a key measure of the success of programs designed to benefit high-risk children. Our findings also support a previous study among school-aged children that found coverage by Medicaid was associated with significant improvement in the use of some preventive health services. Still, many poor children, even those with Medicaid, do not receive adequate preventive care. For example, a study of children with

Medicaid coverage in California found that many had not made an adequate number of visits for preventive care.

Implications of Recent Changes in Medicaid

One option to reduce inequalities in access to care for poor children is the expansion of Medicaid eligibility. Indeed, the Congress has substantially expanded Medicaid eligibility over the last 7 years, culminating in the Omnibus Budget Reconciliation Act (OBRA) of 1990. Our findings suggest that expansion of Medicaid should result in improved access to preventive services and an increased likelihood of finding a medical home. However, further changes are needed to improve the quantity and quality of medical services available to children with Medicaid coverage. Another law, the OBRA of 1989, may address some of the limitations of Medicaid identified in our findings. This legislation makes substantial changes in the preventive care component of Medicaid, the Early and Periodic Screening, Diagnosis, and Treatment (EPSDT) program.

The EPSDT program is a required benefit under state Medicaid programs. It was designed to provide assessment of health needs and treatment of conditions identified during the screening process. Under OBRA 1989, the range of medical services allowable under state Medicaid programs to treat such conditions has been broadened substantially. Also, physician visits are now allowed whenever a medical condition is suspected, regardless of established periodicity schedules. Previously, both the scope of covered benefits and the number of visits allowable through EPSDT were limited. These changes may improve the comprehensiveness and continuity of care provided to children through the EPSDT program.

However, the potential benefits of EPSDT enhancements will be realized only to the degree that states embrace the intent of the legislation to improve preventive care for poor children. Individual states have been slow in implementing the changes mandated by federal law. Despite increasing Medicaid expenditures, still less than 1% of the total Medicaid budget is spent on preventive care through EPSDT. Physicians and other advocates for children can play an important role in improving preventive care for poor children by encouraging each state to fully implement these provisions to expand EPSDT.

Improvements in Medicaid alone, however, are unlikely to solve the access problem for many children living in inner-city and rural areas that have a severe shortage of physicians. Difficulties recruiting physicians to provide care for these children through Medicaid have been well documented. Community clinics play an important role in meeting the health needs of children living in these areas. However, community clinics face increasing demands on their limited resources as the number of uninsured patients seeking their services grows. While there is some potential for increased funding with recently passed legislation, additional funding increases are needed if community clinics are to maintain, or improve, the quality and range of services provided to their patients.

❖ Conclusion

Amidst the most sophisticated and costly health care system in the world, a significant number of children do not have access to even basic preventive care. Even those poor children who gain access to the system do not necessarily have access to the same care as that available to other children. Recent legislation may improve some of these disparities, but inequities are likely to remain. More fundamental changes in the health care system may be needed to ensure that all children have access to comprehensive primary care and the opportunity to lead a healthy, productive life.

In health there is freedom. Health is the first of all liberties.
—Henri Frederic Amie (1879)

❖ About the Authors

Robert F. St. Peter, M.D., is with the Robert Wood Johnson Clinical Scholars Program and a Clinical Instructor in the Department of Pediatrics, School of Medicine, University of California, San Francisco.

Paul. W. Newacheck, DR.P.H., is Professor of Pediatrics in the the Institute for Health Policy Studies and Department of Pediatrics, School of Medicine, University of California, San Francisco.

Neal Halfon, M.D., M.P.H., is Professor of Pediatrics in the Department of Pediatrics, School of Medicine, University of California, Los Angeles.

❖ Chapter 8
Quality, Effectiveness, and Appropriateness of Care

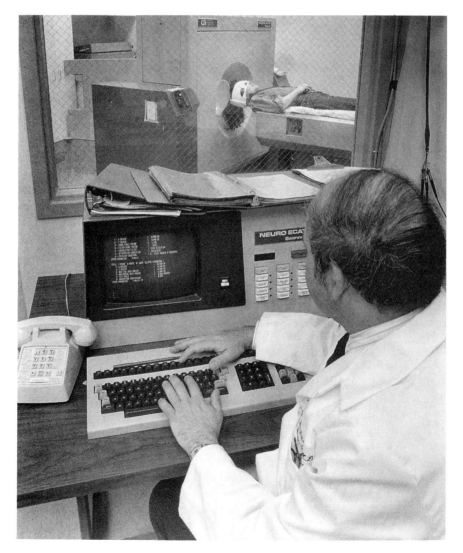

Concerns about access to health care services and the costs of care of necessity raise questions about quality. Initial studies of quality focused on the process of care and the structure of services. In recent years, however, investigators are emphasizing effectiveness, appropriateness, and outcomes of care. Because of the complexity of emerging treatment modes, clinicians face uncertainty about whether the benefits of a particular treatment outweigh the risks. Because our knowledge is incomplete, we see an increased emphasis on outcomes rather than process in order to produce the capacity to better inform clinicians and assist them and their patients in decision making and thus ultimately improve the quality of care.

This initiative in health services places new burdens on the federal government to support studies related to outcomes and to inform clinicians of the findings. All of our authors stress the importance of federal agencies' role in funding studies and disseminating findings in health services research, that have demonstrated usefulness and effectiveness at both the policy and the patient care levels. They acknowledge the contributions of health services research in providing better information to patients and physicians to assist them in engineering the best possible treatment results. Thus far, the level of funding has been sadly inadequate to address the need.

In "Clinical Decision Making: From Theory to Practice," physician/mathematician David M. Eddy discusses the need to reduce uncertainty in medical care and to determine the most efficacious treatments. He describes the factors at play in the uncertain decision making process in medical therapeutics. He says that at present we lack both the information we need to make sound clinical decisions and the skills to process the information, and he makes a strong statement that the goal is not to take decision making power away from physicians, but to improve their capacity to treat their patients.

Noralou P. Roos and Leslie L. Roos point out that it is important that cost-cutting measures do not drive out funding for quality-of-care assessment, outcome assessments, developing practice guidelines, and monitoring the system. They discuss various ways that uncertainty permeates medical practices and the implications that can be drawn from variations in practice style. The authors also caution against the dangers associated with the assumption that more treatment is necessarily better.

In "Cutting Waste by Making Rules: Promises, Pitfalls, and Realistic Prospects," Jan Blustein and Theodore R. Marmor discuss the efforts that some are making to contain costs by eliminating wasteful care. They introduce readers to the proposed policy of designing microallocational rules for the provision of medical care that will be meant to protect patients from receiving wasteful, useless, and potentially dangerous treatments. These would include parameters about routine patient care that could save insurers and the government many millions of dollars every year. The authors discuss methods of investigation, such as clinical epidemiology, the RAND/Value method, and outcomes research, that have contributed to physicians' ability to establish practice guidelines in recent years. They also discuss the implications of "rulemaking," its pitfalls, and its possibilities.

❖ Clinical Decision Making: From Theory to Practice

DAVID M. EDDY

Medical practice is in the middle of a profound transition. Most physicians can remember the day when, armed with a degree, a mission, and confidence, they could set forth to heal the sick. Like Solomon, physicians could receive patients, hear their complaints, and determine the best course of action. While not every patient could be cured, everyone could be confident that whatever was done was the best possible. Most important, each physician was free, trusted, and left alone to determine what was in the best interest of each patient.

All of that is changing. In retrospect, the first changes seem minor— some increased paperwork, "tissue" committees, a few more meetings. These activities were designed to affect the presumably small fraction of physicians who, in fact, deserved to be scrutinized, and the scrutiny was an internal process performed by physicians themselves. But today's activities are aimed at all physicians, are much more anonymous, and seem beyond physician control. Now physicians must deal with second opinions, precertification, skeptical medical directors, variable coverage, outright denials, utilization review, threats of cookbook medicine, and letters out of the blue chiding that Mrs. Smith is on two incompatible drugs. Solomon did not have to call anyone to get permission for his decisions. What is going on?

The rank and file of doctors are no more scientific than their tailors. Doctoring is an art, not a science: Any layman who is interested in science sufficiently to take in one of the scientific journals and follow the literature of the scientific movement, knows more about it than these doctors (probably a large majority) who are not interested in it, and practice it only to earn their bread.
—George Bernard Shaw

What is going on is that one of the basic assumptions underlying the practice of medicine is being challenged. This assumption is not just a theory about cholesterol, antiarrhythmics, or estrogens. This assumption concerns the intellectual foundation of medical care. Simply put, the assumption is that whatever a physician decides is, by definition, correct. The challenge says that while many decisions no doubt are correct, many are not, and

315

elaborate mechanisms are needed to determine which are which. Physicians are slowly being stripped of their decision-making power.

❖ Challenging the Quality of Clinical Decisions

Why is the assumption that physicians' decisions are correct being challenged? At first thought, the challenge might appear to be a pernicious scheme launched by payers, motivated to save money, even at the expense of quality. Actually, while the rapid and apparently uncontrollable rise in health care costs might have been the initial pressure point, the challenge can be justified solely by a concern for quality. The plain fact is that many decisions made by physicians appear to be arbitrary—highly variable, with no obvious explanation. The very disturbing implication is that this arbitrariness represents, for at least some patients, suboptimal or even harmful care.

These are strong words that demand explanation. What is the evidence that decisions are arbitrary? The most impressive clues come in the form of variations across and within physicians with respect to observations, perceptions, reasoning, conclusions, and practices.

Observer variations have been recognized for decades, but the findings are still startling, and the problem has not been solved. A correct decision about an intervention requires that a patient's condition be diagnosed correctly. Substantial variations in what physicians see have been reported in virtually every aspect of the diagnostic process, from taking a history, to doing a physical examination, reading laboratory tests, performing a pathological diagnosis, and recommending a treatment. A 1985 bibliography listed more than 400 articles that describe this problem. In general, observers looking at the same thing will disagree with each other or even with themselves from 10% to 50% of the time.

An example will provide the flavor. When four cardiologists were given high-quality coronary angiograms of representative patients and asked to estimate whether the percentage of stenosis in the proximal and distal left anterior descending artery was greater or less than 50%, they disagreed on 60% of the patients. If the distinction between proximal and distal stenosis is ignored and the question is reduced to whether there is 50% stenosis in *any* segment, they still disagreed on 40% of patients. Another study evaluated the extent to which observers agreed with themselves on two successive readings of the same angiograms. The observers changed their minds from 8% to 37% of the time, depending on the vessel segment.

The evidence of variations in perceptions is equally distressing. The crux of any decision is to estimate the consequences of the available options. It is easy to appreciate that if a physician's perception of the outcomes of alternative interventions is incorrect, the chance that he or she will choose the best intervention for a patient is severely threatened. Now consider the following true story. A specialty society, which by prior agreement will remain anonymous, convened a meeting to set a guideline about one of its most common and important practices. The 57 participants identified one particular outcome as being especially important. They agreed that a practitioner's belief about the magnitude of the outcome would largely determine his or her belief about the proper use of the practice and would determine his or her recommendation to a patient. The practitioners, all specialists in the field, were then asked to write down their beliefs about the probability of the outcome. The 57 respondents provided 27 different estimates that ranged from 0% to 100%.

It is tempting to speculate that nonspecialists would have a wider range of opinions, but the spread can hardly get any wider. Before anyone gets smug, understand that no specialty is immune. For example, after several meetings and a unanimous consensus, experts' estimates of the effect of colon cancer screening on colon cancer mortality ranged from 5% to 95%. Fifty cardiovascular surgeons' estimates of the probabilities of various risks associated with xenografts vs. mechanical heart valves ranged from 0% to about 50%. For one particular risk, the 10-year probability of valve failure with xenografts, the range of estimates was 3% to 95%.

Even if decision-makers' perceptions of the facts were always accurate, that information must be processed to draw conclusions applicable to individual patients. With rare exceptions, physicians depend on their judgment and intuition to do this. But it is easy to be misled. Rather than cite studies, I will ask a question. You have ordered a diagnostic test for a patient to rule out a relatively uncommon but serious disease that, given this patient's signs and symptoms, has a prevalence of approximately 1 in 100. The test, which has a sensitivity of 80% and a specificity of 80%, has positive results. You repeat the test and it has positive results a second time. What is the probability that the patient has the disease? Everyone should get the correct answer: this is one of the most straightforward and common problems encountered in medical practice, the problem has been simplified to the extreme, all of the ingredients have been presented, and the solution method has been described in scores of medical publications during the last 25 years. Yet, it is still a safe bet that at least 20% of physicians will get the wrong answer. (The correct answer is between 4% [if the tests are totally dependent] and 14% [if the tests are independent].) Our intuitions about problems like this are easily fooled by a variety of cognitive biases.

Given the variations in observations, perceptions, and reasoning, it is easy to imagine that when faced with the same information, different physicians can draw different conclusions. A study of second opinions illustrates the point. Surgeons given written descriptions of surgical problems have split down the middle regarding whether to recommend surgery—half recommending surgery, half not. When surveyed again 2 years later, the same surgeons often disagreed with their previous opinions, with as many as 40% changing their recommendations.

But the ultimate question is whether these uncertainties and variations cause patients to be treated differently. It appears that they do. For example, an analysis of procedure rates for Medicare patients in 13 large metropolitan areas in the United States showed that for more than half the procedures studied, the rates varied more than 300% between the areas with high and low rates. Another study that compared utilization rates in 16 large communities in four states found more than threefold differences between the highest and lowest rates for heart bypass, thyroid, and prostate surgery; fivefold differences for specific back and abdominal surgeries; sevenfold differences for knee replacements; and almost 20-fold differences for carotid endarterectomies. In Vermont, the chance of having one's tonsils removed as a child are 8% in one community and 70% in another. In Iowa, 15% of the men younger than 85 years in one region have had prostatectomies compared with more than 60% in another. In Maine, the chance of hysterectomy by the age of 70 years varies across communities from less than 20% to more than 70%. While some of the variations might be explained by differences in disease incidence, available resources, and patient preferences, it is impossible to explain all of them.

These findings conjure up the image of a $650-billion tank rumbling down the road, with, depending on how you look at it, either no hands or a thousand hands on the wheel and the windows fogged over. To be fair, it must be understood that the evidence just given presents a caricature, highlighting the big nose and weak chin. But it is undeniable that at least some decisions about important medical practices are subject to factors that are uncertain and variable. When so many people have such different beliefs and are doing such different things, it is impossible for everyone to be correct. There is a distinct possibility that many decisions made by practitioners are wrong—wrong in the sense that they are based on mistaken perceptions of the facts, and wrong in the sense that they are not in their patients' best interests.

The discovery that many of our decisions are vulnerable to error should not be surprising. The ingredients needed for accurate decisions are simply missing for many medical practices. The first ingredient is evidence—accurate, interpretable, applicable observations of the frequencies with which important outcomes occur with different practices. That type of evidence is not available for a large proportion of medical practices. When there is no formal evidence, practitioners have little choice but to turn to their personal experiences. However, these are notoriously misleading: the number of observations are small, there are no controls, patients' and physicians' decisions about interventions are not random, follow-up is incomplete and usually short-term, and memories are highly selective. The second ingredient is the ability to analyze the evidence. Even if good evidence were available, it is unrealistic, even unfair, to expect people to be able to sort through it all in their heads—especially people who were trained to provide medical care, not to analyze evidence and perform calculations.

❖ Implications for Clinical Practice

In summary, there is good reason to challenge the assumption that every individual practitioner's decision is necessarily correct.

A failure of the assumption has immense implications for the quality of care. It implies that the same patient can go to different physicians, be told different things, and receive different care. No doubt some of the differences will not be important. However, some will surely be important—leading to different chances of benefits, different harms, and different costs. A failure of the assumption also has immense implications for informed consent, expert testimony, consensus development, the concepts of "standard and accepted" or "reasonable and necessary," malpractice, quality assurance programs that are based on statistical norms, and the cost of care.

It is for all these reasons that insurance companies, employers, and the government, as well as the medical profession itself, are aggressively seeking to understand the magnitude of the problem and find solutions. No responsible institution can sit still while patients are subjected to serious interventions and costs fly, knowing that there is such a large random component to the decisions. Without evidence that differences in the intensity of practices yield proportionate increases in value, these institutions are virtually forced to act. The mechanisms that have been developed during the last several years to assure quality and contain costs are not sinister attempts to save money by cutting quality or to seize control. They are conscientious responses to a real problem—a problem that is harming not just the cost, but the quality of care.

Will Second-Guessing Physicians Solve the Problem?

At this point, it is reasonable to ask whether the mechanisms that have been put in place thus far will correct the problem. Can preguessing and second-guessing each physician's decision be counted on to make the ultimate choice correct? Unfortunately, no. While these mechanisms are well intentioned, while they are steps in the right direction, and while they might be the best we can do right now, they will by no means correct every error. There are three main problems. The first is that the mechanisms themselves depend on a questionable assumption. Virtually all of the current quality assurance and cost-containment mechanisms assume that there is "accuracy in numbers." In other words, if the decisions of the individual physicians cannot be trusted, the collective decisions or actions of a larger number of physicians can be trusted. Second opinions expand the basis for a decision to two, precertification expands it to the number of people who defined the indications, searching for outliers expands it to everyone in the database, and so forth. The problem is that each of these mechanisms attempts to correct possible misperceptions of one physician by checking the decision, not against reality, but against the perceptions of other physicians. Why should we assume that the physician offering the second opinion knows the correct answer? Is there reason to believe that the manual used in a precertification program contains the revealed truth? Outliers are not necessarily bad. (Albert Schweitzer was an outlier.) Who can say that a guideline developed by an expert panel is correct? Indeed, what does a consensus of a group whose perceptions might vary from 0% to 100% even mean?

The second problem with current quality assurance and cost-containment mechanisms is that many medical decisions are inherently too subtle to be made at a distance. While these mechanisms vary in their flexibility, they all are based to some degree on a presumption that decisions fall in a definable number of categories that can be addressed in the abstract, and the answers can be applied to individuals. The problem is that the cliché about patients being individuals is true. While it is possible and even desirable to *guide* decisions, it can be dangerous to try to *make* them from a distance.

The third problem is that, even if these quality mechanisms worked in the sense of "correcting" incorrect decisions, they are cumbersome, expensive, and demoralizing for both physicians and patients. They also create an adversarial atmosphere that can only harm patient care. In short, the current mechanisms are unlikely to solve the problem. If applied forcefully enough, these mechanisms will decrease variations in practices, which will decrease our sense of discomfort. But there is no guarantee that the targets these recommendations construct are correct, or that the gains they make are worth the cost in time, money, and hassle.

❖ Four Conclusions

Where does this leave us? First, it must be emphasized that medicine is not practiced at random and is not a fraud. Physicians are not the Keystone Kops. Decisions might be variable but they are not whimsical or flippant. The variability occurs because physicians must make decisions about phenomenally complex problems, under very difficult circumstances, with very little support. They are in the impossible position of not knowing the outcomes of different actions, but having to act anyway.

Second, it is undeniable that many if not most medical practices are effective. A relative of mine is fond of pointing out that she would be blind, deaf, bedridden, and depressed, were it not for her cataract surgery, lens implant, hearing aid, hip replacement, and amitriptyline. While there are undoubtedly some ineffective and unnecessary practices, the real questions pertain to which treatments work best and whether the costs and risks of more risky and expensive practices are matched by proportionate benefits.

A third point is that the problems just described are no one's fault. No one is questioning the sincerity, honesty, or diligence of physicians. Physicians face one of the most difficult social and intellectual problems. In addition to the mysteries of human biology and disease and continually expanding technologies, they must deal with a bewildering variety of other forces: expectations of patients and families; personal, professional, and financial goals; changing reimbursement systems; competition; malpractice; peer pressure; the press; politics; and incomplete information.

These three points, while encouraging, do not allow us to relax. A fourth conclusion is that we can do much better than we are doing now. For example, clinical research is extremely inefficient. Some questions are dissected beyond recognition; others are virtually ignored. A tremendous amount of research energy is wasted on poor designs that yield unusable results. Even good designs are spoiled by poor coordination with other research and with clinical reality.

It is also possible to improve our ability to reason both collectively and as individuals. Our current approach to analyzing evidence, estimating the consequences of our actions, and determining the desirability of those outcomes is primitive. We are trying to solve in our heads problems that far exceed the capacity of the unaided human mind. There are tools, already in use in many other disciplines, to help us.

❖ Where Do We Go from Here?

Ideally, decisions about medical practices should be made between physicians and their patients, with each decision tailored to fit the patient's problems and desires. However, to achieve this ideal, physicians must have solid information about the consequences of different choices and must be able to process that information accurately. Currently, we lack both the information required for decision making and the skills needed to process the information. Quality assurance and cost-containment mechanisms that attempt to preguess and second-guess physicians' decisions from a distance suffer from the same problems. While well intentioned, these mechanisms create one more factor that distorts and strains the ideal process without offering a permanent solution for the problem.

The solution is not to remove the decision-making power from physicians, but to improve the capacity of physicians to make better decisions. To achieve this solution, we must give physicians the information they need; we must institutionalize the skills to use that information; and we must build processes that support, not dictate, decisions.

Challenges are healthy. This one goes deep, but promises great value.

❖ About the Author

David M. Eddy, M.D., PH.D., is Alexander McMahon Professor of Health Policy and Management, Duke University, Durham, NC.

❖ Small Area Variations, Practice Style, and Quality of Care

NORALOU P. ROOS AND LESLIE L. ROOS

Traditionally, medicine has been oriented toward care for the individual patient. Using their knowledge base, physicians are seen to intervene to cure or ameliorate the diagnosed illness. Given a choice of treatments, the one most suitable for the patient is selected. This logical model of medical practice implies a tight linkage among needs, interventions, and outcomes, which is radically inconsistent with the results of extensive research on patterns of medical care utilization in North America and Western Europe. It suggests a degree of precision in both diagnosis and therapy, a knowledge of patient needs and of effective responses, which is beyond the capabilities of individual practitioners and of the health professions collectively. The blunt reality is that little hard evidence is available to evaluate the effectiveness of many medical acts and procedures, within or outside of the acute care sector, including the commonplace, the high tech, the expensive, and the new.

In the absence of such evidence, opinions within the medical profession differ widely both as to how conditions should be diagnosed and how they should be treated when diagnosed. Patterns of practice vary widely. Amid the resulting diversity, patients of particular physicians or in particular regions might sometimes not receive interventions that would likely do them more good than harm. Patients of other physicians in other regions may receive treatment that would be judged inappropriate or unnecessary if subjected to critical peer review. In short, there can be no basis for a general claim that "more is better" when intervention patterns vary so markedly from region to region, hospital to hospital, physician to physician, and when hard evidence of benefit is so often lacking.

Our description of medical practice, which will be documented by a wide range of evidence, will disconcert many readers. This review is not meant as an exposé. No fingers are pointed nor witch-hunts suggested. Physicians' decision making is influenced by a number of factors, including the psychological dynamics and uncertainty surrounding the short- and long-term consequences of different treatment alternatives.

❖ Uncertainty and Variation
Uncertainty Permeates Medical Practices

Deviations from a logical model of medical practice may be caused by uncertainty. Such a model predicts that, when uncertainty is reduced or eliminated, the forces producing practice variation will greatly diminish. Eddy has described both the uncertainties surrounding how conditions are diagnosed in the first place and how they are treated once diagnosed. For example, in the diagnosis of disease, the line between normal and abnormal findings is often unclear. Many signs and symptoms are common, and knowing which will require treatment is difficult to determine. When two (or three) physicians see the same signs, symptoms, x-rays, or other test results, they are likely to interpret them differently.

A similar set of problems surrounds the decision on how to treat diseases once they are diagnosed. For any given patient, a wide variety of procedures "can be ordered in any order and at any time"; the list of procedures that *might* be included in a workup of a patient presenting with chest pain or hypertension could easily take more than a page. Even choices between major treatments are by no means obvious.

Physician consensus panels have also drawn on experts to define the "state of the art" in medical practice. The lack of consensus over appropriate medical treatment in the most common of situations is striking. For example, in a panel examining the appropriateness of various indications for bypass surgery, initial levels of *agreement* among the nine physician panel members ranged from 12.2% to 22.2%, depending upon how stringent the criteria for agreement were. After 2 days of panel discussion, the agreement levels improved somewhat; but, even using the least strict definition of consensus, panel members failed to agree on more than half of the indications for bypass surgery (58.8%).

A major reason for overtreatment of all kinds is the natural optimism that physicians bring to their work and that patients themselves no doubt encourage. Who wants a pessimist for a doctor?
—John P. Bunker, Stanford University

Uncertainty also permeates medical knowledge about outcomes of even the most common of procedures. When patients are observed over long periods of time after treatment, they typically experience more adverse outcomes than the literature suggests. Thus, although a workshop convened by the National Institutes of Health suggested that following transurethral prostatectomy "the need for further operative treatment is uncommon," the cumulative probability at 8 years of having a second operation was found to be 20.2%. When treatments diffuse outside of large hospitals (the site of most evaluations but not where most care is delivered), the outcomes are usually worse.

Variations and Practice Style

Population-based estimates of health care use (regardless of where the care is received) have been developed to compare usage across countries, across states, and across smaller hospital service areas. These variations occur across all age groups—from children, through middle aged, to the elderly. The implications of these variations have been highlighted in several ways. Using the surgical rates to calculate lifetime probabilities of organ loss, Gittelsohn and Wennberg estimated that in the early 1970s the chances of a Vermont child reaching age 20 with tonsils in place ranged from 40% to 90%, depending on community of residence. If the United States' expenditures on seven common surgical procedures (hysterectomy, tonsillectomy, etc.) were based on the rates of low hospital service areas of Vermont and Maine, the costs were estimated to be $2.4 billion, while the bill based on the high-use areas of these two states would be $6.6 billion—in 1975 dollars.

Although a number of factors can influence these patterns, most of the variation seems explained *not* by underlying health differences in the populations of these different areas but by the practice style of the physicians treating patients. Some of the most persuasive evidence of the impact of practice style comes from the work on surgical signatures. Wennberg and Gittelsohn have demonstrated marked differences in rates of surgery for five common procedures across several areas in Maine. Rates of hemorrhoidectomy stayed much below the provincial average over each of the 5 years, whereas prostatectomy rates remained high. Left undisturbed by feedback and review or by the migration of physicians in and out of the area, the surgical signature of a community remained constant from year to year. Although consistent variation in rates across small areas points strongly to the influence of physician practice style (since several physicians typically practice in these areas), the evidence is somewhat indirect.

Marked differences in practice patterns among individual physicians seem to underlie the differences in rates. The rate of primary cesarean section across 11 physicians treating low-risk suburban women ranged from 9.6% to 31.8%. Close examination of the data yielded "no obvious explanation for variations in cesarean section rates across physicians."

Manitoba patients reporting good or excellent health were found to have very different probabilities of being hospitalized in the 2 years after their interview, depending upon the practice style of their physician. Thirty-three percent of the patients of those physicians scoring high on an index of physician hospital practice style (PHPS) were hospitalized in the 2 years following the interview compared with 20% of the patients of physicians who scored low on the index. Even after controlling for such patient characteristics as age, education, self-reported health status, proximity to death or nursing home entry, and for such system characteristics as supply of hospital beds and occupancy rates, a patient of a physician who scored high on the index was twice as likely to be hospitalized as a patient of a physician scoring low on the index.

❖ Is More Better?

Rates, Innovation, and Outcomes

The North American ethos surrounding the health care system is that "more is better." Expenditures rise every year, and yet headlines constantly decry underexpenditures in the health care system. Does this suggest that high rates identify areas delivering the best quality care? Are areas with the highest hospitalization rates or highest hysterectomy rates delivering the best care to area residents? Examining the hospital records of diabetic cases treated in high-, medium-, and low-rate counties, Connell et al. reported that the patients admitted by physicians in high-rate counties were tested substantially less thoroughly than those admitted in low-rate counties. Intravenous insulin treatment for severe metabolic emergencies was also less appropriately used in high-rate counties.

Some practice patterns are not only costly, but probably have negative implications for health. Both a well-publicized clinical trial in Pittsburgh and extensive Manitoba analyses of administrative data emphasized the desirability of conservative standards for tonsillectomy. Nonetheless, differences across areas remain; children resident in Lethbridge, Alberta, are much more likely to have their tonsils removed than are children resident in Edmonton.

Assuming that high rates must be better also overlooks the fact that hospitals can be dangerous places. In Steel et al.'s study of patients admitted to a medical service of a university hospital, 36% of the patients were found to have acquired an iatrogenic illness (one caused by treatment); for 9%, the event was considered major (something which was life-threatening or produced considerable disability). Compared with research done over a decade earlier, the risks associated with hospitalization had not been reduced over time, but had, if anything, gotten worse. This has occurred despite the enormous increase in hospital funding over this period, much of which was justified in terms of improving quality of care.

How could this be possible? Orkin has suggested that even relatively innocuous-sounding improvements in care should not be approved without clear demonstrations that the benefits are greater than the risks.

❖ Types of Evidence

Appropriateness and Discretion

Since definitive evidence is lacking, expert opinion has been used to specify what is, and what is not, appropriate care. Analyses based on such expert opinion show high levels of inappropriate and equivocal medical decision making. North American studies found only 35% of carotid endarterectomies, 14% of tonsillectomies, and 80% of pacemaker insertions to be done for appropriate indications. High rates of inappropriate utilization are found in more general reviews of hospital use. Rates of inappropriate admissions ranged from 6% to 19% and rates of inappropriate days of care ranged from 20% to 39% in the studies reviewed by Payne.

Some evidence supports the idea that high rates identify discretionary decisions about the delivery of health care and overuse, possibly unnecessary use, of the health care system. Dyck et al. found a larger proportion (52%) of hysterectomies were inappropriate in the Saskatchewan city with the higher rate than in the city with the lower rate (17%). In a study of 23 adjacent counties in one state, Leape et al. found that 28% of the variance in rate of coronary angiography was explained by the level of inappropriateness. However, for the other two procedures studied (carotid endarterectomy and upper gastrointestinal tract endoscopy), there was no relationship between surgical rate and rate of appropriately selecting individuals for surgery.

Not only can particular treatments be studied, but hospitalization as a whole can be analyzed in terms of its discretionary or nondiscretionary nature. In Manitoba, the relationship between a physician's practice style and the type of patient hospitalized was examined to determine if physicians more likely to admit patients to hospitals did so for more discretionary indications and for patients who were less ill. We used the index of PHPS described previously; a physician's score on this index was strongly related to the probability of his or her patient being hospitalized after controlling for factors related to patient health status, access to care, etc.

A 197% difference in hospital admission rates was found between those physicians most and least prone to hospitalize their patients. The range for discretionary use is much less. Physicians scoring highest on this index were 6% more likely to admit patients with a high variation condition and 34% more likely to admit patients with a diagnosis judged to be discretionary. Patients of physicians least prone to hospitalize were also somewhat more likely to show a higher illness level—their patients were 32% more likely to be admitted with a high-risk diagnosis.

Perhaps this lack of correspondence between rates of hospitalization (197% range between categories) and rates of discretionary or inappropriate use (6–34% range between categories) should not be surprising. Wennberg has suggested that "precisely because so many accepted theories concerning the treatment of common illnesses have not been adequately assessed, the number of potential patients who can be *appropriately* [our emphasis] treated by medical or surgical alternatives is very large indeed." Brook argues persuasively that the bias inherent in our processes of judging appropriateness "may mean that elimination of inappropriate or equivocal uses would improve a population's health, but that increasing appropriate use may only increase health care expenditures."

Cost-Effectiveness and Need

Funding choices about medical treatments need to be made. Government efforts to deal with pressures for new programs force such choices. Decision analysts try to use data of various kinds to answer such critical questions as

1. Are there treatments providing some benefit to the patient (regardless of cost) that could be expanded?
2. Which treatments are likely to be cost-effective compared with other uses of the funds?

Summarizing information on the comparative cost-effectiveness of a number of programs is difficult. Data from various sources using different methodologies must be forced into a common framework.

The calculated cost-effectiveness of some interventions is probably unduly optimistic. First, the analyses are likely to have been based on efficacy data. Efficacy is concerned with "does a particular treatment work" under ideal conditions, typically on patients selected using a strict protocol in a teaching hospital. Effectiveness studies deal with whether or not a specific treatment works in practice, when the treatment is widely diffused. For example, hospitals where relatively few surgical procedures of a particular type are performed often have poorer outcomes than do those performing larger numbers of the procedure. Bypass surgery in particular shows a very wide range of risk-adjusted mortality among hospitals.

Second, most decision analyses are unclear as to the role of comorbidity and age. For example, the selection criteria used in the major randomized clinical trial of bypass surgery (the CASS study) were applicable to a very low percentage (less than 10%) of the patients receiving bypass surgery in CASS participating centers and other hospitals. The remainder of the patients were either older or sicker than the CASS group. Although the CASS researchers developed a registry to follow individuals who were *not* randomized, most clinical trials do not follow patients with characteristics that may exclude them from randomization.

Generally, surgical interventions are less beneficial for older patients and those with more comorbidity. The risks of surgery are greater, whereas the benefits must be reaped over a shorter life span. Decision analysts need to take this into account.

Third, the baseline population mortality will vary markedly among areas, even across such large areas as American states. Such baseline mortality will affect the judgment as to the benefits and risks of particular interventions. Specifically, quality-adjusted life year calculations are likely to be changed when calculated for different populations. The higher the baseline mortality rate in a given area, the lower is likely to be the benefit of interventions that seem expensive in terms of cost/quality-adjusted life-year.

Fourth, the quality of the information used as input into decision analyses is often poor. Although Detsky's summary used some meta-analyses and randomized trials, this is not always the case with published decision analyses. Population-based, nonrandomized research is scarce. Weak research designs tend to be biased toward showing improved outcomes from a new treatment. Such biases are important because, if the program has a high cost per quality-adjusted life-year, sensitivity testing with small changes in the data may well reveal the new treatment to be of little value.

Patient Preferences

The shared responsibility "among clinicians, patients and policymakers who act as societal agents" increases the complexity of clinical decision making. The expected benefits of any intervention may vary with different patient preferences. Several lines of evidence suggest that patient risk aversion implies lower surgical rates. Specifically, patients seem likely to avoid "a choice that has a high expected utility because it includes a possibility of the worst outcome."

The fact that physicians and medical organizations are more interested in disease than in health might be regarded as an expression of professional bias, but this attitude corresponds in reality to a widespread human trait.
—René Dubos

As Wennberg has emphasized, "when offered a choice, patients often choose differently than their physicians." McNeil et al. found that, when confronted by a choice of treatment for lung cancer, subjects preferred radiation therapy, which had higher probabilities of immediate- and 1-year survival, over surgery, which had a higher probability of 5-year survival. Although McNeil et al. further reported that physicians seemed less risk-averse than patients, when physicians are patients they may behave differently.

❖ Physician Behavior

Increasing information on appropriate treatments or on outcomes associated with different treatments, may, or may not, change physician behavior. Part of the problem may be clinician overconfidence. Baumann et al. noted such overconfidence in two different situations: (a) the treatment of breast cancer by physicians and (b) the management of intensive care patients by nurses. In both situations, clinicians were highly confident that they had made the right decision ("microcertainty") although there was no consensus as to what the optimal treatment would be ("macro-uncertainty").

Although high rates of care are not consistently associated with high rates of inappropriate use, when information on their high-rate practice style is fed back to physicians, rates sometimes fall.

On the other hand, physicians can be reluctant to change established practice patterns in order to improve quality of care.

Physicians ideologically resist the monitoring of their practice, particularly if such monitoring can be labeled "cookbook medicine." However, Hampton has argued:

Clinical freedom is dead, and no one need regret its passing. In the days when investigation was nonexistent and treatment as harmless as it was ineffective, the doctor's opinion was all that there was, but now opinion is not good enough.

❖ What Have We Learned?

What have we learned from the above review? The research summarized above has demonstrated that

1. The practice of medicine is very different from one physician to another.
2. A significant amount of care is inappropriate and the rate of inappropriate care is often as high in the low-rate areas as in high-rate areas.
3. The lack of evidence showing clear benefits from procedures, at least as performed on many patients, suggests that existing rates are often too high.
4. Some of the variation is explained by uncertainty.
5. Even when uncertainty is reduced, there is no guarantee that appropriate care will be delivered.
6. Informed patients are likely to prefer more conservative, rather than more aggressive, treatment (at least where there are risks involved).
7. Both expert panels and cost-effectiveness studies are likely biased such that the benefits of treatments are overestimated. Applying practice guidelines may lower surgical rates in certain areas, but this is not guaranteed.

The politics driving expansion of acute care have been well documented. Continued pressure on health care budgets can certainly be expected. Although the amount of invasive treatment patients wish may be less than that now delivered, informed patients may well value extra information (even if treatment is unlikely to change). Where the risks are very low, and even if efficacy has not been demonstrated to be high, patients and physicians are likely to want better diagnoses. Such interest in extra consultations, laboratory testing, endoscopy, magnetic resonance imaging (MRI), and so on adds to the already existing pressures on the system.

The uncertainties of medical practice and the large variations in the rates of hospitalization for most medical conditions and surgical treatments highlight the interface between population health and the medical care system. Health status (of both individuals and populations) and the effectiveness of medical interventions are related, but "experts" differ greatly in their judgments as to the extent of the relationship and how one affects the other. If the relationship is relatively weak, then funds saved from the health care system can be used for other purposes.

At one extreme, the lack of convincing evidence as to the efficacy and effectiveness of many treatment strategies might suggest that efforts to contain cost can safely focus upon bringing rates of hospitalization for many conditions down toward the lower end of the spectrum of utilization. A more moderate approach would focus on regions whose residents tend to use more resources than others; perhaps utilization in these areas can safely be reduced toward mean levels. This middle-of-the-road strategy may have considerable appeal to government funders in an era of escalating health care costs.

❖ Policy Suggestions

Reduce Utilization in High-Rate Areas

The current practice of medicine clearly does not ensure that appropriate care will be delivered to patients. Surprisingly high rates of inappropriate care have been found in both low- and high-rate areas. Even when care has been designated "appropriate," various biases in the system work to overestimate appropriateness and the effectiveness of care.

Iglehart believes that "as provincial plans restrain the use of technology, (Canadian) physicians increasingly face the difficult choice of providing care on the basis of medical need rather than rendering it to all who could benefit." We have argued that the situation is far more complicated. If a portion of the care delivered is inappropriate or of unknown benefit, funds for procedures of proven effectiveness and for increasing the knowledge base should be available from better management and from efforts to restrain areas of high utilization.

What is the basis for thinking that efforts at reducing utilization in high-rate areas will not adversely affect health? First of all, even though socioeconomic factors may affect both rates of utilization and the associated expenses for hospital care, in New England (as in Manitoba) the regions with low incomes are not those with the highest hospital utilization rates. Dramatic differences in utilization between Boston and New Haven occur despite demographically similar populations receiving most of their care in university hospitals. Most of the higher utilization in Boston "is devoted to the hospital admission of adults with common acute but often minor illnesses or with chronic diseases. . . . These findings indicate that academic standards of care are compatible with widely varying patterns of practice." Most importantly, regions with high utilization have not been shown to differ systematically from regions with low utilization in terms of access to care, health status, or mortality.

Which utilization should be reduced? Targeting *both* areas with high overall utilization and areas that are high in a particular choice of an important surgical or medical treatment identifies a place to start. Such changes need to be done with support—both in terms of information and expertise—to maximize the reduction of what is inappropriate and highly discretionary.

New funds for the health care system are difficult to find. Significant funds will be needed to develop practice guidelines, to do outcome assessments, and to monitor practice. Since much more would seem to be gained from improving the quality of care that we are now delivering than from doing more or from doing new things, policy makers and insurers should with good conscience redirect funds from the existing system into the quality assurance and technology assessment activities proposed here.

Evaluate Treatments

Better information is necessary; Detsky has suggested the (potentially) high cost-effectiveness ratios of clinical trials. Well-designed registry and population-based cohort studies may have similar ratios. New, expensive technologies that *promise* to help at least *some* patients (often without good evidence of benefit) are a particular threat to efforts at cost containment. Their advocates argue that traditional methods of evaluation or technology assessment have been outstripped by the dramatic benefits promised by new technologies. . . .

Practice guidelines seem most needed for controversial interventions that have a significant effect on patients or the health care system. Procedures showing high variation across service areas suggest professional controversy and the potential for both overuse and inappropriate use. Phelps and Parente have developed an index of expected gain from technology assessment, which combines measures of resource use, the coefficient of variation in rates across regions, and the estimated rate at which the incremental value of a medical intervention changes as its rate of use changes. The index provides a dollar-valued welfare loss for variations that can be used for setting priorities for assessment. The highest index score was generated by coronary artery bypass surgery, but most of the high index interventions were nonsurgical (including hospitalizations for psychosis, cardiac catheterization, chronic obstructive lung disease, and angina pectoris).

Quality of Care Assessment Must Include Judgments of Appropriateness

Recent high-profile efforts to monitor quality of care have focused on comparing mortality rates of patients treated at different hospitals. Inhospital reviews often look at deaths, although progress has recently been made in performing target reviews using criteria based on ICD-9-CM diagnostic and procedure codes. Hannan et al. have reported the success of a targeted study (testing 11 explicit criteria) of uniform hospital discharge data when compared with a nontargeted subjective review of the medical record.

Few activities encompassed under quality of care review ask the questions: "Was the admission appropriate in the first place?" "Should the surgery have been done?" "Should the MRI have been performed?" While such questions might be asked as part of utilization review, they are typically not seen as pertinent to reviews of quality of care. Economics aside, modern medical treatments have a significant potential for harm and for producing pain and suffering. Given the enormous variations in physician practice patterns, quality of care assessments must include appropriateness reviews.

Develop Explicit Guidelines Drawing on Nonlocal Sources

If practice guidelines are developed by local practitioners without reference to clinical trial evidence and work done elsewhere, they may well exaggerate local area differences. While the importance of local input to gain acceptance of guidelines should not be underestimated, some education as to the marked variation among well-meaning practitioners must take place.

Leape et al. have reviewed practice guidelines developed in several contexts—by specialty societies, the Clinical Efficacy Assessment Project, the Joint Commission on Accreditation of Healthcare Organizations, etc. These proved to be essentially useless for making assessments as to the appropriateness of a given procedure because such guidelines lack specificity—they are so general as to leave everything up to the judgment of the individual practitioner or review body.

Worthwhile Activities

Pressures for expanding the health care system must not be allowed to drive out funding for other, more worthwhile activities. Three recent studies highlight the various factors at work in trying to both manage health care and ensure good health for all. The higher surgical rates found in the United States are associated neither with greater longevity nor with greater public satisfaction with the health care system. Although the low levels of American satisfaction with their system are not reflected in general dissatisfaction with their personal health care experiences, compared with the United Kingdom and Canada, "the United States has the smallest proportion of its population who are 'very satisfied'" with these experiences.

All countries must look to their health care budgets to find room for outcome assessments, developing practice guidelines, and monitoring the system. Other parts of health care, such as cost-effective health promotion programs that promise to help prevent or postpone major diseases must not be neglected. Perhaps the most important task is to find the political will to manage the health care system in a cost-effective fashion.

❖ About the Authors

Noralou P. Roos, PH.D., is Director of the Manitoba Centre for Health Policy and Evaluation, Department of Community Health Sciences, St. Boniface Hospital Research Centre, Winnipeg, Manitoba, Canada.

Leslie L. Roos, PH.D., is with the Department of Community Health Sciences, Manitoba Centre for Health Policy and Evaluation, St. Boniface Hospital Research Centre, Winnipeg, Manitoba, Canada.

❖ Cutting Waste by Making Rules: Promises, Pitfalls, and Realistic Prospects

JAN BLUSTEIN AND THEODORE R. MARMOR

American medical costs, one hardly needs to say, continue to rise relentlessly. In 1990, health expenditures consumed approximately 12.2% of America's gross national product (GNP). A decade earlier, the share was 9.1%. In 1970, we spent approximately 7.4%. There has developed an apparent consensus—among government, labor, and profession leaders—that costs must be contained. At the same time, there is widespread agreement that access must be universalized. As a result, many believe that excruciatingly hard choices are unavoidable.

This perceived dilemma has led to a great deal of talk about rationing. The tenor of the commentary indicates that it is a fearsome solution to our present troubles—painful and divisive, entailing choices that no one wants to make but which must be faced due to inescapable scarcity. Both contemporary rhetoric and current health policy, however, hold out the hope of a far more agreeable alternative. Galvanized by the realization that much medical care is of uncertain value, and bolstered by findings that show significant variation in medical practice patterns, a coalition of policymakers, politicians, and researchers is now actively engaged in seeking to contain costs by eliminating wasteful care. This appears an attractive course. Waste-cutting, unlike rationing, does not connote the cruel denial of necessary care. On the contrary, it suggests saving people from medical interventions that would not have done them any good. If "rationing" is the fearsome alternative, "cutting waste" is the benign one.

While consensus grows that wasteful practice is a problem, there is considerable disagreement about the solution. Such disagreement is hardly surprising, since cutting waste is merely a goal, not a program. Cutting waste can mean any of a number of things. It can mean regionalizing services, instituting yearly expenditure targets, implementing managed care systems, or developing elaborate review mechanisms to constrain the diffusion of new technologies. Indeed, the idea of "cutting waste" is so broad in its potential scope that it can subsume many hotly debated reforms in the field of health policy. Like health maintenance organizations (HMOs), competition, and diagnostic related groups before it, it is another vaunted panacea, the new great answer to arrive on the American health policy agenda.

This essay critically assesses the widely advertised plan to cut waste by making microallocational rules for the provision of medical care. Such rules, variously denominated "practice parameters," "clinical guidelines," and "standards of care," are aimed at ensuring that no patient is subjected to "wasteful" care by specifying what treatments particular patients should receive. For example, the rule that "healthy patients under 40 years of age without a family history of heart disease should not be given an electrocardiogram" is a practice parameter. It could be used by physicians to guide day-to-day treatment decisions. It could also be used by payers to control reimbursement, and by policymakers to appraise aggregate data about medical care utilization.

Our analysis raises the fundamental but too-little discussed question of what constitutes waste. Our central claim is that so-called "wasteful" practice is a conceptual hodgepodge, which encompasses treatments that are (1) ineffective, (2) of uncertain effectiveness, (3) ethically troubling, or (4) not allocationally efficient. From this starting point, we address issues of rule making and resource allocation and ask the following questions: Can all four of these types of wasteful care be identified in ways that are scientifically defensible and administratively practicable? What obstacles must be faced to make cutting waste by making rules into a *policy* in each case? Are there American institutions and attitudes that would make such rule making more costly, and therefore less attractive, than it seems? And can any (or all) of these four types of waste be cut without confronting the dilemma of difficult choices? But before approaching these questions, we begin by briefly reviewing the ways in which the problem of wasteful care has been framed by health care analysts, providers, and policymakers.

❖ Loose Talk About "Waste"

Terms like "wasteful," "ineffective," "inappropriate," "of unproven effectiveness," "unnecessary," and even "irrational" are used loosely and often interchangeably in the literature that is critical of current medical practice. Commentators have lamented the prevalence of unnecessary elective surgery, gratuitous "little ticket" diagnostic tests, and expensive treatments for acquired immunodeficiency syndrome (AIDS) patients. It is tempting to assume that these practices share some fundamental characteristic that places them within a unified category of wasteful medical treatments.

Making "expensive" synonymous with "medically unnecessary" seems a particularly troubling example of bureaucratically sanctioned linguistic drift. But it is not just linguistic territory that has been invaded by the waste cutters. Utilization review companies have moved beyond the realm of previewing surgical procedures and into the field of making allocational choices in the cases of very sick and dying patients. They employ "case managers" to direct the costly care of their sickest enrollees. This strategy can pay off handsomely. "[M]any cost-management companies are strengthening their 'case management' of patients who are seriously ill, with advanced cancer or

AIDS, for example, or recovering from a stroke. 'The savings can average $10,000 to $15,000 per case and be as high as $400,000.'" While some case managers may be truly well intentioned, intervening to help patients and save them from painful overtreatment, they also represent economic interests that will inevitably conflict at times with the interests of the patient. In the future, we are likely to hear more from case managers about "inappropriate," "ineffective," and "medically unnecessary" care. When we do, it will be hard to know exactly what this means. Is the proposed treatment harmful or worthless? Is it futile or just too costly?

These ambiguities must be faced in formulating a sensible strategy for controlling the cost of medical care in America. It would be enormously agreeable if cost containment could be achieved by cutting out a homogeneous wedge of present practices. But our analysis suggests that waste is heterogeneous, a claim worth exploring at some length. We need to know more about the four different types of waste. How prevalent are they? How do we determine that particular treatments fall into one of the four categories? What political, social, and professional obstacles will arise when standards are introduced forbidding wasteful practices? Will waste-cutting erect barriers to beneficial care, or can waste-cutting bypass such choices in medical care allocation? These four questions are at the core of the following section.

❖ A Taxonomy of "Waste"

Ineffective (or Harmful) Treatment

Some Americans, expert and lay, believe that much of medical care is ineffective or positively harmful.

Academic medicine is trying to answer this criticism. Researchers in a relatively new branch of investigation, clinical epidemiology, are trying to sort out which medical maneuvers are effective. Ideally, the research involves systematic and painstaking testing of therapies through randomized controlled clinical trials. But these experiments, the "gold standard" for determining clinical effectiveness, are events of epic proportion, lasting for years, costing millions of dollars, involving thousands of patients, facing monumental bureaucratic barriers, and raising serious ethical issues. Often, by the time clinical trials are completed, the technology they studied is outmoded. Although other methodologies have been developed and can yield useful information, physicians must regularly weigh the preponderance of imperfect evidence in order to estimate whether a particular patient might benefit from a particular intervention. It is often possible to entertain some reasonable doubt (or to hold out some reasonable hope) that a treatment will be effective. While there is currently a great deal of enthusiasm about improving the scientific basis of medicine, and while there is surely room for improvement, a vast project to make medicine scientific can never keep up with innovations in medical practice. Nor is it likely to provide firm ground for determining correct choices in most clinical situations. Medical decision making is simply too complex.

Given these limitations, how can ineffective treatments be identified? One approach is to augment imperfect information with the judgments of experts. Distinguished physicians, well-versed in the scientific literature, can use their clinical judgment—their beliefs about what works, based on their own past practices—to produce estimates of effectiveness. And groups of physicians can combine their expert judgments to arrive at consensus. A group of researchers at the RAND Corporation has developed a method for generating this kind of professional consensus about what works (and what doesn't work) in medicine. Because their innovative method has been so widely acclaimed and so often held up as a model for cutting waste by making rules, it warrants a brief review.

The RAND group's goal was to develop practice parameters for several widely used operations. They assembled a panel of distinguished physicians for each of the operations, and each panel member reviewed the available scientific literature about the procedure. With a list of all of the possible clinical scenarios in which each procedure might be performed, each panelist made an assessment of the appropriateness of the intervention for each of the scenarios, based on the literature review and clinical judgment. After making independent assessments, the panel members met to discuss the cases and compare their ratings. They found there was substantial disagreement among them about the appropriateness of performing the operations in many clinical settings. And so, after reviewing the cases together, the individual physicians rated each scenario again, and the revised ratings were combined into a group consensus rating of the appropriateness of treatment in each situation.

The ratings have been used successfully in pilot programs to identify "inappropriate" care. Two prominent RAND researchers recently left the Santa Monica think tank to found Value Health Sciences, Inc., bringing along the RAND methodology. They then developed some innovative software that uses the expert consensus on appropriateness to deliver second opinions about physician's treatment choices. Value's clients employ utilization review nurses to quiz physicians about referrals for the selected procedures. Using Value's computer-driven questionnaire while talking over the telephone, the nurses gather information about prospective patients and then match each prospective patient to a previously rated clinical scenario. If the prior consensus suggested the operation was "appropriate" for that patient, the patient's insurance company pays for the hospital admission. If the rules identified the operation as "inappropriate," the procedure is not covered. The referring physician may then appeal the decision regarding coverage with a doctor representing the utilization review company. In a trial run by the Aetna insurance company, 15% of 1,000 referrals for procedures were judged "inappropriate"; physician appeals brought the number of actual refusals down to 9%.

The successful implementation of the RAND/Value method is one of the first achievements of what has been called the "outcomes movement." This informal coalition of academic researchers, government officials, physician professional organizations, and members of the health insurance industry has come together over the past three years in an effort to study what works in medicine, to define "appropriate" care, and to use that definition of appropriateness to eliminate allegedly wasteful care through the use of practice guidelines.

Federal officials have been enthusiastic supporters of what has been hailed—perhaps somewhat grandiosely—as "the third revolution in health care." Former Health Care Financing Administration (HCFA) director William L. Roper, under pressure to contain Medicare's explosive growth, announced a major initiative to "evaluate and improve medical practice" by using HCFA's mammoth databases to study the outcomes of care given under that program. In a related later development, the Department of Health and Human Services' National Center for Health Services Research (NCHSR) was renamed the Agency for Health Care Policy and Research (AHCPR) and charged with "promoting the quality, appropriateness, and effectiveness of health care" and directing studies that would lead to the development of clinical guidelines for "treatments or conditions that account for a significant portion of Medicare expenditures." With the new name came an increase in federal funding.

The American Medical Association (AMA) is perhaps the least likely of the coalition's members. Historically a staunch advocate of physician autonomy, the AMA has teamed up with the RAND Corporation and the Academic Medical Center Consortium, a group of major teaching hospitals, to develop practice guidelines for use by "payers and utilization and medical reviewers to define a range of practice options physicians could use without incurring financial or other sanctions."

In summary, parameters *do* hold some promise in curbing ineffective or harmful care, and there is clearly energetic activity in support of their development. But the amount of time and money required to develop and implement the RAND/Value approach on a large scale, though unknown, is surely substantial. According to AHCPR officials, it has taken three years to move from the process of identifying conditions for guideline development to early pilot testing of those guidelines; the agency released two guidelines in March 1992, intending to make several more available this summer. If such guidelines were to be widely used to audit physician choices, the degree of bureaucratization in medical care would increase substantially. The requirement that physicians "clear" a large proportion of their decisions could impose significant additional costs in a system where, experts estimate, as much as 20% of expenditures already go to administrative matters, and where provider frustration with the micromanagement of care is already intense. Still, the movement has generated tremendous enthusiasm and significant funding. It is worth exploring the probable consequences of extending its approach to other types of "wasteful" care.

Treatment of Uncertain Effectiveness

There is ample room for doubt about the effectiveness of many medical treatments. For some treatments, there is very little data on effectiveness. For most treatments, there is disagreement as to how to interpret the available data. In the face of this uncertainty, how feasible is it to talk about cutting waste with rules prohibiting payment for treatments of undetermined effectiveness?

Most physicians would almost certainly oppose this approach. Because of the lack of scientific knowledge about disease, the practice of medicine is not a "cookbook" endeavor. Clinicians extrapolate beyond scientific data in "the large portion of cases . . . [that] are clinically gray and require clinical judgment". Judging how to proceed in questionable cases is part of what constitutes the art of medicine. Physician Donald Berwick of the Harvard Community Health Plan has rightly warned that in choosing to cut waste by overriding clinical judgment, "we [may] gain control of care patterns only to find that care is being given by doctors who have lost pride and heart." And while the specter of disheartened physicians might not forestall officials intent upon cutting costs, public opinion would likely inhibit this approach to "cutting waste." Some patients would surely be outraged at being denied treatment simply because scientific data is lacking.

Treatment That Is Ethically Troubling

The explosive growth of the bioethics field, an area that was virtually nonexistent a generation ago, testifies to the proliferation of ethically troubling medical treatment. The use of aggressive medical therapies in treating the very old, the very young, and the very sick has engendered some of the most vehement charges of "waste," "inappropriateness," and "irrationality" in American medicine.

Rulemaking in this area requires an ethical consensus concerning an appropriate level of care. For people who are intimately acquainted with instances of gross overtreatment, this often seems a trivial problem. Waste is apparent and outrageous. Something like Justice Stewart's standard for obscenity—"I know it when I see it"—seems to hold. But experience shows that even the seemingly clearest cases can evoke controversy (if not litigation), bringing into conflict those most intimately familiar with the patient's situation. These controversies often reflect fundamental disagreements about the goals and obligations of providers, payers, and patients, or even disputes about the significance of human life, including a "right to life." We will not recapitulate the bioethical debates surrounding these issues. It is enough to note that the term "wasteful" is used here in an entirely different sense than in the previous two sections. No literature search or scientific experiment satisfactorily speaks to this issue of "waste." No consensus panel can settle the ethical question of what is futile, desirable, or even cruel.

What then are the possibilities for policy in this area? What kinds of rules can be made to cut waste in ethically problematic cases? Significant progress has been made in defining when it is *permissible* to terminate care. Guidelines developed in the bioethics community have informed court decisions and state statutes. Such policies undoubtedly can help in guiding individual decisions, but their impact on the overall allocation of medical resources is unknown. Such guidelines, however, are not analogous to the RAND/Value procedures to "cut waste." Little progress has been made in developing analogous rules in this area, rules that would say when wastefulness makes it *obligatory* to deny or terminate care. (It should be emphasized, moreover, that no one connected with the landmark RAND studies has proposed that any such rules be made.)

Treatment That Is Not Allocationally Efficient

Notwithstanding the above difficulties, bread-and-butter medicine is not about complex ethical issues. Rather, increasingly it is about expensive medical care options. Today's physicians must choose daily from among various costly treatments and tests, many of which are unquestionably beneficial.

When do expensive maneuvers become "wasteful"? Traditionally, policymakers have approached this problem from the framework of cost-benefit analysis. Given a rank ordering of medical programs and procedures, beginning with the one with the best cost-to-benefit profile and ending with the one with the least attractive profile, one might simply allocate money from the top down. Above some cutoff point, the listed interventions could be considered "worthwhile"; below that point, "wasteful." There are, however, three significant obstacles to implementing such a plan in American medicine.

The first is the unavailability of a defensible rank ordering. We have scant information about the effectiveness and costs of most clinical interventions. Moreover, we lack a firm conceptual and empirical basis for equating different kinds of medical, social, and financial benefits. In the absence of these two sorts of information, it is difficult to assign meaningful cost-benefit estimates to medical procedures. The second difficulty is that the American medical care system does not operate within a fixed budget (nor do most American physicians). Without a budgetary limit, the borderline between "worthwhile" and "wasteful" simply cannot be defined. It is impossible to say which interventions would fall below a purely hypothetical cut-off. A final obstacle arises from our decentralized system of financing. We have no guarantee that cuts in "wasteful" expenditures will be compensated with shifts toward "worthwhile" expenditures. We may agree that annual mammographic screening for young women is comparatively wasteful, but we have no reason to believe that money saved by abstaining from mammography will be spent on a more worthwhile endeavor, such as universal access to prenatal care.

While rigorous cost-benefit analysis is unlikely to govern the allocation of medical services in the foreseeable future, concerns about costs and benefits will continue to have an important place in discussions of "wasteful" care. This is surely appropriate, since no medical care system can provide all possible services. But when "not cost effective" is taken to be synonymous with "wasteful," some misleading inferences can follow. One of these is the suggestion that treatments that fall below the cost-benefit cutoff point are "wasteful," and therefore do no one much good. This is certainly not true. There are many potentially lifesaving treatments that are very costly, but effective (breast-cancer screening in young women, safer diagnostic tests, and organ transplantation all fall into this category). When cutting waste on economic grounds, we inevitably eliminate some services that do some good. We should therefore not be surprised to find people fighting for access to treatments that are "not cost-effective."

If "waste cutting" means "trimming the fat" and "rationing" means "making rules to limit the use of beneficial services," it will necessarily be the case that in trimming fat we deny some people some beneficial services. What is particularly striking is that the *perception* of benefit determines the political cost of waste cutting.

More generally, economically driven rulemaking runs counter to those American values and institutions favoring aggressive, high-technology, "do something" medicine. Opinion polls show that Americans believe, nearly unanimously, that financial considerations should not enter into life-and-death medical decisions. In the legal arena, technological imperatives dovetail with our shared notions of individual rights and professional responsibilities, meaning that rulemaking could exacerbate an increasingly unacceptable malpractice environment. As people who are injured by denial of care seek retribution, several issues will be at stake: Can care be denied because it is too expensive? When harm results from denial of treatment, who is responsible? What are the responsibilities of payers and providers? Already, some interesting cases have been heard. A Washington state court recently held that a third-party payer had a duty to pay for a man's liver transplant because his life depended on it. A Michigan woman with colon cancer has sued her HMO, maintaining that their cost-containment rules led to a delay in the detection of her malignancy.

While commentators agree that the relationship between the malpractice standard and care cost containment is one of the most important issues confronting medical tort law in the 1990s, they are divided on how the legal system will accommodate rulemaking. Some argue that physicians who prudently adopt recommended sparer practice styles will find protection in the event of adverse outcomes. Others are doubtful that the accommodation can be made so smoothly, and fear that economically based rulemaking will "create enormous confusion and, quite likely, place physicians under inappropriate and unfair economic and legal pressures" as they are forced to make choices between their own professional standards and payers' rules.

Whatsoever the political and legal outcomes, it is clear that economically driven rulemaking could force physicians to redefine their professional roles. Many physicians find such rulemaking unacceptable and many believe that cost containment measures seriously compromise the quality of medical care. Some hold that consideration of costs simply has no place in the practice of medicine.

❖ Realistic Prospects for Rulemaking

This brief survey of the policy to cut waste by rulemaking has revealed that it is really many policies—at least as many policies as there are kinds of waste. Three summary points should be emphasized.

First, there are different senses in which treatments are "wasteful." We know that some treatments are wasteful by looking at their results; in other cases, we need to examine their price tag; in still others, we must make a moral judgment. While this is not a profound point, it is one that is frequently obscured in the rhetoric of waste-cutting. Medicare's rules about medical necessity (and a myriad of similarly disingenuous policies) create confusion, breed cynicism, and offer little promise as long-term strategies to guide the allocation of medical services.

Second, since "waste" is diverse, policies to "cut waste" face different prospects for success. Although some forms of care can probably be prohibited with little resistance, this is not likely to be the case generally. There will be substantial professional, political, ethical, and legal obstacles to cutting waste in many cases. Although identification of wasteful practices may be conceptually straightforward, the costs of rulemaking may be high. Rules can work, but these obstacles must be faced squarely in attempts to develop coherent and realistic health policy.

Third, because the spectrum of "wasteful" care includes care that is effective, cutting waste by making rules will not always circumvent hard choices. Sometimes it may mean eliminating care that is both needed and beneficial. In other cases, it may mean cutting services that are perceived to be beneficial but are of uncertain effectiveness. In either case, we must watch out for immoderate promises about painless "waste cutting."

While doubts about rulemaking are warranted, nihilism is not. We all stand to gain from the knowledge that will flow from the outcomes movement, and rulemaking may work in some situations. As we have shown, *rulemaking is likely to be particularly successful when the treatment in question is clearly ineffective or harmful.* It is, however, far from obvious that such instances are sufficiently prevalent to justify the extravagant optimism surrounding the movement's likely impact.

In the end, the parameters movement may founder—not because of a lack of "wasteful" medical care, but because government and business leaders want a quicker fix to the problem of rising medical care costs. With wasteful care on the public's mind, a coalition of resourceful researchers, government officials, politicians, business leaders, and professional organizations have developed a vision of a world in which scientific know-how aided by computerized wizardry will produce rules for allocating the "right" amount of medical care. But the public's "issue attention cycle" waxes and wanes quickly. As it becomes clear that it would be years before hoped-for economic gains could be realized, and that cuts in "waste" entail significant social costs, the movement could lose some of its momentum and funding.

❖ Is There an Alternative to Rulemaking?

Nothing above is intended to imply that there is a simple solution to the problem of rising medical expenditures. The "professional imperative" that drives physicians to provide more, better, and safer services (and the desire for better health that drives patients to seek the same) will continue. If we are to curb rising costs, powerful countervailing forces must be brought to bear. Rules can certainly help in applying such forces, and the parameters movement is well underway. But is rulemaking the most promising course of action? Any answer must take into account two decades of frustrating failure to contain health expenditures in America. During that time, there were numerous attempts to change the way in which America delivers, pays for, and regulates medical care. None has been demonstrably successful in curbing medical care inflation or in constraining the growth in the intensity of services provided. Neither competition, managed care, prospective payment, nor numerous other purported panaceas has fulfilled its promise. Each in its day was touted as the answer to the problem of rising costs, leading to cycles of delight and disappointment as expenditures resumed their seemingly inexorable rise, or costs were shifted onto other sectors of the medical care economy. To expect more of the outcomes movement would be to ignore the lessons of experience. It is worth sketching what these lessons might be.

During the same 20-year period that costs rose in this country, other nations had substantially greater success in controlling health expenditures. Canada's and Britain's systems are most often cited, but most of Western Europe's achievements are comparable. In each case, the inherently inflationary forces in medical care that Robert Evans has so eloquently described—technological growth, asymmetry of information, uncertainty of evidence, and rising expectations—have been met with policy responses to counter powerful pressures for more spending. In Canada, that has meant the concentration of financial authority in single provincial payers, the use of global hospital budgets, the separate control of capital expenditures by hospitals, and the active setting of prices for physician services. In the United States, reforms failed to address those forces in a concerted fashion, and inflation has continued unabated.

There are indications that America is moving toward universal health insurance. Recent public opinion polls show that a majority of Americans favor a national health insurance system over our present arrangements.

Still, most of these powerful parties are unconvinced that reform should include the kind of concentrated financial and regulatory power that has repeatedly proved successful abroad. In the context of the federal budget deficit and the public's hostility toward increased taxes, it is uncertain whether reform will follow the model of direct governmental financing. Some claim that a system that preserves the present employment-based insurance scheme and maintains some role for private insurance companies is politically more feasible. If such a program could be coupled with strong governmental regulatory powers, some observers believe that we might achieve universal access to medical care, while still containing costs.

As the debate on major reforms heightens over the coming months, one truth will continue to be undeniable: contemporary medicine offers an astonishing array of beneficial therapies. These therapies will be sought by many patients wanting to improve their lives. They will be employed by doctors wanting to help their patients, exercise their craft, and earn their income. There is little hope that either of the intimate partners in the doctor-patient relationship will come to see most medical treatment as "wasteful."

Meanwhile, the "professional imperative" will prevail unless powerfully constrained. While many physicians will refrain from performing procedures known to be ineffective, most will not be willing to unilaterally cut other "wasteful" activities (practices of uncertain effectiveness, activities that are ethically problematic, and therapies that are not allocationally efficient). If doctors will not say "no" to their patients, then we can expect that payers will begin to say "no" to doctors. And indeed they have begun to do so. A new coalition has promised to cut health expenditures by making rules forbidding wasteful treatment. But it is doubtful that "cutting waste" is as straightforward or as painless as the most voluble members of the coalition have suggested. And it is certain that cutting waste by making rules will mean different things to different people.

❖ About the Authors

Jan Blustein, M.D., is a fellow in health policy, Robert F. Wagner Graduate School of Public Service, New York University, New York City.

Theodore R. Marmor, PH.D., is Professor of Public Policy and Management and Chair, Center for Health Studies, Institution for Social and Policy Studies, School of Organization and Management, Yale University, New Haven, Connecticut.

❖ Chapter 9
A Hard Look at Some Neglected Issues

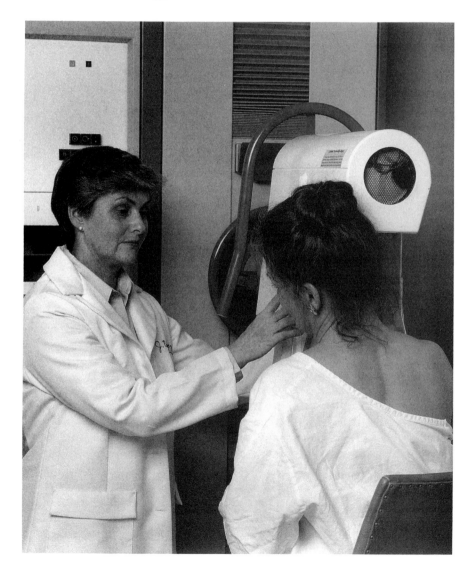

It is well recognized that certain segments of our society bear a disproportionate burden of illness and that there are serious inequities about the availability of care offered to specific groups of people. In this chapter, we set aside the more global approach to health policy, to examine in detail issues faced by some significant groups in our society—African Americans, the elderly, women, and those stricken with acquired immuno-deficiency syndrome (AIDS). All of these groups have received and continue to receive a certain amount of discrimination within the health care system, and this book would not be complete without addressing their particular needs and concerns.

Representing 12 percent of the population and including 32.5 million people in 1990 and projected to reach 21.1 percent or 68 million by 2040, older Americans bear a disproportionate burden of chronic illness and disability. People in the United States are living longer and the burden of chronic illness and disability increases progressively in old age. The problems are growing exponentially as this group grows faster than the rest of the population, and the oldest-old subgroup, aged 85 and over, expands the fastest. This group, numbering 3 million in 1990, is expected to quadruple to 12 million by 2040. Despite the improvement in the economic status of the majority of the elderly in the past 20 years, the situation of many elders in society is precarious.

Advancing age requires difficult life transitions at best. For many, it means an abrupt, sometimes involuntary, retirement and a substantial drop in income, and for others it means the death of a spouse, chronic illness, and increasing disability. The hardships of this major life transition are exacerbated by the lack of social support provided old people just when they are required to give up their employment income. More than one fourth of the old people in this country survive at or near the poverty level. Their health is depleted by their living conditions. Individuals are living longer but face many uncertainties, including the combined effects of poverty, social isolation, ageism, chronic illness, and disability.

In "Long-Term Care: Requiem for Commercial Private Insurance," Thomas Bodenheimer and Carroll L. Estes discuss the inadequacies of long-term care in the United States. They point out that private insurance rests on the principle that people with higher risk are rejected from coverage or are charged higher premiums than those with lower risk. For private long-term care insurance, the underwriting principle creates a dilemma—premiums are affordable for only about 20 percent of the elderly population. The authors propose a social insurance program for long-term care that would provide universal, affordable, and equitable coverage for older Americans.

In the article, "Race in the Health of America," S. M. Miller looks at differential health data between African Americans and white Americans and concludes that, while considerable progress has been made in social and economic conditions for African Americans, "to be poor *and* African American is to run the risk of ill health." The author reviews data on biological, social, economic, and cultural factors as they affect health to explore reasons why differences persist between blacks and whites in both morbidity and mortality rates. He also reviews major policy issues that affect the health of African Americans, not least the question of whether the emphasis should be on improving medical treatment or on raising the standard of living of the poor.

What is "women's health"? Why is there a "women's health movement"? Because many people don't know the answers to these questions, we have included two articles here on this important and neglected issue, which has implications for half the nation's (and world's) population. First, women have their own unique health concerns and, second, even for conditions that affect men and women equally, far too little research has been devoted to female subjects. Another important factor is that although reproduction is only one of the functions of a woman's life, this function has often been the main focus of health care for women.

In "Women's Health: Review and Research Agenda as We Approach the 21st Century," Judith Rodin and Jeannette R. Ickovics review past research and project future research directions regarding women's health, and they examine sex differences in mortality and morbidity, along with evidence that the quality and quantity of these differences are changing. The authors explain why shifting mortality rates in recent years have resulted in a decreasing advantage for women. They also identify neglected areas that require greater research allocations, including women and AIDS, psychopharmacology, substance abuse, hormone replacement therapy, the aging of the female population, and reproductive technologies.

Mary K. Zimmerman raises a number of complex issues in her article describing the women's health movement. She provides a critique of the medical profession and its approach to women over the centuries. She describes how the movement gained momentum in recent decades and began to challenge standard medical practice, which was historically based on the "prevailing male-centered cultural views of women's proper position." Her provocative assessment underscores the vital need for recognition of the necessity to address the many gender imbalances in the health care system.

In 1981, AIDS came to the attention of public health officials in the United States. By December of that year, some 200 cases had been identified, and many of those stricken with *Pneumocystis carinii* pneumonia, Kaposi's sarcoma, and other diseases that are hallmarks of infection with the human immunodeficiency virus (HIV) had already died. The number of cases reported in the United States increased to epidemic proportions in the decade that followed, and the disease has now been reported in more than 70 countries on six continents. In 1983, the U.S. Department of Health and Human Services declared AIDS to be the nation's "number one health priority." In September 1993, 339,250 people in the nation had been reported with AIDS, and 201,775 had died. It is estimated that over a million Americans are infected with HIV, and it is likely that all of them will eventually develop AIDS and die as a result. Overall, HIV infection ranks as the tenth leading cause of death. For the African American population, it ranked seventh. The crisis of the AIDS epidemic has stimulated responses from all levels of government as well as from the private sector. Because of the nature and magnitude of this epidemic and its implications for public health and health care, AIDS has had a major impact on the nation's health care system.

The HIV epidemic has generated the need for a broad spectrum of public health, medical, social, and educational services in communities throughout the country. The financial impact has been felt by individuals stricken with the disease, by families and friends of persons with HIV disease, by nonprofit community-based health and social service agencies in areas with a concentration of high-risk groups, by hospitals and physicians caring for persons with HIV disease, by the private and commercial insurance industry, by employers, and by every level of government.

The economic costs of HIV disease are both direct and indirect. The major component of direct costs is the cost of care of patients in and out of the hospital, including physician services, drugs, ancillary services, home health and hospice care, and nursing home care. Other expenditures related to disease reporting and surveillance are for tracking the epidemic, for establishing routes of HIV transmission, and for laying the epidemiologic groundwork to develop prevention strategies. Funds for prevention are for information and education directed toward the general public, particularly sexually active adults, as well as risk reduction programs aimed at changing high-risk behaviors in special populations—sexually active homosexual and bisexual men, intravenous drug users, sexual partners of IV drug users, and adolescents who may engage in such high-risk behaviors as IV drug use—and protecting the blood supply. Direct costs of care are high if hospital and nursing home care loom large in patient treatment. Indirect costs reflect the economic loss to society, generally measured by lost wages due to sickness and early death. Indirect costs are high if illness and death occur in young people at the peak of their earning power. Both of these circumstances are characteristic of HIV infection.

Although AIDS became known in the early 1980s as a disease of homosexuals, patterns of the disease are shifting, and more and more it is manifesting as a disease of the disadvantaged—of poor, inner city African Americans and Hispanics. Since the early 1980s, the transmission of HIV among homosexual men in cities such as San Francisco has declined, but this has not been the case among IV drug users, where the prevalence of HIV infection has continued to increase. This is because of the many complexities related to combating the disease among drug addicts and their sex partners. In addition, many babies in the United States were infected at birth and later developed AIDS, almost all of them the offspring of drug addicts or their sex partners. By late 1993, over 4,906 U.S. children under the age of 13 had been diagnosed with AIDS, and 2,615 had died.

The policy issues related to AIDS loom large; primary among them is the effort to curb the spread of HIV. Issues related to treatment, needle exchange for drug addicts, HIV drug treatment availability, costs, research, and ethics also pose great challenges.

Included in this chapter is the introduction to the 1991 report of the National Commission on Acquired Immune Deficiency Syndrome, "America Living with AIDS: Transforming Anger, Fear, and Indifference into Action." A major goal of the commission is to awaken the nation to the enormity of the HIV crisis, and this report, with its numbers alone, makes a great contribution in that direction. For example, it predicted that by 1993, AIDS would outstrip all other diseases in lost human potential. The introduction reprinted here also includes 30 recommendations or concrete proposals for action, urging the nation not to give in to the epidemic.

❖ Long-Term Care: Requiem for Commercial Private Insurance

THOMAS BODENHEIMER AND CARROLL L. ESTES

In 1990, Americans over 65 years of age numbered 31 million; this figure is expected to reach 52 million by the year 2020 and 68 million by 2040. Three million Americans were over 85 years in 1990; this number will more than double to 7 million by the year 2020 and will quadruple to 12 million by 2040. These startling projections should direct the attention of health policymakers to the paramount issue of long-term care.

In this chapter, we describe the realities of long-term care; we examine the difficulties faced in applying private insurance principles to long-term care; and we evaluate three options for financing long-term care—private insurance, public-private partnership, and social insurance. We conclude that social insurance is the most reasonable approach to finance long-term care for all Americans.

Health is a continuing property in the sense that it is present from the ovum until death; it does not disappear during an illness to return on recovery, but the level of health changes throughout life.
—J.R. Audy and F.L. Dunn

❖ The Reality of Long-Term Care in America

- ❖ Nine and a half million Americans need long-term care (LTC); of these, 3.9 million are disabled people below age 65.
- ❖ Americans over 85 are the group most likely to need LTC since about half are disabled or need help performing one or more activities of daily living (ADLs).
- ❖ Males over 65 have a 30 percent chance of entering a nursing home at some time in their lives, while for women—who more often outlive their spouses—the chance is 52 percent.
- ❖ Medicare was designed primarily to cover the costs of hospital care and offers almost no coverage for LTC. Private LTC insurance scarcely exists. Only 6 percent of LTC costs are covered by Medicare, and only 4 percent by private insurance; 42 percent comes from Medicaid and 43 percent from the life savings of patients and their families. At least 100,000 Americans became impoverished in 1985 paying for LTC.

❖ Out-of-pocket expenses for health care paid by the elderly approximated 17 percent of after-tax income in 1991. One third of these expenses went for nursing home costs. For poor, minority, and female elders and those living alone, health costs are an even greater proportion of income. Single older women living alone may spend up to 42 percent of their income for health care.

❖ The United States spent about $60 billion on LTC in 1989, including $48 billion on nursing home care. The average cost of nursing home care is $23,000 a year and for many exceeds $55,000. Spending on nursing home and home health care is expected to triple from 1990 to 2020.

Given these facts, a widespread consensus has developed that our nation must create a system to finance LTC. Yet, there is disagreement on whether LTC should be financed in the public arena or whether private health insurance should be involved.

❖ The Underwriting Principle

Insurance is a social mechanism by which people reduce the adverse financial consequences of a costly event by paying small amounts in advance to an institution, which, in turn, pays all or part of the costs incurred by the event. Insurance can be divided into private insurance, which is voluntary, and social insurance, which is compulsory.

Western industrialized nations finance health care through varied combinations of four major mechanisms: private insurance, social security, out-of-pocket payments, and taxes. Social insurance—often combining social security and tax revenues—is a popular approach in Western Europe and underlies the Medicare program in the United States. Because coverage is compulsory, social insurance spreads the risk of illness among the entire population. In most cases, social insurance is based on the "ability-to-pay principle," which includes two features: lower-income people receive more benefits relative to their income and to their payments than higher-income people, and people requiring large amounts of health care receive more benefits relative to their payments than people who rarely utilize health services.

The United States—with its 41 percent governmental share of health care financing, far below that of other industrialized nations—relies heavily on private health insurance, which is structured in a manner quite distinct from the ability-to-pay principle. Whereas American private health insurance as initially offered by Blue Cross and Blue Shield in the 1930s charged its subscribers the same premium regardless of risk of illness (community rating), an increasing proportion of private insurance plans now charge higher premiums for those at greater risk of contracting illness (experience rating). Private health insurance usually finances health care using the "underwriting principle," by which the population is divided into homogeneous groups and classified according to the risk of creating a claim against the insurer. For example, young healthy people are considered preferred risks and charged relatively low premiums, healthy middle-aged people are standard risks with somewhat higher premiums, and the elderly are substandard risks with the highest premiums. The chronically disabled may be classified as unacceptable risks who are uninsurable.

Underwriting has also been called "risk-rating, the practice of setting premiums and other terms of policies for groups and individuals according to the age, sex, occupation, health status, and health risks of policyholders." It is widespread in individual and small group markets, and has entered large groups as well. Underwriting has three negative consequences for health consumers: the denial of coverage for individuals or groups found to have a high risk of illness, the imposition of preexisting condition exclusions, and the setting of premium rates that increase with the risk of illness (experience rating). Donald Light has characterized the underwriting principle as

> the inverse coverage law: the more people need coverage, the less coverage they are likely to get or the more they are likely to pay for what they get.

Can a competitive private market exist without underwriting? Two central characteristics of underwriting are the prerogative of insurers to reject applicants and the practice of charging higher premiums for higher-risk individuals or groups (experience rating). Mary Nell Lehnhard, a Blue Cross/Blue Shield executive, explains why a competitive market forces insurers to retain the right to reject applicants:

> In a competitive market, insurers that accept all risks, or have even marginally more liberal enrollment practices, find themselves with a worse mix of risks, and consequently, higher premiums than insurers that have been more selective.

Mark Hall, past research fellow at the Health Insurance Association of America, explains why a competitive market pressures insurers to utilize experience rating and to oppose a single premium for the entire community (community rating):

> Insurers are concerned that community rating in a market of many competing carriers will randomly produce winners and losers according to which companies happen to have relatively older, sicker subscribers. Flat community rating may arbitrarily drive some insurance companies out of business.

Economist Henry Aaron agrees that "free competition among insurance companies is unimaginable without widespread experience rating."

❖ Can Private Insurance Provide Universal Long-Term Care Protection?

How does the underwriting principle bear on the problem of LTC financing? The largest market for LTC insurance consists of the elderly, who—because of their age—are at risk of requiring LTC services. Under the underwriting principle, the elderly are charged high premiums or are rejected as unacceptable risks. Moreover, the chief market for LTC insurance contains people with an average income only 62 percent that of the general population. Thus, people requiring or likely to require LTC are placed in serious jeopardy by the underwriting principle: if they can obtain insurance at all, they must pay more than younger people even though their incomes are likely to be less. Given these realities, the private financing of LTC presents difficulties both for private insurers and for those needing insurance.

Problems for Private Insurers

A central tenet of underwriting is the capacity to predict the health care costs of different groups.

> A major difficulty in the expansion of long-term care insurance is that there has been relatively little direct actuarial or plan experience on which to base rates.

Calculating costs is problematic because the need for LTC may not occur until 20 years or more after the insurance is purchased. A continued rise in average life expectancy would greatly increase costs for LTC insurers. Serious disability for the elderly, especially for those over 85, is a common and often costly event. At the same time, the population likely to purchase LTC insurance—the elderly—has a lower average income than the general population. Thus, LTC insurance is difficult to market because premiums must be high enough to cover costs, but low enough to attract clients.

The LTC insurance market lacks a large population of preferred risks by which insurers can adequately spread LTC costs. The market for LTC insurance consists of (1) individuals over 65 whose age places them at higher risk and heightens their urgency for insurance coverage, and (2) younger healthy groups that might obtain LTC insurance through employment. The severely disabled under age 65 belong to neither market since they are generally uninsurable. If the latter market is small, the former faces a critical problem of affordability. In fact, the latter market is tiny, comprising in June 1990 only 5 percent of all LTC policies. Insurance offerings to younger healthy groups through employers have attracted little interest among young workers for whom the prospects of long-term disability are remote. By mid-1990, only 150 employers had agreed to offer LTC plans and, when offered such policies on an employee-pay-all basis, only 5.2 percent of employees elected to enroll.

It is doubtful whether the younger market will ever blossom. Few employers wish to involve themselves in LTC insurance; they are having sufficient difficulties with the cost of health insurance. Employees have more pressing financial needs than LTC coverage, the benefits of which are decades away. While premiums in the young market are low, benefits shrink with inflation. Thirty or 40 years hence, nursing home daily rates will exceed $200, meaning that a 90-day deductible would translate into $18,000 in out-of-pocket payments for the first three months of a nursing home stay.

Without making LTC insurance compulsory, younger people will not purchase this product in large numbers, thereby leaving insurers to market high-cost policies to high-risk elderly individuals—an improbable task.

Only 1.65 million private LTC policies were in force in 1990. While the insurance industry points to a recent increase in LTC policies, this growth is concentrated among healthier and wealthier customers, and will come to a halt as the small potential market is saturated. The insurance industry itself optimistically predicts that only 42 percent of people over 65 could afford LTC insurance, thereby admitting that private insurance cannot provide universal LTC coverage. Even as the number of policies grows, the number of people needing LTC insurance will likely increase even faster; between 1990 and 2030, the number of people requiring assistance with ADLs will almost double.

Problems for Consumers

High premiums price many people out of the LTC insurance market. Even people who can afford LTC policies may be unable to renew their coverage; while policies generally claim to have a premium that does not increase with age, companies can raise rates as long as they do so for broad categories of policy holders. According to a 1990 Health Insurance Association of America survey, the average annual premium for $80 of nursing home benefits a day, with a 20-day deductible and inflation protection, was $1,395 for an individual at age 65, rising to $4,199 at age 79. Half of elderly couples live on less than $20,000 per year. If a couple of 65 at the $20,000 income level purchased low-cost policies for $2,000 ($1,000 for each person), their LTC insurance would account for 10 percent of their income. It has been estimated that LTC policies whose premiums exceed 5 percent of income are unaffordable. By that criterion, couples over age 65 would need to earn $40,000 or more to be able to purchase LTC coverage; only 18 percent of elderly couples earn above that amount. The General Accounting Office cites LTC insurance affordability at 20 percent for the 65 to 79 age group.

Individually paid premiums are a regressive way to provide LTC protection; as a flat dollar amount, a premium represents a greater burden on lower-income people than on the well-to-do.

People with illness or high risk of illness may be denied coverage. According to a study published by the Health Insurance Association of

America, 15 percent of the elderly have disabilities that cause them to be rejected for LTC insurance. Some companies have rejection rates of 30 percent.

In order to protect themselves from catastrophic losses, private LTC insurers sell policies with limited benefits. Most private policies specify that a policy holder must be dependent in three or more ADLs before receiving benefits for home health services. Less than 10 percent of the population under 85 and less than 30 percent over 85 have impairment in three or more ADLs.

LTC policies generally pay a fixed fee rather than reimbursing actual charges, with most policies paying between $50 and $100 for a nursing home day. About 70 percent of policies have optional inflation protection, generally increasing benefits at 5 percent per year; such protection will likely be inadequate since from 1965 to 1990, nursing home costs have inflated at an average rate of 10 percent per year and home health care costs at 9.5 percent per year. While inflation protection generally increases premiums by about 25 percent, the added premium cost can reach 90 percent. Nursing home deductibles range from 0 to 100 days. A typical policy provides $50 per day after a 20-day deductible. Assuming the daily cost to be $80, a year's stay would require an out-of-pocket expenditure of $11,950 over and above payment of the insurance premium.

Maximum benefit periods, often four or five years, limit the duration of care, and some policies have a maximum lifetime payout. While most policies are guaranteed renewable, companies can evade this guarantee by dropping an entire class of policy holders.

In summary, the underwriting principle segments the market such that groups are required to "pay their own way" in the purchase of insurance. Because the majority of elderly and disabled people are unable to pay their own way and because younger and healthier people are unlikely to buy the product, the market price of LTC insurance is out of the reach of most of its potential customers. In this sense, universal commercial LTC insurance is unworkable for both the insurance industry and the health consumer.

❖ Does a Public-Private Partnership Provide the Answer?

People who agree with the above analysis may argue that the solution to LTC coverage is a public-private partnership. The public-private partnership is likely to perpetuate a two-class system of LTC. While government subsidies do enlarge the pool of buyers for LTC insurance, former Social Security Commissioner Robert Ball predicts that

> the industry still could not provide coverage to the great majority. . . and millions of higher-risk older consumers will still be unable to meet the expense of even a subsidized premium.

Moreover, the public-private partnership, with multiple competing insurers, is structurally incapable of controlling costs and is likely to replicate for the LTC sector the "runaway inflation that accompanied the expansion of hospital insurance." Even if states are able to control the Medicaid contribution to LTC, it will be difficult to contain the private insurance portion of the program's costs. In the mixed public-private health sector of the U.S. economy, 11 serious cost control measures introduced during the past two decades have been unable to stop the growth in national health care expenditures. The experience of developed nations over the past 10 to 15 years demonstrates that a centralized financing mechanism setting global expenditure caps is the most effective method for controlling costs. Without effective cost control, the public-private partnership is likely to experience over time the erosion of access to LTC—with its greatest impact on the low-income elderly—that inevitably accompanies rising costs.

We are concerned that private insurance for the higher-income population coexisting with public insurance for those with lower incomes will perpetuate and worsen inequality in LTC services.

❖ The Social Insurance Alternative

In a competitive market, insurers who wish to survive must employ the underwriting principle. That principle, by its very nature, places an onerous financial burden on those with lower incomes and greater risks of illness, thereby limiting access to the insurance process for the majority of elderly and disabled people who truly require long-term care. The public-private partnership concept, relying on partial government subsidies, is beset—in somewhat muted form—by the same difficulties. While private LTC insurance and the public-private partnership can alleviate the financial suffering created by long-term care costs for some people, these solutions are not capable of providing universal and equitable LTC insurance for the United States.

What is the alternative? Social insurance is widely utilized in developed nations to finance such programs as retirement, unemployment, disability, and health care. Under social insurance, as exemplified by the U.S. Social Security program, a large proportion of the population is placed together in one single risk pool. Contributions are compulsory and are earmarked such that everyone who contributes is eligible for benefits. Lower-income families tend to receive somewhat greater benefits relative to their level of contribution than those with higher incomes. Most significantly, social insurance represents a transfer of income from younger employed people to older retired people or to people who become prematurely disabled; in that sense, social insurance is in the individual self-interest of contributors, most of whom will require its benefits as they grow older or become disabled.

Large numbers of younger employed people at low risk for needing LTC services are highly unlikely to purchase LTC insurance voluntarily, but they can be called on to pay a compulsory contribution to their own future needs.

In this way, LTC costs can be broadly spread throughout society rather than concentrated—as with private LTC insurance—among a small higher-risk and lower- and fixed-income grouping. Thus, the demography of LTC allows it to fit comfortably within the fabric of social insurance. Social insurance for LTC obviates the underwriting principle inherent in private insurance and bases its payment structure on the ability-to-pay principle—whether through Social Security or income tax financing—by which lower-income persons and those with more severe disability receive more benefits for less cost.

Market failure for private retirement pensions made necessary the enactment of Social Security in 1935. We predict that market failure in the arena of private health and LTC insurance will lead to the development of social insurance in the 1990s. Public LTC insurance ensures that (1) equitable protection and coverage will be provided for the entire population; (2) the right to LTC will be experienced as an earned benefit rather than as a welfare handout; (3) because there is equality, there will be broad support for maintaining and improving the program; (4) the problems of "adverse selection" disappear because there is no need to screen out adverse risks; and (5) with financing through earmarked payments, everyone contributes and the risk is spread across the entire population.

❖ Is Public Long-Term Care Insurance Politically Feasible?

Supporters of the public-private partnership generally cite one reason for failing to embrace public LTC insurance: fear of imposing new taxes or of further straining government deficits. The flaw in this reasoning is that dollars spent on LTC insurance premiums can empty people's wallets as fast or faster than dollars generated through taxes or Social Security payments.

Although public opinion is favorable to social insurance financing for LTC, the public has far less influence than providers and insurers on U.S. health policy. The insurance and nursing home industries oppose public LTC insurance. Moreover, under the special-interest politics traditional in the United States, a minority of elders with ample funds to purchase private LTC insurance may be coopted by the promise of subsidized insurance and asset protection and may thus be reluctant to stand up for the concerns of lower-income seniors.

The political environment is increasingly ripe for health insurance reform and strong cost containment measures. Many Americans expect the federal government, not the private sector, to lead the way. Moreover, the benefits of publicly financed LTC insurance will become clearer with the evolution of current economic trends: the conjuncture of rising LTC costs and declining real family incomes.

❖ Summary

LTC is inadequately financed in the United States. Should such financing be accomplished using the private insurance mechanism, relying on the public sector, or combining public and private approaches? Private insurance rests on the underwriting principle that people with higher risk of illness are rejected from coverage or are charged higher premiums than those with lower risk. In the arena of LTC financing, the underwriting principle creates a dilemma for both insurers and consumers: most policies are purchased by the elderly who face a high risk of needing LTC services; thus premiums are affordable for a relatively small percentage of those who need policies. A public-private partnership, by which the government partially subsidizes private LTC insurance, will be unable to extend affordable LTC insurance to all Americans. The problem is likely to worsen with increases in the number of people requiring LTC and the costs of such care. The economic realities of LTC financing will set the stage for broad public acceptance of social insurance for LTC.

❖ About the Authors

Carroll L. Estes, PH.D., is Director of the Institute for Health and Aging and Professor, Department of Social and Behaviorial Sciences, School of Nursing, University of California, San Francisco.

Thomas S. Bodenheimer, M.D., is Assistant Clinical Professor of Family and Community Medicine, School of Medicine, University of California, San Francisco

❖ Race in the Health of America

S.M. MILLER

At the beginning of this century, W.E.B. DuBois prophetically declared that "the problem of the twentieth century is the problem of the color line—the relation of the darker to the lighter races of men in Asia and Africa, in America and the islands of the sea." Much has happened since DuBois first published his stirring, brilliant essays, but the color line continues to be a disturbing force in the United States as well as in South Africa. Certainly, the issue of race is different today in America from what it is in South Africa, but progress in the United States has not erased racial divisiveness.

❖ Patterns

Health cannot be understood simply as a biological phenomenon. Consequently, the health of African Americans is first discussed in terms of economic and social conditions and racial attitudes, and, then, in terms of the differential data between African Americans and whites.

Economic Conditions

Poverty, as it is now understood in the United States, is defined by a simple measurement: a poverty line is determined by 30-year-old food expenditure data; those with incomes below that line are officially designated as poor. The result is that the poor are probably worse off relative to the rest of society today than they were in 1960.

Racial inequality is measured by comparing African Americans and whites on a variety of conditions. Some view the last 20 years as a movement toward a "melting pot" that has narrowed economic and social differences between the races, so that African Americans are now experiencing the pattern of various ethnic groups who began as poor immigrants and achieved sizable economic gains over time. In this view, race is becoming less important; class-linked factors like schooling are pointed to to explain income differences among African Americans. Others see increasing "polarization"; for them, the differences between African Americans and whites are widening rather than declining. Farley sees both of these perspectives as misleading. My own view is that evolving and revolving sets of relationships form "jagged changes," with some reductions in inequalities, small changes, and some widening inequalities all occurring at the same time.

Poverty and unemployment are two economic areas in which wide racial differences are disturbingly apparent. The white poverty rate in 1986 was 11 percent while the African-American rate was 31 percent. Between 1985 and 1986, the poverty rate declined slightly for both African Americans and whites but was higher than it was in 1978. The percentage of the African-American population below the poverty line was higher in 1986 than in 1969. The most dismal statistic is that 45.6 percent of African-American children were living in households with incomes below the poverty line in 1986; this compares with a figure of 17.7 percent for white children. A broader measure of the poor is the near-poverty line, which refers to all those whose household incomes are below 125 percent of the poverty line; in 1984, more than two-fifths of African Americans lived below this standard compared to somewhat more than one of six whites. While African-American and white rates are closer than they were in 1959, the percentage of African Americans living in poverty or near poverty today does not support a melting-pot interpretation.

The median family income of African-American households is a smaller percentage of white household income today than it was in 1969, 1974, or 1979. The continuing difference is partially due to the growth of single-parent households among African Americans but, controlling for this factor, African-American household incomes are still only 80 percent of those of whites.

The greatest relative gain for African Americans is in the occupational earnings distribution for women. The differences have declined to close to zero; in some comparisons, employed African-American women do better than employed white women. Two limitations should be noted, however. Women, both African American and white, still substantially lag behind white men who have a big income advantage even when differences in education are controlled. When attention shifts to one-parent families, African-American female heads of households have smaller incomes than do their white counterparts.

Unemployment continues to plague African-American communities. The African-American unemployment rate is twice that of whites and has remained at that multiple for 30 years. The unemployment rate among young African-American males is staggering: over 30 percent of those in the labor force. Perhaps of greater damage is the high percentage of young African-American males who are not considered to be looking for employment, those "out of the labor force." "Indeed, all indicators report," according to R. Farley, "that the employment situation of young blacks vis-à-vis that of whites has deteriorated since 1960."

Social Conditions

African-American fertility rates have declined very dramatically and are much closer to those of whites than in 1960. While the number of African-American teenage births has not increased, they are a larger percentage of all African-American births. In part, the importance of these teenage births is due to what sociologist Cheryl Townsend Gilkes terms the "constrained fertility" of older and/or middle-class African-American women who do not have children or have only one. The concern about African-American teenaged mothers is not misplaced but has narrowed the analysis of what is occurring. Some analysts partially attribute the large number of unmarried African-American mothers to a shortage of suitable males—men who are not in jail and are employed at a decent wage.

Housing has decidedly improved, partly because fewer African Americans live in the rural South, but even there African-American housing has advanced. This overall gain may mask the deterioration of housing in many center-city areas and ignores the fact that African Americans spend a higher proportion of their incomes for housing than whites. The general housing gain has been accompanied by continuing and perhaps increasing residential segregation.

Differences between African Americans and whites in years of schooling have decreased markedly, especially for women. A warning sign is that the percentage of African Americans in colleges and universities has declined in recent years, possibly due to the contraction of funds available to minority students. The overall improvement in years of schooling of African Americans is not as positive as it appears, for the gap between African Americans and whites in school skills has not diminished and may have increased. School segregation has been reduced in the South but not in the North.

What is to be made of these changes in economic and social conditions? A sizable slice of the African-American population has improved its economic position, but a large, perhaps larger, group of African Americans is living under very inadequate conditions. American society is less occupationally segregated than in the past, but it is still residentially and (especially in the North) school segregated.

Health Differences

Health is a key indicator of well-being, and health statistics a measure of both progress and continuing inequalities. The health of African Americans has improved considerably, but inequalities between African Americans and whites are still significant.

Mortality Differences   African-American longevity has certainly increased, but a 50 percent difference remains in adjusted death rates for African Americans and whites. If African Americans had the same death rates as whites, 59,000 African-American deaths a year would not occur. Infant mortality is almost twice as frequent among African Americans as whites; this difference is not completely attributable to more young African-American mothers. Except for stomach cancer, the cancer survival rate of African Americans is lower than that of whites.

That considerable progress has been made (and presumably could be made) is revealed in the relative change in mortality rates in the Carolinas between 1900 and 1940. In the earlier year, African-American mortality rates were 40 percent higher in the more urban northern state; by 1940, the New York State African-American mortality rate was at least 25 percent lower than that of the more rural Carolinas. Various influences were involved, but improved housing, water supply, and other public measures in New York undoubtedly contributed to the absolute and relative decline in mortality rates.

Morbidity Differences   African Americans have more undetected diseases than whites, and African-American children may be in worse health than white children. The incidence of low-weight births (and their attendant difficulties) is almost twice as frequent among African Americans as whites. This difference, as with infant mortality, is not completely attributable to more young African-American mothers. Older African Americans suffer from more functional limitations than older whites, a situation of "accelerated" or "unequal" aging, which is associated with poverty, low education, and low-level occupations. At the young end of the age ladder, African-American children seem in worse health than whites.

Self-report data indicate that 50 percent more African Americans than whites are likely to regard themselves as only in fair or poor health. African Americans report more frequently that they feel "little" satisfaction with their health and physical conditions. Yet, there is more undetected disease among African Americans than whites. While whites report more acute conditions, African Americans report more chronic conditions. The statement by Manton et al. that "differentials in health between blacks and whites are pervasive and long-standing, despite recent advances in black life expectancy" summarizes what the morbidity and mortality data record.

To be poor *and* African American is to run the risk of ill health; those who are African American alone share the same health risks.

Use of Facilities   Medicaid has made a difference in access to and use of physicians and hospitals. Differences in utilization (as measured by visits to physicians) between African Americans and whites have been eliminated. A further indication of the importance of financing mechanisms to provide access to and use of medical care is that poor African Americans with health coverage make twice as many visits to physicians as do poor uncovered African Americans.

Nonetheless, some important differences persist. Whites receive more skilled nursing home care than African Americans, although the differences are decreasing. African Americans have a lower cancer survival rate than whites, except for stomach cancer.

Despite Medicaid, 22 percent of African Americans are without any medical insurance coverage, compared to 15 percent of whites. Furthermore, in terms of physician contact, the factors of emergency room and hospital treatment are almost twice as important among African Americans as whites.

While the number of African-American physicians has increased, the rate of increase is diminishing. The fear is that the number of African-American physicians will not expand as a percentage of all physicians as market pressures become more significant and financial aid to African-American student physicians does not expand. Since African-American physicians are more likely to serve African-American patients than do white physicians, this limitation could prove important.

The utilization issue has three important components: (1) Does medical care make a difference? An influential survey by Levine and associates argues the importance of medical attention. The improvement in the survival rates of low-weight babies is attributed to advances in hospital care, not to other conditions. (2) Will African Americans, and especially the African-American poor, take advantage of opportunities for care? Again, surveys show that when poor individuals are provided services that are accessible and appear to them to be useful they will be used, undermining the notion of under-utilization of services by the uneducated or resistant poor. (3) Do finance and delivery systems affect utilization? A strong conclusion is that they "have played a critical role in improvements in health and access to care."

The clear inference is that health conditions of African Americans and the poor can be influenced by governmental actions. The distribution of medical resources relative to need affects causality and successful treatment. General economic gains, the reduction of barriers to African Americans, and governmental programs including occupational health regulations have improved the health situation of African Americans. Some important differences still persist. African-American mortality and morbidity could be reduced by further government-sponsored economic and health programs.

❖ Interpretations

Studies show that racial differences in health exist; numerous investigations report that class or income level influence health conditions. Surprisingly few analyses try to discern whether race is related to health conditions when differences in income levels are controlled. Studies that have made this type of cross-tabulation point to the significance for health of being African American, even at higher income levels.

In Oakland, California, a comparison by Haan et al. of age-specific mortality rates in poverty and nonpoverty areas shows that differences between African Americans are much less than between whites. Improved housing, a lower concentration of poor people, and more income seem to have less effect on African Americans than on whites.

A study of stress found its severity highest in lower-class African Americans and lowest in middle-class whites. This result would confirm the importance of class factors, but an additional comparison by Dohrenwend and

Dohrenwend points to the significance of racial experience: middle-class African Americans and lower-class whites had similar levels of stress.

We turn from the limited data on the important question of whether race as well as class is important in health conditions to interpretations of why African-Americans and white health differences persist despite distinct improvements in African-American health. Five sets of explanations are examined: biological, cultural, economic, social, and service.

Biology

Sickle cell anemia is often cited as a genetic factor among African Americans. But such genetic influences would by themselves not explain higher mortality and morbidity rates for particular disease conditions. A somewhat more compelling argument is that certain African-American genetic characteristics conduce toward disease. But if such biological influences were important, they would interact with economic, social, or psychological situations to produce effects.

It is difficult to explain African-American women's pronounced gains in health without introducing nonbiological influences. Nor would it be easy to contend that African-American health could not be further improved because it has met the limits placed by genetic factors. For example, "there does not appear to be any inherent biological reason for the differences in cervical cancer rates between blacks and whites" according to Baquet and Ringer. Extending this point to other diseases and afflictions, we need to rethink health policy in broader than strictly medical terms. The cloudiness of the concept of race and the many genetic strains among African Americans make purely biological explanations questionable.

Culture

Cultural explanations of health problems have even reached the extreme concept of "health criminals." African Americans and others, because they do not take proper care of themselves (e.g., poor diet, lack of exercise, homicide) are indicted as the producers of their sad fate, driving up medical expenditures and exacting tribute from the careful healthy. Certainly, a healthy life is in large measure produced by what people do for themselves, but not completely. It is too easy to blame a group's behavior rather than to look for broader or deeper causes and outcomes.

Where cultural influences might be significant, the questions become: Why the pattern? What maintains it? Since not all practices of one generation are exhibited in the next, continuity has to be explained rather than taken for granted. In the case of African-American and white health differences, the implication is that African Americans do not behave in ways that are as conducive to health as do whites. The further implication is that conditions for African Americans and whites are the same and that health differences are due to malperformance on the part of African Americans.

A cultural explanation does not adequately reveal the dynamics of at least one health hazard, particularly important for African Americans, which seems particularly suited for such an explanation—the high incidence of obesity. The continuation of eating habits of a poor childhood that relied on cheap, fattening food; work and family tensions that make planned, diet-conscious eating difficult; inadequate incomes that reduce possibilities and choices; a low sense of destiny control; and limited knowledge are all implicated in obesity. Even in this most personal of behavior, simply relying on an explanation in terms of habit and attitudes may be inadequate. Nor does the cultural approach lead to a comprehensive strategy for dealing with the issue.

Economic Factors

"To be a poor man is hard, but to be a poor race in a land of dollars is the very bottom of hardships," according to W.E.B. DuBois. African-American and white disparities in economic conditions contribute to health differentials despite African-American gains. Since a much larger and very sizable slice of African Americans is poor, economic conditions and their ramifications undoubtedly adversely affect African-American health. Inadequate incomes affect many aspects of daily life that impinge on health. These range from housing problems (e.g., rat-infested neighborhoods and over-crowding, which quicken the spread of communicable diseases), malnutrition, the stress of struggling to make ends meet, and dangerous jobs. Job and housing conditions may expose African Americans to certain cancers to a much greater extent than whites.

The emphasis on improvements in economic gains for African Americans ignores the possibility that early deprivation can affect later health states. Nutritional deprivation of children during World War I affected their health, especially of women, in later life. Recent advances in material circumstances of African Americans may not overcome the effect of earlier life experiences. With perhaps one half of African-American children under the age of 6 living in poverty, this current deprivation may maintain later health differences, even if many of these children later improve their economic conditions.

Social Explanations

The problem is not only that of poverty but of economic and social inequalities associated with race. A British study provides a suggestive line of thought: a pronounced difference in mortality risk exists between high- and low-level members of the white-collar civil service. Both groups had secure tenure, relatively good pay, and fringe benefits. The author's point is that hierarchy produces tensions and stresses even where individuals seem somewhat similarly situated. For African Americans in the United States the sense of economic inequality, social distance, discrimination, and hierarchy—of not being accorded full equality—is undoubtedly strong and persisting. In the words of H.W. Neighbors, racial discrimination probably "exacerbates the mental health-damaging effects of poverty status among blacks."

In the health area, then, the call for individuals to change to more positive health practices may not be effective among African Americans because the shift requires exploration of new roles, norms, and practices, as well as access to facilities, information, and support: "Maladaptive patterns of coping . . . and hazardous forms of consumption . . . can be seen to reflect the molding of social and cultural life by contemporary economic (and race) relations," according to M. Susser and associates.

A more specific influence on African Americans may be widespread and disturbing uprooting and resettlement. Although the African-American population of center-city areas is declining, it may be that new African Americans are moving in as long-time residents move out. The data on this point are uncertain. The new residents may experience heavy pressures in accommodating to a difficult set of center-city circumstances and lack the social supports that would be helpful.

What is clear is that African-American neighborhoods suffer disruption resulting from urban renewal, abandonment, and arson. People are forced to move, severing networks of relationships, which are important for social well-being and which impinge on health, especially of the aged.

Some investigators believe that racial discrimination is almost inevitable in a market economy and infer that the stress resulting from discrimination continues to affect health. Many successful African Americans point not only to limitations on their occupational progress but to stressful encounters around the job.

Medical Services

Despite noticeable improvements in health care for the poor and African Americans resulting from Medicare and Medicaid, there is still less adequate medical attention for African Americans than whites. The quality of health care is likely to be better in white areas, especially in access to physicians and hospitals. At every income level, African Americans have substantially higher reliance on emergency room and outpatient departments for contacts with physicians than do whites. Indeed, racial differences are greater above the $10,000 annual income level than below it. Since 1980, African Americans have experienced decreased medical attention as a result of federal cutbacks. If such patterns continue, African-American and white differences in health services will not be reduced.

❖ Policy

The burdens of knowledge are heavy. Knowing that health care can be improved and health inequalities reduced, it is immoral as well as economically wasteful to refuse to pursue these goals. For in the realm of health, rights to equal consideration and conditions are much less controversial than in the realm of employment. In the 1960s, a president of the American Medical Association declared that health care was a privilege, not a right. Today, few would agree. There is now a consensus that African Americans should have mortality and morbidity rates much closer to those of whites. Much less agreement exists about what to do to close the gaps.

An everchanging, rhythmic biotic adventure of varying individuals, health is a part of the weave of life, coloring it brightly here, subtly shading it there, obvious in one place, obscure—almost lost—in another.
    —Benjamin A. Kogan

Policy Criteria

In this section, we deal with three policy issues: creaming, poverty or inequality reduction, and universality vs. targeting.

Creaming The jagged progress characteristic of African Americans can be partly considered a result of creaming. Creaming is a policy, intentional or unintended, of concentrating on the "easiest cases." Where the poor or disadvantaged are involved, it improves the situation of the better-off of the badly-off population—those least disadvantaged of a disadvantaged group. The expectation is that as each layer moves up, those worse off gradually become the recipients of attention and will then improve their situation.

The methods which led to the improvement among the better-off of the badly-off will be equally useful for the worse-off who were left behind; the departure of the better-off will not adversely affect the worst-off who remain. Both assumptions are frequently, perhaps usually, wrong.

Poverty Reduction or Equality Is the objective only to reduce poverty or unemployment among African Americans because of the damage inflicted by that economic condition? Or is it to reduce economic inequalities between African Americans and whites? In the latter case, it would be unsatisfactory if African-American poverty rates were reduced while white household income increased and widened the gap between African Americans and whites. Despite strong disagreements about the goal of economic equality, the dismay when economic inequality between African Americans and whites is increasing indicates widespread agreement that these inequalities should be decreasing, even if complete equality is not the objective.

The consensus seems to be that poverty and inequality should not be disproportionately concentrated in an ascriptive group (ie., one characterized by unchangeable characteristics like race, ethnicity, or gender), and should be dwindling rather than expanding. While this outlook is not as demanding as the right to equal health and health care, it demands reductions in inequalities as well as in poverty.

The underlying issue from the perspective of health policy is the strong likelihood that the persistence of economic, social, and political inequalities, even if African-American poverty is reduced, is injurious to the health of African Americans. This outlook treats equality as instrumental to health; the deeper question is, of course, the moral one of the nature of our obligations to one another.

African-American and white equality may be insufficient in some health respects. The concept of "excess deaths" points to American mortality rates for certain diseases that exceed those of other nations. More effective interventions would be likely to lower American rates. If African-American rates were the same as white rates, that achievement would be unsatisfactory. The case of "excess deaths" illustrates a general point about equality: incorporating the excluded or disadvantaged into existing structures and improving their situation may be inadequate; the general situation for all may have to be improved. American medical care may have to face that challenge.

Universality or Targeting The specific policy questions of how to improve the situation of African Americans is part of the general policy debate about the competing principles of, on one hand, universality or comprehensiveness and, on the other, targeting, selectivity, or means-testing. The first set of terms refers to programs available to (almost) all; by virtue of being a citizen, resident, or wage earner, one receives benefits from a program. In practice, no program is available to everybody, but Social Security and Medicare come closest to it. Age and past contributions for the former and age alone for the latter make one eligible for benefits. The targeted principle sets out conditions, usually of income inadequacy, that must be met in order to receive benefits. Eligibility is not on the basis of a noneconomic characteristic like age or sickness alone; rather, one must show need, the inability to provide for one's household, or to seek the needed service in the marketplace. Targeted programs like Medicaid are aimed at "needy" persons; untargeted or universal programs do not require that the individual or household demonstrate a lack of means to cover needs.

The advantage of a universal-type program available to (almost) all is that it builds support because so many, especially politically potent nonpoor persons, benefit from it. Other gains are that it avoids stigmatization of beneficiaries, may promote social solidarity by establishing institutions and activities in which all are involved (at least at some point in their lives), and is likely to promote higher quality service because of the threat of widespread political discontent if quality is low or deteriorating.

The negative side, emphasized by economists in their benefit-cost calculations, is "leakage," diffusion of program resources, which reduces the "target efficiency" of a program because it aids those not in need. By providing to all rather than to only those with insufficient resources, less is available to low-income people who need more substantial aid. Public resources are "wasted" or "leaked" to those who could handle the burden of the costs that they face. By eliminating this diffusion and concentrating the public program on those with real resource needs, more funds would be available to those who need them.

The assumption is that cost savings resulting from targeting and removal of benefits from those who do not lack resources would lead to a practice where greater resources are expended on those who lack means. No iron law of policy or politics dictates that result.

Indeed, the argument against selectivity or targeting goes further and contends that participants in means-tested programs tend to be or feel stigmatized, so that some of the benefits to them of the program may be lost because of the burden of the disgrace.

Programs that are seen as for the poor, the underclass, welfare cheats, and African Americans in general face political, financial, and operational obstacles. The contrast between a universal program like Social Security and a targeted program like Aid to Families with Dependent Children (AFDC) is instructive: in the 1970s and 1980s, Social Security payments more than kept up with inflation while AFDC suffered real income losses as many states did not increase benefits at all despite the high rise in prices.

The Reagan administration's objectives of drastic reductions in the levels of and eligibility for means-tested programs were largely unsuccessful. That is not to say that they achieved no significant reductions, but they could not institute the depth of cuts that were initially predicted. Considerable public and political pressure for maintenance of these programs blocked many Reagan efforts. While many people are critical of something called "the welfare state," they often recognize the usefulness of specific programs.

The first line of defense or improvement should be universal programs; they are likely to be better programs and to have strong political constituencies. The general principle is to make the needs of the African-American low-income population part of efforts to improve the situation of all or most Americans. Where that principle is inadequate, then targeting within the universal program can be a desirable and effective instrument. The outstanding example of the merger of these approaches is the Social Security program, which favors low-income participants. Their benefits are greater relative to their contributions than are those with higher income. Differences in preretirement wage incomes are narrowed in postretirement Social Security benefits. Elderly African Americans who suffered from low wages during their working lives are somewhat improved relative to those who were in a better situation in the preretirement period. Yet, elderly African Americans are not singled out for this gain, a situation which makes that advance more politically secure.

In practice, both universality and targeting have to be utilized. When and how are the issues. Universality is the policy of first resort, but such programs often cream, are more effectively utilized by those with more education and resources, provide inadequate resources for those in greatest need, and have only a limited effect on reducing economic inequalities. Universality reduces the likelihood of two Americas or two sets of institutions—one for the "disadvantaged," the other for those who are better off. It improves the political chances of maintaining and improving funding for programs and enhancing their quality. Nonetheless, universality has to be supplemented and sometimes supplanted by targeting on those who are disadvantaged and discriminated against.

Economic and Social Policies

Employment is a prime area for improvement of the situation of African Americans—more and better jobs and a more effective upgrading of existing jobs are all needed. Following the approach just discussed, the first step is an expanding economy that produces more jobs and good jobs at that. African Americans do better in an expanding than in a contracting economy. An effective macroeconomic policy that stimulates the economy is an important first step. At issue within job growth is the quality of jobs produced. Many of the new jobs of the 1970s and 1980s have been low-paying, part-time, and devoid of fringe benefits; many of the good blue-collar jobs in mass-production industries have disappeared.

An increase in jobs, especially good jobs, does not assure that African Americans will get them. Affirmative action, to which we shall return, is one route. Encouraging African-American entrepreneurship is another. But education, training, improved transportation, and child care are of greater importance in helping African Americans to move into good jobs in greater numbers.

The current emphasis on higher standards in public education may worsen the schooling of many poor and African American children if particular effort is not put into improving their learning. Federal aid to education has diminished; the downward cycle should be reversed. The Elementary and Secondary Education Act, which provides funding to school districts with many low-income children, should be better funded and strengthened to insure that the funds are spent in ways that benefit low-income students.

A difficulty within the dual pressures on schools today—pressures toward "excellence" as well as on general learning and vocational preparation—is that schools for the poor, especially the African-American poor, may become so heavily vocationalized that students learn little of the world around them. If the vocational training does not lead to a good job and provides few adaptable skills, then poor African Americans will be doubly handicapped—ill-prepared for employment and uninformed about significant matters. And, if they fail to measure up to "excellence," they will drop out or be pushed out of school.

The United States lacks a comprehensive, accessible, well-funded system of worker training and development like the permanent or recurrent education schemes of France and Sweden. We have community colleges, adult education programs, and nationally funded and state and locally operated job training programs. They do not add up to a national program with priorities and direction. A comprehensive national program is needed with specific targeting to improve the employment prospects of those who are more difficult to place. At the same time, access to higher education should be facilitated by expanding aid and loan programs for low-income students. Where higher education is concerned, targeted financial help is not stigmatizing nor politically unattractive.

Affirmative action has a definite role to play, but it is certainly not the most important item on the economic agenda for African Americans. Without affirmative action, many educated and trained African Americans would not have attained middle-class positions. Indeed, they might not have been willing to seek further education and training if they did not believe that affirmative action would open up positions that had been closed to their parents.

A charge against it is that it has not improved the situation much for those African Americans with limited schooling and training and low initial job motivation and capacity. To benefit the African-American poor, not only does affirmative action need to be strengthened, but programs going beyond it need to be devised.

Even with a successful welfare-type program, direct aid or transfers to low-income people would still be necessary. Again, if universal programs reduced the need for targeted transfer, the poor would benefit. Improving Social Security benefits for low-wage earners would benefit the aged African-American poor without invoking a special system for them. If unemployment insurance payments were weighted so that not only previous wage income but the number of members in the household influenced the benefit, some large unemployed white and African-American families would gain.

Health Services

The attention to improving financial access to medical personnel and hospital care draws concern away from the advancement of public health measures (e.g., reduction of air and water pollution, improved regulation of food and drugs, reduction of work injuries and diseases, elimination of dangerous dumps). Public health measures are particularly important for lower-income citizens. Good health is not only a result of what physicians and hospitals do for us, or what we do for ourselves; our environments, broadly viewed, are implicated in our health status.

A final, difficult-to-resolve issue is how much should be spent on health measures to improve health and how much on improving economic and social conditions that affect health. Class and race data point inevitably to the conclusion that improving incomes and social conditions would enhance the health of African Americans, especially low-income African Americans. Even those who espouse the importance of personal health practices (e.g., quitting smoking, good nutrition, exercise) have to question whether improved incomes or social conditions will do more for health outcomes than medical interventions or health education. It is difficult to change practices without changing circumstances. Is the way to improve the health of African Americans through the economy and society rather than through the clinic, hospital, or health maintenance organization? Reducing economic and social inequalities may be the road to the achievement of individual health and a healthy society.

❖ About the Author

Seymour M. Miller, PH.D., is a professor emeritusof sociology, Boston University, Boston, Massachusetts

❖ Women's Health: Review and Research Agenda as We Approach the 21st Century

JUDITH RODIN AND JEANNETTE R. ICKOVICS

❖ Review of the Literature

Health is a complex and multidetermined issue, influenced by a wide variety of factors: physiological, biochemical, psychological, environmental, and social. As society approaches the 21st century, we believe that it is an important time to assess what we know—and what we do not know—regarding women's health in particular. One may ask, "Why a focus on *women's* health?" The answers are clear. Certain health concerns are unique to women (e.g., hysterectomy, dysmenorrhea, cesarean section, breast cancer) or disproportionately affect women (e.g, rheumatoid arthritis, lupus, osteoporosis, eating disorders). Even for health issues that affect both women and men, most research has been limited to male subjects, leaving a large gap in our knowledge base concerning women's health. Sex differences in morbidity and mortality have been documented. Furthermore, health risks and enhancements may operate differently for women and men, thereby confirming the need to examine women's health as distinct from men's health.

Psychosocial factors are also likely to differentially affect women's and men's health. Women and men engage in social roles that often differ, if not in quantity, certainly in quality. Sex differences in role expectations, environmental qualities, role burdens related to the domains of work and family, and abilities to adapt and cope with stressful situations may also have a distinctive impact on health. Imbalances in social roles, and subsequently in power, equality, and control, are likely to affect women's health adversely. Within these roles, women are more likely than men to be subjected to interpersonal violence, sexual discrimination, and harassment.

Health treatment also raises concerns specific to women. For instance, 70% of all psychoactive medications (e.g., antidepressants, tranquilizers) are prescribed to women, in part because of the stereotype that women's health complaints are more emotionally laden and psychosomatic than men's. In addition, two thirds of all surgical procedures in this country are performed on women. Obstetrical and gynecological surgery is the most frequent category, with 1,700 hysterectomies performed daily. The medical benefits of these surgeries do not seem to outweigh the health and psychological risks. Ironically, although in the reproductive area women are exposed to a large number of technologies, in other areas of medical practice such as coronary health, they may inappropriately receive fewer technological interventions. Inadequate access to quality health care and health insurance is more likely to affect women, in large part because women are more likely than men to be poor. Finally, women are underrepresented as health care professionals. Although women are entering medical school in greater numbers, sex biases persist in training and professional status: furthermore, the sex of the physician does affect treatment and patient-doctor interaction.

Perhaps there has been less study of women's health because, despite the risks just specified, women live longer. Although women continue to maintain a mortality advantage over men, this advantage has been steadily declining over the past decade. Moreoever, regardless of whether this declining trend continues, the future portends major changes that will significantly affect women's health. For instance, looking toward the 21st century, we must now begin to consider threats to women's health because of environmental factors such as acquired immunodeficiency syndrome (AIDS) and scientific developments such as reproductive technologies. Psychosocial factors that have a major impact on health—social roles, social support, self-efficacy, stress, and coping—are also likely to change in their degree and complexion over the coming decade. These reasons provide a strong rationale for the urgent need to study women's health.

Sex Differentials in Mortality and Morbidity

Mortality As Strickland has noted, "At every moment across the life span, from conception to death, girls and women are on the average biologically more advantaged and live longer than boys and men." Approximately 125 male fetuses are conceived for every 100 female fetuses, and 27% more boys than girls die in the first year of life. For those who celebrate a century of life, only one man is alive for every five women. At every age in between, more men than women die. These data vary according to social class and ethnic backgrounds, but, nonetheless, African-American women still have lower overall mortality rates than both African-American and white men.

Men and women also differ by cause of death. In the United States in 1980, the age-adjusted mortality rate for each of the 12 leading causes of death was higher for men than women. The sex ratio, men to women, varied, respectively, from 3.86:1 for homicide to 1.02:1 for diabetes. Those causes, with nearly a twofold or greater difference in the sex ratio in decreasing order after homicide, were respiratory cancer, suicide, chronic obstructive pulmonary disease, accidents, cirrhosis of the liver, and heart disease. Although the actual number of men who die of coronary heart disease (CHD) is greater than the number of women who die of coronary disease, it is important to note that CHD is the leading cause of death for both women and men.

Two major categories of explanation have been proposed to account for the sex differential in mortality: first, a biological explanation that women are biologically more advantaged than men and, second, a social or lifestyle explanation that men behave in ways more damaging to their health. There are many ways that biological protection could be conferred for women. Some investigators suggest that genetic differences are one mechanism: the additional and redundant genetic material furnished by females' second X chromosome may be protective. In contrast, the male Y chromosome is specialized solely for the development of the male reproductive tract, and it carries no significant additional information. Others believe that understanding hormonal differences between women and men across the life cycle may be the pivotal element in understanding sex differences in health.

Morbidity In spite of women's biological and behavioral advantage with regard to mortality, women appear to have greater morbidity than men. *Morbidity* can be defined as generalized poor health, a specific illness, or the sum of a number of illnesses. These may be identified by self-reported occurrence, restricted activity, number of doctor visits or hospitalizations, or actual screening examinations. In a review of morbidity figures, Wingard found that most categories of self-reported chronic conditions and all acute conditions were more common for women than men, except injuries. Hypertension is usually more common in men before the age of 60 and in women after the age of 60. Obesity is higher for women in most samples, and results from most studies indicate that women have poorer vision and dental status, whereas men have poorer hearing. Higher proportions of women than men have diabetes, anemia, and respiratory and gastrointestinal problems. Rheumatoid arthritis is three times more common in women than men, and systemic lupus erythematosus (lupus) is 10 times more likely among women than men.

Considering health behaviors, women report more acute symptoms than do men, and the epidemiological evidence supports this. Women have higher rates of restricted activity, disability, and physician visits; they also have higher levels of prescription and nonprescription drug use. On the other hand, men have longer hospital stays, and there is no difference in total work-loss days. In an attempt to reconcile these seemingly contradictory data on morbidity and mortality, the following interpretation has been put forth. Although women are more frequently ill, they suffer from problems that are serious but not life-threatening: these conditions lead to symptoms, disability, and medical care, but not death. Men are sick less often, but their illnesses and injuries are more severe: men have higher rates of chronic diseases that are the leading causes of death.

Explanations for the sex differences in morbidity come from a variety of sources. Some are more clearly psychological. For example, there are thought to be differences between women and men in how they judge their own health and in subsequent health-reporting behavior. However, these beliefs about gender differences in health perceptions and reporting behavior have not received consistent empirical support. Second, stress has emerged as a central explanatory construct to account for sex differences in physical health. This is not surprising inasmuch as stress has a prominent place in the conceptual frameworks of research into psychological distress. Demographic variables have also been invoked as explanations. For instance, socioeconomic status is clearly related to morbidity: poverty rates are significantly higher for women than for men, compounding the rates of women's morbidity. Furthermore, the sex differential in age, with many more women than men in the oldest age groups, also contributes to women's excess morbidity.

Changing Trends in Mortality and Morbidity

Although women continue to hold a mortality advantage, this advantage has decreased in recent years. The sex-mortality ratio has taken a clear turn downward and has been slowly but steadily declined during the 1980s. This indicates a declining advantage for women. The sex-mortality ratio has been declining especially for persons aged 45 years and older. There are several changes in the epidemiology of the major diseases that appear to have caused this shifting mortality trend. The death rate from heart disease has been decreasing steadily across the last 30 years for men, and staying about the same for women. Cancer rates, which rose more rapidly for men than for women until 1979, declined more rapidly for men than for women in the 1980s.

We propose that these epidemiologic shifts are attributable, in large part, to the psychological and behavioral effects of major social trends—in particular, changes that women and men have undergone during the past few decades in social structure and roles. To the extent that variations in health are related to variations in life-style, there should be corresponding shifts in the rates of disorder. As reported earlier, these changes are evident. We consider two major social and life-style changes—women's increased substance use and work-force participation—that have led to psychological and behavioral outcomes with consequences for health.

Substance Use and Health

Epidemiologic Trends In recent years, there has been a striking increase in smoking among women, followed by a great increase in women's rates of lung cancer. Smoking rates among women continue to increase, whereas smoking rates among men are decreasing substantially. Overall, women's smoking rates began to decline later than men's, and they are declining at a slower rate: this has resulted in converging rates of smoking for women and men. These trends are largely responsible for the narrowing gap in lung cancer deaths: smoking accounts for 85% of lung cancer deaths. The Centers for Disease Control (CDC) reported that between 1979 and 1986 lung cancer deaths rose 7 percent among men and 44 percent among women. In 1986, lung cancer surpassed breast cancer as the leading cause of cancer death for U.S. women.

National data also show changes in alcohol consumption. Although men continue to drink more and in greater quantities than women, the number of women (particularly younger women) who drink has increased slightly over the past three decades. Moreover, problem drinking has significantly increased among women. The increased use of alcohol among women is especially distressing in light of recent evidence suggesting that even moderate alcohol consumption is associated with up to a 50 percent elevation in the risk of breast cancer. Another recent study suggested that alcohol abuse puts women at a dramatically increased risk of suicide; alcoholic women were nearly 5 times more likely than nonalcoholic women to attempt suicide.

Psychological and Behavioral Determinants and Consequences In the past, adherence to traditional sex role expectations concerning appropriate female and male behavior had a dramatic effect on producing sex differences in health-related behaviors and subsequent health. For example, expectations that men more than women use guns, take physical risks in recreation, and have certain types of physically risky jobs have contributed to men's engaging in these behaviors, and have resulted in higher rates of accidents among men. Until relatively recently, a major reason for sex differences in smoking and drinking has been traditional expectations concerning appropriate behavior of women and men. Although there had been widespread social disapproval for women engaging in smoking and drinking, for men these behaviors have often been considered a rite of passage. These expectations have changed: women are now smoking and drinking with no social risk of doing something inappropriate. In fact, given the sharp increase in smoking and drinking among young women, it appears that these behaviors have also become a rite of passage for women. As the cigarette advertisers would like us to believe, women have come a long way, baby!

Work-Force Participation and Health

Epidemiologic Trends Since World War II there has been a dramatic movement of women into the labor force. In 1986, two thirds of all women aged 20 to 64 were in the labor force. This rate is expected to increase to 81% by the year 2000, with 66 million women projected to be in the labor force at that time. Contributing to this trend is the rapidly increasing workforce participation of married women and those with young children. It is no longer viable to discuss women's traditional roles: less than 7% of all families consist of a father working and a mother at home with one or more children. Although the impact of these changes is far-reaching, we focus on the health effects in particular.

LaCroix and Haynes have summarized the results of recent studies comparing risk factors for chronic diseases and health-status indicators among employed and nonemployed women. In almost all studies, employed women are healthier than nonemployed women. The evidence showing similar or more favorable health profiles among employed women is strengthened by the consistency of results, using both nationally representative and geographically circumscribed community populations and a variety of health outcome variables.

Verbrugge provided striking support for the importance of the psychological benefits of work-force participation on health. She showed that women who have less employment are at greater risk, especially those with greater felt stress and unhappiness, stronger feelings of vulnerability to illness and formal time constraints, and less physical activity or exercise. Other studies have also demonstrated that the lack of employment is a risk factor for women's health.

It is difficult to establish the direction of causality in these relationships. Employment may be directly health-promoting and risk-reducing for women (i.e., social causation), or women in poor health may be unable to obtain or keep jobs (i.e., social selection). The social causation approach has been supported in the San Antonio Heart Study, in which the relations between employment status and cardiovascular risk factors (e.g., triglyceride levels, lipoprotein profiles) were examined. Even after excluding all women with any history of medically diagnosed chronic conditions, the health advantage of employed women persists.

Psychological and Behavioral Determinants and Consequences Sorensen and Verbrugge reviewed three theoretical models by which the changes in work-force participation might lead to changes in health outcomes. The *job stress model* posits that the stress and strain of employment will ultimately harm women's health. Although the data thus far do not support this alternative, theoretically it is possible that longer term health-damaging effects may occur or that health effects other than cardiovascular disease may be important to consider. In opposition is the *health benefits model*, emphasizing the direct advantages of employment (e.g., financial remuneration, self-esteem, control, social support) that maintain and enhance women's health. Finally, the *role expansion model* considers the indirect advantages of employment, suggesting that adding the work role enhances health through increased opportunities for reward and satisfaction; furthermore, satisfaction in one role may provide protection against strain in another role.

Multiple Roles Women are not only workers but also parents and spouses who have increasing demands for a variety of productive activities. Of course, women and men have always had multiple roles. However, women experience greater interrole conflict and overload than do men.

One key difference appears to be women's greater family responsibilities. Even when both spouses work, wives perform a disproportionate share of child care and household tasks, regardless of social class.

Studies examining multiple roles in relation to both perceived and objective health status have shown that on the average, in spite of household and other strains, the more roles a woman occupies, the healthier she is likely to be. Employed married parents have the best health profile, whereas people with none of these roles have the worst profile. Involvement in multiple roles expands potential resources and rewards, including alternate sources of self-esteem, control, and social support; in turn, these benefits may enhance both mental and physical health. Multiple roles may also provide cognitive cushioning in the face of stress.

Role Quality   The nature and quality of a woman's experiences within roles, not merely role occupancy per se, are critical to understanding the processes that affect her health. Not all roles are good for women. When role context or quality is ignored, one may inaccurately attribute findings to individual differences rather than to differences in structural factors or the quality of roles. For instance, in a study of midlife women, Baruch and Barnett found that qualitative aspects of role involvement were more strongly related to dimensions of well-being than either role occupancy or the number of roles occupied. Verbrugge suggested that having low quality roles such as those with time constraints, irregular schedules, and low control may jeopardize health, whereas having high quality roles, even if they are numerous, may help maintain or enhance health. Assessment of these psychological variables illuminates our understanding of the relation between multiple roles and health, and of gender differences in this relationship.

Summary

The existence of sex differences in morbidity and mortality, and in the psychological and social processes that influence these indicators of health, support the need to examine women's health independently of men's health. Biological differences between the sexes have been thought to play a major role in the sex differentials in health. Although they undoubtedly do, social factors—particularly as they relate to life-style and roles— may be more powerful predictors of current changes in health trends. Increased substance use has certainly had an adverse impact on women's health, resulting in higher cancer rates. In contrast, and contrary to expectations, increased work-force participation has had a beneficial impact on women's health. These changes in gender-related trends in substance use and work-force participation have influenced perceived adequacy of roles, access to social support, and opportunities for challenges to and enhancement of self-efficacy. Examination of psychological and behavioral consequences of both social and biological factors, as well as their interaction, must continue to be the focus of research attention.

❖ An Agenda for Women's Health Research

Current trends and projections have guided the development of this research agenda. As the review demonstrated, the profiles and patterns of risk factors and illness by gender appear to be changing. If this trend continues, psychological research will be urgently needed to help identify its causes. Moreover, the future portends additional changes that will have significant effects on women's health. These also demand research attention.

In this section, we point to some overriding issues that impact upon a scientific research agenda for women's health. These recommendations apply to research on a variety of specific topics. We then turn to a selective review of health concerns facing women as we approach the 21st century: AIDS, uses of clinical psychopharmacology, the increased use of exogenous steroid hormones (i.e., oral contraceptives, hormone replacement therapy), the aging of the population, and reproductive technologies.

These topics reflect a sampling of issues that deserve significant research attention; they are not intended to serve as an exhaustive list.

General Recommendations for Research

First and foremost, women must be included as subjects in health research. Despite a policy established more than three years ago by the National Institutes of Health that urged that women be included in study populations, the U.S. General Accounting Office recently reported that this policy has not yet been adequately implemented. As in the past, white men continue to be almost exclusively studied in major health care and pharmacological research. Even in animal-model research, male animals are almost always used. Female animals and humans are often dismissed as study subjects because their normal hormonal fluctuations are seen as potentially contaminating research results. An additional explanation for women's exclusion from this research includes avoiding possible toxic exposure to women of childbearing age. Although this policy is well intended, it has limited women's participation as research subjects. The consequence is that we do not know whether many of these research findings can be generalized to women. However, there are groups of women who are at little or no risk of becoming pregnant (e.g., women with hysterectomies, women whose monogamous partner has had a vasectomy, lesbians not planning to have children, celibate women), and informed consent can protect all research subjects. Finally, the expense of increasing sample size to include women has often effectively served to exclude them.

Unfortunately, health results from studies of men may not be reliably extended to women. Research must include outcome measures differentially associated with women and men in order to clarify how sex differences may operate. Although it might seem ideal to undertake large-scale, multisite, nationally representative, prospective studies on women's health, cost and feasibility would likely be prohibitive. Therefore, smaller, well-designed studies that focus on sex and gender in creative ways are also encouraged.

Second, research on health concerns that uniquely or disproportionately affect women must be the focus of increased research attention. Institutional funding at equitable levels should be allocated to study related health and illness factors. Funding is an issue of cost-benefit determination. The devaluation of women's health research precludes spending funds that would adequately address women's health needs. When women are included in research, health has been examined in the major disease categories (e.g., cancer, cardiovascular disease). What have not yet been examined in depth are other causes of the increasing trends in the physical disorders that disproportionately affect women, such as menstrual dysfunction, rheumatoid arthritis, lupus, and gastrointestinal disorders. Morbidity and mortality rates depend upon which illness or disease is specified. Researchers must choose health-outcome measures with sensitivity to sex differences in prevalence.

Third, gender-comparative research is particularly important if we are to move toward a more comprehensive understanding of health. Although often rejected because of inherent methodological difficulties, gender-comparative research is an extension of the long, empirical tradition of comparative methods in neuroscience and physiology. This type of research would likely lead to improvements in the health and health care of both women and men. Only through the use of methodologically sound gender-comparative research can we begin to disentangle the complex interaction between biological and social factors and their impact on health.

Fourth, women cannot be treated as a homogeneous group. Striking health differences exist on the basis of race and ethnicity. According to U.S. population data on disease prevalence, minority women experience higher rates of maternal and infant mortality and higher incidence of diabetes, hypertension, cardiovascular disease, AIDS, and certain types of cancer. Furthermore, they have a lower life expectancy than their white counterparts. Sociocultural factors such as lower socioeconomic status, limited access to health care, lower levels of education and employment, and higher stress have an adverse effect on the health of minority women. Clearly, continued research and intervention must focus on the special needs of minority women. Otherwise, their health status will continue to fall further behind other members of this society.

Fifth, in addition to health differences by race and ethnicity, differences also exist across the life cycle. There is a complex interaction between sex and age that varies with both cause and outcome (morbidity vs. mortality). In order to enhance and more accurately predict women's future health, longitudinal and life-course perspectives must be incorporated into research plans. Changes between cohorts and within cohorts across time must be evaluated.

Although health and illness can be measured cross-sectionally, longitudinal data are necessary in order to identify patterns of stability or change that influence women's health outcomes over time. For instance, there has been only minimal analysis of the health effects of multiple roles at various points in the family cycle; however, the demands of family and career fluctuate according to children's ages and stages of career development. Each phase of the individual and family life cycle should be analyzed separately to enhance our understanding of the link between roles and health, and so that appropriate service interventions and policies can be developed.

Conclusions

This article raises a number of issues for serious consideration. Women have higher morbidity rates, yet lower mortality rates. Both social and biological factors account for this seeming contradiction. But recently, concurrent with dramatic changes in life-style and social roles for women, mortality rates have shifted, resulting in a decreasing advantage for women. Explaining the health consequences of these dynamic changes requires understanding of the health effects of psychological and social variables such as perceived control, the experience of life roles, social support, and the redefinition of gender roles.

In advocating new research issues and questions, we have emphasized that women must be included in health research, from broad-perspective health trials to clinical pharmacology studies. Furthermore, institutional funding at equitable levels should be allocated to research on health issues that disproportionately or uniquely affect women. In order to best prepare for the 21st century, we must also look ahead to future trends that will have significant impact on women's health, such as the spread of AIDS, the extension of the life span, and the development of reproductive technologies.

Finally, research findings must be responsibly integrated into treatment approaches and public policy. Eliminating sex bias in health status, health research, health care, and health policies can be the first step toward eliminating other inequities in the home and workplace. We must be bold and ambitious in our aspirations for women's health, now and in the future.

❖ About the Authors

Judith Rodin, PH.D., is Provost of Yale University and the Philip R. Allen Professor of Psychology and Professor of Psychiatry and Medicine at Yale University, New Haven, Connecticut.

Jeannette R. Ickovics, PH.D., is Associate Research Scientist, Department of Psychology, Yale University, New Haven, Connecticut.

❖ The Women's Health Movement: A Critique of Medical Enterprise and the Position of Women

MARY K. ZIMMERMAN

Methods and conclusions formed by one half the race only must necessarily require revision as the other half of humanity rises into conscious responsibility.
—Elizabeth Blackwell, M.D. (1889)

In this chapter, we examine the women's health movement as a challenge to many of the assumptions and practices of mainstream modern medicine. In so doing, we not only learn about a significant health care development in its own right, but we also expand our understanding of the social nature of medical knowledge, institutions, and practice. The Women's Health Movement is not the only current challenge to modern medicine, but it is the most deeply rooted historically as well as the most analytically sophisticated. Catherine Reissman sees the women's health movement as exemplary of a broad critique of contemporary medicine that calls into question (1) "medicalization," the increasing tendency to apply medical definitions and control to phenomena not previously thought of as medical problems; (2) standard treatments that rely heavily on intervention and technology rather than prevention and self-care; and (3) typical medical power relations, which are highly asymmetric and where professional authority prevails with minimal reciprocity between doctor and patient and little involvement of family or friends. In addition, the feminist critique of medicine shows how the medical care system contributes to the control and maintenance of conventional status hierarchies and role relationships, mirroring and reproducing gender inequality in society.

Throughout history, human beings have developed numerous ways of interpreting and assigning meaning to diseases and other health problems. These definitions emerge from group interaction as members jointly construct their shared reality. The dominant system of medical knowledge and practice in the Western world today, deeply embedded in the institutions of our society and largely taken for granted, is an excellent example of such a "reality." We tend to see it as *the* reality rather than as only one of many possible ways of making sense of illness, disease, and health. Yet medicine is very much a product of socially constructed values, customs, and roles as well as their interpretations and reinterpretations. It is not the clear-cut, objective, scientific endeavor it is often thought to be.

Thus, the women's health movement is important for its analysis of the contemporary medical care system, for the questions it raises about the nature of medical knowledge, and for its insights into how health care relationships and services affect the health and well-being of individuals. Furthermore, it is important to study because it shows medicine as an agent of social control with respect to key statuses and roles in society, such as those based on gender. We begin by exploring the viewpoint of the women's health movement—its basic assumptions and arguments—and how these ideas have developed historically. We then review its key strategies and issues, and close by considering these in relation to feminist theory and ideas about social change.

❖ The Perspective of the Women's Health Movement

The women's health movement gathered momentum and became a recognizable force for social change along with the reemergence of the feminist movement in the late 1960s and early 1970s. It continued into the 1980s to provide serious challenges to central aspects of standard medical practice, such as the scientific objectivity of diagnosis and treatment, the economic exploitation of patients, and the efficacy and humaneness of the traditional doctor-patient relationship. The women's health movement offers an alternative perspective on health care values and beliefs. It also provides a system of direct services as an alternative to much mainstream health care, an extensive network of self-help groups, education and advocacy organizations, and women's clinics.

A fundamental assumption underlying the women's health movement is that women have not had ultimate control over their own bodies and their own health. With few exceptions, contemporary women live in social worlds where men occupy the vast majority of powerful, decision-making positions. Health policy, health legislation, health care planning and administration, health-related research, and the influential clinical roles that govern the creation of health knowledge and the delivery of health and medical services are all dominated by men or, more precisely, by male-centered thinking, whether from men or women. In addition, this androcentric system also controls the business and industrial corporations that heavily influence both environmental risks to human health and the nature of the technology developed to improve health. An important corollary assumption to the notion of male control is that men have many life experiences and interests unique from women's. Out of these distinctive experiences men develop interpretations of reality and agendas for action that serve male priorities. The preeminence of male-centered views means they also may be adopted by women.

From a feminist perspective, the belief systems and supporting institutions created and perpetuated through the dominance of one sex determine the health of the other in three basic ways. In terms of disease *etiology* or causation, women are affected by corporate and government environmental decisions that encourage (or prevent) exposure to risk and the development of disease. These decisions, in turn, may lead to social policies designed to "protect" women but which at the same time segregate and exclude them. Dominant belief systems and institutions also affect women in terms of disease *diagnosis* by controlling which health problems are officially recognized and who ultimately is designated sick or healthy. Finally, they affect women in terms of medical *treatment*, by determining the nature of treatment regimens and rehabilitation programs as well as decisions regarding to whom these are applied. Since class and racial groups also are subject to conditions of dominance and exploitation, poor working-class women and women of color experience double or, frequently, triple jeopardy in such a system.

The lack of women's power relative to men in these critical areas is considered by feminists to be unjust, undesirable, and in need of change. On a more practical level, however, one can reasonably ask if it really has made a difference that men have been in control. If medicine is based on scientific fact and administered professionally, then how could gender matter? The response of the women's health movement is that gender *has* made a difference. Male dominance in the health system has jeopardized women through a pattern of actions that have been harmful rather than beneficial to women's health. It is important to point out that the feminist critique is based on the *impact* of these actions rather than their intent. Implicit in the perspective of the women's health movement is the belief that if women shared control, were more centrally involved in health decision making, and brought female-oriented perspectives to balance male views, there would be changes in the environment and in the structure of health care that would substantially improve the health of all persons.

A Critical Perspective on the Diagnosis of Women's Health Problems

Mainstream medicine, in the critical perspective, has constructed its scientific knowledge around prevailing male-centered cultural views of women's proper position. Diagnosis of medical problems and disease therefore can be used as an instrument of social control to keep women in their places. As the work of feminist historians demonstrates, medical authorities have claimed the right to define what a woman is or should be since at least the nineteenth century.

Physiological signs and symptoms can be interpreted in any number of ways. Symptoms also can be experienced differently depending on how medical authorities react to them. Thus, in effect, the response of professionals can "create" diseases. Physicians do not create the actual physiological symptoms, but they negotiate and define which symptoms are important, which are to be disregarded, which should be treated, and which should not. In addition to organizing certain signs and symptoms into "diseases," physicians use these categories of *diagnoses* to designate people as sick or well. Once a person is diagnosed as sick, physicians then have the authority, through law and custom, to invade the person's body with drugs, surgery, or other manipulations that alter their anatomical and/or physiological condition. In some cases, these interventions may result in health improvement; in others, not.

Because of the totality of the power of diagnosis and the magnitude of its implications for individuals over whom it is exercised, critics of modern medicine—feminists in particular—have strongly questioned the validity of the knowledge on which diagnosis is based and through which intervention is justified.

Objectivity and Medical Knowledge

Activists in the women's health movement claim that medical knowledge is not objective, scientifically derived, or free of value judgments.

The central criticism of medical diagnosis to develop out of the women's health movement is that physicians tend to view women's health problems, whatever their type, location, or symptoms, in terms of reproductive function. Thus cardiovascular problems, bone and skeletal disorders, cancer, skin problems, as well as emotional and psychiatric disorders—only to name a few—are first and foremost viewed as linked to or caused by female hormones. This preoccupation of physicians with the menopausal status of their patients has endured for over a century.

This reproductive-centered view also helps explain a seeming paradox in the feminist critique of medicine—that, on the one hand, physicians are all too willing to diagnose and intervene medically in health areas where women are unique in relation to men and, on the other, ignore or minimize women's problems in areas where men also have problems.

Viewing women in terms of their uniquely female reproductive functions has other serious implications. First, the underlying cause of a health problem may be masked if the physician thinks only of reproductive functions. If the reproductive system is *not* the source of the problem, then treatments directed there will be fruitless and, in fact, may be quite harmful (as in the use of estrogen therapy in mid-life or the current debate over progesterone as a remedy for "premenstrual syndrome").

A second implication of medical preoccupation with the female reproductive system is that, since this is a normal part of the female body, if it also is considered to be a source of illness and disability then it follows that women are "normally abnormal" and, therefore, unfit (in comparison to men) for responsible, demanding, and authoritative roles in society. Such views have been used to support the exclusion of women from public life, thereby legitimating gender discrimination and inequality. The study of societal reaction to menstruation, for example, reveals it is used as a basis for the separation of men and women and the exclusion of females from key societal activities in ancient Hebrew cultures and perhaps earlier. In the nineteenth century also, physicians linked the common ailments of women to the vulnerability of their reproductive systems and actively campaigned against women who in various ways endeavored to enter public life. These physicians accepted the culturally predominant view that women should confine themselves to the domesticity of private households and avoid the public arenas of work and politics. Not only did physicians accept this view, but they developed elaborate justifications for it with their theories, clinical opinions, and "scientific" facts. Moreover, it was clearly in their interest to do so. Medical theories and evidence were used to keep women from competing with men in many areas—not the least of which was the field of medicine itself—and ensured their supportive role in nurturing their families and maintaining domestic order.

❖ The Origins of the Women's Health Movement

Differing male and female views on health and health care have existed for much of human history, even though these differences have gone largely unrecognized by scholars. They reflect the fact that men and women, while living in physical proximity, have lived in quite different social worlds. As a consequence, health problems perceived and experienced, as well as lay and professional reactions to them, have been gender specific. Women's unique experiences in childbearing account for some but by no means all of this variation.

In Western societies, male domination and gender-specific views have created the conditions for women's dissatisfaction and ultimate struggle for change. In this sense, the women's health movement did not begin in 1969 or 1971, but emerged out of the sociopolitical relationship between men and women that, in terms of health and health care, became accentuated with industrialization, the growth of technology, and the rise of "scientific" medicine in the nineteenth century.

Several recent sources trace the contemporary American women's health movement to the 1820s and 1830s and the then popular Ladies Physiological Societies, an outgrowth of a broad-based "popular health movement," which emphasized demystifying medicine through self-awareness and self-knowledge, preventive measures, and acceptance of women as trained health practitioners. The popular health movement was opposed to interventionist techniques, the so-called heroic medicine of the time. This activism was different than today's in that challenging the traditional sphere of women was not the central issue. In fact, the domestic role of woman as wife and mother was emphasized by the physiological societies. Women largely supported the idea that they were the "morally superior" sex and should be educated in proper health and hygiene for the benefit of their families.

Since some of the conditions for a full-scale social movement in the area of women's health had existed for decades, why did such a movement emerge only in the late 1960s and early 1970s? One possible answer is that although problems and grievances existed, the structural conditions were lacking. Specifically, organizational capabilities and opportunities for collective action were not effectively in place for women before the civil rights and student movements of the 1960s. Women were active participants in these movements, developing a heightened sensitivity to injustice and inequity and a growing belief in the rights of people—all people—to govern their own lives and destinies. They became increasingly aware of how they themselves were oppressed within these movements, at the same time that they were discovering their own capabilities. The public self-confidence of women activists as a group plus their concrete political experience stimulated the rebirth of feminism and, more specifically, the rise of the women's health movement. Widespread concern for consumer control and more individual responsibility in health matters also contributed to these efforts.

A series of events in these years, including the Thalidomide scandal, thrust the grievances of women concerning the modern health system into sharper focus. It is important to underscore that these developments in themselves did not *cause* the women's health movement. The conditions for its development, as I have argued, were much more long-standing and dependent on long-term structural and institutional changes. Nevertheless, these more immediate events served as metaphors and rallying points for women's claims of injustice.

The legal availability of abortion is the issue commonly cited as pivotal in the development of feminist concern over health matters in the 1960s. Reproductive choice was seen as one of the most basic of all issues for women, based on the assumption that as long as the fundamental female functions of pregnancy and childbearing were outside the control of women, women would remain subservient. Lack of power in reproductive matters necessarily precludes women from control over their own lives, limiting their involvement in public life. Access to safe abortions was seen as essential for the empowerment of women; the prohibition of abortion was viewed as an attempt to perpetuate women's limited societal influence. As this issue generated increasing awareness of the lack of control women had over all aspects of their bodies and their health, the women's health movement's early focus on abortion, childbirth, birth control, hysterectomy, menopause, and sterilization was extended to other health concerns such as mental health, heart disease, cancer, diabetes, osteoporosis, eating disorders, and treatment of disability and impairment.

In the course of recognizing and examining this wide array of problems, similar patterns among them emerged. Because the corpus of medical knowledge had been developed with many built-in stereotypes and biases regarding women, the process of medical education had to be challenged. And, as it became clear that the relationship between doctor and patient and between male and female health workers paralleled the dominant-submissive pattern of relationships in the traditional patriarchal family, new forms of interaction within the health care context had to be developed.

❖ Strategies within the Women's Health Movement

During the beginning phase of the women's health movement, from the early to mid-1970s, two organizational strategies emerged to realize the goals of this growing critique: self-help groups and political action organizations.

Self-Help

The most innovative of the two strategies was the concept of feminist *self-help*, eventually manifest in the existence of hundreds, perhaps thousands, of grass-roots self-help groups located throughout the United States. Self-help both exemplified the aims of the movement and fueled its growth and development.

Feminist self-help groups appear on the surface to be the health equivalent of the feminist consciousness-raising groups of the late 1960s and early 1970s. The concept refers to any gathering of women who share common experiences, health care information, and skills. Usually these groups are small, with half a dozen to a dozen participants. Some groups focus on a particular subject such as fertility detection, breast examination, vaginal infection, or menopause, and have a finite time span of approximately 8 or 10 weeks. Other groups are broader in focus and continue indefinitely. The immediate purpose of the self-help group is for women to learn about themselves through mutual discussion and sharing information, including personal experiences. The most widely known of these groups is the Boston Women's Health Book Collective, whose efforts produced the popular health manual for women, *Our Bodies, Ourselves*, first published in 1971.

The process of feminist self-help is now found in diverse areas such as cancer treatment, diabetes, and eating disorders, carrying out the objectives of the women's health movement in a variety of ways. First, it is a reciprocal, participatory situation, nonhierarchical in principle, in stark contrast to the traditional dominance-passivity of most doctor-patient relationships. Second, its purpose is to help women learn about their bodies in a firsthand way without having to rely on the androcentric approaches frequently found in standard medical sources.

Political Action Organizations

The other type of organizational structure adopted by the women's health movement has been the *political action organization*. These groups have been mainly concerned with effecting political, legal, and institutional changes through activities such as public information campaigns, lobbying, community organizing, and mobilization. One of the most successful of these groups, with an international membership of several thousand, is California's Coalition for the Medical Rights of Women, founded in 1974. Coalition activities have been a powerful force in California politics and have affected national health policy in a number of ways. One of the coalition's early projects was to press for more stringent California standards for the regulation and labeling of drugs and medical devices. Once successful, these efforts in turn forced national manufacturers to comply—for example, by adding warning labels to over-the-counter drugs for pregnant women. The coalition's activities also have resulted in stronger regulations for intrauterine contraceptive devices (IUDs), the establishment of informed consent procedures for sterilization, and increased public and professional awareness of the medical and legal consequences of diethylstilbestrol (DES) exposure.

Another notable example of political action organizations within the women's health movement is the National Women's Health Network. Established in 1975 and located in Washington, D.C., where it closely monitors Congress and government agencies, the network functions primarily as an information clearinghouse and a consumer advocacy and lobbying group. Members have organized demonstrations, pressured governmental agencies, and testified at congressional hearings on behalf of such issues as national health insurance, examination of dangerous obstetrical practices, forced sterilization, and the elimination under the Medicaid program of federal funds for abortions.

Political action organizations rely on support from private donations as well as on volunteer help. Those that have survived have done so against significant odds and under constant financial pressure. As in the case of self-help, feminist commitment has been a key ingredient in the persistence of these organizations.

❖ About the Author

Mary K. Zimmerman, PH.D., is Associate Professor of Health Services Administration and Sociology at the University of Kansas, Lawrence, Kansas.

E ❖ America Living with AIDS: Transforming Anger, Fear, and Indifference into Action

The National Commission on Acquired Immune Deficiency Syndrome, 1991

Since scientists first began to understand the dynamics that govern transmission of the human immunodeficiency virus (HIV), it has been possible to predict with chilling accuracy the toll the epidemic would exact in sickness and in lives lost. As the nation enters the second decade of the HIV epidemic, the accuracy of predictions made in the mid-1980s stands as a silent rebuke. One need take only a brief look at these statistics to understand the impact that acquired immunodeficiency syndrome (AIDS) has had in the United States.

By the end of 1990, more than 100,000 people in the United States had died of AIDS, and nearly a third of those deaths occurred that year. Now more than a hundred people die in the United States every day of AIDS—one every 15 minutes—and the pace is accelerating. As of June 1991, 182,834 cases of AIDS in the United States and its commonwealths and territories had been reported to the federal Centers for Disease Control (CDC). Between March 1990 and March 1991, the reported number of new cases in the United States rose by more than one third. These numbers are a telling indication that our efforts at prevention must be redoubled.

The lethality of AIDS has been its most impressive and dismaying feature.
—American College of Physicians

During the earliest years of the epidemic, from 1981 to 1982, nearly 80 percent of all reported AIDS cases were from six large metropolitan areas in five states—New York City, San Francisco, Los Angeles, Miami, Newark, and Houston. So far in 1991, 31 metropolitan areas and 25 states and the Commonwealth of Puerto Rico have reported 1,000 or more cumulative AIDS cases—and the number of communities, counties, and states affected by HIV disease continues to expand.

While the majority of new AIDS cases has been from metropolitan areas, there has been a significant increase in new cases in municipalities with populations less than 500,000. Lack of access to adequate health care has denied the benefits of advances in treatment to many in these smaller cities and rural communities, despite the dedication of stalwart health care providers and volunteers. More ominous still, failure to acknowledge the dimensions of the crisis has resulted in insufficient attention to AIDS education and prevention programs.

HIV disease has had a disproportionate impact on some communities. The HIV epidemic continues to affect gay and bisexual men more than any other single group of Americans; these individuals compose 64 percent of the cases of AIDS reported since the beginning of the epidemic. African Americans constitute 12 percent of the United States population, but nearly 28 percent of AIDS cases. Hispanics constitute 9 percent of the population, but 16 percent of AIDS cases. Unless sustained support for targeted interventions that facilitate access to a broad range of health and social services is given, there is every indication that these communities will continue to be disproportionately represented among AIDS cases in the future.

The number of women and children infected with HIV—particularly within communities of color—continues to grow dramatically. In fact, AIDS cases among women are growing faster than AIDS cases among men. As of June 1991, women accounted for 10 percent of all AIDS cases. AIDS is projected to become one of the top five causes of death for young women.

Increasingly, parents who are themselves infected are forced to make agonizing choices for themselves, their infected children, and their uninfected children. Parents may sacrifice their own health as they seek care for their children and must struggle with issues of how to provide for both sick and healthy children after their death. New York City officials project an "orphan burden" of approximately 20,000 children who will need to be cared for by relatives or placed in foster homes when their parents die of AIDS in the next few years. About one fourth of these children will be HIV positive themselves. Intravenous drug use has contributed significantly to this new trend. Approximately 70 percent of all pediatric AIDS cases are directly related to maternal exposure to HIV through intravenous drug use or sex with an intravenous drug user.

Communities all across the United States are struggling to confront the twin epidemics of HIV and substance use. The nexus between HIV and substance use is unarguable. Already, approximately 31 percent of all AIDS cases can be linked, either directly or indirectly, to intravenous drug use. Cases of HIV infection related to unprotected sexual activity under the influence of crack cocaine, alcohol, or other substances is another disturbing trend, especially among adolescents. Drug treatment centers are ill equipped to deal with the growing numbers of substance users with HIV disease. The lack of treatment slots, training, and funding only perpetuates this insidious link.

The number of reported AIDS cases does not, however, accurately portray the scope of the epidemic because such figures represent only 10 to 15 percent of the total number of people now infected with HIV in the United

States. CDC estimates that, at present, approximately one adult male in 100 in the United States is HIV positive and one adult female in 600 is similarly infected. In all, CDC estimates that at least one million people in this country have HIV infection.

Moreover, HIV affects people of all ages. Adolescents are often forgotten as discussions center on adults and children. Presently, adolescents with hemophilia represent a majority of reported AIDS cases among those aged 13 to 19. In addition, adolescents practice many of the same behaviors that put adults at risk. Given the length of time between infection and diagnosis, it is clear that the large numbers of individuals diagnosed with AIDS in their mid to late twenties were infected during their teens. The disproportionate impact of AIDS on young people is further dramatized by the "years of potential life lost." *Health economists have tallied up the years of potential life lost before age 65 to describe the extent to which deaths from AIDS occur primarily in young people. In 1987, the years of potential life lost due to AIDS was 432,000. This figure compared with 246,000 for stroke, 1.5 million for heart disease, and 1.8 million for cancer. While the rates for these other major diseases remain stable, the years of potential life lost due to AIDS continues to increase. In 1991, estimates place the years of potential life lost due to AIDS between 1.2 and 1.4 million, ranking it third among all diseases. By 1993, AIDS will clearly outstrip all other diseases in lost human potential.*

HIV disease has a devastating impact on those who are already marginalized members of society. Growing numbers of HIV infection and AIDS cases occur among poor residents of inner cities.

A mere tally of cases only sketches part of the picture. It quickly became clear that HIV disease could not be understood outside the context of racism, homophobia, poverty, and unemployment—pervasive factors that foster the spread of the disease. This web of associated social ills has been referred to as "a synergy of plagues."

AIDS exposes the underbelly of many enduring social problems— lack of access to health care, prostitution, drug use, discrimination, and poverty.
> —Mervyn F. Silverman, President, American Foundation for AIDS Research

---

The association of poverty, homelessness, and disease is perhaps best dramatized by the impact of the HIV epidemic on those in inner cities who are living at the margins of society. Without permanent addresses or steady incomes, the homeless and many of America's poor often are isolated from all but the most rudimentary health care. Public hospitals that serve low-income communities and the overwhelming majority of people with AIDS in large cities are over crowded, their staffs are beleaguered, and their substandard funding is shrinking with each additional municipal budget crisis. Those most in need of health care are typically the ones who can least afford it. When illness strikes, the emergency room becomes the "family physician." The increase in numbers of HIV cases is placing a strain on a system already on the verge of collapse.

In some areas of the country the sheer number of people with AIDS has forced a greater awareness and understanding of the challenges people with HIV disease face. However, although recent opinion polls reflect a moderation of harsh attitudes toward people living with HIV disease, HIV-related discrimination has not disappeared. This discrimination reflects the racism and homophobia that pervade our society and, like poverty, limit people's access to care and compassion. AIDS has been sufficiently controversial to have earned the status of the most litigated disease in American history. There is, moreover, a further disquieting trend. Surveys of court cases and complaints to human rights commissions show that rather than disappearing, AIDS discrimination is changing. Subtle prejudices involving denial of basic health services are replacing overt forms of bias, and these subtle biases are more difficult to fight legally.

As the epidemic worsens, opportunities to mobilize effective responses diminish each day that we fail to act decisively. Education for prevention of further HIV spread through the avoidance of risk behavior has been greatly underutilized. Despite a slow start, there is much that can be done now to prevent new HIV infections from occurring and to enhance the quality and length of life of those already infected. In recent years, there have been heartening developments in treatments for HIV disease. Guaranteeing access to all of these treatments is essential.

The nation must be awakened to the enormity of the HIV crisis and to the potential for individual and collective action. There is no lack of options or remedies. We are not without hope. The nation's response must be commensurate with the threat posed by the epidemic.

❖ Recommendations

1. A comprehensive national HIV plan should be developed with the full participation of involved federal agencies and with input from national organizations representing various levels of government to identify priorities and resources necessary for preventing and treating HIV disease.

2. Universal health care coverage should be provided for all persons living in the United States to ensure access to quality health care services.

3. The federal government should establish a comprehensive national HIV prevention initiative.

4. Government should assure access to a system of health care for all people with HIV disease.

5. Medicaid should cover all low-income people with HIV disease.
6. States and/or the federal government should pay the Consolidated Omnibus Budget Reconciliation Act (COBRA) premiums for low-income people with HIV disease who have left their jobs and cannot afford to pay the health insurance premium.
7. Medicaid payment rates for providers should be increased sufficiently to ensure adequate participation in the Medicaid program.
8. Social Security Disability Insurance (SSDI) beneficiaries who are disabled and have HIV disease or another serious chronic health condition should have the option of purchasing Medicare during the current two-year waiting period.
9. Congress and the Administration should work together to adequately raise the Medicaid cap on funds directed to the Commonwealth of Puerto Rico to ensure equal access to care and treatment.
10. Policies should be developed now to address future plans for the distribution of AIDS vaccines and the ethical and liability issues that will arise when vaccines become available.
11. The federal government should fund the Ryan White CARE Act at the fully authorized level.
12. Congress should remove the government restrictions that have been imposed on the use of funds for certain kinds of HIV education, services, and research.
13. The Secretary of Health and Human Services should direct the National Institutes of Health, the Health Care Financing Administration, and the Health Resources and Services Administration to work together to develop a series of recommendations to address the obstacles that keep many people from participating in HIV-related clinical trials, as well as the variables that force some people to seek participation in trials because they have no other health care options.
14. HIV-related services should be expanded to facilities where underserved populations receive health care and human services, in part to ensure their increased participation in trials of investigational new therapies.
15. Current efforts at the National Institutes of Health (NIH) to expand the recruitment of underrepresented populations in the AIDS Clinical Trials Group should be continued and increased.
16. HIV education and training programs for health care providers should be improved and expanded and better methods should be developed to disseminate state-of-the-art clinical information about HIV disease, as well as drug and alcohol use, to the full range of health care providers.
17. Greater priority and funding should be given to behavioral, social science, and health services research.
18. The Food and Drug Administration should aggressively pursue all options for permitting the early use of promising new therapies for

conditions for which there is no standard therapy or for patients who have failed or are intolerant of standard therapy.

19. The National Institutes of Health should develop a formal mechanism for disseminating state-of-the-art treatment information in an expeditious and far-reaching manner.

20. The Department of Health and Human Services should conduct a study to determine the policies of third-party payers regarding the payments of certain health service costs that are provided as part of an individual's participation in clinical trials conducted in the development of HIV-related drugs.

21. Implementation of the Americans with Disabilities Act should be carefully monitored, and states and localities should evaluate the adequacy of existing state and local antidiscrimination laws and ordinances for people with disabilities, including people living with HIV disease.

22. The federal government should expand drug abuse treatment so that all who apply for treatment can be accepted into treatment programs. The federal government should also continually work to improve the quality and effectiveness of drug abuse treatment.

23. Legal barriers to the purchase and possession of injection equipment should be removed.

24. The following interim steps to improve access to expensive HIV-related drugs should be taken:
    a. adequately reimburse for the purchase of drugs required in the prevention and treatment of HIV disease, including clotting factor for hemophilia;
    b. undertake, through the Department of Health and Human Services, a consolidated purchase and distribution of drugs used in the prevention and treatment of HIV disease;
    c. amend the Orphan Drug Act to set a maximum sales cap for covered drugs.

25. All levels of government should develop comprehensive HIV plans that establish priorities, ensure consistent and comprehensive policies, and allocate resources.

26. Federal, state, and local governments should join forces with the private sector in providing long-term support to community-based organizations.

27. The U.S. Public Health Service should expand and promote comprehensive programs for technical assistance and capacity building for effective long-term prevention efforts.

28. Federal, state, and local entities should provide support for training, technical assistance, supervisory staff, and program coordination to acknowledge and support the family members, friends, and volunteers who are an integral part of the care system of a person with HIV disease.

29. The federal government should develop an evaluation and technical assistance component for all federally funded HIV-related programs.
30. Elected officials at all levels of government have the responsibility to be leaders in this time of health care crisis and should exercise leadership in the HIV epidemic based on sound science and informed public health practices.

❖ Suggested Readings

❖ Chapter 1 Health Status and Its Determinants

Banister, E.W. et al. *Contemporary Health Issues*. Boston: Jones and Bartlett, 1988.

Aiken, L.H., and Mechanic, D., eds. *Applications of Social Science to Clinical Medicine and Health Policy*. New Brunswick, N.J.: Rutgers University Press, 1986.

Berkman, L.F., and Syme, S.L. "Social Networks, Host Resistance and Mortality: A Nine-Year Follow-Up of Alameda County Residents." *American Journal of Epidemiology* 109 (1979): 186–204.

Behrman, R.E. "Scientific Medicine, Social Ills, and Child Health. " *Western Journal of Medicine* 157 (1992): 74–76.

Bunker, J.R., Gomby, D.S., and Kehrer, B.H. *Pathways to Health: The Role of Social Factors*. Menlo Park, Calif: The Henry J. Kaiser Family Foundation, 1989.

Dubos, R. *Mirage of Health*. New York: Harper & Row, 1979.

Guralnik, J.M., and Kaplan, G.A. "Predictors of Healthy Aging: Prospective Evidence from the Alameda County Study." *American Journal of Public Health* 79 (1989): 703–708.

Institute of Medicine. *The Second Fifty Years: Promoting Health and Preventing Disability*. Washington, D.C.: National Academy Press, 1990.

Lewis, T. *The Lives of a Cell*. New York: Viking, 1974.

McGinnis, J.M., Richmond, J.B., Brandt, E.N., Windom, R.E., and Mason, J.O. "Health Progress in the United States: Results of the 1990 Objectives for the Nation." *Journal of the American Medical Association* 268, No. 18 (1992): 2545.

McKeown, T. *The Role of Medicine: Dream Mirage or Nemesis*, 2nd edition. Oxford: Blackwell, 1979.

McKinlay, J.B. "A Case for Refocussing Upstream: The Political Economy of Illness." In *The Sociology of Health and Illness: Critical Perspectives*, 2nd edition, edited by Conrad, P., and Kern, R. New York: St. Martin's, 1986, pp. 484–498.

National Center for Health Statistics. *Health United States, 1991, and Prevention Profile*. Hyattsville: U.S. Department of Health and Human Services, 1992, DHHS publication (PHS) 92–1232.

Ries, P. "Americans Assess Their Health: United States, 1987." National Center for Health Statistics. *Vital Health Statistics* 10, No. 174, (1990).

Roos, N.P., and Havens, B. "Predictors of Successful Aging: A Twelve-Year Study of Manitoba Elderly." *American Journal of Public Health* 81, No. 1 (1991): 63.

U.S. Department of Health and Human Services. *Healthy People 2000: National Health Promotion and Disease Prevention Objectives*. Washington D.C.: Office of the Assistant Secretary for Health, Department of Health and Human Services, 1991, DHHS publication (PHS) 91-50213.

U.S. Senate Special Committee on Aging, American Association of Retired Persons, The Federal Council on Aging, and the U.S. Administration on Aging. *Aging America: Trends and Projections*, 1991.

White, K.L., Williams, T.F., and Greenberg, B.G. "The Ecology of Medical Care." *New England Journal of Medicine* 265 (1961): 885–892.

❖ Chapter 2 Shaping the Health Care System

Bradford, L., and Kirkman-Liff. "Health Insurance Values and Implementation in the Netherlands and the Federal Republic of Germany: An Alternative Path to Universal Coverage." *Journal of the American Medical Association* 265 (1991): 2496.

Breslow, L., Fielding, J.E., and Lave, L.B., eds. *Annual Review of Public Health*, Vol. 10. Palo Alto: Annual Reviews, Inc., 1989.

Butler, S.M. and Hais/Maier, E.S., eds. *Critical Issues: A National Health System for America*, Washington, D.C., Heritage Foundation, 1990.

Ginzberg, E. *From Physician Shortage to Patient Shortage*. Boulder, Colo.: Westview, 1986.

Iglehart, J.K. "Health Policy Report: Germany's Health Care System (part 1)." *New England Journal of Medicine* 324 (1991): 503, and (part 2). 324 (1991): 1750.

Marmor, T.R., "Canada's Health-Care System: A Model for the United States?" *Current History* 90 (1991): 422.

Merlis, M. "Health Insurance," *CRS Issue Brief, Major Planning Issue.* Congressional Research Service, The Library of Congress, Order Code IB91093, October 1992.

Showstack, J., et al. "Health of the Public: The Academic Response." *Journal of the American Medical Association* 267, No. 18 (1992): No. 2497.

Spencer, G. *Projections of the Population of the United States by Age, Sex and Race: 1988 to 2080*. Current Population Reports, Series P-25, No. 1018. Washington, D.C.: U.S. Bureau of the Census, 1989.

Taylor, H., and Reinhardt, U.E. "Does the System Fit?" *Health Management Quarterly* 2 (1991): 6.

Williams, S.J., and Torrens, P.R., eds. *Introduction to Health Services*, 4th ed. Albany: Delmar Publishers, 1993.

❖ Chapter 3 The Politics of Health: Establishing Policies and Setting Priorities

Aaron, H.J. and Schultze, L., eds. *Setting Domestic Priorities.* Brookings, 1992

Alford, R.R., ed. *Health Care Politics: Ideological and Interest Group Barriers to Reform.* Chicago: The University of Chicago Press, 1975.

Conrad, P., and Kern, R., eds. *The Sociology of Health and Illness: Critical Perspectives,* 2nd ed. New York, St. Martin's: 1986.

Downs, A. *An Economic Theory of Democracy.* New York: Harper & Row, 1957.

Iglehart, J., ed. "Rationing: Oregon's Plan (Special Section)." *Health Affairs* 10: (1991): 5–51, 78–95.

Lamm, R.D. "Rationing of Health Care: Inevitable and Desirable." *University of Pennsylvania Law Review* 140, No.5 (1992): 1511.

Public Health Service, Office of Disease Prevention and Health Promotion, U.S. Department of Health and Human Services. "Strategies for Promoting Health for Specific Populations." *Journal of Public Health Policy* 8, No. 3 (1987): 369–423.

Relman, A.S. "Is Rationing Inevitable?" *New England Journal of Medicine* 322 (1990): 1809.

1

❖ Chapter 4 The Critical Role of Nurses

Aiken, L.H., and Fagin, C., eds. *Charting Nursing's Future: Agenda for the 1990s.* Philadelphia: Lippincott, 1992.

Aiken, L.H. "The Hospital Nursing Shortage: A Paradox of Increasing Supply and Increasing Vacancy Rates." *Western Journal of Medicine* 151(1989): 87–92.

Friss, L. "The Nursing Shortage: Do We Dislike It Enough to Cure It?" *Inquiry* 25 (1988):232–242.

Jameton, A. "Duties to Self: Professional Nursing in the Critical Care Unit." In *Ethics at the Bedside: A Source Book for the Critical Care Nurse,* edited by Fowler, M., and Levine-Ariff, J. Philadelphia: Lippincott, 1987, pp. 115–135.

Makaden, H.J., and Gibbons, T. "Nurses and Physicians: Prospects for Collaboration." *Ann Inter Med* 103 (1985): 134–135.

McKibbin, R.C. *The Nursing Shortage and the 1990s: Realities and Remedies.* Kansas City: American Nurses' Association, 1990.

Muyskens, J.L. "The Role of the Nurse." *Moral Problems in Nursing.* Totowa, N.J.: Rowman and Littlefield, 1982, pp. 30–40.

Robert Wood Johnson Foundation. *Challenges in Health Care: A Chartbook Perspective.* Princeton: Robert Wood Johnson Foundation, 1991.

Small, N., and Walsh, M., eds. *Teaching Nursing Homes, the Nursing Perspective.* Owings Mill, Md.: National Health Publishers, 1988.

Stein, L.I., Watts, D.T., and Howell, T. "The Doctor-Nurse Game Revisited." *New England Journal of Medicine* 322 (1990): 546.

Vance, C., Talbott, S.W., McBride, A.B., and Mason, D.J. "Coming of Age: The Women's Movement and Nursing." *Political Action Handbook for Nurses: Changing the Workplace, Government, Organizations, and Community.* Menlo Park, Calif.: Addison-Wesley, 1985, pp. 23–37.

❖ Chapter 5 Initiatives for Reform

Blendon, R.J., Edwards, J.N., and Hyams, A.L. "Making the Critical Choices." *Journal of the American Medical Association* 267, No.18 (1992): 2509.

Blendon, R.J., Leitman, R., Morrison, I., and Donelan, K. "Satisfaction with Health Systems in Ten Nations." *Health Affairs* 9 (1990): 185.

Clinton, W. "The Clinton Health Care Plan." *New England Journal of Medicine* 327, No. 11 (1992): 804.

Clinton, W. "Clinton"s Health Plan: Taking His Message to Congress." *The New York Times* 1993.

Davis, K. "Health Care Financing Reform: The Next Century." *Resident and Staff Physician* 37, No. 2 (1991): 86.

Enthoven, A., and Kronick, R. "A Consumer Choice Health Plan for the 1990s." *New England Journal of Medicine* 320 (1989): 29.

Etzioni, A. "Health Care Rationing: A Critical Evaluation." *Health Affairs* 88 (1991).

Feder, J., Holahan, J., and Marmor, T., eds. *National Health Insurance: Conflicting Goals and Policy Choices.* Washington, D.C.: The Urban Institute, 1980.

Fein, R. "The Health Security Partnership: A Federal-State Universal Insurance and Cost-Containment Program." *Journal of the American Medical Association* 265 (1991): 2555.

Grumbach, K., et al. "Liberal Benefits, Conservative Spending: The Physicians for a

National Health Program Proposal." *Journal of the American Medical Association* 265 (1991): 2549.

Harvard Community Health Plan. *An International Comparison of Health-Care Systems. Annual Report.* Brookline, Mass.: Harvard Community Health Plan, 1990.

Harvey, L.K., and Shubat, S.C. *Public Opinion on Health Care Issues, 1991 Edition.* Chicago: American Medical Association, 1991.

Health Affairs Supplement 1993. Project Hope, 7500 Old Georgetown Road, Bethesda, M.D. 20814

The Health Debate: Special Section, *The New York Times,* 11/14/93.

Holahan, J., and Zedlewski, S. "Who Pays for Health in the United States? Implications for Health System Reform." *Inquiry,* Blue Cross and Blue Shield Association, 29 (Summer 1992): 231–248.

Marmor, T.R., and Barr, M.S. "Making Sense of the National Health Insurance Reform Debate." *Yale Law & Policy Review* 10, No.2 (1992).

Robinson, J.C. "Philosophical Origins of the Economic Valuation of Life." *The Milbank Quarterly* 64, No.1 (1986): 133–155.

Schieber, G.J., et al. "Health Care Systems in 24 Countries." *Health Affairs* 10, (1991):22.

Smith, M., et al., "Taking the Public's Pulse on Health System Reform." *Health Affairs* 11 (Summer 1992).

Sullivan, L.W. "The Bush Administration's Health Care Plan." *New England Journal of Medicine* 327, No.11 (1992): 801.

U.S. Bipartisan Commission on Comprehensive Health Care. *A Call for Action.* Washington, D.C.: The Pepper Commission on Comprehensive Health Care, 1990.

"Who Pays for Health Care?" *The Urban Institute: Policy and Research Report* (Summer 1992): 12–14.

❖ Chapter 6 Health Care Cost Containment

Davis, K., Anderson, G.F., Rowland, D., and Steinberg, E.P. *Health Care Cost Containment.* Baltimore: Johns Hopkins University Press, 1990.

Enthoven, A.C. *Health Plan: The Only Practical Solution to the Soaring Cost of Medical Care.* Reading, Mass.: Addison-Wesley, 1980.

Enthoven, A.C. "Managed Competition: An Agenda for Action." *Health Affairs* 7, No. 3 (1988): 25.

Evans, R.G., Barer, M.L., and Hertzman, C. "The 20-Year Experiment Accounting for, Explaining, and Evaluating Health Care Cost Containment in Canada and the United States." *Annual Review of Public Health* 12 (1991): 481–518.

Fein, R. *Medical Care, Medical Costs: The Search for a Health Insurance Policy:* Harvard University Press, 1989.

Fuchs, V.R. "National Health Insurance Revisited." *Health Affairs* 10 (1991): 1–11.

Fuchs, V.R. "The Health Sector's Share of the Gross National Product." *Science* (1990): 534.

Fuchs, W.R. *Who Shall Live? Economics and Social Choice.* New York: Basic Books, 1974.

Physician Payment Review Commission. *Annual Report to Congress, 1992.* Washington, D.C.: Physician Payment Review Commission, 1992.

Schieber, G.J., and Poullier, J.P. "International Health Spending Issues and Trends." *Health Affairs* 10 (1991): 106.

Sonnefeld, S.T., et al. "Projections of Health Expenditures through the Year 2000." *Health Care Financing Review* 13 (1991): 1–27.

Waldo, D.R., Sonnefeld, S.T., Lemieus, J.A., and McKusick, D.R. "Health Spending through 2030: Three Scenarios." *Health Affairs* 10, No. 4 (1991): 231–242.

❖ Chapter 7 Inequities in Access to Health Services

Aday, L.A. "Access to What? for Whom?" *Health Management Quarterly* 12, No. 4 (1990): 18–22.

Blendon, R.J., and Edwards, J.N. "Caring for the Uninsured: Choices for Reform." *Journal of the American Medical Association* 265 (1991): 2563.

Butler, S.M. "A Tax Reform Strategy to Deal with the Uninsured." *Journal of the American Medical Association* 265 (1991): 2541.

Davis, K. "Inequality and Access to Health Care." *The Milbank Quarterly* 69, No. 2 (1991): 253.

Davis, K. "Medicaid and the Working Poor." *Health Affairs* 10, No. 3 (1991): 273.

Friedman, E. "Doctors, Doctors Everywhere: and Patients Who Can't Get Care." *Health Business* 6 (January 4, 1991): 1T–2T.

Friedman, E. "Medicare and Medicaid at 25." *Hospitals* 64 (1990): 38–54.

Fuchs, V.R. *Poverty and Health: Asking the Right Questions.* Presented at the 1992 Cornell University Medical College Health Policy Conference, New York, N.Y., February 27–28, 1992.

Hadley, J., Steinberg, E.P., and Feder, J. "Comparison of Uninsured and Privately Insured Hospital Patients: Condition on Admission, Resource Use, and Outcome." *Journal of the American Medical Association* 265(1991): 374–379.

Hill, I.T., and Breyel, J.M. *Caring for Kids.* Washington, D.C.: National Governors' Association, 1991.

Lundberg, G.D., and Blendon, R.J., eds. "Caring for the Uninsured and Underinsured," (special issue). *Journal of the American Medical Association* 265 (1991): 2491.

Marmor, T.R., Mashaw, J., and Haravey, P. *America's Misunderstood Welfare State: Persistent Myths and Continuing Realities.* New York: Basic Books, 1990.

National Association of Community Health Centers. *Access to Community Health Care: A Data Book, 1991.* Washington, D.C.: National Association of Community Health Centers, 1991, pp. 9–11.

Palmer, J.L., Smeeding, T., and Torrey, B.B., eds. *The Vulnerable.* Washington, D.C.: Urban Institute Press, 1988.

Rogers, D.E., and Ginzberg, E., eds. *Medical Care and the Health of the Poor.* Cornell University Medical College, Eighth Conference on Health Policy. Boulder: Westview, 1993.

Springer, M.D., and Lundberg, G.D., eds. *Caring for the Uninsured and Underinsured.* Chicago: American Medical Association, 1991.

❖ Chapter 8 Quality, Effectiveness, and Appropriateness of Care

Brook, R.H., and Appel, F.A. "Quality-of-Care Assessment: Choosing a Method for Peer Review." *New England Journal of Medicine* 288 (1973): 1323.

Caper, P. "The Epidemiologic Surveillance of Medical Care." *American Journal of Public Health* 77 (1987): 669–670.

Eddy, D.M. "Medicine, Money, and Mathematics." *American College of Surgeons Bulletin* 77, No.6 (1992).

Eddy, D.M. "Cost-Effectiveness Analysis. Will It Be Accepted?" *Journal of the American Medical Association* 268 (1992): 132.

Eddy, D.M. "Cost-Effectiveness Analysis. Is It Up to the Task?" *Journal of the American Medical Association* 267 (1992): 3342.

Ellwood, P.M. "Outcomes Management: A Technology of Patient Experience." *New England Journal of Medicine* 318 (1988): 1549–1556.

Epstein, A.M., Stern, R.S., Weissman, J.S. "Do the Poor Cost More? A Multihospital Study of Patients' Socioeconomic Status and Use of Hospital Resources." *New England Journal of Medicine* 322 (1990): 1122.

Gelijns, A.C., ed. *Medical Innovation at the Crossroads, Vol I. Modern Methods of Clinical Investigation.* Washington, D.C.: National Academy Press, 1990.

Holden, K.C., and Smeeding, T. "The Poor, the Rich and the Insecure Elderly Caught in Between." *The Milbank Quarterly* 68, No.2 (1990): 191.

Hopkins, A., and Costain, D., eds. *Measuring the Outcomes of Medical Care.* London: King's Fund Centre for Health Services Development, 1990.

Katz, M. *In the Shadow of the Poorhouse: A Social History of Welfare in America.* New York: Basic Books, 1986.

Luft, H.S., et al. "Does Quality Influence Choice of Hospital?" *Journal of the American Medical Association* 263, No. 21 (1990): 2899.

Luft, H.L. "HMOs and the Quality of Care." *Inquiry* 25, No. 1 (1988): 147–156.

Luft, H.S., Bunker, J.P., and Enthoven, A.C. "Should Operations Be Regionalized? The Empirical Relation Between Surgical Volume and Mortality." *New England Journal of Medicine* 301 (1979): 1364.

Measuring Quality of Care: A Resource Guide. Chicago: American Medical Association, 1987.

Relman, A.S. "Assessment and Accountability: The Third Revolution in Medical Care." *New England Journal of Medicine* 319 (1988): 1220–1222.

Roos, L.L., et al. "Health and Surgical Outcomes in Canada and the United States." *Health Affairs* 16 (1992): 45.

Roper, W.L., et al. "Effectiveness in Health Care." *New England Journal of Medicine* 319, No. 18(1988): 1197–1202.

Wyszewianski, L. "Quality of Care: Past Achievements and Future Challenges." *Inquiry* 25, No.1 (1988): 13–22.

❖ Chapter 9 A Hard Look at Some Neglected Issues

Angell, M. "A Dual Approach to the AIDS Epidemic." *New England Journal of Medicine* 324 (1991): 1498-1500.

Arno, P.S., Shenson, D., Siegal, N.F., Franks, P., and Lee, P.R. "Economic and Policy Implications of Early Intervention in HIV Disease." *Journal of the American Medical Association* 262 (1989): 1493–1498.

Bayer, R. *Private Acts, Social Consequences: AIDS and the Politics of Public Health.* New Brunswick, N.J.: Rutgers University Press, 1991.

Bowman, M., and Gross, M.L. "Overview of Research on Women in Medicine— Issues for Public Policymakers." *Public Health Reports* 101 (1986): 513–521.

Cooper, R., and David, R. "The Biological Concept of Race and Its Application to Public Health and Epidemiology." *Journal of Health Politics, Policy and Law* 11, No. 1 (1986): 97.

Corless, I.B., and Pittman-Lindeman, M., eds. *AIDS: Principles, Practices and Politics.* Reference Edition. New York: Hemisphere Publishing, 1989.

Fox, P.J. "Alzheimer's Disease: An Historical Overview." *The American Journal of Alzheimer's Care* (Fall 1986): 18–24.

Gong, V., and Rudnick, N., eds. *AIDS: Facts and Issues.* New Brunswick, N.J.: Rutgers University Press, 1986, pp 167–178.

Gostin, L.O. "The AIDS Litigation Project: A National Review of Courts and Human Rights Decisions. Part I: The Social Impact of AIDS." *Journal of the American Medical Association* 263 (1990): 1461.

Hess, B.B., and Markson, E.W., eds. *Growing Old in America*, 4th ed. New Brunswick, N.J.: Transaction Publishers, 1991.

Institute of Medicine. *Mobilizing Against AIDS.* Cambridge: Harvard University Press, 1989.

Jecker, N.S. "Age-Based Rationing and Women." *Journal of the American Medical Association* 266, No. 21 (1991): 3012.

Margois, R.J. *Risking Old Age in America.* Boulder, Colo.: Westview, 1990.

Milbank Quarterly. *Currents of Health Policy: Impacts on Black Americans* (Part 1). Cambridge University Press, *The Milbank Quarterly* 65, Supplement 1, (1987).

Muller, H.J., and Cocotas, C. "Women in Power: New Leadership in the Health Industry." In *Health Care for Women International.* Hemisphere Publishing Corporation, 1988.

Murphy, T.F. "No Time for an AIDS Backlash." *Hastings Center Report* 21, No. 2 (1991): 7–11.

National Research Council. *AIDS: Sexual Behavior and Intravenous Drug Use.* Washington, D.C.: National Academy Press, 1989.

Osborn, J.E. "AIDS: Politics and Science." *New England Journal of Medicine* 318, No. 7 (1988): 444–447.

Shaffer, M. "Women's Health Comes to the Forefront of Medicine." *Medical World News* 33, No. 11 (1992): 18.

Shilts, R. *And the Band Played On.* New York: St. Martin's, 1988.

Stone, D.A. "AIDS and the Moral Economy of Insurance." *American Prospect* 62 (Spring 1990).

Sullivan, S., and Lewin, M.E., eds. *The Economics and Ethics of Long Term Care and Disability.* Washington, D.C.: American Enterprise Institute for Public Policy Research, 1988.

Verbrugge, L.M. "Recent, Present, and Future Health of American Adults." In *Annual Review of Public Health.* Vol. 10, edited by Breslow, L., Fielding, J.E., and Lave, L.B. Palo Alto, Calif.: Annual Reviews, Inc., 1989, pp. 333–361.

Wachter, R.M. "AIDS, Activism, and the Politics of Health." *New England Journal of Medicine* 326, No. 2 (1992): 128.

❖ Index